Course Booklet

Switching, Routing, and Wireless Essentials

CCNAv7

Cisco Press

ı|ı.ı|ı. Networking
CISCO Academy

Switching, Routing, and Wireless Essentials Course Booklet (CCNAv7)

Copyright © 2020 Cisco Systems, Inc.

Published by:
Cisco Press
Hoboken, New Jersey

1 2020

Library of Congress Control Number: 2020936830

ISBN-13: 978-0-13-663472-0

ISBN-10: 0-13-663472-9

Warning and Disclaimer

This book is designed to provide information about Switching, Routing, and Wireless Essentials. Every effort has been made to make this book as complete and as accurate as possible, but no warranty or fitness is implied.

The information is provided on an "as is" basis. The authors, Cisco Press, and Cisco Systems, Inc. shall have neither liability nor responsibility to any person or entity with respect to any loss or damages arising from the information contained in this book or from the use of the discs or programs that may accompany it.

The opinions expressed in this book belong to the author and are not necessarily those of Cisco Systems, Inc.

Editor-in-Chief
Mark Taub

**Alliances Manager,
Cisco Press**
Arezou Gol

Product Line Manager
Brett Bartow

Senior Editor
James Manly

Managing Editor
Sandra Schroeder

Senior Project Editor
Tonya Simpson

Editorial Assistant
Cindy Teeters

Cover Designer
Chuti Prasertsith

Composition
codeMantra

Indexer
Cheryl Ann Lenser

This book is part of the Cisco Networking Academy® series from Cisco Press. The products in this series support and complement the Cisco Networking Academy curriculum. If you are using this book outside the Networking Academy, then you are not preparing with a Cisco trained and authorized Networking Academy provider.

For more information on the Cisco Networking Academy or to locate a Networking Academy, Please visit www.netacad.com

ıllıılıı
CISCO.

Trademark Acknowledgments

All terms mentioned in this book that are known to be trademarks or service marks have been appropriately capitalized. Cisco Press or Cisco Systems, Inc., cannot attest to the accuracy of this information. Use of a term in this book should not be regarded as affecting the validity of any trademark or service mark.

Special Sales

For information about buying this title in bulk quantities, or for special sales opportunities (which may include electronic versions; custom cover designs; and content particular to your business, training goals, marketing focus, or branding interests), please contact our corporate sales department at corpsales@pearsoned.com or (800) 382-3419.

For government sales inquiries, please contact governmentsales@pearsoned.com.

For questions about sales outside the U.S., please contact intlcs@pearson.com.

Feedback Information

At Cisco Press, our goal is to create in-depth technical books of the highest quality and value. Each book is crafted with care and precision, undergoing rigorous development that involves the unique expertise of members from the professional technical community.

Readers' feedback is a natural continuation of this process. If you have any comments regarding how we could improve the quality of this book, or otherwise alter it to better suit your needs, you can contact us through email at feedback@ciscopress.com. Please make sure to include the book title and ISBN in your message.

We greatly appreciate your assistance.

Americas Headquarters
Cisco Systems, Inc.
San Jose, CA

Asia Pacific Headquarters
Cisco Systems (USA) Pte. Ltd.
Singapore

Europe Headquarters
Cisco Systems International BV Amsterdam,
The Netherlands

Cisco has more than 200 offices worldwide. Addresses, phone numbers, and fax numbers are listed on the Cisco Website at **www.cisco.com/go/offices.**

Cisco and the Cisco logo are trademarks or registered trademarks of Cisco and/or its affiliates in the U.S. and other countries. To view a list of Cisco trademarks, go to this URL: www.cisco.com/go/trademarks. Third party trademarks mentioned are the property of their respective owners. The use of the word partner does not imply a partnership relationship between Cisco and any other company. (1110R)

Contents at a Glance

Contents

Command Syntax Conventions

The conventions used to present command syntax in this book are the same conventions used in the IOS Command Reference. The Command Reference describes these conventions as follows:

- **Boldface** indicates commands and keywords that are entered literally as shown. In actual configuration examples and output (not general command syntax), boldface indicates commands that are manually input by the user (such as a **show** command).

- *Italic* indicates arguments for which you supply actual values.

- Vertical bars (|) separate alternative, mutually exclusive elements.

- Square brackets ([ ]) indicate an optional element.

- Braces ({ }) indicate a required choice.

- Braces within brackets ([{ }]) indicate a required choice within an optional element.

About This Course Booklet

Your Cisco Networking Academy Course Booklet is designed as a study resource you can easily read, highlight, and review on the go, wherever the Internet is not available or practical:

- The text is extracted directly, word-for-word, from the online course so you can highlight important points and take notes in the "Your Chapter Notes" section.

- Headings with the exact page correlations provide a quick reference to the online course for your classroom discussions and exam preparation.

- An icon system directs you to the online curriculum to take full advantage of the images embedded within the Networking Academy online course interface and reminds you to do the labs, interactive activities, packet tracer activities, watch videos, and take the chapter quizzes.

 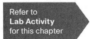

Refer to **Online Course** for Illustration | Refer to **Lab Activity** for this chapter | Go to the online course to take the quiz and exam. | Refer to **Interactive Graphic** in online course | Refer to **Packet Tracer Activity** for this chapter | Refer to **Video** in online course

The Course Booklet is a basic, economical paper-based resource to help you succeed with the Cisco Networking Academy online course.

Introduction

Networking Academy CCNAv7

Welcome to the second course of the Cisco Networking Academy CCNAv7 curriculum, Switching, Routing, and Wireless Essentials (SRWE). This is the second of three courses that are aligned to the CCNA Certification Exam. SRWE contains 16 modules, each with a series of topics.

Switching, Routing, and Wireless Essentials advances your knowledge of the operation of routers and switches in small networks. SRWE will introduce you to wireless local area networks (WLANs) and network security concepts.

By the end of this course you will be able to configure advanced functionality in routers and switches. You will also be able to perform basic troubleshooting of these components. Using security best practices, you will troubleshoot and resolve common protocol issues in both IPv4 and IPv6 networks.

The skills and knowledge you gain in SRWE will prepare you for the final course in CCNA. With Cisco Networking Academy, there is no better time than *now*. Let's go!

CHAPTER 1

Basic Device Configuration

Introduction - 1.0

Why should I take this module? - 1.0.1

Welcome to Basic Device Configuration!

Welcome to the first module in CCNA Switching, Routing, and Wireless Essentials! You know that switches and routers come with some built-in configuration, so why would you need to learn to further configure switches and routers?

Imagine that you purchased a model train set. After you had set it up, you realized that the track was just a simple oval shape and that the train cars only ran clockwise. You might want the track to be a figure eight shape with an overpass. You might want to have two trains that operate independently of each other and are able to move in different directions. How could you make that happen? You would need to reconfigure the track and the controls. It is the same with network devices. As a network administrator you need detailed control of the devices in your network. This means precisely configuring switches and routers so that your network does what you want it to do. This module has many Syntax Checker and Packet Tracer activities to help you develop these skills. Let's get started!

What will I learn to do in this module? - 1.0.2

Module Title: Basic Device Configuration

Module Objective: Configure devices using security best practices.

Topic Title	Topic Objective
Configure a Switch with Initial Settings	Configure initial settings on a Cisco switch.
Configure Switch Ports	Configure switch ports to meet network requirements.
Secure Remote Access	Configure secure management access on a switch.
Basic Router Configuration	Configure basic settings on a router to route between two directly-connected networks, using CLI.
Verify Directly Connected Networks	Verify connectivity between two networks that are directly connected to a router.

Configure a Switch with Initial Settings - 1.1

Switch Boot Sequence - 1.1.1

Before you can configure a switch, you need to turn it on and allow it to go through the five-step boot sequence. This topic covers the basics of configuring a switch and includes a lab at the end.

After a Cisco switch is powered on, it goes through the following five-step boot sequence:

Step 1.   First, the switch loads a power-on self-test (POST) program stored in ROM. POST checks the CPU subsystem. It tests the CPU, DRAM, and the portion of the flash device that makes up the flash file system.

Step 2.   Next, the switch loads the boot loader software. The boot loader is a small program stored in ROM that is run immediately after POST successfully completes.

Step 3.   The boot loader performs low-level CPU initialization. It initializes the CPU registers, which control where physical memory is mapped, the quantity of memory, and its speed.

Step 4.   The boot loader initializes the flash file system on the system board.

Step 5.   Finally, the boot loader locates and loads a default IOS operating system software image into memory and gives control of the switch over to the IOS.

The boot system Command - 1.1.2

The switch attempts to automatically boot by using information in the BOOT environment variable. If this variable is not set, the switch attempts to load and execute the first executable file it can find. On Catalyst 2960 Series switches, the image file is normally contained in a directory that has the same name as the image file (excluding the .bin file extension).

The IOS operating system then initializes the interfaces using the Cisco IOS commands found in the startup-config file. The startup-config file is called **config.text** and is located in flash.

In the example, the BOOT environment variable is set using the **boot system** global configuration mode command. Notice that the IOS is located in a distinct folder and the folder path is specified. Use the command **show boot** to see what the current IOS boot file is set to.

```
S1(config)# boot system flash:/c2960-lanbasek9-mz.150-2.SE/c2960-
lanbasek9-mz.150-2.SE.bin
```

The table defines each part of the **boot system** command.

Command	Definition
`boot system`	The main command
`flash:`	The storage device
`c2960-lanbasek9-mz.150-2.SE/`	The path to the file system
`c2960-lanbasek9-mz.150-2.SE.bin`	The IOS file name

Refer to
Online Course
for Illustration

Refer to
Interactive Graphic
in online course

Switch LED Indicators - 1.1.3

Cisco Catalyst switches have several status LED indicator lights. You can use the switch LEDs to quickly monitor switch activity and performance. Switches of different models and feature sets will have different LEDs and their placement on the front panel of the switch may also vary.

The figure shows the switch LEDs and the Mode button for a Cisco Catalyst 2960 switch.

The Mode button (7 in the figure) is used to toggle through port status, port duplex, port speed, and if supported, the Power over Ethernet (PoE) status of the port LEDs (8 in the figure).

Click each button to learn the purpose of the LED indicators (1-6 in the figure), and the meaning of their colors:

1 SYST

System LED

Shows whether the system is receiving power and is functioning properly. If the LED is off, it means the system is not powered on. If the LED is green, the system is operating normally. If the LED is amber, the system is receiving power but is not functioning properly.

2 RPS

Redundant Power System (RPS) LED

Shows the RPS status. If the LED is off, the RPS is off, or it is not properly connected. If the LED is green, the RPS is connected and ready to provide backup power. If the LED is blinking green, the RPS is connected but is unavailable because it is providing power to another device. If the LED is amber, the RPS is in standby mode, or in a fault condition. If the LED is blinking amber, the internal power supply in the switch has failed, and the RPS is providing power.

3 STAT

Port Status LED

Indicates that the port status mode is selected when the LED is green. This is the default mode. When selected, the port LEDs will display colors with different meanings. If the LED is off, there is no link, or the port was administratively shut down. If the LED is green, a link is present. If the LED is blinking green, there is activity and the port is sending or receiving data. If the LED is alternating green-amber, there is a link fault. If the LED is amber, the port is blocked to ensure that a loop does not exist in the forwarding domain and is not forwarding data (typically, ports will remain in this state for the first 30 seconds after being activated). If the LED is blinking amber, the port is blocked to prevent a possible loop in the forwarding domain.

4 DUPLX

Port Duplex LED

Indicates that the port duplex mode is selected when the LED is green. When selected, port LEDs that are off are in half-duplex mode. If the port LED is green, the port is in full-duplex mode.

5 SPEED

Port Speed LED

Indicates that the port speed mode is selected. When selected, the port LEDs will display colors with different meanings. If the LED is off, the port is operating at 10 Mbps. If the LED is green, the port is operating at 100 Mbps. If the LED is blinking green, the port is operating at 1000 Mbps.

6 PoE

Power over Ethernet (PoE) Mode LED

If PoE is supported, a PoE mode LED will be present. If the LED is off, it indicates the PoE mode is not selected and that none of the ports have been denied power or placed in a fault condition. If the LED is blinking amber, the PoE mode is not selected but at least one of the ports has been denied power or has a PoE fault. If the LED is green, it indicates the PoE mode is selected and the port LEDs will display colors with different meanings. If the port LED is off, the PoE is off. If the port LED is green, the PoE is on. If the port LED is alternating green-amber, PoE is denied because providing power to the powered device will exceed the switch power capacity. If the LED is blinking amber, PoE is off because of a fault. If the LED is amber, PoE for the port has been disabled.

Recovering from a System Crash - 1.1.4

The boot loader provides access into the switch if the operating system cannot be used because of missing or damaged system files. The boot loader has a command-line that provides access to the files stored in flash memory.

The boot loader can be accessed through a console connection following these steps:

Step 1. Connect a PC by console cable to the switch console port. Configure terminal emulation software to connect to the switch.

Step 2. Unplug the switch power cord.

Step 3. Reconnect the power cord to the switch and, within 15 seconds, press and hold down the **Mode** button while the System LED is still flashing green.

Step 4. Continue pressing the **Mode** button until the System LED turns briefly amber and then solid green; then release the **Mode** button.

Step 5. The boot loader **switch:** prompt appears in the terminal emulation software on the PC.

Type the **help** or **?** at the boot loader prompt to view a list of available commands.

By default, the switch attempts to automatically boot up by using information in the BOOT environment variable. To view the path of the switch BOOT environment variable type the **set** command. Then, initialize the flash file system using the **flash_init** command to view the current files in flash, as shown in the output.

```
switch: set
BOOT=flash:/c2960-lanbasek9-mz.122-55.SE7/c2960-lanbasek9-mz.122-
  55.SE7.bin

(output omitted)

switch: flash_init

Initializing Flash...

flashfs[0]: 2 files, 1 directories

flashfs[0]: 0 orphaned files, 0 orphaned directories

flashfs[0]: Total bytes: 32514048
```

```
flashfs[0]: Bytes used: 11838464

flashfs[0]: Bytes available: 20675584

flashfs[0]: flashfs fsck took 10 seconds.

...done Initializing Flash.
```

After flash has finished initializing you can enter the **dir flash:** command to view the directories and files in flash, as shown in the output.

```
switch: dir flash:

Directory of flash:/

     2   -rwx   11834846            c2960-lanbasek9-mz.150-2.SE8.bin

     3   -rwx   2072                multiple-fs
```

Enter the **BOOT=flash** command to change the BOOT environment variable path the switch uses to load the new IOS in flash. To verify the new BOOT environment variable path, issue the **set** command again. Finally, to load the new IOS type the **boot** command without any arguments, as shown in the output.

```
switch: BOOT=flash:c2960-lanbasek9-mz.150-2.SE8.bin

switch: set

BOOT=flash:c2960-lanbasek9-mz.150-2.SE8.bin

(output omitted)

switch: boot
```

The boot loader commands support initializing flash, formatting flash, installing a new IOS, changing the BOOT environment variable and recovery of lost or forgotten passwords.

Refer to
Online Course
for Illustration

Switch Management Access - 1.1.5

To prepare a switch for remote management access, the switch must be configured with an IP address and a subnet mask. Keep in mind that to manage the switch from a remote network, the switch must be configured with a default gateway. This is very similar to configuring the IP address information on host devices. In the figure, the switch virtual interface (SVI) on S1 should be assigned an IP address. The SVI is a virtual interface, not a physical port on the switch. A console cable is used to connect to a PC so that the switch can be initially configured.

Refer to
Interactive Graphic
in online course

Refer to
Online Course
for Illustration

Switch SVI Configuration Example - 1.1.6

By default, the switch is configured to have its management controlled through VLAN 1. All ports are assigned to VLAN 1 by default. For security purposes, it is considered a best practice to use a VLAN other than VLAN 1 for the management VLAN, such as VLAN 99 in the example.

Click each button to learn the steps to configure switch management access.

Step 1

Configure the Management Interface

From VLAN interface configuration mode, an IPv4 address and subnet mask is applied to the management SVI of the switch.

Note: The SVI for VLAN 99 will not appear as "up/up" until VLAN 99 is created and there is a device connected to a switch port associated with VLAN 99.

Note: The switch may need to be configured for IPv6. For example, before you can configure IPv6 addressing on a Cisco Catalyst 2960 running IOS version 15.0, you will need to enter the global configuration command **sdm prefer dual-ipv4-and-ipv6 default** and then **reload** the switch.

Step 2

Configure the Default Gateway

The switch should be configured with a default gateway if it will be managed remotely from networks that are not directly connected.

Note: Because, it will receive its default gateway information from a router advertisement (RA) message, the switch does not require an IPv6 default gateway.

Step 3

Verify Configuration

The **show ip interface brief** and **show ipv6 interface brief** commands are useful for determining the status of both physical and virtual interfaces. The output shown confirms that interface VLAN 99 has been configured with an IPv4 and IPv6 address.

Note: An IP address applied to the SVI is only for remote management access to the switch; this does not allow the switch to route Layer 3 packets.

```
S1# show ip interface brief

Interface       IP-Address       OK? Method   Status     Protocol

Vlan99          172.17.99.11     YES manual   down       down

(output omitted)

S1# show ipv6 interface brief

Vlan99                          [down/down]

    FE80::C27B:BCFF:FEC4:A9C1

    2001:DB8:ACAD:99::1

(output omitted)
```

Refer to
Lab Activity
for this chapter

Lab: Basic Switch Configuration - 1.1.7

In this lab, you will complete the following objectives:

■ Part 1: Cable the Network and Verify the Default Switch Configuration

- Part 2: Configure Basic Network Device Settings
- Part 3: Verify and Test Network Connectivity
- Part 4: Manage the MAC Address Table

Configure Switch Ports - 1.2

Refer to
Online Course
for Illustration

Duplex Communication - 1.2.1

The ports of a switch can be configured independently for different needs. This topic covers how to configure switch ports, how to verify your configurations, common errors, and how to troubleshoot switch configuration issues.

Full-duplex communication increases bandwidth efficiency by allowing both ends of a connection to transmit and receive data simultaneously. This is also known as bidirectional communication and it requires microsegmentation. A microsegmented LAN is created when a switch port has only one device connected and is operating in full-duplex mode. There is no collision domain associated with a switch port operating in full-duplex mode.

Unlike full-duplex communication, half-duplex communication is unidirectional. Half-duplex communication creates performance issues because data can flow in only one direction at a time, often resulting in collisions. Half-duplex connections are typically seen in older hardware, such as hubs. Full-duplex communication has replaced half-duplex in most hardware.

The figure illustrates full-duplex and half-duplex communication.

Gigabit Ethernet and 10 Gb NICs require full-duplex connections to operate. In full-duplex mode, the collision detection circuit on the NIC is disabled. Full-duplex offers 100 percent efficiency in both directions (transmitting and receiving). This results in a doubling of the potential use of the stated bandwidth.

Refer to
Online Course
for Illustration

Configure Switch Ports at the Physical Layer - 1.2.2

Switch ports can be manually configured with specific duplex and speed settings. Use the **duplex** interface configuration mode command to manually specify the duplex mode for a switch port. Use the **speed** interface configuration mode command to manually specify the speed. For example, both switches in the topology should always operate in full-duplex at 100 Mbps.

The table shows the commands for S1. The same commands can be applied to S2.

Task	IOS Commands
Enter global configuration mode.	S1# `configure terminal`
Enter interface configuration mode.	S1(config)# `interface FastEthernet 0/1`
Configure the interface duplex.	S1(config-if)# `duplex full`
Configure the interface speed.	S1(config-if)# `speed 100`
Return to the privileged EXEC mode.	S1(config-if)# `end`
Save the running config to the startup config.	S1# `copy running-config startup-config`

The default setting for both duplex and speed for switch ports on Cisco Catalyst 2960 and 3560 switches is auto. The 10/100/1000 ports operate in either half- or full-duplex mode when they are set to 10 or 100 Mbps and operate only in full-duplex mode when it is set to 1000 Mbps (1 Gbps). Autonegotiation is useful when the speed and duplex settings of the device connecting to the port are unknown or may change. When connecting to known devices such as servers, dedicated workstations, or network devices, a best practice is to manually set the speed and duplex settings.

When troubleshooting switch port issues, it is important that the duplex and speed settings should be checked.

Note: Mismatched settings for the duplex mode and speed of switch ports can cause connectivity issues. Autonegotiation failure creates mismatched settings.

All fiber-optic ports, such as 1000BASE-SX ports, operate only at one preset speed and are always full-duplex

Auto-MDIX - 1.2.3

Until recently, certain cable types (straight-through or crossover) were required when connecting devices. Switch-to-switch or switch-to-router connections required using different Ethernet cables. Using the automatic medium-dependent interface crossover (auto-MDIX) feature on an interface eliminates this problem. When auto-MDIX is enabled, the interface automatically detects the required cable connection type (straight-through or crossover) and configures the connection appropriately. When connecting to switches without the auto-MDIX feature, straight-through cables must be used to connect to devices such as servers, workstations, or routers. Crossover cables must be used to connect to other switches or repeaters.

With auto-MDIX enabled, either type of cable can be used to connect to other devices, and the interface automatically adjusts to communicate successfully. On newer Cisco switches, the **mdix auto** interface configuration mode command enables the feature. When using auto-MDIX on an interface, the interface speed and duplex must be set to **auto** so that the feature operates correctly.

The command to enable auto-MDIX is issued in interface configuration mode on the switch as shown:

```
S1(config-if)# mdix auto
```

Note: The auto-MDIX feature is enabled by default on Catalyst 2960 and Catalyst 3560 switches but is not available on the older Catalyst 2950 and Catalyst 3550 switches.

To examine the auto-MDIX setting for a specific interface, use the **show controllers ethernet-controller** command with the **phy** keyword. To limit the output to lines referencing auto-MDIX, use the **include Auto-MDIX** filter. As shown the output indicates On or Off for the feature.

```
S1# show controllers ethernet-controller fa0/1 phy | include MDIX
  Auto-MDIX            :  On   [AdminState=1   Flags=0x00052248]
```

Switch Verification Commands - 1.2.4

The table summarizes some of the more useful switch verification commands.

Task	IOS Commands
Display interface status and configuration.	S1# **show interfaces** [*interface-id*]
Display current startup configuration.	S1# **show startup-config**
Display current running configuration.	S1# **show running-config**
Display information about flash file system.	S1# **show flash**
Display system hardware and software status.	S1# **show version**
Display history of command entered.	S1# **show history**
Display IP information about an interface.	S1# **show ip interface** [*interface-id*] OR S1# **show ipv6 interface** [*interface-id*]
Display the MAC address table.	S1# **show mac-address-table** OR S1# **show mac address-table**

Verify Switch Port Configuration - 1.2.5

The **show running-config** command can be used to verify that the switch has been correctly configured. From the sample abbreviated output on S1, some important information is shown in the figure:

- Fast Ethernet 0/18 interface is configured with the management VLAN 99

- VLAN 99 is configured with an IPv4 address of 172.17.99.11 255.255.255.0

- The default gateway is set to 172.17.99.1

```
S1# show running-config

Building configuration...

Current configuration : 1466 bytes

!

interface FastEthernet0/18

 switchport access vlan 99

 switchport mode access

!

(output omitted)

!

interface Vlan99

 ip address 172.17.99.11 255.255.255.0

 ipv6 address 2001:DB8:ACAD:99::1/64

!

ip default-gateway 172.17.99.1
```

The **show interfaces** command is another commonly used command, which displays status and statistics information on the network interfaces of the switch. The **show interfaces** command is frequently used when configuring and monitoring network devices.

The first line of the output for the **show interfaces fastEthernet 0/18** command indicates that the FastEthernet 0/18 interface is up/up, meaning that it is operational. Further down, the output shows that the duplex is full and the speed is 100 Mbps.

```
S1# show interfaces fastEthernet 0/18

FastEthernet0/18 is up, line protocol is up (connected)

  Hardware is Fast Ethernet, address is 0025.83e6.9092 (bia
0025.83e6.9092)

  MTU 1500 bytes, BW 100000 Kbit/sec, DLY 100 usec,

      reliability 255/255, txload 1/255, rxload 1/255

  Encapsulation ARPA, loopback not set

  Keepalive set (10 sec)

  Full-duplex, 100Mb/s, media type is 10/100BaseTX
```

Network Access Layer Issues - 1.2.6

The output from the **show interfaces** command is useful for detecting common media issues. One of the most important parts of this output is the display of the line and data link protocol status, as shown in the example.

```
S1# show interfaces fastEthernet 0/18

FastEthernet0/18 is up, line protocol is up (connected)

Hardware is Fast Ethernet, address is 0025.83e6.9092 (bia
0025.83e6.9092)MTU 1500 bytes, BW 100000 Kbit/sec, DLY 100 usec,
```

The first parameter (FastEthernet0/18 is up) refers to the hardware layer and indicates whether the interface is receiving a carrier detect signal. The second parameter (line protocol is up) refers to the data link layer and indicates whether the data link layer protocol keepalives are being received.

Based on the output of the **show interfaces** command, possible problems can be fixed as follows:

- If the interface is up and the line protocol is down, a problem exists. There could be an encapsulation type mismatch, the interface on the other end could be error-disabled, or there could be a hardware problem.

- If the line protocol and the interface are both down, a cable is not attached, or some other interface problem exists. For example, in a back-to-back connection, the other end of the connection may be administratively down.

- If the interface is administratively down, it has been manually disabled (the **shutdown** command has been issued) in the active configuration.

The **show interfaces** command output displays counters and statistics for the FastEthernet0/18 interface, as highlighted in the example.

```
S1# show interfaces fastEthernet 0/18
FastEthernet0/18 is up, line protocol is up (connected)
  Hardware is Fast Ethernet, address is 0025.83e6.9092 (bia 0025.83e6.9092)
  MTU 1500 bytes, BW 100000 Kbit/sec, DLY 100 usec,
     reliability 255/255, txload 1/255, rxload 1/255
  Encapsulation ARPA, loopback not set
  Keepalive set (10 sec)
  Full-duplex, 100Mb/s, media type is 10/100BaseTX
  input flow-control is off, output flow-control is unsupported
  ARP type: ARPA, ARP Timeout 04:00:00
  Last input never, output 00:00:01, output hang never
  Last clearing of "show interface" counters never
  Input queue: 0/75/0/0 (size/max/drops/flushes); Total output drops: 0
  Queueing strategy: fifo
  Output queue: 0/40 (size/max)
  5 minute input rate 0 bits/sec, 0 packets/sec
  5 minute output rate 0 bits/sec, 0 packets/sec
     2295197 packets input, 305539992 bytes, 0 no buffer
     Received 1925500 broadcasts (74 multicasts)
     0 runts, 0 giants, 0 throttles
     3 input errors, 3 CRC, 0 frame, 0 overrun, 0 ignored
     0 watchdog, 74 multicast, 0 pause input
     0 input packets with dribble condition detected
     3594664 packets output, 436549843 bytes, 0 underruns
     8 output errors, 1790 collisions, 10 interface resets
     0 unknown protocol drops
     0 babbles, 235 late collision, 0 deferred
```

Some media errors are not severe enough to cause the circuit to fail but do cause network performance issues. The table explains some of these common errors which can be detected using the **show interfaces** command.

Error Type	Description
Input Errors	Total number of errors. It includes runts, giants, no buffer, CRC, frame, overrun, and ignored counts.
Runts	Packets that are discarded because they are smaller than the minimum packet size for the medium. For instance, any Ethernet packet that is less than 64 bytes is considered a runt.
Giants	Packets that are discarded because they exceed the maximum packet size for the medium. For example, any Ethernet packet that is greater than 1,518 bytes is considered a giant.
CRC	CRC errors are generated when the calculated checksum is not the same as the checksum received.
Output Errors	Sum of all errors that prevented the final transmission of datagrams out of the interface that is being examined.
Collisions	Number of messages retransmitted because of an Ethernet collision.
Late Collisions	A collision that occurs after 512 bits of the frame have been transmitted.

Interface Input and Output Errors - 1.2.7

"Input errors" is the sum of all errors in datagrams that were received on the interface being examined. This includes runts, giants, CRC, no buffer, frame, overrun, and ignored counts. The reported input errors from the **show interfaces** command include the following:

- **Runt Frames** - Ethernet frames that are shorter than the 64-byte minimum allowed length are called runts. Malfunctioning NICs are the usual cause of excessive runt frames, but they can also be caused by collisions.

- **Giants** - Ethernet frames that are larger than the maximum allowed size are called giants.

- **CRC errors** - On Ethernet and serial interfaces, CRC errors usually indicate a media or cable error. Common causes include electrical interference, loose or damaged connections, or incorrect cabling. If you see many CRC errors, there is too much noise on the link and you should inspect the cable. You should also search for and eliminate noise sources.

"Output errors" is the sum of all errors that prevented the final transmission of datagrams out the interface that is being examined. The reported output errors from the **show interfaces** command include the following:

- **Collisions** - Collisions in half-duplex operations are normal. However, you should never see collisions on an interface configured for full-duplex communication.

- **Late collisions** - A late collision refers to a collision that occurs after 512 bits of the frame have been transmitted. Excessive cable lengths are the most common cause of late collisions. Another common cause is duplex misconfiguration. For example, you could have one end of a connection configured for full-duplex and the other for half-duplex. You would see late collisions on the interface that is configured for half-duplex. In that case, you must configure the same duplex setting on both ends. A properly designed and configured network should never have late collisions.

Refer to
Online Course
for Illustration

Troubleshooting Network Access Layer Issues - 1.2.8

Most issues that affect a switched network are encountered during the original implementation. Theoretically, after it is installed, a network continues to operate without problems. However, cabling gets damaged, configurations change, and new devices are connected to the switch that require switch configuration changes. Ongoing maintenance and troubleshooting of the network infrastructure is required.

To troubleshoot scenarios involving no connection, or a bad connection, between a switch and another device, follow the general process shown in the figure.

Use the **show interfaces** command to check the interface status.

If the interface is down:

- Check to make sure that the proper cables are being used. Additionally, check the cable and connectors for damage. If a bad or incorrect cable is suspected, replace the cable.

- If the interface is still down, the problem may be due to a mismatch in speed setting. The speed of an interface is typically autonegotiated; therefore, even if it is manually applied to one interface, the connecting interface should autonegotiate accordingly. If a speed mismatch does occur through misconfiguration, or a hardware or software issue, then that may result in the interface going down. Manually set the same speed on both connection ends if a problem is suspected.

If the interface is up, but issues with connectivity are still present:

- Using the **show interfaces** command, check for indications of excessive noise. Indications may include an increase in the counters for runts, giants, and CRC errors. If there is excessive noise, first find and remove the source of the noise, if possible. Also, verify that the cable does not exceed the maximum cable length and check the type of cable that is used.

- If noise is not an issue, check for excessive collisions. If there are collisions or late collisions, verify the duplex settings on both ends of the connection. Much like the speed setting, the duplex setting is usually autonegotiated. If there does appear to be a duplex mismatch, manually set the duplex to full on both ends of the connection.

Refer to
Interactive Graphic
in online course

Syntax Checker - Configure Switch Ports - 1.2.9

Configure a switch interface based on the specified requirements

Secure Remote Access - 1.3

Refer to
Online Course
for Illustration

Telnet Operation - 1.3.1

You might not always have direct access to your switch when you need to configure it. You need to be able to access it remotely and it is imperative that your access is secure. This topic discusses how to configure Secure Shell (SSH) for remote access. A Packet Tracer activity gives you the opportunity to try this yourself.

Telnet uses TCP port 23. It is an older protocol that uses unsecure plaintext transmission of both the login authentication (username and password) and the data transmitted between the communicating devices. A threat actor can monitor packets using Wireshark. For example, in the figure the threat actor captured the username **admin** and password **ccna** from a Telnet session.

Refer to
Online Course
for Illustration

SSH Operation - 1.3.2

Secure Shell (SSH) is a secure protocol that uses TCP port 22. It provides a secure (encrypted) management connection to a remote device. SSH should replace Telnet for management connections. SSH provides security for remote connections by providing strong encryption when a device is authenticated (username and password) and also for the transmitted data between the communicating devices.

For example, the figure shows a Wireshark capture of an SSH session. The threat actor can track the session using the IP address of the administrator device. However, unlike Telnet, with SSH the username and password are encrypted.

Verify the Switch Supports SSH - 1.3.3

To enable SSH on a Catalyst 2960 switch, the switch must be using a version of the IOS software including cryptographic (encrypted) features and capabilities. Use the **show version** command on the switch to see which IOS the switch is currently running. An IOS filename that includes the combination "k9" supports cryptographic (encrypted) features and capabilities. The example shows the output of the **show version** command.

```
S1# show version

Cisco IOS Software, C2960 Software (C2960-LANBASEK9-M), Version 15.0(2)
SE7, RELEASE SOFTWARE (fc1)
```

Refer to
Interactive Graphic
in online course

Configure SSH - 1.3.4

Before configuring SSH, the switch must be minimally configured with a unique hostname and the correct network connectivity settings.

Click each button to learn the steps to configure SSH.

Step 1

Verify SSH support.

Use the **show ip ssh** command to verify that the switch supports SSH. If the switch is not running an IOS that supports cryptographic features, this command is unrecognized.

```
S1# show ip ssh
```

Step 2

Configure the IP domain.

Configure the IP domain name of the network using the **ip domain-name** *domain-name* global configuration mode command. In the figure, the *domain-name* value is **cisco.com**.

```
S1(config)# ip domain-name cisco.com
```

Step 3

Generate RSA key pairs.

Not all versions of the IOS default to SSH version 2, and SSH version 1 has known security flaws. To configure SSH version 2, issue the **ip ssh version 2** global configuration mode command. Generating an RSA key pair automatically enables SSH. Use the **crypto key generate rsa** global configuration mode command to enable the SSH server on the switch and generate an RSA key pair. When generating RSA keys, the administrator is prompted to enter a modulus length. The sample configuration in the figure uses a modulus size of 1,024 bits. A longer modulus length is more secure, but it takes longer to generate and to use.

Note: To delete the RSA key pair, use the **crypto key zeroize rsa** global configuration mode command. After the RSA key pair is deleted, the SSH server is automatically disabled.

```
S1(config)# crypto key generate rsa

How many bits in the modulus [512]: 1024
```

Step 4

Configure user authentication.

The SSH server can authenticate users locally or using an authentication server. To use the local authentication method, create a username and password pair using the **username** *username* **secret** *password* global configuration mode command. In the example, the user admin is assigned the password ccna.

```
S1(config)# username admin secret ccna
```

Step 5

Configure the vty lines.

Enable the SSH protocol on the vty lines by using the **transport input ssh** line configuration mode command. The Catalyst 2960 has vty lines ranging from 0 to 15. This configuration prevents non-SSH (such as Telnet) connections and limits the switch to accept only SSH connections. Use the **line vty** global configuration mode command and then the **login local** line configuration mode command to require local authentication for SSH connections from the local username database.

```
S1(config)z# line vty 0 15

S1(config-line)# transport input ssh

S1(config-line)# login local

S1(config-line)# exit
```

Step 6

Enable SSH version 2.

By default, SSH supports both versions 1 and 2. When supporting both versions, this is shown in the **show ip ssh** output as supporting version 2. Enable SSH version using the **ip ssh version 2** global configuration command.

```
S1(config)# ip ssh version 2
```

Refer to
Online Course
for Illustration

Verify SSH is Operational - 1.3.5

On a PC, an SSH client such as PuTTY, is used to connect to an SSH server. For example, assume the following is configured:

- SSH is enabled on switch S1

- Interface VLAN 99 (SVI) with IPv4 address 172.17.99.11 on switch S1

- PC1 with IPv4 address 172.17.99.21

The figure shows the PuTTy settings for PC1 to initiate an SSH connection to the SVI VLAN IPv4 address of S1.

When connected, the user is prompted for a username and password as shown in the example. Using the configuration from the previous example, the username **admin** and password **ccna** are entered. After entering the correct combination, the user is connected via SSH to the command line interface (CLI) on the Catalyst 2960 switch.

```
Login as: admin
Using keyboard-interactive
Authentication.
Password:
S1> enable
Password:
S1#
```

To display the version and configuration data for SSH on the device that you configured as an SSH server, use the **show ip ssh** command. In the example, SSH version 2 is enabled.

```
S1# show ip ssh
SSH Enabled - version 2.0
Authentication timeout: 120 secs; Authentication retries: 3
```

To check the SSH connections to the device, use the show ssh command as shown.

```
S1# show ssh
%No SSHv1 server connections running.

Connection Version Mode Encryption  Hmac       State           Username
0          2.0     IN   aes256-cbc  hmac-sha1  Session started  admin
0          2.0     OUT  aes256-cbc  hmac-sha1  Session started  admin
S1#
```

Refer to **Packet
Tracer Activity**
for this chapter

Packet Tracer - Configure SSH - 1.3.6

SSH should replace Telnet for management connections. Telnet uses insecure plaintext communications. SSH provides security for remote connections by providing strong encryption of all transmitted data between devices. In this activity, you will secure a remote switch with password encryption and SSH.

Basic Router Configuration - 1.4

Configure Basic Router Settings - 1.4.1

Up to now, this module has only covered switches. If you want devices to be able to send and receive data outside of your network, you will have to configure routers. This topic teaches you basic router configuration and provides two Syntax Checkers and a Packet Tracer activity so you can practice these skills.

Cisco routers and Cisco switches have many similarities. They support a similar modal operating system, similar command structures, and many of the same commands. In addition, both devices have similar initial configuration steps. For example, the following configuration tasks should always be performed. Name the device to distinguish it from other routers and configure passwords, as shown in the example.

```
Router# configure terminal
Enter configuration commands, one per line.  End with CNTL/Z.
Router(config)# hostname R1
R1(config)# enable secret class
R1(config)# line console 0
R1(config-line)# password cisco
R1(config-line)# login
R1(config-line)# exit
R1(config)# line vty 0 4
R1(config-line)# password cisco
R1(config-line)# login
R1(config-line)# exit
R1(config)# service password-encryption
R1(config)#
```

Configure a banner to provide legal notification of unauthorized access, as shown in the example.

```
R1(config)# banner motd $ Authorized Access Only! $
R1(config)#
```

Save the changes on a router, as shown in the example.

```
R1# copy running-config startup-config
Destination filename [startup-config]?
Building configuration...
[OK]
```

Refer to
Interactive Graphic
in online course

Syntax Checker - Configure Basic Router Settings - 1.4.2

In this Syntax Activity, you will configure basic settings for R2.

Refer to
Online Course
for Illustration

Dual Stack Topology - 1.4.3

One distinguishing feature between switches and routers is the type of interfaces supported by each. For example, Layer 2 switches support LANs; therefore, they have multiple FastEthernet or Gigabit Ethernet ports. The dual stack topology in the figure is used to demonstrate the configuration of router IPv4 and IPv6 interfaces.

Configure Router Interfaces - 1.4.4

Routers support LANs and WANs and can interconnect different types of networks; therefore, they support many types of interfaces. For example, G2 ISRs have one or two integrated Gigabit Ethernet interfaces and High-Speed WAN Interface Card (HWIC) slots to accommodate other types of network interfaces, including serial, DSL, and cable interfaces.

To be available, an interface must be:

- **Configured with at least one IP address** - Use the **ip address** *ip-address subnet-mask* and the **ipv6 address** *ipv6-address/prefix* interface configuration commands.

- **Activated** - By default, LAN and WAN interfaces are not activated (**shutdown**). To enable an interface, it must be activated using the **no shutdown** command. (This is similar to powering on the interface.) The interface must also be connected to another device (a hub, a switch, or another router) for the physical layer to be active.

- **Description** - Optionally, the interface could also be configured with a short description of up to 240 characters. It is good practice to configure a description on each interface. On production networks, the benefits of interface descriptions are quickly realized as they are helpful in troubleshooting and in identifying a third-party connection and contact information.

The following example shows the configuration for the interfaces on R1.

```
R1(config)# interface gigabitethernet 0/0/0
R1(config-if)# ip address 192.168.10.1 255.255.255.0
R1(config-if)# ipv6 address 2001:db8:acad:1::1/64
R1(config-if)# description Link to LAN 1
R1(config-if)# no shutdown
R1(config-if)# exit
R1(config)# interface gigabitethernet 0/0/1
R1(config-if)# ip address 192.168.11.1 255.255.255.0
R1(config-if)# ipv6 address 2001:db8:acad:2::1/64
R1(config-if)# description Link to LAN 2
```

```
R1(config-if)# no shutdown

R1(config-if)# exit

R1(config)# interface serial 0/0/0

R1(config-if)# ip address 209.165.200.225 255.255.255.252

R1(config-if)# ipv6 address 2001:db8:acad:3::225/64

R1(config-if)# description Link to R2

R1(config-if)# no shutdown

R1(config-if)# exit

R1(config)#
```

Refer to
Interactive Graphic
in online course

Syntax Checker - Configure Router Interfaces - 1.4.5

In this Syntax Checker activity, you will configure R2 with its IPv4 and IPv6 interfaces.

IPv4 Loopback Interfaces - 1.4.6

Another common configuration of Cisco IOS routers is enabling a loopback interface.

The loopback interface is a logical interface that is internal to the router. It is not assigned to a physical port and can never be connected to any other device. It is considered a software interface that is automatically placed in an "up" state, as long as the router is functioning.

The loopback interface is useful in testing and managing a Cisco IOS device because it ensures that at least one interface will always be available. For example, it can be used for testing purposes, such as testing internal routing processes, by emulating networks behind the router.

Loopback interfaces are also commonly used in lab environments to create additional interfaces. For example, you can create multiple loopback interfaces on a router to simulate more networks for configuration practice and testing purposes. In this curriculum, we often use a loopback interface to simulate a link to the internet.

Enabling and assigning a loopback address is simple:

```
Router(config)# interface loopback number

Router(config-if)# ip address ip-address subnet-mask
```

Multiple loopback interfaces can be enabled on a router. The IPv4 address for each loopback interface must be unique and unused by any other interface, as shown in the example configuration of loopback interface 0 on R1.

```
R1(config)# interface loopback 0

R1(config-if)# ip address 10.0.0.1 255.255.255.0

R1(config-if)# exit

R1(config)#

%LINEPROTO-5-UPDOWN: Line protocol on Interface Loopback0, changed state
to up
```

Refer to **Packet Tracer Activity** for this chapter

Packet Tracer - Configure Router Interfaces - 1.4.7

In this Packet Tracer activity, you will configure routers with IPv4 and IPv6 addressing.

Verify Directly Connected Networks - 1.5

Refer to **Online Course** for Illustration

Interface Verification Commands - 1.5.1

There is no point in configuring your router unless you verify the configuration and connectivity. This topic covers the commands to use to verify directly connected networks. It includes two Syntax Checkers and a Packet Tracer.

There are several **show** commands that can be used to verify the operation and configuration of an interface. The topology in the figure is used to demonstrate the verification of router interface settings.

The following commands are especially useful to quickly identify the status of an interface:

- **show ip interface brief** and **show ipv6 interface brief** - These display a summary for all interfaces including the IPv4 or IPv6 address of the interface and current operational status.

- **show running-config interface** *interface-id* - This displays the commands applied to the specified interface.

- **show ip route** and **show ipv6 route** - These display the contents of the IPv4 or IPv6 routing table stored in RAM. In Cisco IOS 15, active interfaces should appear in the routing table with two related entries identified by the code 'C' (Connected) or 'L' (Local). In previous IOS versions, only a single entry with the code 'C' will appear.

Verify Interface Status - 1.5.2

The output of the **show ip interface brief** and **show ipv6 interface brief** commands can be used to quickly reveal the status of all interfaces on the router. You can verify that the interfaces are active and operational as indicated by the Status of "up" and Protocol of "up", as shown in the example. A different output would indicate a problem with either the configuration or the cabling.

```
R1# show ip interface brief

Interface              IP-Address       OK? Method Status                Protocol

GigabitEthernet0/0/0   192.168.10.1     YES manual up                         up

GigabitEthernet0/0/1   192.168.11.1     YES manual up                         up

Serial0/1/0            209.165.200.225 YES manual up                         up

Serial0/1/1            unassigned       YES unset  administratively down down

R1# show ipv6 interface brief

GigabitEthernet0/0/0   [up/up]
```

```
    FE80::7279:B3FF:FE92:3130

    2001:DB8:ACAD:1::1

GigabitEthernet0/0/1 [up/up]

    FE80::7279:B3FF:FE92:3131

    2001:DB8:ACAD:2::1

Serial0/1/0            [up/up]

    FE80::7279:B3FF:FE92:3130

    2001:DB8:ACAD:3::1

Serial0/1/1            [down/down]        Unassigned
```

Verify IPv6 Link Local and Multicast Addresses - 1.5.3

The output of the **show ipv6 interface brief** command displays two configured IPv6 addresses per interface. One address is the IPv6 global unicast address that was manually entered. The other address, which begins with FE80, is the link-local unicast address for the interface. A link-local address is automatically added to an interface whenever a global unicast address is assigned. An IPv6 network interface is required to have a link-local address, but not necessarily a global unicast address.

The **show ipv6 interface gigabitethernet 0/0/0** command displays the interface status and all of the IPv6 addresses belonging to the interface. Along with the link local address and global unicast address, the output includes the multicast addresses assigned to the interface, beginning with prefix FF02, as shown in the example.

```
R1# show ipv6 interface gigabitethernet 0/0/0

GigabitEthernet0/0/0 is up, line protocol is up

  IPv6 is enabled, link-local address is FE80::7279:B3FF:FE92:3130

  No Virtual link-local address(es):

  Global unicast address(es):

    2001:DB8:ACAD:1::1, subnet is 2001:DB8:ACAD:1::/64

  Joined group address(es):

    FF02::1

    FF02::1:FF00:1

    FF02::1:FF92:3130

  MTU is 1500 bytes

  ICMP error messages limited to one every 100 milliseconds

  ICMP redirects are enabled

  ICMP unreachables are sent

  ND DAD is enabled, number of DAD attempts: 1

  ND reachable time is 30000 milliseconds (using 30000)

  ND advertised reachable time is 0 (unspecified)
```

```
ND advertised retransmit interval is 0 (unspecified)

ND router advertisements are sent every 200 seconds

ND router advertisements live for 1800 seconds

ND advertised default router preference is Medium
```

Verify Interface Configuration - 1.5.4

The output of the **show running-config interface** command displays the current commands applied to the specified interface as shown.

```
R1 show running-config interface gigabitethernet 0/0/0

Building configuration...

Current configuration : 158 bytes

!

interface GigabitEthernet0/0/0

 description Link to LAN 1

 ip address 192.168.10.1 255.255.255.0

 negotiation auto

 ipv6 address 2001:DB8:ACAD:1::1/64

end

R1#
```

The following two commands are used to gather more detailed interface information:

- **show interfaces** - Displays interface information and packet flow count for all interfaces on the device.

- **show ip interface** and **show ipv6 interface** - Displays the IPv4 and IPv6 related information for all interfaces on a router.

Verify Routes - 1.5.5

The output of the **show ip route** and **show ipv6 route** commands reveal the three directly connected network entries and the three local host route interface entries, as shown in the example. The local host route has an administrative distance of 0. It also has a /32 mask for IPv4, and a /128 mask for IPv6. The local host route is for routes on the router that owns the IP address. It is used to allow the router to process packets destined to that IP.

```
R1# show ip route

Codes: L - local, C - connected, S - static, R - RIP, M - mobile, B - BGP


Gateway of last resort is not set

      192.168.10.0/24 is variably subnetted, 2 subnets, 2 masks

C        192.168.10.0/24 is directly connected, GigabitEthernet0/0/0
```

```
L        192.168.10.1/32 is directly connected, GigabitEthernet0/0/0
      192.168.11.0/24 is variably subnetted, 2 subnets, 2 masks
C        192.168.11.0/24 is directly connected, GigabitEthernet0/0/1
L        192.168.11.1/32 is directly connected, GigabitEthernet0/0/1
      209.165.200.0/24 is variably subnetted, 2 subnets, 2 masks
C        209.165.200.224/30 is directly connected, Serial0/1/0
L        209.165.200.225/32 is directly connected, Serial0/1/0
R1# show ipv6 route
IPv6 Routing Table - default - 7 entries
Codes: C - Connected, L - Local, S - Static, U - Per-user Static route


C    2001:DB8:ACAD:1::/64 [0/0]
     via GigabitEthernet0/0/0, directly connected
L    2001:DB8:ACAD:1::1/128 [0/0]
     via GigabitEthernet0/0/0, receive
C    2001:DB8:ACAD:2::/64 [0/0]
     via GigabitEthernet0/0/1, directly connected
L    2001:DB8:ACAD:2::1/128 [0/0]
     via GigabitEthernet0/0/1, receive
C    2001:DB8:ACAD:3::/64 [0/0]
     via Serial0/1/0, directly connected
L    2001:DB8:ACAD:3::1/128 [0/0]
     via Serial0/1/0, receive
L    FF00::/8 [0/0]
     via Null0, receive
R1#
```

A 'C' next to a route within the routing table indicates that this is a directly connected network. When the router interface is configured with a global unicast address and is in the "up/up" state, the IPv6 prefix and prefix length are added to the IPv6 routing table as a connected route.

The IPv6 global unicast address applied to the interface is also installed in the routing table as a local route. The local route has a /128 prefix. Local routes are used by the routing table to efficiently process packets with the interface address of the router as the destination.

The **ping** command for IPv6 is identical to the command used with IPv4 except that an IPv6 address is used. As shown in the example, the **ping** command is used to verify Layer 3 connectivity between R1 and PC1.

```
R1# ping 2001:db8:acad:1::10

Type escape sequence to abort.

Sending 5, 100-byte ICMP Echos to 2001:DB8:ACAD:1::10, timeout is
2 seconds:

!!!!!

Success rate is 100 percent (5/5), round-trip min/avg/max = 1/1/1 ms
```

Refer to
Interactive Graphic
in online course

Filter Show Command Output - 1.5.6

Commands that generate multiple screens of output are, by default, paused after 24 lines. At the end of the paused output, the --More-- text displays. Pressing **Enter** displays the next line and pressing the spacebar displays the next set of lines. Use the **terminal length** command to specify the number of lines to be displayed. A value of 0 (zero) prevents the router from pausing between screens of output.

Another very useful feature that improves the user experience in the CLI is the filtering of **show** output. Filtering commands can be used to display specific sections of output. To enable the filtering command, enter a pipe (l) character after the **show** command and then enter a filtering parameter and a filtering expression.

There are four filtering parameters that can be configured after the pipe.

Click each button to learn about the filtering commands.

section

Shows the entire section that starts with the filtering expression, as shown in the example.

```
R1# show running-config | section line vty

line vty 0 4
 password 7 110A1016141D
 login
 transport input all
```

include

Includes all output lines that match the filtering expression, as shown in the example.

```
R1# show ip interface brief
Interface              IP-Address      OK? Method Status        Protocol
GigabitEthernet0/0/0   192.168.10.1    YES manual up                  up
GigabitEthernet0/0/1   192.168.11.1    YES manual up                  up
Serial0/1/0            209.165.200.225 YES manual up                  up
Serial0/1/1            unassigned      NO  unset  down              down
R1#

R1# show ip interface brief | include up
```

```
GigabitEthernet0/0/0    192.168.10.1    YES manual up              up

GigabitEthernet0/0/1    192.168.11.1    YES manual up              up

Serial0/1/0             209.165.200.225 YES manual up              up
```

exclude

Excludes all output lines that match the filtering expression, as shown in the example.

```
R1# show ip interface brief

Interface               IP-Address      OK? Method Status     Protocol

GigabitEthernet0/0/0    192.168.10.1    YES manual up              up

GigabitEthernet0/0/1    192.168.11.1    YES manual up              up

Serial0/1/0             209.165.200.225 YES manual up              up

Serial0/1/1             unassigned      NO  unset  down          down

R1#

R1# show ip interface brief | exclude unassigned

Interface               IP-Address      OK? Method Status     Protocol

GigabitEthernet0/0/0    192.168.10.1    YES manual up              up

GigabitEthernet0/0/1    192.168.11.1    YES manual up              up

Serial0/1/0             209.165.200.225 YES manual up              up
```

begin

Shows all the output lines from a certain point, starting with the line that matches the filtering expression, as shown in the example.

```
R1# show ip route | begin Gateway

Gateway of last resort is not set

      192.168.10.0/24 is variably subnetted, 2 subnets, 2 masks

C        192.168.10.0/24 is directly connected, GigabitEthernet0/0/0

L        192.168.10.1/32 is directly connected, GigabitEthernet0/0/0

      192.168.11.0/24 is variably subnetted, 2 subnets, 2 masks

C        192.168.11.0/24 is directly connected, GigabitEthernet0/0/1

L        192.168.11.1/32 is directly connected, GigabitEthernet0/0/1

      209.165.200.0/24 is variably subnetted, 2 subnets, 2 masks

C        209.165.200.224/30 is directly connected, Serial0/1/0

L        209.165.200.225/32 is directly connected, Serial0/1/0
```

Note: Output filters can be used in combination with any **show** command.

Refer to
Interactive Graphic
in online course

Syntax Checker - Filter Show Command Output - 1.5.7

In this Syntax Checker activity, you will filter output for show commands.

Command History Feature - 1.5.8

The command history feature is useful because it temporarily stores the list of executed commands to be recalled.

To recall commands in the history buffer, press **Ctrl+P** or the **Up Arrow** key. The command output begins with the most recent command. Repeat the key sequence to recall successively older commands. To return to more recent commands in the history buffer, press **Ctrl+N** or the **Down Arrow** key. Repeat the key sequence to recall successively more recent commands.

By default, command history is enabled and the system captures the last 10 command lines in its history buffer. Use the **show history** privileged EXEC command to display the contents of the buffer.

It is also practical to increase the number of command lines that the history buffer records during the current terminal session only. Use the **terminal history size** user EXEC command to increase or decrease the size of the buffer.

An example of the **terminal history size** and **show history** commands is shown in the figure.

```
R1# terminal history size 200

R1# show history

  show ip int brief

  show interface g0/0/0

  show ip route

  show running-config

  show history

  terminal history size 200
```

Refer to
Interactive Graphic
in online course

Syntax Checker - Command History Features - 1.5.9

In this Syntax Check activity, you will use the command history feature.

Refer to **Packet
Tracer Activity**
for this chapter

Packet Tracer - Verify Directly Connected Networks - 1.5.10

In this Packet Tracer activity, routers R1 and R2 each have two LANs. Your task is to verify the addressing on each device and verify connectivity between the LANs.

Go to the online course to take the quiz and exam.

Check Your Understanding - Verify Directly Connected Networks - 1.5.11

Module Practice and Quiz - 1.6

Refer to **Packet Tracer Activity** for this chapter

Packet Tracer - Implement a Small Network - 1.6.1

In this Packet Tracer activity, routers R1 and R2 each have two LANs. Your task is to verify the addressing on each device and verify connectivity between the LANs.

Refer to **Lab Activity** for this chapter

Lab - Configure Basic Router Settings - 1.6.2

This is a comprehensive lab to review previously covered IOS router commands. You will cable the equipment and complete basic configurations and IPv4 interface settings on the router. You will then use SSH to connect to the router remotely and use IOS commands to retrieve information from the device to answer questions about the router.

What did I learn in this module? - 1.6.3

Configure a Switch with Initial Settings

After a Cisco switch is powered on, it goes through a five-step boot sequence. The BOOT environment variable is set using the **boot system** global configuration mode command. The IOS is located in a distinct folder and the folder path is specified. Use the switch LEDs to monitor switch activity and performance: SYST, RPS, STAT, DUPLX, SPEED, and PoE. The boot loader provides access into the switch if the operating system cannot be used because of missing or damaged system files. The boot loader has a command line that provides access to the files stored in flash memory. To prepare a switch for remote management access, the switch must be configured with an IP address and a subnet mask. To manage the switch from a remote network, the switch must be configured with a default gateway. To configure the switch SVI, you must first configure the management interface, then configure the default gateway, and finally, verify your configuration.

Configure Switch Ports

Full-duplex communication increases effective bandwidth by allowing both ends of a connection to transmit and receive data simultaneously. Half-duplex communication is unidirectional. Switch ports can be manually configured with specific duplex and speed settings. Use autonegotiation when the speed and duplex settings of the device connecting to the port are unknown or may change. When auto-MDIX is enabled, the interface automatically detects the required cable connection type (straight-through or crossover) and configures the connection appropriately. There are several **show** commands to use when verifying switch configurations. Use the **show running-config** command and the **show interfaces** command to verify a switch port configuration. The output from the **show interfaces** command is also useful for detecting common network access layer issues because it displays the line and data link protocol status. The reported input errors from the **show interfaces** command include: runt frames, giants, CRC errors, along with collisions and late collisions. Use **show interfaces** to determine if your network has no connection or a bad connection between a switch and another device.

Secure Remote Access

Telnet (using TCP port 23) is an older protocol that uses unsecure plaintext transmission of both the login authentication (username and password) and the data transmitted between the communicating devices. SSH (using TCP port 22) is a secure protocol that provides an encrypted management connection to a remote device. SSH provides security for remote connections by providing strong encryption when a device is authenticated (username and password) and also for the transmitted data between the communicating devices. Use the **show version** command on the switch to see which IOS the switch is currently running. An IOS filename that includes the combination "k9" supports cryptographic features and capabilities. To configure SSH you must verify that the switch supports it, configure the IP domain, generate RSA key pairs, configure use authentication, configure the VTY lines, and enable SSH version 2. To verify that SSH is operational, use the **show ip ssh** command to display the version and configuration data for SSH on the device.

Basic Router Configuration

The following initial configuration tasks should always be performed: name the device to distinguish it from other routers and configure passwords, configure a banner to provide legal notification of unauthorized access, and save the changes on a router. One distinguishing feature between switches and routers is the type of interfaces supported by each. For example, Layer 2 switches support LANs and, therefore, have multiple FastEthernet or Gigabit Ethernet ports. The dual stack topology is used to demonstrate the configuration of router IPv4 and IPv6 interfaces. Routers support LANs and WANs and can interconnect different types of networks; therefore, they support many types of interfaces. For example, G2 ISRs have one or two integrated Gigabit Ethernet interfaces and High-Speed WAN Interface Card (HWIC) slots to accommodate other types of network interfaces, including serial, DSL, and cable interfaces. The IPv4 loopback interface is a logical interface that is internal to the router. It is not assigned to a physical port and can never be connected to any other device.

Verify Directly Connected Networks

Use the following commands to quickly identify the status of an interface: **show ip interface brief** and **show ipv6 interface brief** to see summary all interfaces (IPv4 and IPv6 addresses and operational status), **show running-config interface interface-id** to see the commands applied to a specified interface, and **show ip route** and **show ipv6 route** to see the contents of the IPv4 or IPv6 routing table stored in RAM. The output of the **show ip interface brief** and **show ipv6 interface brief** commands can be used to quickly reveal the status of all interfaces on the router. The **show ipv6 interface gigabitethernet 0/0/0** command displays the interface status and all of the IPv6 addresses belonging to the interface. Along with the link local address and global unicast address, the output includes the multicast addresses assigned to the interface. The output of the **show running-config interface** command displays the current commands applied to a specified interface. The **show interfaces** command displays interface information and packet flow count for all interfaces on the device. Verify interface configuration using the **show ip interface** and **show ipv6 interface** commands, which display the IPv4 and IPv6 related information for all interfaces on a router. Verify routes using the **show ip route** and **show ipv6 route** commands. Filter show command output using the pipe (|) character. Use filter expressions: section, include, exclude, and begin. By default, command history is enabled, and the system captures the last 10 command lines in its history buffer. Use the **show history** privileged EXEC command to display the contents of the buffer.

Go to the online course to take the quiz and exam.

Chapter Quiz - Basic Device Configuration

Your Chapter Notes

CHAPTER 2

Switching Concepts

Introduction - 2.0

Why should I take this module? - 2.0.1

Welcome to Switching Concepts!

You can connect and configure switches, that's great! But even a network with the newest technology develops its own problems eventually. If you have to troubleshoot your network, you need to know how switches work. This module gives you the fundamentals of switches and switch operation. Luckily, switch operation is easy to understand!

What will I learn to do in this module? - 2.0.2

Module Title: Switching Concepts

Module Objective: Explain how Layer 2 switches forward data.

Topic Title	Topic Objective
Frame Forwarding	Explain how frames are forwarded in a switched network.
Switching Domains	Compare a collision domain to a broadcast domain.

Frame Forwarding - 2.1

Refer to
Interactive Graphic
in online course

Switching in Networking - 2.1.1

The concept of switching and forwarding frames is universal in networking and telecommunications. Various types of switches are used in LANs, WANs, and in the public switched telephone network (PSTN).

The decision on how a switch forwards traffic is made based on the flow of that traffic. There are two terms associated with frames entering and leaving an interface:

- **Ingress** - This is used to describe the port where a frame enters the device.
- **Egress** - This is used to describe the port that frames will use when leaving the device.

A LAN switch maintains a table that is referenced when forwarding traffic through the switch. The only intelligence of a LAN switch is its ability to use its table to forward traffic. A LAN switch forwards traffic based on the ingress port and the destination MAC address of an Ethernet frame. With a LAN switch, there is only one master switching table that describes a strict association between MAC addresses and ports; therefore, an Ethernet frame with a given destination address always exits the same egress port, regardless of the ingress port it enters.

Note: An Ethernet frame will never be forwarded out the same port it was on which it was received.

Click Play to see an animation of the switching process.

The Switch MAC Address Table - 2.1.2

A switch is made up of integrated circuits and the accompanying software that controls the data paths through the switch. Switches use destination MAC addresses to direct network communications through the switch, out the appropriate port, toward the destination.

For a switch to know which port to use to transmit a frame, it must first learn which devices exist on each port. As the switch learns the relationship of ports to devices, it builds a table called a MAC address table. This table is stored in content addressable memory (CAM) which is a special type of memory used in high-speed searching applications. For this reason, the MAC address table is sometimes also called the CAM table.

LAN switches determine how to handle incoming data frames by maintaining the MAC address table. A switch populates its MAC address table by recording the source MAC address of each device connected to each of its ports. The switch references the information in the MAC address table to send frames destined for a specific device out of the port which has been assigned to that device.

The Switch Learn and Forward Method - 2.1.3

The following two-step process is performed on every Ethernet frame that enters a switch.

Step 1.   **Learn - Examining the Source MAC Address**

Every frame that enters a switch is checked for new information to learn. It does this by examining the source MAC address of the frame and port number where the frame entered the switch:

- If the source MAC address does not exist in the MAC address table, the MAC address and incoming port number are added to the table.

- If the source MAC address does exist, the switch updates the refresh timer for that entry. By default, most Ethernet switches keep an entry in the table for five minutes. If the source MAC address does exist in the table but on a different port, the switch treats this as a new entry. The entry is replaced using the same MAC address, but with the more current port number.

Step 2.   **Forward - Examining the Destination MAC Address**

If the destination MAC address is a unicast address, the switch will look for a match between the destination MAC address of the frame and an entry in its MAC address table:

- If the destination MAC address is in the table, it will forward the frame out of the specified port.

- If the destination MAC address is not in the table, the switch will forward the frame out all ports except the incoming port. This is called an unknown unicast. If the destination MAC address is a broadcast or a multicast, the frame is also flooded out all ports except the incoming port.

Refer to **Video**
in online course

Video - MAC Address Tables on Connected Switches - 2.1.4

Click Play in the figure to view a demonstration of how two connected switches build MAC address tables.

Switching Forwarding Methods - 2.1.5

Switches make Layer 2 forwarding decisions very quickly. This is because of software on application-specific-integrated circuits (ASICs). ASICs reduce the frame-handling time within the device and allow the device to manage an increased number of frames without degrading performance.

Layer 2 switches use one of two methods to switch frames:

- **Store-and-forward switching** - This method makes a forwarding decision on a frame after it has received the entire frame and checked the frame for errors using a mathematical error-checking mechanism known as a cyclic redundancy check (CRC). Store-and-forward switching is Cisco's primary LAN switching method.

- **Cut-through switching** - This method begins the forwarding process after the destination MAC address of an incoming frame and the egress port have been determined.

Refer to
Online Course
for Illustration

Store-and-Forward Switching - 2.1.6

Store-and-forward switching, as distinguished from cut-through switching, has the following two primary characteristics:

- **Error checking** - After receiving the entire frame on the ingress port, the switch compares the frame check sequence (FCS) value in the last field of the datagram against its own FCS calculations. The FCS is an error checking process that helps to ensure that the frame is free of physical and data-link errors. If the frame is error-free, the switch forwards the frame. Otherwise, the frame is dropped.

- **Automatic buffering** - The ingress port buffering process used by store-and-forward switches provides the flexibility to support any mix of Ethernet speeds. For example, handling an incoming frame traveling into a 100 Mbps Ethernet port that must be sent out a 1 Gbps interface would require using the store-and-forward method. With any mismatch in speeds between the ingress and egress ports, the switch stores the entire frame in a buffer, computes the FCS check, forwards it to the egress port buffer and then sends it.

The figure illustrates how store-and-forward makes a decision based on the Ethernet frame.

Refer to
Online Course
for Illustration

Cut-Through Switching - 2.1.7

The store-and-forward switching method drops frames that do not pass the FCS check. Therefore, it does not forward invalid frames.

By contrast, the cut-through switching method may forward invalid frames because no FCS check is performed. However, cut-through switching has the ability to perform rapid frame switching. This means the switch can make a forwarding decision as soon as it has looked up the destination MAC address of the frame in its MAC address table, as shown in the figure.

The switch does not have to wait for the rest of the frame to enter the ingress port before making its forwarding decision.

Fragment free switching is a modified form of cut-through switching in which the switch only starts forwarding the frame after it has read the Type field. Fragment free switching provides better error checking than cut-through, with practically no increase in latency.

The lower latency speed of cut-through switching makes it more appropriate for extremely demanding, high-performance computing (HPC) applications that require process-to-process latencies of 10 microseconds or less.

The cut-through switching method can forward frames with errors. If there is a high error rate (invalid frames) in the network, cut-through switching can have a negative impact on bandwidth, thereby clogging up bandwidth with damaged and invalid frames.

Refer to
Lab Activity
for this chapter

Activity - Switch It!

Use this activity to check your understanding of how a switch learns and forwards frames.

Switching Domains - 2.2

Refer to
Online Course
for Illustration

Collision Domains - 2.2.1

In the previous topic, you gained a better understanding of what a switch is and how it operates. This topic discusses how switches work with each other and with other devices to eliminate collisions and reduce network congestion. The terms collisions and congestion are used here in the same way that you use them in street traffic.

In legacy hub-based Ethernet segments, network devices competed for the shared medium. The network segments that share the same bandwidth between devices are known as collision domains. When two or more devices within the same collision domain try to communicate at the same time, a collision will occur.

If an Ethernet switch port is operating in half-duplex, each segment is in its own collision domain. There are no collision domains when switch ports are operating in full-duplex. However, there could be a collision domain if a switch port is operating in half-duplex.

By default, Ethernet switch ports will autonegotiate full-duplex when the adjacent device can also operate in full-duplex. If the switch port is connected to a device operating in half-duplex, such as a legacy hub, then the switch port will operate in half-duplex. In the case of half-duplex, the switch port will be part of a collision domain.

As shown in the figure, full-duplex is chosen if both devices have the capability along with their highest common bandwidth.

Refer to
Interactive Graphic
in online course

Broadcast Domains - 2.2.2

A collection of interconnected switches forms a single broadcast domain. Only a network layer device, such as a router, can divide a Layer 2 broadcast domain. Routers are used to segment broadcast domains, but will also segment a collision domain.

When a device sends a Layer 2 broadcast, the destination MAC address in the frame is set to all binary ones.

The Layer 2 broadcast domain is referred to as the MAC broadcast domain. The MAC broadcast domain consists of all devices on the LAN that receive broadcast frames from a host.

Click Play in the figure to see this in the first half of the animation.

When a switch receives a broadcast frame, it forwards the frame out each of its ports, except the ingress port where the broadcast frame was received. Each device connected to the switch receives a copy of the broadcast frame and processes it.

Broadcasts are sometimes necessary for initially locating other devices and network services, but they also reduce network efficiency. Network bandwidth is used to propagate the broadcast traffic. Too many broadcasts and a heavy traffic load on a network can result in congestion, which slows down network performance.

When two switches are connected together, the broadcast domain is increased, as seen in the second half of the animation. In this case, a broadcast frame is forwarded to all connected ports on switch S1. Switch S1 is connected to switch S2. The frame is then also propagated to all devices connected to switch S2.

Alleviate Network Congestion - 2.2.3

LAN switches have special characteristics that help them alleviate network congestion. By default, interconnected switch ports attempt to establish a link in full-duplex, therefore eliminating collision domains. Each full-duplex port of the switch provides the full bandwidth to the device or devices that are connected to that port. Full-duplex connections have dramatically increased LAN network performance, and are required for 1 Gbps Ethernet speeds and higher.

Switches interconnect LAN segments, use a MAC address table to determine egress ports, and can lessen or eliminate collisions entirely. Characteristics of switches that alleviate network congestion include the following:

- **Fast port speeds** - Ethernet switch port speeds vary by model and purpose. For instance, most access layer switches support 100 Mbps and 1 Gbps port speeds. Distribution layer switches support 100 Mbps, 1 Gbps, and 10 Gbps port speeds and core layer and data center switches may support 100 Gbps, 40 Gbps, and 10 Gbps port speeds. Switches with faster port speeds cost more but can reduce congestion.

- **Fast internal switching** - Switches use a fast internal bus or shared memory to provide high performance.

- **Large frame buffers** - Switches use large memory buffers to temporarily store more received frames before having to start dropping them. This enables ingress traffic from a faster port (e.g., 1 Gbps) to be forwarded to a slower (e.g., 100 Mbps) egress port without losing frames.

- **High port density** - A high port density switch lowers overall costs because it reduces the number of switches required. For instance, if 96 access ports were required, it would be less expensive to buy two 48-port switches instead of four 24-port switches. High port density switches also help keep traffic local, which helps alleviate congestion.

Go to the online course to take the quiz and exam.

Check Your Understanding - Switching Domains - 2.2.4

Module Practice and Quiz - 2.3

What did I learn in this module? - 2.3.1

Frame Forwarding

The decision on how a switch forwards traffic is based on the flow of that traffic. The term ingress describes the port where a frame enters a device. The term egress describes the port that frames will use when leaving the device. An Ethernet frame will never be forwarded out the port where it entered. For a switch to know which port to use to transmit a frame, it must first learn which devices exist on each port. As the switch learns the relationship of ports to devices, it builds a table called a MAC address table. Every frame that enters a switch is checked for new information to learn by examining the source MAC address of the frame and port number where the frame entered the switch. If the destination MAC address is a unicast address, the switch will look for a match between the destination MAC address of the frame and an entry in its MAC address table. Switch forwarding methods include store-and-forward and cut-through. Store-and-forward uses error-checking and automatic buffering. Cut-through does not error check. Instead it performs rapid frame switching. This means the switch can make a forwarding decision as soon as it has looked up the destination MAC address of the frame in its MAC address table.

Switching Domains

If an Ethernet switch port is operating in half-duplex, each segment is in its own collision domain. There are no collision domains when switch ports are operating in full-duplex. By default, Ethernet switch ports will autonegotiate full-duplex when the adjacent device can also operate in full-duplex. A collection of interconnected switches forms a single broadcast domain. Only a network layer device, such as a router, can divide a Layer 2 broadcast domain. The Layer 2 broadcast domain is referred to as the MAC broadcast domain. The MAC broadcast domain consists of all devices on the LAN that receive broadcast frames from a host. When a switch receives a broadcast frame, it forwards the frame out each of its ports, except the ingress port where the broadcast frame was received. Each device connected to the switch receives a copy of the broadcast frame and processes it. Switches can: interconnect LAN segments, use a MAC address table to determine egress ports, and can lessen or eliminate collisions entirely. Characteristics of switches that alleviate network congestion are fast port speeds, fast internal switching, large frame buffers, and high port density.

Go to the online course to take the quiz and exam.

Chapter Quiz - Switching Concepts

Your Chapter Notes

CHAPTER 3

VLANs

Introduction - 3.0

Why should I take this module? - 3.0.1

Welcome to VLANs!

Imagine that you are in charge of a very large conference. There are people from all over who share a common interest and some who also have special expertise. Imagine if each expert who wanted to present their information to a smaller audience had to do that in the same large room with all the other experts and their smaller audiences. Nobody would be able to hear anything. You would have to find separate rooms for all the experts and their smaller audiences. The Virtual LAN (VLAN) does something similar in a network. VLANs are created at Layer 2 to reducing or eliminate broadcast traffic. VLANs are how you break up your network into smaller networks, so that the devices and people within a single VLAN are communicating with each other and not having to manage traffic from other networks. The network administrator can organize VLANs by location, who is using them, the type of device, or whatever category is needed. You know you want to learn how to do this, so don't wait!

What will I learn to do in this module? - 3.0.2

Module Title: VLANs

Module Objective: Implement VLANs and trunking in a switched network.

Topic Title	Topic Objective
Overview of VLANs	Explain the purpose of VLANs in a switched network
VLANs in a Multi-Switched Environment	Explain how a switch forwards frames based on VLAN configuration in a multi-switch environment.
VLAN Configuration	Configure a switch port to be assigned to a VLAN based on requirements.
VLAN Trunks	Configure a trunk port on a LAN switch.
Dynamic Trunking Protocol	Configure Dynamic Trunking Protocol (DTP).

Overview of VLANs - 3.1

Refer to **Online Course** for Illustration

VLAN Definitions - 3.1.1

Of course organizing your network into smaller networks is not as simple as separating screws and putting them into jars. But it will make your network easier to manage. Virtual LANs (VLANs) provide segmentation and organizational flexibility in a switched network. A group of devices within a VLAN communicate as if each device was attached to the same cable. VLANs are based on logical connections, instead of physical connections.

As shown in the figure, VLANs in a switched network enable users in various departments (i.e., IT, HR, and Sales) to connect to the same network regardless of the physical switch being used or location in a campus LAN.

VLANs allow an administrator to segment networks based on factors such as function, team, or application, without regard for the physical location of the users or devices. Each VLAN is considered a separate logical network. Devices within a VLAN act as if they are in their own independent network, even if they share a common infrastructure with other VLANs. Any switch port can belong to a VLAN.

Unicast, broadcast, and multicast packets are forwarded and flooded only to end devices within the VLAN where the packets are sourced. Packets destined for devices that do not belong to the VLAN must be forwarded through a device that supports routing.

Multiple IP subnets can exist on a switched network, without the use of multiple VLANs. However, the devices will be in the same Layer 2 broadcast domain. This means that any Layer 2 broadcasts, such as an ARP request, will be received by all devices on the switched network, even by those not intended to receive the broadcast.

A VLAN creates a logical broadcast domain that can span multiple physical LAN segments. VLANs improve network performance by separating large broadcast domains into smaller ones. If a device in one VLAN sends a broadcast Ethernet frame, all devices in the VLAN receive the frame, but devices in other VLANs do not.

Using VLANs, network administrators can implement access and security policies according to specific groupings of users. Each switch port can be assigned to only one VLAN (except for a port connected to an IP phone or to another switch).

Refer to
Online Course
for Illustration

Benefits of a VLAN Design - 3.1.2

Each VLAN in a switched network corresponds to an IP network. Therefore, VLAN design must take into consideration the implementation of a hierarchical network-addressing scheme. Hierarchical network addressing means that IP network numbers are applied to network segments or VLANs in a way that takes the network as a whole into consideration. Blocks of contiguous network addresses are reserved for and configured on devices in a specific area of the network, as shown in the figure.

The table lists the benefits of designing a network with VLANs.

Benefit	Description
Smaller broadcast domains	• Dividing a network into VLANs reduces the number of devices in the broadcast domain.
	• In the figure, there are six computers in the network but only three broadcast domains (i.e., Faculty, Student, and Guest).
Improved security	• Only users in the same VLAN can communicate together.
	• In the figure, faculty network traffic on VLAN 10 is completely separated and secured from users on other VLANs.
Improved IT efficiency	• VLANs simplify network management because users with similar network requirements can be configured on the same VLAN.
	• VLANs can be named to make them easier to identify.
	• In the figure, VLAN 10 was named "Faculty", VLAN 20 "Student", and VLAN 30 "Guest."

Benefit	Description
Reduced cost	VLANs reduce the need for expensive network upgrades and use the existing bandwidth and uplinks more efficiently, resulting in cost savings.
Better performance	Smaller broadcast domains reduce unnecessary traffic on the network and improve performance.
Simpler project and application management	• VLANs aggregate users and network devices to support business or geographic requirements. • Having separate functions makes managing a project or working with a specialized application easier; an example of such an application is an e-learning development platform for faculty.

Refer to **Interactive Graphic** in online course

Refer to **Online Course** for Illustration

Types of VLANs - 3.1.3

VLANs are used for different reasons in modern networks. Some VLAN types are defined by traffic classes. Other types of VLANs are defined by the specific function that they serve.

Click each VLAN type for more information.

Default VLAN

The default VLAN on a Cisco switch is VLAN 1. Therefore, all switch ports are on VLAN 1 unless it is explicitly configured to be on another VLAN. By default, all Layer 2 control traffic is associated with VLAN 1.

Important facts to remember about VLAN 1 include the following:

- All ports are assigned to VLAN 1 by default.

- The native VLAN is VLAN 1 by default.

- The management VLAN is VLAN 1 by default.

- VLAN 1 cannot be renamed or deleted.

For instance, in the **show vlan brief** output, all ports are currently assigned to the default VLAN 1. No native VLAN is explicitly assigned and no other VLANs are active; therefore, the network is designed with the native VLAN the same as the management VLAN. This is considered a security risk.

```
Switch# show vlan brief

VLAN Name              Status   Ports
---- ---------------- ------- --------------------
1    default           active   Fa0/1,  Fa0/2,  Fa0/3,  Fa0/4
                                Fa0/5,  Fa0/6,  Fa0/7,  Fa0/8
                                Fa0/9,  Fa0/10, Fa0/11, Fa0/12
                                Fa0/13, Fa0/14, Fa0/15, Fa0/16
                                Fa0/17, Fa0/18, Fa0/19, Fa0/20
                                Fa0/21, Fa0/22, Fa0/23, Fa0/24
```

```
                                    Gi0/1,   Gi0/2
1002  fddi-default                           act/unsup

1003  token-ring-default                     act/unsup

1004  fddinet-default                        act/unsup

1005  trnet-default                          act/unsup
```

Data VLAN

Data VLANs are VLANs configured to separate user-generated traffic. They are referred to as user VLANs because they separate the network into groups of users or devices. A modern network would have many data VLANs depending on organizational requirements. Note that voice and network management traffic should not be permitted on data VLANs.

Native VLAN

User traffic from a VLAN must be tagged with its VLAN ID when it is sent to another switch. Trunk ports are used between switches to support the transmission of tagged traffic. Specifically, an 802.1Q trunk port inserts a 4-byte tag in the Ethernet frame header to identify the VLAN to which the frame belongs.

A switch may also have to send untagged traffic across a trunk link. Untagged traffic is generated by a switch and may also come from legacy devices. The 802.1Q trunk port places untagged traffic on the native VLAN. The native VLAN on a Cisco switch is VLAN 1 (i.e., default VLAN).

It is a best practice to configure the native VLAN as an unused VLAN, distinct from VLAN 1 and other VLANs. In fact, it is not unusual to dedicate a fixed VLAN to serve the role of the native VLAN for all trunk ports in the switched domain.

Management VLAN

A management VLAN is a data VLAN configured specifically for network management traffic including SSH, Telnet, HTTPS, HHTP, and SNMP. By default, VLAN 1 is configured as the management VLAN on a Layer 2 switch.

Voice VLAN

A separate VLAN is needed to support Voice over IP (VoIP). VoIP traffic requires the following:

- Assured bandwidth to ensure voice quality

- Transmission priority over other types of network traffic

- Ability to be routed around congested areas on the network

- Delay of less than 150 ms across the network

To meet these requirements, the entire network has to be designed to support VoIP.

In the figure, VLAN 150 is designed to carry voice traffic. The student computer PC5 is attached to the Cisco IP phone, and the phone is attached to switch S3. PC5 is in VLAN 20, which is used for student data.

Refer to **Packet Tracer Activity** for this chapter

Packet Tracer - Who Hears the Broadcast? - 3.1.4

In this Packet Tracer activity, you will complete the following objectives:

- Part 1: Observe Broadcast Traffic in a VLAN Implementation
- Part 2: Complete Review Questions

Go to the online course to take the quiz and exam.

Check Your Understanding - Overview of VLANs - 3.1.5

VLANs in a Multi-Switched Environment - 3.2

Refer to **Online Course** for Illustration

Defining VLAN Trunks - 3.2.1

VLANs would not be very useful without VLAN trunks. VLAN trunks allow all VLAN traffic to propagate between switches. This enables devices connected to different switches but in the same VLAN to communicate without going through a router.

A trunk is a point-to-point link between two network devices that carries more than one VLAN. A VLAN trunk extends VLANs across an entire network. Cisco supports IEEE 802.1Q for coordinating trunks on Fast Ethernet, Gigabit Ethernet, and 10-Gigabit Ethernet interfaces.

A VLAN trunk does not belong to a specific VLAN. Instead, it is a conduit for multiple VLANs between switches and routers. A trunk could also be used between a network device and server or another device that is equipped with an appropriate 802.1Q-capable NIC. By default, on a Cisco Catalyst switch, all VLANs are supported on a trunk port.

In the figure, the highlighted links between switches S1 and S2, and S1 and S3 are configured to transmit traffic coming from VLANs 10, 20, 30, and 99 (i.e., native VLAN) across the network. This network could not function without VLAN trunks.

Refer to **Interactive Graphic** in online course

Network without VLANs - 3.2.2

When a switch receives a broadcast frame on one of its ports, it forwards the frame out all other ports except the port where the broadcast was received. In the animation, the entire network is configured in the same subnet (172.17.40.0/24) and no VLANs are configured. As a result, when the faculty computer (PC1) sends out a broadcast frame, switch S2 sends that broadcast frame out all of its ports. Eventually the entire network receives the broadcast because the network is one broadcast domain.

Refer to **Interactive Graphic** in online course

Network with VLANs - 3.2.3

Click Play in the animation to see that the same network has now been segmented using two VLANs. Faculty devices are assigned to VLAN 10 and student devices are assigned to VLAN 20. When a broadcast frame is sent from the faculty computer, PC1, to switch S2, the switch forwards that broadcast frame only to those switch ports configured to support VLAN 10.

The ports that comprise the connection between switches S2 and S1 (ports F0/1), and between S1 and S3 (ports F0/3) are trunks and have been configured to support all the VLANs in the network.

When S1 receives the broadcast frame on port F0/1, S1 forwards that broadcast frame out of the only other port configured to support VLAN 10, which is port F0/3. When S3 receives the broadcast frame on port F0/3, it forwards that broadcast frame out the only other port configured to support VLAN 10, which is port F0/11. The broadcast frame arrives at the only other computer in the network configured in VLAN 10, which is faculty computer PC4.

When VLANs are implemented on a switch, the transmission of unicast, multicast, and broadcast traffic from a host in a particular VLAN are restricted to the devices that are in that VLAN.

Refer to
Online Course
for Illustration

VLAN Identification with a Tag - 3.2.4

The standard Ethernet frame header does not contain information about the VLAN to which the frame belongs. Therefore, when Ethernet frames are placed on a trunk, information about the VLANs to which they belong must be added. This process, called tagging, is accomplished by using the IEEE 802.1Q header, specified in the IEEE 802.1Q standard. The 802.1Q header includes a 4-byte tag inserted within the original Ethernet frame header, specifying the VLAN to which the frame belongs.

When the switch receives a frame on a port configured in access mode and assigned a VLAN, the switch inserts a VLAN tag in the frame header, recalculates the Frame Check Sequence (FCS), and sends the tagged frame out of a trunk port.

VLAN Tag Field Details

As shown in the figure, the VLAN tag control information field consists of a Type field, a Priority field, a Canonical Format Identifier field, and VLAN ID field:

- **Type** - A 2-byte value called the tag protocol ID (TPID) value. For Ethernet, it is set to hexadecimal 0x8100.

- **User priority** - A 3-bit value that supports level or service implementation.

- **Canonical Format Identifier (CFI)** - A 1-bit identifier that enables Token Ring frames to be carried across Ethernet links.

- **VLAN ID (VID)** - A 12-bit VLAN identification number that supports up to 4096 VLAN IDs.

After the switch inserts the tag control information fields, it recalculates the FCS values and inserts the new FCS into the frame.

Refer to
Online Course
for Illustration

Native VLANs and 802.1Q Tagging - 3.2.5

The IEEE 802.1Q standard specifies a native VLAN for trunk links, which defaults to VLAN 1. When an untagged frame arrives on a trunk port it is assigned to the native VLAN. Management frames that are sent between switches is an example of traffic that is typically untagged. If the link between two switches is a trunk, the switch sends the untagged traffic on the native VLAN.

Tagged Frames on the Native VLAN

Some devices that support trunking add a VLAN tag to native VLAN traffic. Control traffic sent on the native VLAN should not be tagged. If an 802.1Q trunk port receives a tagged frame with the VLAN ID that is the same as the native VLAN, it drops the frame. Consequently, when configuring a switch port on a Cisco switch, configure devices so that they do not send tagged frames on the native VLAN. Devices from other vendors that support tagged frames on the native VLAN include IP phones, servers, routers, and non-Cisco switches.

Untagged Frames on the Native VLAN

When a Cisco switch trunk port receives untagged frames (which are unusual in a well-designed network), it forwards those frames to the native VLAN. If there are no devices associated with the native VLAN (which is not unusual) and there are no other trunk ports (which is not unusual), then the frame is dropped. The default native VLAN is VLAN 1. When configuring an 802.1Q trunk port, a default Port VLAN ID (PVID) is assigned the value of the native VLAN ID. All untagged traffic coming in or out of the 802.1Q port is forwarded based on the PVID value. For example, if VLAN 99 is configured as the native VLAN, the PVID is 99 and all untagged traffic is forwarded to VLAN 99. If the native VLAN has not been reconfigured, the PVID value is set to VLAN 1.

In the figure, PC1 is connected by a hub to an 802.1Q trunk link.

PC1 sends untagged traffic, which the switches associate with the native VLAN configured on the trunk ports, and forward accordingly. Tagged traffic on the trunk received by PC1 is dropped. This scenario reflects poor network design for several reasons: it uses a hub, it has a host connected to a trunk link, and it implies that the switches have access ports assigned to the native VLAN. It also illustrates the motivation for the IEEE 802.1Q specification for native VLANs as a means of handling legacy scenarios.

Refer to
Online Course
for Illustration

Voice VLAN Tagging - 3.2.6

A separate voice VLAN is required to support VoIP. This enables quality of service (QoS) and security policies to be applied to voice traffic.

A Cisco IP phone connects directly to a switch port. An IP host can connect to the IP phone to gain network connectivity as well. The access port connected to the Cisco IP phone can be configured to use two separate VLANs. One VLAN is for voice traffic and the other is a data VLAN to support the host traffic. The link between the switch and the IP phone simulates a trunk link to carry both voice VLAN traffic and data VLAN traffic.

Specifically, the Cisco IP Phone contains an integrated three-port 10/100 switch. The ports provide dedicated connections to the following devices:

- Port 1 connects to the switch or other VoIP device.

- Port 2 is an internal 10/100 interface that carries the IP phone traffic.

- Port 3 (access port) connects to a PC or other device.

The switch access port sends CDP packets instructing the attached IP phone to send voice traffic in one of three ways. The method used varies based on the type of traffic:

- Voice VLAN traffic must be tagged with an appropriate Layer 2 class of service (CoS) priority value

- Access VLAN traffic can also be tagged with a Layer 2 CoS priority value

- Access VLAN is not tagged (no Layer 2 CoS priority value)

In the figure, the student computer PC5 is attached to a Cisco IP phone, and the phone is attached to switch S3. VLAN 150 is designed to carry voice traffic, while PC5 is in VLAN 20, which is used for student data.

Voice VLAN Verification Example - 3.2.7

The example output for the **show interface fa0/18 switchport** command is shown. The highlighted areas in the sample output show the F0/18 interface configured with a VLAN that is configured for data (VLAN 20), and a VLAN configured for voice (VLAN 150).

```
S1# show interfaces fa0/18 switchport

Name: Fa0/18

Switchport: Enabled

Administrative Mode: static access

Operational Mode: static access

Administrative Trunking Encapsulation: negotiate

Operational Trunking Encapsulation: native

Negotiation of Trunking: Off

Access Mode VLAN: 20 (student)

Trunking Native Mode VLAN: 1 (default)

Administrative Native VLAN tagging: enabled

Voice VLAN: 150 (voice)
```

Refer to **Packet Tracer Activity** for this chapter

Packet Tracer - Investigate a VLAN Implementation - 3.2.8

In this activity, you will observe how broadcast traffic is forwarded by the switches when VLANs are configured and when VLANs are not configured.

Refer to **Interactive Graphic** in online course

Check Your Understanding - VLANs in a Multi-Switch Environment - 3.2.9

Go to the online course to take the quiz and exam.

VLAN Configuration - 3.3

VLAN Ranges on Catalyst Switches - 3.3.1

Creating VLANs, like most other aspects of networking, is a matter of entering the appropriate commands. This topic details how to configure and verify different types of VLANs.

Different Cisco Catalyst switches support various numbers of VLANs. The number of supported VLANs is large enough to accommodate the needs of most organizations. For example, the Catalyst 2960 and 3650 Series switches support over 4,000 VLANs. Normal range VLANs on these switches are numbered 1 to 1,005 and extended range VLANs are numbered 1,006 to 4,094. The figure illustrates the default VLANs on a Catalyst 2960 switch running Cisco IOS Release 15.x.

```
Switch# show vlan brief

VLAN Name                Status    Ports
---- ------------------  -------   --------------------
1    default             active    Fa0/1,  Fa0/2,  Fa0/3,  Fa0/4
                                   Fa0/5,  Fa0/6,  Fa0/7,  Fa0/8
                                   Fa0/9,  Fa0/10, Fa0/11, Fa0/12
                                   Fa0/13, Fa0/14, Fa0/15, Fa0/16
                                   Fa0/17, Fa0/18, Fa0/19, Fa0/20
                                   Fa0/21, Fa0/22, Fa0/23, Fa0/24
                                   Gi0/1,  Gi0/2
1002 fddi-default                  act/unsup
1003 token-ring-default            act/unsup
1004 fddinet-default               act/unsup
1005 trnet-default                 act/unsup
```

Normal Range VLANs

The following are characteristics of normal range VLANs:

- They are used in all small- and medium-sized business and enterprise networks.

- They are identified by a VLAN ID between 1 and 1005.

- IDs 1002 through 1005 are reserved for legacy network technologies (i.e., Token Ring and Fiber Distributed Data Interface).

- IDs 1 and 1002 to 1005 are automatically created and cannot be removed.

- Configurations are stored in the switch flash memory in a VLAN database file called vlan.dat.

- When configured, VLAN trunking protocol (VTP), helps synchronize the VLAN database between switches.

Extended Range VLANs

The following are characteristics of extended range VLANs:

- They are used by service providers to service multiple customers and by global enterprises large enough to need extended range VLAN IDs.

- They are identified by a VLAN ID between 1006 and 4094.

- Configurations are saved, by default, in the running configuration.

- They support fewer VLAN features than normal range VLANs.

- Requires VTP transparent mode configuration to support extended range VLANs.

Note: 4096 is the upper boundary for the number of VLANs available on Catalyst switches, because there are 12 bits in the VLAN ID field of the IEEE 802.1Q header.

VLAN Creation Commands - 3.3.2

When configuring normal range VLANs, the configuration details are stored in flash memory on the switch in a file called vlan.dat. Flash memory is persistent and does not require the **copy running-config startup-config** command. However, because other details are often configured on a Cisco switch at the same time that VLANs are created, it is good practice to save running configuration changes to the startup configuration.

The table displays the Cisco IOS command syntax used to add a VLAN to a switch and give it a name. Naming each VLAN is considered a best practice in switch configuration.

Task	IOS Command
Enter global configuration mode.	Switch# **configure terminal**
Create a VLAN with a valid ID number.	Switch(config)# **vlan** *vlan-id*
Specify a unique name to identify the VLAN.	Switch(config-vlan)# **name** *vlan-name*
Return to the privileged EXEC mode.	Switch(config-vlan)# **end**

Refer to **Online Course** for Illustration

VLAN Creation Example - 3.3.3

In the topology, the student computer (PC2) has not been associated with a VLAN yet, but it does have an IP address of 172.17.20.22, which belongs to VLAN 20.

The example shows how the student VLAN (VLAN 20) is configured on switch S1.

```
S1# configure terminal
S1(config)# vlan 20
S1(config-vlan)# name student
S1(config-vlan)# end
```

Note: In addition to entering a single VLAN ID, a series of VLAN IDs can be entered separated by commas, or a range of VLAN IDs separated by hyphens using the **vlan** *vlan-id* command. For example, entering the **vlan 100,102,105-107** global configuration command would create VLANs 100, 102, 105, 106, and 107.

VLAN Port Assignment Commands - 3.3.4

After creating a VLAN, the next step is to assign ports to the VLAN.

The table displays the syntax for defining a port to be an access port and assigning it to a VLAN. The **switchport mode access** command is optional, but strongly recommended as a security best practice. With this command, the interface changes to permanent access mode.

Task	IOS Command
Enter global configuration mode.	Switch# **configure terminal**
Enter interface configuration mode.	Switch(config)# **interface** *interface-id*
Set the port to access mode.	Switch(config-if)# **switchport mode access**
Assign the port to a VLAN.	Switch(config-if)# **switchport access vlan** *vlan-id*
Return to the privileged EXEC mode.	Switch(config-if)# **end**

Note: Use the **interface range** command to simultaneously configure multiple interfaces.

Refer to **Online Course** for Illustration

VLAN Port Assignment Example - 3.3.5

In the figure, port F0/6 on switch S1 is configured as an access port and assigned to VLAN 20. Any device connected to that port will be associated with VLAN 20. Therefore, in our example, PC2 is in VLAN 20.

The example shows the configuration for S1 to assign F0/6 to VLAN 20.

```
S1# configure terminal
S1(config)# interface fa0/6
S1(config-if)# switchport mode access
S1(config-if)# switchport access vlan 20
S1(config-if)# end
```

VLANs are configured on the switch port and not on the end device. PC2 is configured with an IPv4 address and subnet mask that is associated with the VLAN, which is configured on the switch port. In this example, it is VLAN 20. When VLAN 20 is configured on other switches, the network administrator must configure the other student computers to be in the same subnet as PC2 (172.17.20.0/24).

Refer to **Online Course** for Illustration

Data and Voice VLANs - 3.3.6

An access port can belong to only one data VLAN at a time. However, a port can also be associated to a voice VLAN. For example, a port connected to an IP phone and an end device would be associated with two VLANs: one for voice and one for data.

Consider the topology in the figure. PC5 is connected to the Cisco IP phone, which in turn is connected to the FastEthernet 0/18 interface on S3. To implement this configuration, a data VLAN and a voice VLAN are created.

Data and Voice VLAN Example - 3.3.7

Use the **switchport voice vlan** *vlan-id* interface configuration command to assign a voice VLAN to a port.

LANs supporting voice traffic typically also have quality of service (QoS) enabled. Voice traffic must be labeled as trusted as soon as it enters the network. Use the **mls qos trust [cos | device cisco-phone | dscp | ip-precedence]** interface configuration command to set the trusted state of an interface, and to indicate which fields of the packet are used to classify traffic.

The configuration in the example creates the two VLANs (i.e., VLAN 20 and VLAN 150) and then assigns the F0/18 interface of S3 as a switchport in VLAN 20. It also assigns voice traffic to VLAN 150 and enables QoS classification based on the class of service (CoS) assigned by the IP phone.

```
S3(config)# vlan 20
S3(config-vlan)# name student
S3(config-vlan)# vlan 150
S3(config-vlan)# name VOICE
S3(config-vlan)# exit
S3(config)# interface fa0/18
S3(config-if)# switchport mode access
S3(config-if)# switchport access vlan 20
S3(config-if)# mls qos trust cos
S3(config-if)# switchport voice vlan 150
S3(config-if)# end
S3#
```

Note: The implementation of QoS is beyond the scope of this course.

The **switchport access vlan** command forces the creation of a VLAN if it does not already exist on the switch. For example, VLAN 30 is not present in the **show vlan brief** output of the switch. If the **switchport access vlan 30** command is entered on any interface with no previous configuration, then the switch displays the following:

```
% Access VLAN does not exist. Creating vlan 30
```

Verify VLAN Information - 3.3.8

After a VLAN is configured, VLAN configurations can be validated using Cisco IOS **show** commands.

The **show vlan** command displays a list of all configured VLANs. The **show vlan** command can also be used with options. The complete syntax is **show vlan [brief | id** *vlan-id* **| name** *vlan-name* **| summary]**.

The table describes the **show vlan** command options.

Task	Command Option
Display VLAN name, status, and its ports one VLAN per line.	`brief`
Display information about the identified VLAN ID number. For *vlan-id*, the range is 1 to 4094.	`id vlan-id`
Display information about the identified VLAN name. The *vlan-name* is an ASCII string from 1 to 32 characters.	`name vlan-name`
Display VLAN summary information.	`summary`

The **show vlan summary** command displays the count of all configured VLANs.

```
S1# show vlan summary

Number of existing VLANs          : 7

Number of existing VTP VLANs      : 7

Number of existing extended VLANS : 0
```

Other useful commands are the **show interfaces** *interface-id* **switchport** and the **show interfaces vlan** *vlan-id* command. For example, the **show interfaces fa0/18 switchport** command can be used to confirm that the FastEthernet 0/18 port has been correctly assigned to data and voice VLANs.

```
S1# show interfaces fa0/18 switchport

Name: Fa0/18

Switchport: Enabled

Administrative Mode: static access

Operational Mode: static access

Administrative Trunking Encapsulation: dot1q

Operational Trunking Encapsulation: native

Negotiation of Trunking: Off

Access Mode VLAN: 20 (student)

Trunking Native Mode VLAN: 1 (default)

Voice VLAN: 150

Administrative private-vlan host-association: none

(Output omitted)
```

Change VLAN Port Membership - 3.3.9

There are a number of ways to change VLAN port membership.

If the switch access port has been incorrectly assigned to a VLAN, then simply re-enter the **switchport access vlan** *vlan-id* interface configuration command with the correct VLAN ID. For instance, assume Fa0/18 was incorrectly configured to be on the default VLAN 1 instead of VLAN 20. To change the port to VLAN 20, simply enter **switchport access vlan 20**.

To change the membership of a port back to the default VLAN 1, use the **no switchport access vlan** interface configuration mode command as shown.

In the output for example, Fa0/18 is configured to be on the default VLAN 1 as confirmed by the **show vlan brief** command.

```
S1(config)# interface fa0/18

S1(config-if)# no switchport access vlan

S1(config-if)# end

S1#
```

```
S1# show vlan brief

VLAN Name               Status    Ports
---- ------------------ --------- ------------------------------

1    default            active    Fa0/1,  Fa0/2,  Fa0/3,  Fa0/4

                                  Fa0/5,  Fa0/6,  Fa0/7,  Fa0/8

                                  Fa0/9,  Fa0/10, Fa0/11, Fa0/12

                                  Fa0/13, Fa0/14, Fa0/15, Fa0/16

                                  Fa0/17, Fa0/18, Fa0/19, Fa0/20

                                  Fa0/21, Fa0/22, Fa0/23, Fa0/24

                                  Gi0/1,  Gi0/2

20   student            active
1002 fddi-default       act/unsup
1003 token-ring-default act/unsup
1004 fddinet-default    act/unsup
1005 trnet-default      act/unsup
```

Notice that VLAN 20 is still active, even though no ports are assigned to it.

The **show interfaces f0/18 switchport** output can also be used to verify that the access VLAN for interface F0/18 has been reset to VLAN 1 as shown in the output.

```
S1# show interfaces fa0/18 switchport

Name: Fa0/18

Switchport: Enabled

Administrative Mode: static access

Operational Mode: static access

Administrative Trunking Encapsulation: negotiate

Operational Trunking Encapsulation: native

Negotiation of Trunking: Off

Access Mode VLAN: 1 (default)

Trunking Native Mode VLAN: 1 (default)
```

Delete VLANs - 3.3.10

The **no vlan** *vlan-id* global configuration mode command is used to remove a VLAN from the switch vlan.dat file.

Caution: Before deleting a VLAN, reassign all member ports to a different VLAN first. Any ports that are not moved to an active VLAN are unable to communicate with other hosts after the VLAN is deleted and until they are assigned to an active VLAN.

The entire vlan.dat file can be deleted using the **delete flash:vlan.dat** privileged EXEC mode command. The abbreviated command version (**delete vlan.dat**) can be used if the vlan.dat file has not been moved from its default location. After issuing this command and reloading the switch, any previously configured VLANs are no longer present. This effectively places the switch into its factory default condition with regard to VLAN configurations.

Note: To restore a Catalyst switch to its factory default condition, unplug all cables except the console and power cable from the switch. Then enter the **erase startup-config** privileged EXEC mode command followed by the **delete vlan.dat** command.

Refer to **Interactive Graphic** in online course

Syntax Checker - VLAN Configuration - 3.3.11

In this Syntax Checker activity, you will implement and verify a VLAN configuration for switch interfaces based on the specified requirements.

Refer to **Packet Tracer Activity** for this chapter

Packet Tracer - VLAN Configuration - 3.3.12

In this Packet Tracer activity, you will perform the following:

- Verify the Default VLAN Configuration
- Configure VLANs
- Assign VLANs to Ports

VLAN Trunks - 3.4

Trunk Configuration Commands - 3.4.1

Now that you have configured and verified VLANs, it is time to configure and verify VLAN trunks. A VLAN trunk is a Layer 2 link between two switches that carries traffic for all VLANs (unless the allowed VLAN list is restricted manually or dynamically).

To enable trunk links, configure the interconnecting ports with the set of interface configuration commands shown in the table.

Task	IOS Command
Enter global configuration mode.	Switch# **configure terminal**
Enter interface configuration mode.	Switch(config)# **interface** *interface-id*
Set the port to permanent trunking mode.	Switch(config-if)# **switchport mode trunk**
Sets the native VLAN to something other than VLAN 1.	Switch(config-if)# **switchport trunk native vlan** *vlan-id*
Specify the list of VLANs to be allowed on the trunk link.	Switch(config-if)# **switchport trunk allowed vlan** *vlan-list*
Return to the privileged EXEC mode.	Switch(config-if)# **end**

Refer to
Online Course
for Illustration

Trunk Configuration Example - 3.4.2

In the figure, VLANs 10, 20, and 30 support the Faculty, Student, and Guest computers (PC1, PC2, and PC3). The F0/1 port on switch S1 is configured as a trunk port and forwards traffic for VLANs 10, 20, and 30. VLAN 99 is configured as the native VLAN.

The example shows the configuration of port F0/1 on switch S1 as a trunk port. The native VLAN is changed to VLAN 99 and the allowed VLAN list is restricted to 10, 20, 30, and 99.

```
S1(config)# interface fastEthernet 0/1
S1(config-if)# switchport mode trunk
S1(config-if)# switchport trunk native vlan 99
S1(config-if)# switchport trunk allowed vlan 10,20,30,99
S1(config-if)# end
```

Note: This configuration assumes the use of Cisco Catalyst 2960 switches which automatically use 802.1Q encapsulation on trunk links. Other switches may require manual configuration of the encapsulation. Always configure both ends of a trunk link with the same native VLAN. If 802.1Q trunk configuration is not the same on both ends, Cisco IOS Software reports errors.

Verify Trunk Configuration - 3.4.3

The switch output displays the configuration of switch port F0/1 on switch S1. The configuration is verified with the **show interfaces** *interface-ID* **switchport** command.

```
S1# show interfaces fa0/1 switchport
Name: Fa0/1
Switchport: Enabled
Administrative Mode: trunk
Operational Mode: trunk
Administrative Trunking Encapsulation: dot1q
Operational Trunking Encapsulation: dot1q
Negotiation of Trunking: On
Access Mode VLAN: 1 (default)
Trunking Native Mode VLAN: 99 (VLAN0099)
Administrative Native VLAN tagging: enabled
Voice VLAN: none
Administrative private-vlan host-association: none
Administrative private-vlan mapping: none
Administrative private-vlan trunk native VLAN: none
Administrative private-vlan trunk Native VLAN tagging: enabled
Administrative private-vlan trunk encapsulation: dot1q
```

```
Administrative private-vlan trunk normal VLANs: none

Administrative private-vlan trunk associations: none

Administrative private-vlan trunk mappings: none

Operational private-vlan: none

Trunking VLANs Enabled: ALL

Pruning VLANs Enabled: 2-1001
```

(output omitted)

The top highlighted area shows that port F0/1 has its administrative mode set to **trunk**. The port is in trunking mode. The next highlighted area verifies that the native VLAN is VLAN 99. Further down in the output, the bottom highlighted area shows that VLANs 10, 20, 30, and 99 are enabled on the trunk.

Reset the Trunk to the Default State - 3.4.4

Use the **no switchport trunk allowed vlan** and the **no switchport trunk native vlan** commands to remove the allowed VLANs and reset the native VLAN of the trunk. When it is reset to the default state, the trunk allows all VLANs and uses VLAN 1 as the native VLAN. The example shows the commands used to reset all trunking characteristics of a trunking interface to the default settings.

```
S1(config)# interface fa0/1

S1(config-if)# no switchport trunk allowed vlan

S1(config-if)# no switchport trunk native vlan

S1(config-if)# end
```

The **show interfaces f0/1 switchport** command reveals that the trunk has been reconfigured to a default state.

```
S1# show interfaces fa0/1 switchport

Name: Fa0/1

Switchport: Enabled

Administrative Mode: trunk

Operational Mode: trunk

Administrative Trunking Encapsulation: dot1q

Operational Trunking Encapsulation: dot1q

Negotiation of Trunking: On

Access Mode VLAN: 1 (default)

Trunking Native Mode VLAN: 1 (default)

Administrative Native VLAN tagging: enabled

Voice VLAN: none

Administrative private-vlan host-association: none

Administrative private-vlan mapping: none
```

```
Administrative private-vlan trunk native VLAN: none

Administrative private-vlan trunk Native VLAN tagging: enabled

Administrative private-vlan trunk encapsulation: dot1q

Administrative private-vlan trunk normal VLANs: none

Administrative private-vlan trunk associations: none

Administrative private-vlan trunk mappings: none

Operational private-vlan: none

Trunking VLANs Enabled: ALL

Pruning VLANs Enabled: 2-1001
```

(output omitted)

This sample output shows the commands used to remove the trunk feature from the F0/1 switch port on switch S1. The **show interfaces f0/1 switchport** command reveals that the F0/1 interface is now in static access mode.

```
S1(config)# interface fa0/1

S1(config-if)# switchport mode access

S1(config-if)# end

S1# show interfaces fa0/1 switchport

Name: Fa0/1

Switchport: Enabled

Administrative Mode: static access

Operational Mode: static access

Administrative Trunking Encapsulation: dot1q

Operational Trunking Encapsulation: native

Negotiation of Trunking: Off

Access Mode VLAN: 1 (default)

Trunking Native Mode VLAN: 1 (default)

Administrative Native VLAN tagging: enabled
```

(output omitted)

Refer to **Packet Tracer Activity** for this chapter

Packet Tracer - Configure Trunks - 3.4.5

In this Packet Tracer activity, you will perform the following:

- Verify VLANs
- Configure Trunks

Refer to
Lab Activity
for this chapter

Lab - Configure VLANs and Trunking - 3.4.6

In this lab, you will perform the following:

- Build the Network and Configure Basic Device Settings
- Create VLANs and Assign Switch Ports
- Maintain VLAN Port Assignments and the VLAN Database
- Configure an 802.1Q Trunk between the Switches
- Delete the VLAN Database

Dynamic Trunking Protocol - 3.5

Introduction to DTP - 3.5.1

Some Cisco switches have a proprietary protocol that lets them automatically negotiate trunking with a neighboring device. This protocol is called Dynamic Trunking Protocol (DTP). DTP can speed up the configuration process for a network administrator. Ethernet trunk interfaces support different trunking modes. An interface can be set to trunking or nontrunking, or to negotiate trunking with the neighbor interface. Trunk negotiation is managed by DTP, which operates on a point-to-point basis only, between network devices.

DTP is a Cisco proprietary protocol that is automatically enabled on Catalyst 2960 and Catalyst 3650 Series switches. DTP manages trunk negotiation only if the port on the neighbor switch is configured in a trunk mode that supports DTP. Switches from other vendors do not support DTP.

Caution: Some internetworking devices might forward DTP frames improperly, which can cause misconfigurations. To avoid this, turn off DTP on Cisco switch interfaces that are connected to devices that do not support DTP.

The default DTP configuration for Cisco Catalyst 2960 and 3650 switches is dynamic auto.

To enable trunking from a Cisco switch to a device that does not support DTP, use the **switchport mode trunk** and **switchport nonegotiate** interface configuration mode commands. This causes the interface to become a trunk, but it will not generate DTP frames.

```
S1(config-if)# switchport mode trunk
S1(config-if)# switchport nonegotiate
```

To re-enable dynamic trunking protocol use the **switchport mode dynamic auto** command.

```
S1(config-if)# switchport mode dynamic auto
```

If the ports connecting two switches are configured to ignore all DTP advertisements with the **switchport mode trunk** and the **switchport nonegotiate** commands, the ports will stay in trunk port mode. If the connecting ports are set to dynamic auto, they will not negotiate a trunk and will stay in the access mode state, creating an inactive trunk link.

When configuring a port to be in trunk mode, use the **switchport mode trunk** command. Then there is no ambiguity about which state the trunk is in; it is always on.

Negotiated Interface Modes - 3.5.2

The **switchport mode** command has additional options for negotiating the interface mode. The full command syntax is the following:

```
Switch(config)# switchport mode { access | dynamic { auto | desirable } |
trunk }
```

The options are described in the table.

Option	Description
access	• Puts the interface (access port) into permanent nontrunking mode and negotiates to convert the link into a nontrunk link. • The interface becomes a nontrunk interface, regardless of whether the neighboring interface is a trunk interface.
dynamic auto	• Makes the interface able to convert the link to a trunk link. • The interface becomes a trunk interface if the neighboring interface is set to trunk or desirable mode. • The default switchport mode for all Ethernet interfaces is **dynamic auto**.
dynamic desirable	• Makes the interface actively attempt to convert the link to a trunk link. • The interface becomes a trunk interface if the neighboring interface is set to trunk, desirable, or dynamic auto mode.
trunk	• Puts the interface into permanent trunking mode and negotiates to convert the neighboring link into a trunk link. • The interface becomes a trunk interface even if the neighboring interface is not a trunk interface.

Use the **switchport nonegotiate** interface configuration command to stop DTP negotiation. The switch does not engage in DTP negotiation on this interface. You can use this command only when the interface switchport mode is **access** or **trunk**. You must manually configure the neighboring interface as a trunk interface to establish a trunk link.

Results of a DTP Configuration - 3.5.3

The table illustrates the results of the DTP configuration options on opposite ends of a trunk link connected to Catalyst 2960 switch ports. Best practice is to configure trunk links statically whenever possible.

	Dynamic Auto	Dynamic Desirable	Trunk	Access
Dynamic Auto	Access	Trunk	Trunk	Access
Dynamic Desirable	Trunk	Trunk	Trunk	Access
Trunk	Trunk	Trunk	Trunk	Limited connectivity
Access	Access	Access	Limited connectivity	Access

Verify DTP Mode - 3.5.4

The default DTP mode is dependent on the Cisco IOS Software version and on the platform. To determine the current DTP mode, issue the **show dtp interface** command as shown in the output.

```
S1# show dtp interface fa0/1
DTP information for FastEthernet0/1:
TOS/TAS/TNS: ACCESS/AUTO/ACCESS
TOT/TAT/TNT: NATIVE/NEGOTIATE/NATIVE
Neighbor address 1: C80084AEF101
Neighbor address 2: 000000000000
Hello timer expiration (sec/state): 11/RUNNING
Access timer expiration (sec/state): never/STOPPED
Negotiation timer expiration (sec/state): never/STOPPED
Multidrop timer expiration (sec/state): never/STOPPED
FSM state: S2:ACCESS
# times multi & trunk 0
Enabled: yes
In STP: no
```

Note: A general best practice is to set the interface to **trunk** and **nonegotiate** when a trunk link is required. On links where trunking is not intended, DTP should be turned off.

Packet Tracer - Configure DTP - 3.5.5

In this Packet Tracer activity, you will configure and verify DTP.

Check Your Understanding - Dynamic Trunking Protocol - 3.5.6

Module Practice and Quiz - 3.6

Packet Tracer - Implement VLANs and Trunking - 3.6.1

In this Packet Tracer activity, you will perform the following:

- Configure VLANs
- Assign Ports to VLANs
- Configure Static Trunking
- Configure Dynamic Trunking

Refer to
Lab Activity
for this chapter

Lab - Implement VLANs and Trunking - 3.6.2

In this lab, you will perform the following:

- Build the Network and Configure Basic Device Settings

- Create VLANs and Assign Switch Ports

- Configure an 802.1Q Trunk between the Switches

What did I learn in this module? - 3.6.3

Overview of VLANs

Virtual LANs (VLANs) are a group of devices that can communicate as if each device was attached to the same cable. VLANs are based on logical instead of physical connections. Administrators use VLANs to segment networks based on factors such as function, team, or application. Each VLAN is considered a separate logical network. Any switch port can belong to a VLAN. A VLAN creates a logical broadcast domain that can span multiple physical LAN segments. VLANs improve network performance by separating large broadcast domains into smaller ones. Each VLAN in a switched network corresponds to an IP network; therefore, VLAN design must use a hierarchical network-addressing scheme. Types of VLANs include the default VLAN, data VLANs, the native VLAN, management VLANs. and voice VLANs.

VLANs in a Multi-Switched Environment

A VLAN trunk does not belong to a specific VLAN. It is a conduit for multiple VLANs between switches and routers. A VLAN trunk is a point-to-point link between two network devices that carries more than one VLAN. A VLAN trunk extends VLANs across an entire network. When VLANs are implemented on a switch, the transmission of unicast, multicast, and broadcast traffic from a host in a particular VLAN are restricted to the devices that are in that VLAN. VLAN tag fields include the type, user priority, CFI and VID. Some devices add a VLAN tag to native VLAN traffic. If an 802.1Q trunk port receives a tagged frame with the VID that is the same as the native VLAN, it drops the frame. A separate voice VLAN is required to support VoIP. QoS and security policies can be applied to voice traffic. Voice VLAN traffic must be tagged with an appropriate Layer 2 CoS priority value.

VLAN Configuration

Different Cisco Catalyst switches support various numbers of VLANs including normal range VLANs and extended range VLANs. When configuring normal range VLANs, the configuration details are stored in flash memory on the switch in a file called vlan.dat. Although it is not required, it is good practice to save running configuration changes to the startup configuration. After creating a VLAN, the next step is to assign ports to the VLAN. There are several commands for defining a port to be an access port and assigning it to a VLAN. VLANs are configured on the switch port and not on the end device. An access port can belong to only one data VLAN at a time. However, a port can also be associated to a voice VLAN. For example, a port connected to an IP phone and an end device would be associated with two VLANs: one for voice and one for data. After a VLAN is configured, VLAN configurations can be validated using Cisco IOS **show** commands. If the switch access port has been incorrectly assigned to a VLAN, then simply re-enter the **switchport access vlan** *vlan-id* interface configuration command with the correct VLAN ID. The **no vlan** *vlan-id* global configuration mode command is used to remove a VLAN from the switch vlan.dat file.

VLAN Trunks

A VLAN trunk is an OSI Layer 2 link between two switches that carries traffic for all VLANs. There are several commands to configure the interconnecting ports. To verify VLAN trunk configuration use the **show interfaces** *interface-ID* **switchport** command. Use the **no switchport trunk allowed vlan** and the **no switchport trunk native vlan** commands to remove the allowed VLANs and reset the native VLAN of the trunk.

Dynamic Trunking Protocol

An interface can be set to trunking or nontrunking, or to negotiate trunking with the neighbor interface. Trunk negotiation is managed by the Dynamic Trunking Protocol (DTP), which operates on a point-to-point basis only, between network devices. DTP is a Cisco proprietary protocol that manages trunk negotiation only if the port on the neighbor switch is configured in a trunk mode that supports DTP. To enable trunking from a Cisco switch to a device that does not support DTP, use the **switchport mode trunk** and **switchport nonegotiate** interface configuration mode commands. The **switchport mode** command has additional options for negotiating the interface mode including access, dynamic auto, dynamic desirable, and trunk. To verify the current DTP mode, issue the **show dtp interface** command.

Go to the online course to take the quiz and exam.

Chapter Quiz - VLANs

Your Chapter Notes

CHAPTER 4

Inter-VLAN Routing

Introduction - 4.0

Why should I take this module? - 4.0.1

Welcome to Inter-VLAN Routing!

Now you know how to segment and organize your network into VLANs. Hosts can communicate with other hosts in the same VLAN, and you no longer have hosts sending out broadcast messages to every other device in your network, eating up needed bandwidth. But what if a host in one VLAN needs to communicate with a host in a different VLAN? If you are a network administrator, you know that people will want to communicate with other people outside of your network. This is where inter-VLAN routing can help you. Inter-VLAN routing uses a Layer 3 device such as a router or a Layer 3 switch. Let's take your VLAN expertise and combine it with your network layer skills and put them to the test!

What will I learn to do in this module? - 4.0.2

Module Title: Inter-VLAN Routing

Module Objective: Troubleshoot inter-VLAN routing on Layer 3 devices.

Topic Title	Topic Objective
Inter-VLAN Routing Operation	Describe options for configuring inter-VLAN routing.
Router-on-a-Stick Inter-VLAN Routing	Configure router-on-a-stick inter-VLAN routing.
Inter-VLAN Routing using Layer 3 Switches	Configure inter-VLAN routing using Layer 3 switching.
Troubleshoot Inter-VLAN Routing	Troubleshoot common inter-VLAN configuration issues.

Inter-VLAN Routing Operation - 4.1

What is Inter-VLAN Routing? - 4.1.1

VLANs are used to segment switched Layer 2 networks for a variety of reasons. Regardless of the reason, hosts in one VLAN cannot communicate with hosts in another VLAN unless there is a router or a Layer 3 switch to provide routing services.

Inter-VLAN routing is the process of forwarding network traffic from one VLAN to another VLAN.

There are three inter-VLAN routing options:

- **Legacy Inter-VLAN routing** - This is a legacy solution. It does not scale well.

- **Router-on-a-Stick** - This is an acceptable solution for a small to medium-sized network.

■ **Layer 3 switch using switched virtual interfaces (SVIs)** - This is the most scalable solution for medium to large organizations.

Refer to
Online Course
for Illustration

Legacy Inter-VLAN Routing - 4.1.2

The first inter-VLAN routing solution relied on using a router with multiple Ethernet interfaces. Each router interface was connected to a switch port in different VLANs. The router interfaces served as the default gateways to the local hosts on the VLAN subnet.

For example, refer to the topology where R1 has two interfaces connected to switch S1.

Notice in the example MAC address table of S1 is populated as follows:

■ Fa0/1 port is assigned to VLAN 10 and is connected to the R1 G0/0/0 interface.

■ Fa0/11 port is assigned to VLAN 10 and is connected to PC1.

■ Fa0/12 port is assigned to VLAN 20 and is connected to the R1 G0/0/1 interface.

■ Fa0/11 port is assigned to VLAN 20 and is connected to PC2.

MAC Address table for S1

Port	MAC Address	VLAN
F0/1	R1 G0/0/0 MAC	10
F0/11	PC1 MAC	10
F0/12	R1 G0/0/1 MAC	20
F0/24	PC2 MAC	20

When PC1 sends a packet to PC2 on another network, it forwards it to its default gateway 192.168.10.1. R1 receives the packet on its G0/0/0 interface and examines the destination address of the packet. R1 then routes the packet out its G0/0/1 interface to the F0/12 port in VLAN 20 on S1. Finally, S1 forwards the frame to PC2.

Legacy inter-VLAN routing using physical interfaces works, but it has a significant limitation. It is not reasonably scalable because routers have a limited number of physical interfaces. Requiring one physical router interface per VLAN quickly exhausts the physical interface capacity of a router.

In our example, R1 required two separate Ethernet interfaces to route between VLAN 10 and VLAN 20. What if there were six (or more) VLANs to interconnect? A separate interface would be required for each VLAN. Obviously, this solution is not scalable.

Note: This method of inter-VLAN routing is no longer implemented in switched networks and is included for explanation purposes only.

Refer to
Interactive Graphic
in online course

Router-on-a-Stick Inter-VLAN Routing - 4.1.3

The 'router-on-a-stick' inter-VLAN routing method overcomes the limitation of the legacy inter-VLAN routing method. It only requires one physical Ethernet interface to route traffic between multiple VLANs on a network.

A Cisco IOS router Ethernet interface is configured as an 802.1Q trunk and connected to a trunk port on a Layer 2 switch. Specifically, the router interface is configured using subinterfaces to identify routable VLANs.

The configured subinterfaces are software-based virtual interfaces. Each is associated with a single physical Ethernet interface. Subinterfaces are configured in software on a router. Each subinterface is independently configured with an IP address and VLAN assignment. Subinterfaces are configured for different subnets that correspond to their VLAN assignment. This facilitates logical routing.

When VLAN-tagged traffic enters the router interface, it is forwarded to the VLAN subinterface. After a routing decision is made based on the destination IP network address, the router determines the exit interface for the traffic. If the exit interface is configured as an 802.1q subinterface, the data frames are VLAN-tagged with the new VLAN and sent back out the physical interface.

Click Play in the figure to view an animation of how a router-on-a-stick performs its routing function.

As seen in the animation, PC1 on VLAN 10 is communicating with PC3 on VLAN 30. When R1 accepts the tagged unicast traffic on VLAN 10, it routes that traffic to VLAN 30, using its configured subinterfaces. Switch S2 removes the VLAN tag of the unicast frame and forwards the frame out to PC3 on port F0/23.

Note: The router-on-a-stick method of inter-VLAN routing does not scale beyond 50 VLANs.

Refer to **Online Course** for Illustration

Inter-VLAN Routing on a Layer 3 Switch - 4.1.4

The modern method of performing inter-VLAN routing is to use Layer 3 switches and switched virtual interfaces (SVI). An SVI is a virtual interface that is configured on a Layer 3 switch, as shown in the figure.

Note: A Layer 3 switch is also called a multilayer switch as it operates at Layer 2 and Layer 3. However, in this course we use the term Layer 3 switch.

Inter-VLAN SVIs are created the same way that the management VLAN interface is configured. The SVI is created for a VLAN that exists on the switch. Although virtual, the SVI performs the same functions for the VLAN as a router interface would. Specifically, it provides Layer 3 processing for packets that are sent to or from all switch ports associated with that VLAN.

The following are advantages of using Layer 3 switches for inter-VLAN routing:

- They are much faster than router-on-a-stick because everything is hardware switched and routed.

- There is no need for external links from the switch to the router for routing.

- They are not limited to one link because Layer 2 EtherChannels can be used as trunk links between the switches to increase bandwidth.

■ Latency is much lower because data does not need to leave the switch in order to be routed to a different network.

■ They more commonly deployed in a campus LAN than routers.

The only disadvantage is that Layer 3 switches are more expensive.

Go to the online course to take the quiz and exam.

Check Your Understanding - Inter-VLAN Routing Operation - 4.1.5

Router-on-a-Stick Inter-VLAN Routing - 4.2

Refer to **Online Course** for Illustration

Router-on-a-Stick Scenario - 4.2.1

In the previous topic, three different ways to create inter-VLAN routing were listed, and legacy inter-VLAN routing was detailed. This topic details how to configure router-on-a-stick inter-VLAN routing. You can see in the figure that the router is not in the center of the topology but instead, appears to be on a stick near the border, hence the name.

In the figure, the R1 GigabitEthernet 0/0/1 interface is connected to the S1 FastEthernet 0/5 port. The S1 FastEthernet 0/1 port is connected to the S2 FastEthernet 0/1 port. These are trunk links that are required to forward traffic within and between VLANs.

To route between VLANs, the R1 GigabitEthernet 0/0/1 interface is logically divided into three subinterfaces, as shown in the table. The table also shows the three VLANs that will be configured on the switches.

Router R1 Subinterfaces

Subinterface	VLAN	IP Address
G0/0/1.10	10	192.168.10.1/24
G0/0/1.20	20	192.168.20.1/24
G0/0/1.30	99	192.168.99.1/24

Assume that R1, S1, and S2 have initial basic configurations. Currently, PC1 and PC2 cannot **ping** each other because they are on separate networks. Only S1 and S2 can **ping** each other, but they but are unreachable by PC1 or PC2 because they are also on different networks.

To enable devices to ping each other, the switches must be configured with VLANs and trunking, and the router must be configured for inter-VLAN routing.

Refer to **Online Course** for Illustration

S1 VLAN and Trunking Configuration - 4.2.2

Complete the following steps to configure S1 with VLANs and trunking:

Refer to **Interactive Graphic** in online course

Step 1.   Create and name the VLANs.

Step 2.   Create the management interface.

Step 3.   Configure access ports.

Step 4.   Configure trunking ports.

Click each button for details of the configuration step.

1. Create and name the VLANs.

First, the VLANs are created and named. VLANs are only created after you exit out of VLAN subconfiguration mode.

```
S1(config)# vlan 10
S1(config-vlan)# name LAN10
S1(config-vlan)# exit
S1(config)# vlan 20
S1(config-vlan)# name LAN20
S1(config-vlan)# exit
S1(config)# vlan 99
S1(config-vlan)# name Management
S1(config-vlan)# exit
S1(config)#
```

2. Create the management interface.

Next, the management interface is created on VLAN 99 along with the default gateway of R1.

```
S1(config)# interface vlan 99
S1(config-if)# ip add 192.168.99.2 255.255.255.0
S1(config-if)# no shut
S1(config-if)# exit
S1(config)# ip default-gateway 192.168.99.1
S1(config)#
```

3. Configure access ports.

Next, port Fa0/6 connecting to PC1 is configured as an access port in VLAN 10. Assume PC1 has been configured with the correct IP address and default gateway.

```
S1(config)# interface fa0/6
S1(config-if)# switchport mode access
S1(config-if)# switchport access vlan 10
S1(config-if)# no shut
S1(config-if)# exit
S1(config)#
```

4. Configure trunking ports.

Finally, ports Fa0/1 connecting to S2 and Fa05 connecting to R1 are configured as trunk ports.

```
S1(config)# interface fa0/1

S1(config-if)# switchport mode trunk

S1(config-if)# no shut

S1(config-if)# exit

S1(config)# interface fa0/5

S1(config-if)# switchport mode trunk

S1(config-if)# no shut

S1(config-if)# end

*Mar  1 00:23:43.093: %LINEPROTO-5-UPDOWN: Line protocol on Interface
FastEthernet0/1, changed state to up

*Mar  1 00:23:44.511: %LINEPROTO-5-UPDOWN: Line protocol on Interface
FastEthernet0/5, changed state to up
```

Refer to
Online Course
for Illustration

S2 VLAN and Trunking Configuration - 4.2.3

The configuration for S2 is similar to S1.

```
S2(config)# vlan 10

S2(config-vlan)# name LAN10

S2(config-vlan)# exit

S2(config)# vlan 20

S2(config-vlan)# name LAN20

S2(config-vlan)# exit

S2(config)# vlan 99

S2(config-vlan)# name Management

S2(config-vlan)# exit

S2(config)#

S2(config)# interface vlan 99

S2(config-if)# ip add 192.168.99.3 255.255.255.0

S2(config-if)# no shut

S2(config-if)# exit

S2(config)# ip default-gateway 192.168.99.1

S2(config)# interface fa0/18

S2(config-if)# switchport mode access

S2(config-if)# switchport access vlan 20

S2(config-if)# no shut
```

```
S2(config-if)# exit

S2(config)# interface fa0/1

S2(config-if)# switchport mode trunk

S2(config-if)# no shut

S2(config-if)# exit

S2(config-if)# end

*Mar  1 00:23:52.137: %LINEPROTO-5-UPDOWN: Line protocol on Interface
FastEthernet0/1, changed state to up
```

Refer to
Online Course
for Illustration

R1 Subinterface Configuration - 4.2.4

The router-on-a-stick method requires you to create a subinterface for each VLAN to be routed.

A subinterface is created using the **interface** *interface_id subinterface_id* global configuration mode command. The subinterface syntax is the physical interface followed by a period and a subinterface number. Although not required, it is customary to match the subinterface number with the VLAN number.

Each subinterface is then configured with the following two commands:

- **encapsulation dot1q** *vlan_id* [**native**] - This command configures the subinterface to respond to 802.1Q encapsulated traffic from the specified *vlan-id*. The **native** keyword option is only appended to set the native VLAN to something other than VLAN 1.

- **ip address** *ip-address subnet-mask* - This command configures the IPv4 address of the subinterface. This address typically serves as the default gateway for the identified VLAN.

Repeat the process for each VLAN to be routed. Each router subinterface must be assigned an IP address on a unique subnet for routing to occur.

When all subinterfaces have been created, enable the physical interface using the **no shutdown** interface configuration command. If the physical interface is disabled, all subinterfaces are disabled.

In the following configuration, the R1 G0/0/1 subinterfaces are configured for VLANs 10, 20, and 99.

```
R1(config)# interface G0/0/1.10

R1(config-subif)# description Default Gateway for VLAN 10

R1(config-subif)# encapsulation dot1Q 10

R1(config-subif)# ip add 192.168.10.1 255.255.255.0

R1(config-subif)# exit

R1(config)#

R1(config)# interface G0/0/1.20

R1(config-subif)# description Default Gateway for VLAN 20

R1(config-subif)# encapsulation dot1Q 20
```

```
R1(config-subif)# ip add 192.168.20.1 255.255.255.0

R1(config-subif)# exit

R1(config)#

R1(config)# interface G0/0/1.99

R1(config-subif)# description Default Gateway for VLAN 99

R1(config-subif)# encapsulation dot1Q 99

R1(config-subif)# ip add 192.168.99.1 255.255.255.0

R1(config-subif)# exit

R1(config)#

R1(config)# interface G0/0/1

R1(config-if)# description Trunk link to S1

R1(config-if)# no shut

R1(config-if)# end

R1#

*Sep 15 19:08:47.015: %LINK-3-UPDOWN: Interface GigabitEthernet0/0/1,
changed state to down

*Sep 15 19:08:50.071: %LINK-3-UPDOWN: Interface GigabitEthernet0/0/1,
changed state to up

*Sep 15 19:08:51.071: %LINEPROTO-5-UPDOWN: Line protocol on Interface
GigabitEthernet0/0/1, changed state to up

R1#
```

Verify Connectivity Between PC1 and PC2 - 4.2.5

The router-on-a-stick configuration is complete after the switch trunk and the router sub-interfaces have been configured. The configuration can be verified from the hosts, router, and switch.

From a host, verify connectivity to a host in another VLAN using the **ping** command. It is a good idea to first verify the current host IP configuration using the **ipconfig** Windows host command.

```
C:\Users\PC1> ipconfig

Windows IP Configuration

Ethernet adapter Ethernet0:

   Connection-specific DNS Suffix . :

   Link-local IPv6 Address         : fe80::5c43:ee7c:2959:da68%6

   IPv4 Address                    : 192.168.10.10

   Subnet Mask                     : 255.255.255.0

   Default Gateway                 : 192.168.10.1

C:\Users\PC1>
```

The output confirms the IPv4 address and default gateway of PC1. Next, use **ping** to verify connectivity with PC2 and S1, as shown in the figure. The **ping** output successfully confirms inter-VLAN routing is operating.

```
C:\Users\PC1> ping 192.168.20.10

Pinging 192.168.20.10 with 32 bytes of data:

Reply from 192.168.20.10: bytes=32 time<1ms TTL=127

Reply from 192.168.20.10: bytes=32 time<1ms TTL=127

Reply from 192.168.20.10: bytes=32 time<1ms TTL=127

Reply from 192.168.20.10: bytes=32 time<1ms TTL=127

Ping statistics for 192.168.20.10:

    Packets: Sent = 4, Received = 4, Lost = 0 (0% loss).

Approximate round trip times in milli-seconds:

    Minimum = 0ms, Maximum = 0ms, Average = 0ms

C:\Users\PC1>

C:\Users\PC1> ping 192.168.99.2

Pinging 192.168.99.2 with 32 bytes of data:

Request timed out.

Request timed out.

Reply from 192.168.99.2: bytes=32 time=2ms TTL=254

Reply from 192.168.99.2: bytes=32 time=1ms TTL=254    |

Ping statistics for 192.168.99.2:

    Packets: Sent = 4, Received = 2, Lost = 2 (50% loss).

Approximate round trip times in milli-seconds:

    Minimum = 1ms, Maximum = 2ms, Average = 1ms

C:\Users\PC1>
```

Refer to
Interactive Graphic
in online course

Router-on-a-Stick Inter-VLAN Routing Verification - 4.2.6

In addition to using **ping** between devices, the following **show** commands can be used to verify and troubleshoot the router-on-a-stick configuration.

- **show ip route**
- **show ip interface brief**
- **show interfaces**
- **show interfaces trunk**

Click each button for example output for these commands.

show ip route

Verify that the subinterfaces are appearing in the routing table of R1 by using the **show ip route** command. Notice that there are three connected routes (C) and their respective exit interfaces for each routable VLAN. The output confirms that the correct subnets, VLANs, and subinterfaces are active.

```
R1# show ip route | begin Gateway

Gateway of last resort is not set

        192.168.10.0/24 is variably subnetted, 2 subnets, 2 masks
C         192.168.10.0/24 is directly connected, GigabitEthernet0/0/1.10
L         192.168.10.1/32 is directly connected, GigabitEthernet0/0/1.10
        192.168.20.0/24 is variably subnetted, 2 subnets, 2 masks
C         192.168.20.0/24 is directly connected, GigabitEthernet0/0/1.20
L         192.168.20.1/32 is directly connected, GigabitEthernet0/0/1.20
        192.168.99.0/24 is variably subnetted, 2 subnets, 2 masks
C         192.168.99.0/24 is directly connected, GigabitEthernet0/0/1.99
L         192.168.99.1/32 is directly connected, GigabitEthernet0/0/1.99
R1#
```

show ip interface brief

Another useful router command is **show ip interface brief,** as shown in the output. The output confirms that the subinterfaces have the correct IPv4 address configured, and that they are operational.

```
R1# show ip interface brief | include up

GigabitEthernet0/0/1    unassigned      YES unset  up              up
Gi0/0/1.10              192.168.10.1    YES manual up              up
Gi0/0/1.20              192.168.20.1    YES manual up              up
Gi0/0/1.99              192.168.99.1    YES manual up              up
R1#
```

show interfaces

Subinterfaces can be verified using the **show interfaces** *subinterface-id* command, as shown.

```
R1# show interfaces g0/0/1.10

GigabitEthernet0/0/1.10 is up, line protocol is up
   Hardware is ISR4221-2x1GE, address is 10b3.d605.0301 (bia 10b3.d605.0301)
   Description: Default Gateway for VLAN 10
   Internet address is 192.168.10.1/24
   MTU 1500 bytes, BW 100000 Kbit/sec, DLY 100 usec,
```

```
        reliability 255/255, txload 1/255, rxload 1/255
     Encapsulation 802.1Q Virtual LAN, Vlan ID  10.
     ARP type: ARPA, ARP Timeout 04:00:00
     Keepalive not supported
     Last clearing of "show interface" counters never
R1#
```

show interfaces trunk

The misconfiguration could also be on the trunking port of the switch. Therefore, it is also useful to verify the active trunk links on a Layer 2 switch by using the **show interfaces trunk** command, as shown in the output. The output confirms that the link to R1 is trunking for the required VLANs.

Note: Although VLAN 1 was not explicitly configured, it was automatically included because control traffic on trunk links will always be forwarded on VLAN 1.

```
S1# show interfaces trunk

Port         Mode             Encapsulation   Status        Native vlan

Fa0/1        on               802.1q          trunking      1

Fa0/5        on               802.1q          trunking      1

Port         Vlans allowed on trunk

Fa0/1        1-4094

Fa0/5        1-4094

Port         Vlans allowed and active in management domain

Fa0/1        1,10,20,99

Fa0/5        1,10,20,99

Port         Vlans in spanning tree forwarding state and not pruned

Fa0/1        1,10,20,99

Fa0/5        1,10,20,99

S1#
```

Refer to **Packet Tracer Activity** for this chapter

Packet Tracer - Configure Router-on-a-Stick Inter-VLAN Routing - 4.2.7

In this activity, you will check for connectivity prior to implementing inter-VLAN routing. Then you will configure VLANs and inter-VLAN routing. Finally, you will enable trunking and verify connectivity between VLANs.

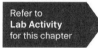

Refer to
Lab Activity
for this chapter

Lab - Configure Router-on-a-Stick Inter-VLAN Routing - 4.2.8

In this lab, you will complete the following objectives:

- Part 1: Build the Network and Configure Basic Device Settings
- Part 2: Configure Switches with VLANs and Trunking
- Part 3: Configure Trunk-Based Inter-VLAN Routing

Inter-VLAN Routing using Layer 3 Switches - 4.3

Layer 3 Switch Inter-VLAN Routing - 4.3.1

Modern, enterprise networks rarely use router-on-a-stick because it does not scale easily to meet requirements. In these very large networks, network administrators use Layer 3 switches to configure inter-VLAN routing.

Inter-VLAN routing using the router-on-a-stick method is simple to implement for a small to medium-sized organization. However, a large enterprise requires a faster, much more scalable method to provide inter-VLAN routing.

Enterprise campus LANs use Layer 3 switches to provide inter-VLAN routing. Layer 3 switches use hardware-based switching to achieve higher-packet processing rates than routers. Layer 3 switches are also commonly implemented in enterprise distribution layer wiring closets.

Capabilities of a Layer 3 switch include the ability to do the following:

- Route from one VLAN to another using multiple switched virtual interfaces (SVIs).
- Convert a Layer 2 switchport to a Layer 3 interface (i.e., a routed port). A routed port is similar to a physical interface on a Cisco IOS router.

To provide inter-VLAN routing, Layer 3 switches use SVIs. SVIs are configured using the same **interface vlan** *vlan-id* command used to create the management SVI on a Layer 2 switch. A Layer 3 SVI must be created for each of the routable VLANs.

Refer to
Online Course
for Illustration

Layer 3 Switch Scenario - 4.3.2

In the figure, the Layer 3 switch, D1, is connected to two hosts on different VLANs. PC1 is in VLAN 10 and PC2 is in VLAN 20, as shown. The Layer 3 switch will provide inter-VLAN routing services to the two hosts.

The table shows the IP addresses for each VLAN.

D1 VLAN IP Addresses

VLAN Interface	IP Address
10	192.168.10.1/24
20	192.168.20.1/24

Refer to
Interactive Graphic
in online course

Layer 3 Switch Configuration - 4.3.3

Complete the following steps to configure S1 with VLANs and trunking:

Step 1.   Create the VLANs.

Step 2.   Create the SVI VLAN interfaces.

Step 3.   Configure access ports.

Step 4.   Enable IP routing.

Click each button for details of the configuration step.

1. Create the VLANs.

First, create the two VLANs as shown in the output.

```
D1(config)# vlan 10
D1(config-vlan)# name LAN10
D1(config-vlan)# vlan 20
D1(config-vlan)# name LAN20
D1(config-vlan)# exit
D1(config)#
```

2. Create the SVI VLAN interfaces.

Configure the SVI for VLANs 10 and 20. The IP addresses that are configured will serve as the default gateways to the hosts in the respective VLANs. Notice the informational messages showing the line protocol on both SVIs changed to up.

```
D1(config)# interface vlan 10
D1(config-if)# description Default Gateway SVI for 192.168.10.0/24
D1(config-if)# ip add 192.168.10.1 255.255.255.0
D1(config-if)# no shut
D1(config-if)# exit
D1(config)#
D1(config)# int vlan 20
D1(config-if)# description Default Gateway SVI for 192.168.20.0/24
D1(config-if)# ip add 192.168.20.1 255.255.255.0
D1(config-if)# no shut
D1(config-if)# exit
D1(config)#
*Sep 17 13:52:16.053: %LINEPROTO-5-UPDOWN: Line protocol on Interface
Vlan10, changed state to up
*Sep 17 13:52:16.160: %LINEPROTO-5-UPDOWN: Line protocol on Interface
Vlan20, changed state to up
```

3. Configure access ports.

Next, configure the access ports connecting to the hosts and assign them to their respective VLANs.

```
D1(config)# interface GigabitEthernet1/0/6

D1(config-if)# description Access port to PC1

D1(config-if)# switchport mode access

D1(config-if)# switchport access vlan 10

D1(config-if)# exit

D1(config)#

D1(config)# interface GigabitEthernet1/0/18

D1(config-if)# description Access port to PC2

D1(config-if)# switchport mode access

D1(config-if)# switchport access vlan 20

D1(config-if)# exit
```

4. Enable IP routing.

Finally, enable IPv4 routing with the **ip routing** global configuration command to allow traffic to be exchanged between VLANs 10 and 20. This command must be configured to enable inter-VAN routing on a Layer 3 switch for IPv4.

```
D1(config)# ip routing

D1(config)#
```

Layer 3 Switch Inter-VLAN Routing Verification - 4.3.4

Inter-VLAN routing using a Layer 3 switch is simpler to configure than the router-on-a-stick method. After the configuration is complete, the configuration can be verified by testing connectivity between the hosts.

From a host, verify connectivity to a host in another VLAN using the **ping** command. It is a good idea to first verify the current host IP configuration using the **ipconfig** Windows host command. The output confirms the IPv4 address and default gateway of PC1.

```
C:\Users\PC1> ipconfig

Windows IP Configuration

Ethernet adapter Ethernet0:

   Connection-specific DNS Suffix . :

   Link-local IPv6 Address          : fe80::5c43:ee7c:2959:da68%6

   IPv4 Address                     : 192.168.10.10

   Subnet Mask                      : 255.255.255.0

   Default Gateway                  : 192.168.10.1

C:\Users\PC1>
```

Next, verify connectivity with PC2 using the **ping** Windows host command, as shown in the output. The **ping** output successfully confirms inter-VLAN routing is operating.

```
C:\Users\PC1> ping 192.168.20.10

Pinging 192.168.20.10 with 32 bytes of data:

Reply from 192.168.20.10: bytes=32 time<1ms TTL=127

Reply from 192.168.20.10: bytes=32 time<1ms TTL=127

Reply from 192.168.20.10: bytes=32 time<1ms TTL=127

Reply from 192.168.20.10: bytes=32 time<1ms TTL=127

Ping statistics for 192.168.20.10:
    Packets: Sent = 4, Received = 4, Lost = 0 (0% loss),
Approximate round trip times in milli-seconds:
    Minimum = 0ms, Maximum = 0ms, Average = 0ms

C:\Users\PC1>
```

Routing on a Layer 3 Switch - 4.3.5

If VLANs are to be reachable by other Layer 3 devices, then they must be advertised using static or dynamic routing. To enable routing on a Layer 3 switch, a routed port must be configured.

A routed port is created on a Layer 3 switch by disabling the switchport feature on a Layer 2 port that is connected to another Layer 3 device. Specifically, configuring the **no switchport** interface configuration command on a Layer 2 port converts it into a Layer 3 interface. Then the interface can be configured with an IPv4 configuration to connect to a router or another Layer 3 switch.

Refer to **Online Course** for Illustration

Routing Scenario on a Layer 3 Switch - 4.3.6

In the figure, the previously configured D1 Layer 3 switch is now connected to R1. R1 and D1 are both in an Open Shortest Path First (OSPF) routing protocol domain. Assume inter-VLAN has been successfully implemented on D1. The G0/0/1 interface of R1 has also been configured and enabled. Additionally, R1 is using OSPF to advertise its two networks, 10.10.10.0/24 and 10.20.20.0/24.

Note: OSPF routing configuration is covered in another course. In this module, OSPF configuration commands will be given to you in all activities and assessments. It is not required that you understand the configuration in order to enable OSPF routing on the Layer 3 switch.

Refer to **Interactive Graphic** in online course

Routing Configuration on a Layer 3 Switch - 4.3.7

Complete the following steps to configure D1 to route with R1:

Step 1. Configure the routed port.

Step 2. Enable routing.

Step 3.   Configure routing.

Step 4.   Verify routing.

Step 5.   Verify connectivity.

Click each button for details of the configuration step.

1. Configure the routed port.

Configure G1/0/1 to be a routed port, assign it an IPv4 address, and enable it.

```
D1(config)# interface GigabitEthernet1/0/1

D1(config-if)# description routed Port Link to R1

D1(config-if)# no switchport

D1(config-if)# ip address 10.10.10.2 255.255.255.0

D1(config-if)# no shut

D1(config-if)# exit

D1(config)#
```

2. Enable routing.

Ensure IPv4 routing is enabled with the **ip routing** global configuration command.

```
D1(config)# ip routing

D1(config)#
```

3. Configure routing.

Configure the OSPF routing protocol to advertise the VLAN 10 and VLAN 20 networks, along with the network that is connected to R1. Notice the message informing you that an adjacency has been established with R1.

```
D1(config)# router ospf 10

D1(config-router)# network 192.168.10.0 0.0.0.255 area 0

D1(config-router)# network 192.168.20.0 0.0.0.255 area 0

D1(config-router)# network 10.10.10.0 0.0.0.3 area 0

D1(config-router)# ^Z

D1#

*Sep 17 13:52:51.163: %OSPF-5-ADJCHG: Process 10, Nbr 10.20.20.1 on
GigabitEthernet1/0/1 from LOADING to FULL, Loading Done

D1#
```

4. Verify routing.

Verify the routing table on D1. Notice that D1 now has a route to the 10.20.20.0/24 network.

```
D1# show ip route | begin Gateway

Gateway of last resort is not set

      10.0.0.0/8 is variably subnetted, 3 subnets, 3 masks
C        10.10.10.0/30 is directly connected, GigabitEthernet1/0/1

L        10.10.10.2/32 is directly connected, GigabitEthernet1/0/1

O        10.20.20.0/24 [110/2] via 10.10.10.1, 00:00:06,
GigabitEthernet1/0/1

      192.168.10.0/24 is variably subnetted, 2 subnets, 2 masks
C        192.168.10.0/24 is directly connected, Vlan10

L        192.168.10.1/32 is directly connected, Vlan10

      192.168.20.0/24 is variably subnetted, 2 subnets, 2 masks
C        192.168.20.0/24 is directly connected, Vlan20

L        192.168.20.1/32 is directly connected, Vlan20

D1#
```

5. Verify connectivity.

At this time, PC1 and PC2 are able to ping the server connected to R1.

```
C:\Users\PC1> ping 10.20.20.254

Pinging 10.20.20.254 with 32 bytes of data:

Request timed out.

Reply from 10.20.20.254: bytes=32 time<1ms TTL=127

Reply from 10.20.20.254: bytes=32 time<1ms TTL=127

Reply from 10.20.20.254: bytes=32 time<1ms TTL=127

Ping statistics for 10.20.20.254:

    Packets: Sent = 4, Received = 3, Lost = 1 (25% loss).

Approximate round trip times in milli-seconds:

    Minimum = 1ms, Maximum = 2ms, Average = 1ms

C:\Users\PC1>

!=====================================================

C:\Users\PC2> ping 10.20.20.254

Pinging 10.20.20.254 with 32 bytes of data:

Reply from 10.20.20.254: bytes=32 time<1ms TTL=127

Reply from 10.20.20.254: bytes=32 time<1ms TTL=127

Reply from 10.20.20.254: bytes=32 time<1ms TTL=127
```

```
Reply from 10.20.20.254: bytes=32 time<1ms TTL=127

Ping statistics for 10.20.20.254:

    Packets: Sent = 4, Received = 4, Lost = 0 (0% loss).

Approximate round trip times in milli-seconds:

    Minimum = 1ms, Maximum = 2ms, Average = 1ms

C:\Users\PC2>
```

Refer to **Packet Tracer Activity** for this chapter

Packet Tracer - Configure Layer 3 Switching and Inter-VLAN Routing - 4.3.8

In this activity, you will configure Layer 3 switching and Inter-VLAN routing on a Cisco 3560 switch.

Troubleshoot Inter-VLAN Routing - 4.4

Common Inter-VLAN Issues - 4.4.1

By now, you know that when you configure and verify, you must also be able to troubleshoot. This topic discusses some common network problems associated with inter-VLAN routing.

There are a number of reasons why an inter-VAN configuration may not work. All are related to connectivity issues. First, check the physical layer to resolve any issues where a cable might be connected to the wrong port. If the connections are correct, then use the list in the table for other common reasons why inter-VLAN connectivity may fail.

Issue Type	How to Fix	How to Verify

Missing VLANs	• Create (or re-create) the VLAN if it does not exist.
	• Ensure host port is assigned to the correct VLAN.
		`show vlan [brief]`
		`show interfaces switchport`
		`ping`

Switch Trunk Port Issues	• Ensure trunks are configured correctly. • Ensure port is a trunk port and enabled.	`show interfaces trunk` `show running-config`

Switch Access Port Issues	• Assign correct VLAN to access port.
	• Ensure port is an access port and enabled.
	• Host is incorrectly configured in the wrong subnet.
		`show interfaces switchport`
		`show running-config interface`
		`ipconfig`

Router Configuration Issues	• Router subinterface IPv4 address is incorrectly configured. • Router subinterface is assigned to the VLAN ID.	`show ip interface brief` `show interfaces`

Refer to
Online Course
for Illustration

Troubleshoot Inter-VLAN Routing Scenario - 4.4.2

Examples of some of these inter-VLAN routing problems will now be covered in more detail.

This topology will be used for all of these issues.

The VLAN and IPv4 addressing information for R1 is shown in the table.

Router R1 Subinterfaces

Subinterface	VLAN	IP Address
G0/0/0.10	10	192.168.10.1/24
G0/0/0.20	20	192.168.20.1/24
G0/0/0.30	99	192.168.99.1/24

Missing VLANs - 4.4.3

An inter-VLAN connectivity issue could be caused by a missing VLAN. The VLAN could be missing if it was not created, it was accidently deleted, or it is not allowed on the trunk link.

For example, PC1 is currently connected to VLAN 10, as shown in the **show vlan brief** command output.

```
S1# show vlan brief

VLAN Name                     Status    Ports
---- ----------------------- --------- -------------------------------

1    default                  active    Fa0/2,  Fa0/3,  Fa0/4,  Fa0/7
                                        Fa0/8,  Fa0/9,  Fa0/10, Fa0/11
                                        Fa0/12, Fa0/13, Fa0/14, Fa0/15
                                        Fa0/16, Fa0/17, Fa0/18, Fa0/19
                                        Fa0/20, Fa0/21, Fa0/22, Fa0/23
                                        Fa0/24, Gi0/1,  Gi0/2

10   LAN10                    active    Fa0/6

20   LAN20                    active

99   Management               active

1002 fddi-default             act/unsup

1003 token-ring-default       act/unsup

1004 fddinet-default          act/unsup

1005 trnet-default            act/unsup

S1#
```

Now assume that VLAN 10 is accidently deleted, as shown in the following output.

```
S1(config)# no vlan 10
S1(config)# do show vlan brief
```

VLAN	Name	Status	Ports
1	default	active	Fa0/2, Fa0/3, Fa0/4, Fa0/7
			Fa0/8, Fa0/9, Fa0/10, Fa0/11
			Fa0/12, Fa0/13, Fa0/14, Fa0/15
			Fa0/16, Fa0/17, Fa0/18, Fa0/19
			Fa0/20, Fa0/21, Fa0/22, Fa0/23
			Fa0/24, Gi0/1, Gi0/2
20	LAN20	active	
99	Management	active	
1002	fddi-default	act/unsup	
1003	token-ring-default	act/unsup	
1004	fddinet-default	act/unsup	
1005	trnet-default	act/unsup	

```
S1(config)#
```

Notice VLAN 10 is now missing from the output. Also notice that port Fa0/6 has not been reassigned to the default VLAN. The reason is because when you delete a VLAN, any ports assigned to that VLAN become inactive. They remain associated with the VLAN (and thus inactive) until you assign them to a new VLAN or recreate the missing VLAN.

Use the **show interface** *interface-id* **switchport** command to verify the VLAN membership.

```
S1(config)# do show interface fa0/6 switchport
Name: Fa0/6
Switchport: Enabled
Administrative Mode: static access
Operational Mode: static access
Administrative Trunking Encapsulation: dot1q
Operational Trunking Encapsulation: native
Negotiation of Trunking: Off
Access Mode VLAN: 10 (Inactive)
Trunking Native Mode VLAN: 1 (default)
Administrative Native VLAN tagging: enabled
Voice VLAN: none
(Output omitted)
```

Recreating the missing VLAN would automatically reassign the hosts to it, as shown in the following output.

```
S1(config)# vlan 10
S1(config-vlan)# do show vlan brief

VLAN Name                             Status     Ports
-------------------------------       ---------  ------------------------------
1    default                          active     Fa0/2,  Fa0/3,  Fa0/4,  Fa0/7
                                                 Fa0/8,  Fa0/9,  Fa0/10, Fa0/11
                                                 Fa0/12, Fa0/13, Fa0/14, Fa0/15
                                                 Fa0/16, Fa0/17, Fa0/18, Fa0/19
                                                 Fa0/20, Fa0/21, Fa0/22,cFa0/23
                                                 Fa0/24, Gi0/1,  Gi0/2

20   LAN20                            active
99   Management                       active
1002 fddi-default                     act/unsup
1003 token-ring-default               act/unsup
1004 fddinet-default                  act/unsup
1005 trnet-default                    act/unsup
S1(config-vlan)#
```

Notice that the VLAN has not been created as expected. The reason is because you must exit from VLAN sub-configuration mode to create the VLAN, as shown in the following output.

```
S1(config-vlan)# exit
S1(config)# do show vlan brief

VLAN Name                             Status     Ports
-------------------------------       ---------  ------------------------------
1    default                          active     Fa0/2,  Fa0/3,  Fa0/4,  Fa0/7
                                                 Fa0/8,  Fa0/9,  Fa0/10, Fa0/11
                                                 Fa0/12, Fa0/13, Fa0/14, Fa0/15
                                                 Fa0/16, Fa0/17, Fa0/18, Fa0/19
                                                 Fa0/20, Fa0/21, Fa0/22, Fa0/23
                                                 Fa0/24, Gi0/1,  Gi0/2

10   VLAN0010                         active     Fa0/6
20   LAN20                            active
99   Management                       active
1002 fddi-default                     act/unsup
1003 token-ring-default               act/unsup
```

```
1004 fddinet-default              act/unsup

1005 trnet-default               act/unsup

S1(config)#
```

Now notice that the VLAN is included in the list and that the host connected to Fa0/6 is on VLAN 10.

Refer to
Online Course
for Illustration

Switch Trunk Port Issues - 4.4.4

Another issue for inter-VLAN routing includes misconfigured switch ports. In a legacy inter-VLAN solution, this could be caused when the connecting router port is not assigned to the correct VLAN.

However, with a router-on-a-stick solution, the most common cause is a misconfigured trunk port.

For example, assume PC1 was able to connect to hosts in other VLANs until recently. A quick look at maintenance logs revealed that the S1 Layer 2 switch was recently accessed for routine maintenance. Therefore, you suspect the problem may be related to that switch.

On S1, verify that the port connecting to R1 (i.e., F0/5) is correctly configured as a trunk link using the **show interfaces trunk** command, as shown.

```
S1# show interfaces trunk

Port          Mode              Encapsulation  Status         Native vlan

Fa0/1         on                802.1q         trunking       1

Port          Vlans allowed on trunk

Fa0/1         1-4094

Port          Vlans allowed and active in management domain

Fa0/1         1,10,20,99

Port          Vlans in spanning tree forwarding state and not pruned

Fa0/1         1,10,20,99

S1#
```

The Fa0/5 port connecting to R1 is mysteriously missing from the output. Verify the interface configuration using the **show running-config interface fa0/5** command, as shown.

```
S1# show running-config interface fa0/5

Building configuration...

Current configuration : 96 bytes

!

interface FastEthernet0/5

 description Trunk link to R1

 switchport mode trunk

 shutdown

end

S1#
```

As you can see, the port was accidently shut down. To correct the problem, re-enable the port and verify the trunking status, as shown in the output.

```
S1(config)# interface fa0/5

S1(config-if)# no shut

S1(config-if)#

*Mar  1 04:46:44.153: %LINK-3-UPDOWN: Interface FastEthernet0/5, changed
state to up

S1(config-if)#

*Mar  1 04:46:47.962: %LINEPROTO-5-UPDOWN: Line protocol on Interface
FastEthernet0/5, changed state to up

S1(config-if)# do show interface trunk

Port        Mode              Encapsulation   Status       Native vlan

Fa0/1       on                802.1q          trunking     1

Fa0/5       on                802.1q          trunking     1

Port        Vlans allowed on trunk

Fa0/1       1-4094

Fa0/5       1-4094

Port        Vlans allowed and active in management domain

Fa0/1       1,10,20,99

Fa0/5       1,10,20,99

Port        Vlans in spanning tree forwarding state and not pruned

Fa0/1       1,10,20,99

Fa0/1       1,10,20,99

S1(config-if)#
```

To reduce the risk of a failed inter-switch link disrupting inter-VLAN routing, redundant links and alternate paths should be part of the network design.

Refer to
Online Course
for Illustration

Switch Access Port Issues - 4.4.5

When a problem is suspected with a switch access port configuration, use verification commands to examine the configuration and identify the problem.

Assume PC1 has the correct IPv4 address and default gateway but is not able to **ping** its own default gateway. PC1 is supposed to be connected to a VLAN 10 port.

Verify the port configuration on S1 using the **show interfaces** *interface-id* **switchport** command.

```
S1# show interface fa0/6 switchport

Name: Fa0/6

Switchport: Enabled

Administrative Mode: static access
```

```
Operational Mode: static access

Administrative Trunking Encapsulation: dot1q

Operational Trunking Encapsulation: native

Negotiation of Trunking: Off

Access Mode VLAN: 1 (default)

Trunking Native Mode VLAN: 1 (default)

Administrative Native VLAN tagging: enabled

Voice VLAN: none
```

The Fa0/6 port has been configured as an access port as indicated by "static access". However, it appears that it has not been configured to be in VLAN 10. Verify the configuration of the interface.

```
S1# show running-config interface fa0/6

Building configuration...

Current configuration : 87 bytes

!

interface FastEthernet0/6

 description PC-A access port

 switchport mode access

end

S1#
```

Assign port Fa0/6 to VLAN 10 and verify the port assignment.

```
S1# configure terminal

S1(config)# interface fa0/6

S1(config-if)# switchport access vlan 10

S1(config-if)#

S1(config-if)# do show interface fa0/6 switchport

Name: Fa0/6

Switchport: Enabled

Administrative Mode: static access

Operational Mode: static access

Administrative Trunking Encapsulation: dot1q

Operational Trunking Encapsulation: native

Negotiation of Trunking: Off

Access Mode VLAN: 10 (VLAN0010)

Trunking Native Mode VLAN: 1 (default)

Administrative Native VLAN tagging: enabled
```

```
Voice VLAN: none

(Output omitted)
```

PC1 is now able to communicate with hosts on other VLANs.

Refer to
Online Course
for Illustration

Router Configuration Issues - 4.4.6

Router-on-a-stick configuration problems are usually related to subinterface misconfigurations. For example, an incorrect IP address was configured or the wrong VLAN ID was assigned to the subinterface.

For example, R1 should be providing inter-VLAN routing for users in VLANs 10, 20, and 99. However, users in VLAN 10 cannot reach any other VLAN.

You verified the switch trunk link and all appears to be in order. Verify the subinterface status using the **show ip interface brief** command.

```
R1# show ip interface brief

Interface              IP-Address    OK? Method Status                 Protocol

GigabitEthernet0/0/0   unassigned    YES unset  administratively down down

GigabitEthernet0/0/1   unassigned    YES unset  up                        up

Gi0/0/1.10             192.168.10.1  YES manual up                        up

Gi0/0/1.20             192.168.20.1  YES manual up                        up

Gi0/0/1.99             192.168.99.1  YES manual up                        up

Serial0/1/0            unassigned    YES unset  administratively down down

Serial0/1/1            unassigned    YES unset  administratively down down

R1#
```

The subinterfaces have been assigned the correct IPv4 addresses and they are operational.

Verify which VLANs each of the subinterfaces is on. To do so, the **show interfaces** command is useful but it generates a great deal of additional unrequired output. The command output can be reduced using IOS command filters as shown in the output.

```
R1# show interfaces | include Gig|802.1Q

GigabitEthernet0/0/0 is administratively down, line protocol is down

GigabitEthernet0/0/1 is up, line protocol is up

  Encapsulation 802.1Q Virtual LAN, Vlan ID  1., loopback not set

GigabitEthernet0/0/1.10 is up, line protocol is up

  Encapsulation 802.1Q Virtual LAN, Vlan ID  100.

GigabitEthernet0/0/1.20 is up, line protocol is up

  Encapsulation 802.1Q Virtual LAN, Vlan ID  20.

GigabitEthernet0/0/1.99 is up, line protocol is up

  Encapsulation 802.1Q Virtual LAN, Vlan ID  99.

R1#
```

The pipe symbol (|) along with some select keywords is a useful method to help filter command output. In this example, the keyword **include** was used to identify that only lines containing the letters "Gig" or "802.1Q" will be displayed. Because of the way the **show interface** output is naturally listed, using these filters produces a condensed list of interfaces and their assigned VLANs.

Notice that the G0/0/1.10 interface has been incorrectly assigned to VLAN 100 instead of VLAN 10. This is confirmed by looking at the configuration of the R1 GigabitEthernet 0/0/1.10 subinterface, as shown.

```
R1# show running-config interface g0/0/1.10

Building configuration...

Current configuration : 146 bytes

!

interface GigabitEthernet0/0/1.10

 description Default Gateway for VLAN 10

 encapsulation dot1Q 100

 ip address 192.168.10.1 255.255.255.0

end

R1#
```

To correct this problem, configure subinterface G0/0/1.10 to be on the correct VLAN using the **encapsulation dot1q 10** subinterface configuration mode command.

```
R1# conf t

Enter configuration commands, one per line.  End with CNTL/Z.

R1(config)# interface gigabitEthernet 0/0/1.10

R1(config-subif)# encapsulation dot1Q 10

R1(config-subif)# end

R1#

R1# show interfaces | include Gig|802.1Q

GigabitEthernet0/0/0 is administratively down, line protocol is down

GigabitEthernet0/0/1 is up, line protocol is up

   Encapsulation 802.1Q Virtual LAN, Vlan ID  1., loopback not set

GigabitEthernet0/0/1.10 is up, line protocol is up

   Encapsulation 802.1Q Virtual LAN, Vlan ID  10.

GigabitEthernet0/0/1.20 is up, line protocol is up

   Encapsulation 802.1Q Virtual LAN, Vlan ID  20.

GigabitEthernet0/0/1.99 is up, line protocol is up

R1#
```

When the subinterface has been assigned to the correct VLAN, it is accessible by devices on that VLAN and the router can perform inter-VLAN routing.

With verification, router configuration problems are quickly addressed, allowing inter-VLAN routing to function properly.

Go to the online course to take the quiz and exam.

Check Your Understanding - Troubleshoot Inter-VLAN Routing - 4.4.7

Refer to **Packet Tracer Activity** for this chapter

Packet Tracer - Troubleshoot Inter-VLAN Routing - 4.4.8

In this Packet Tracer activity, you will complete the following objectives:

- Part 1: Locate Network Problems
- Part 2: Implement the Solution
- Part 3: Verify Network Connectivity

Refer to **Lab Activity** for this chapter

Lab - Troubleshoot Inter-VLAN Routing - 4.4.9

In this lab, you will complete the following objectives:

- Part 1: Build the Network and Load Device Configurations
- Part 2: Troubleshoot the Inter-VLAN Routing Configuration
- Part 3: Verify VLAN Configuration, Port Assignment and Trunking
- Part 4: Test Layer 3 Connectivity

Module Practice and Quiz - 4.5

Refer to **Packet Tracer Activity** for this chapter

Packet Tracer - Inter-VLAN Routing Challenge - 4.5.1

In this activity, you will demonstrate and reinforce your ability to implement inter-VLAN routing, including configuring IP addresses, VLANs, trunking, and subinterfaces.

Refer to **Lab Activity** for this chapter

Lab - Implement Inter-VLAN Routing - 4.5.2

In this lab, you will complete the following objectives:

- Part 1: Build the Network and Configure Basic Device Settings
- Part 2: Create VLANs and Assign Switch Ports
- Part 3: Configure an 802.1Q Trunk between the Switches
- Part 4: Configure Inter-VLAN Routing on the S1 Switch
- Part 5: Verify Inter-VLAN Routing is Working

What did I learn in this module? - 4.5.3

Inter-VLAN Routing Operation

Hosts in one VLAN cannot communicate with hosts in another VLAN unless there is a router or a Layer 3 switch to provide routing services. Inter-VLAN routing is the process of forwarding network traffic from one VLAN to another VLAN. Three options include legacy, router-on-a-stick, and Layer 3 switch using SVIs. Legacy used a router with multiple Ethernet interfaces. Each router interface was connected to a switch port in different VLANs. Requiring one physical router interface per VLAN quickly exhausts the physical interface capacity of a router. The 'router-on-a-stick' inter-VLAN routing method only requires one physical Ethernet interface to route traffic between multiple VLANs on a network. A Cisco IOS router Ethernet interface is configured as an 802.1Q trunk and connected to a trunk port on a Layer 2 switch. The router interface is configured using subinterfaces to identify routable VLANs. The configured subinterfaces are software-based virtual interfaces, associated with a single physical Ethernet interface. The modern method is Inter-VLAN routing on a Layer 3 switch using SVIs. The SVI is created for a VLAN that exists on the switch. The SVI performs the same functions for the VLAN as a router interface. It provides Layer 3 processing for packets being sent to or from all switch ports associated with that VLAN.

Router-on-a-Stick Inter-VLAN Routing

To configure a switch with VLANs and trunking, complete the following steps: create and name the VLANs, create the management interface, configure access ports, and configure trunking ports. The router-on-a-stick method requires a subinterface to be created for each VLAN to be routed. A subinterface is created using the **interface** *interface_id subinterface_id* global configuration mode command. Each router subinterface must be assigned an IP address on a unique subnet for routing to occur. When all subinterfaces have been created, the physical interface must be enabled using the **no shutdown** interface configuration command. From a host, verify connectivity to a host in another VLAN using the **ping** command. Use **ping** to verify connectivity with the host and the switch. To verify and troubleshoot use the **show ip route**, **show ip interface brief**, **show interfaces**, and **show interfaces trunk** commands.

Inter-VLAN Routing using Layer 3 Switches

Enterprise campus LANs use Layer 3 switches to provide inter-VLAN routing. Layer 3 switches use hardware-based switching to achieve higher-packet processing rates than routers. Capabilities of a Layer 3 switch include routing from one VLAN to another using multiple switched virtual interfaces (SVIs) and converting a Layer 2 switchport to a Layer 3 interface (i.e., a routed port). To provide inter-VLAN routing, Layer 3 switches use SVIs. SVIs are configured using the same interface vlan vlan-id command used to create the management SVI on a Layer 2 switch. A Layer 3 SVI must be created for each of the routable VLANs. To configure a switch with VLANS and trunking, complete the following steps: create the VLANS, create the SVI VLAN interfaces, configure access ports, and enable IP routing. From a host, verify connectivity to a host in another VLAN using the **ping** command. Next, verify connectivity with the host using the **ping** Windows host command. VLANs must be advertised using static or dynamic routing. To enable routing on a Layer 3 switch, a routed port must be configured. A routed port is created on a Layer 3 switch by disabling the switchport feature on a Layer 2 port that is connected to another Layer 3 device. The interface can be configured with an IPv4 configuration to connect to a router or another Layer 3 switch. To configure a Layer 3 switch to route with a router, follow these steps: configure the routed port, enable routing, configure routing, verify routing, and verify connectivity.

Troubleshoot Inter-VLAN Routing

There are a number of reasons why an inter-VAN configuration may not work. All are related to connectivity issues such as missing VLANs, switch trunk port issues, switch access port issues, and router configuration issues. A VLAN could be missing if it was not created, it was accidently deleted, or it is not allowed on the trunk link. Another issue for inter-VLAN routing includes misconfigured switch ports. In a legacy inter-VLAN solution, a misconfigured switch port could be caused when the connecting router port is not assigned to the correct VLAN. With a router-on-a-stick solution, the most common cause is a misconfigured trunk port. When a problem is suspected with a switch access port configuration, use **ping** and **show interfaces** *interface-id* **switchport** commands to identify the problem. Router configuration problems with router-on-a-stick configurations are usually related to subinterface misconfigurations. Verify the subinterface status using the **show ip interface brief** command.

Go to the online course to take the quiz and exam.

Chapter Quiz - Inter-VLAN Routing

Your Chapter Notes

CHAPTER 5

STP Concepts

Introduction - 5.0

Why should I take this module? - 5.0.1

Welcome to STP Concepts!

A well-designed Layer 2 network will have redundant switches and paths to ensure that if one switch goes down, another path to a different switch is available to forward data. Users of the network would not experience any disruption of service. Redundancy in a hierarchical network design fixes the problem of a single point of failure, yet it can create a different kind of problem called Layer 2 loops.

What is a loop? Imagine that you are at a concert. The singer's microphone and the amplified loudspeaker can, for a variety of reasons, create a feedback loop. What you hear is an amplified signal from the microphone that comes out of the loudspeaker which is then picked up again by the microphone, amplified further, and passed again through the loudspeaker. The sound quickly becomes very loud, unpleasant, and makes it impossible to hear any actual music. This continues until the connection between the microphone and the loudspeaker is cut.

A Layer 2 loop creates similar chaos in a network. It can happen very quickly and make it impossible to use the network. There are a few common ways that a Layer 2 loop can be created and propagated. Spanning Tree Protocol (STP) is designed specifically to eliminate Layer 2 loops in your network. This module discusses causes of loops and the various types of spanning tree protocols. It includes a video and a Packet Tracer activity to help you understand STP concepts.

What will I learn to do in this module? - 5.0.2

Module Title: STP Concepts

Module Objective: Explain how STP enables redundancy in a Layer 2 network.

Topic Title	Topic Objective
Purpose of STP	Explain common problems in a redundant, L2 switched network.
STP Operations	Explain how STP operates in a simple switched network.
Evolution of STP	Explain how Rapid PVST+ operates.

Purpose of STP - 5.1

Redundancy in Layer 2 Switched Networks - 5.1.1

This topic covers the causes of loops in a Layer 2 network and briefly explains how spanning tree protocol works. Redundancy is an important part of the hierarchical design for eliminating single points of failure and preventing disruption of network services to users. Redundant networks require the addition of physical paths, but logical redundancy must also be part of the design. Having alternate physical paths for data to traverse the network makes it possible for users to access network resources, despite path disruption. However, redundant paths in a switched Ethernet network may cause both physical and logical Layer 2 loops.

Ethernet LANs require a loop-free topology with a single path between any two devices. A loop in an Ethernet LAN can cause continued propagation of Ethernet frames until a link is disrupted and breaks the loop.

Refer to
Interactive Graphic
in online course

Spanning Tree Protocol - 5.1.2

Spanning Tree Protocol (STP) is a loop-prevention network protocol that allows for redundancy while creating a loop-free Layer 2 topology. IEEE 802.1D is the original IEEE MAC Bridging standard for STP.

Click Play in the figure to view an animation of STP in action.

Refer to
Interactive Graphic
in online course

STP Recalculation - 5.1.3

Click Play in the next figure to view an animation of STP recalculation when a failure occurs.

Issues with Redundant Switch Links - 5.1.4

Path redundancy provides multiple network services by eliminating the possibility of a single point of failure. When multiple paths exist between two devices on an Ethernet network, and there is no spanning tree implementation on the switches, a Layer 2 loop occurs. A Layer 2 loop can result in MAC address table instability, link saturation, and high CPU utilization on switches and end-devices, resulting in the network becoming unusable.

Unlike the Layer 3 protocols, IPv4 and IPv6, Layer 2 Ethernet does not include a mechanism to recognize and eliminate endlessly looping frames. Both IPv4 and IPv6 include a mechanism that limits the number of times a Layer 3 networking device can retransmit a packet. A router will decrement the TTL (Time to Live) in every IPv4 packet, and the Hop Limit field in every IPv6 packet. When these fields are decremented to 0, a router will drop the packet. Ethernet and Ethernet switches have no comparable mechanism for limiting the number of times a switch retransmits a Layer 2 frame. STP was developed specifically as a loop prevention mechanism for Layer 2 Ethernet.

Refer to
Interactive Graphic
in online course

Layer 2 Loops - 5.1.5

Without STP enabled, Layer 2 loops can form, causing broadcast, multicast and unknown unicast frames to loop endlessly. This can bring down a network within a very short amount of time, sometimes in just a few seconds. For example, broadcast frames, such as an ARP Request are forwarded out all of the switch ports, except the original ingress port. This ensures that all devices in a broadcast domain are able to receive the frame. If there is more than one path for the frame to be forwarded out of, an endless loop can result. When a loop occurs, the MAC address table on a switch will constantly change with the updates from the broadcast frames, which results in MAC database instability. This can cause high CPU utilization, which makes the switch unable to forward frames.

Broadcast frames are not the only type of frames that are affected by loops. Unknown unicast frames sent onto a looped network can result in duplicate frames arriving at the destination device. An unknown unicast frame is when the switch does not have the destination MAC address in its MAC address table and must forward the frame out all ports, except the ingress port.

Click Play in the figure to view the animation. When the animation pauses, read the text describing the action. The animation will continue after the short pause.

Refer to
Interactive Graphic
in online course

Broadcast Storm - 5.1.6

A broadcast storm is an abnormally high number of broadcasts overwhelming the network during a specific amount of time. Broadcast storms can disable a network within seconds by overwhelming switches and end devices. Broadcast storms can be caused by a hardware problem such as a faulty NIC or from a Layer 2 loop in the network.

Layer 2 broadcasts in a network, such as ARP Requests are very common. A Layer 2 loop is likely to have immediate and disabling consequences on the network. Layer 2 multicasts are typically forwarded the same way as a broadcast by the switch. So, although IPv6 packets are never forwarded as a Layer 2 broadcast, ICMPv6 Neighbor Discovery uses Layer 2 multicasts.

Click Play in the figure to view an animation that shows the increasingly adverse effects of a loop as the broadcast and unknown unicast frames continue to propagate indefinitely in a broadcast storm.

A host caught in a Layer 2 loop is not accessible to other hosts on the network. Additionally, due to the constant changes in its MAC address table, the switch does not know out of which port to forward unicast frames. In the previous animation, the switches will have the incorrect ports listed for PC1. Any unknown unicast frame destined for PC1 loops around the network, just as the broadcast frames do. More and more frames looping around the network eventually creates a broadcast storm.

To prevent these issues from occurring in a redundant network, some type of spanning tree must be enabled on the switches. Spanning tree is enabled, by default, on Cisco switches to prevent Layer 2 loops from occurring.

Refer to
Interactive Graphic
in online course

Refer to
Online Course
for Illustration

The Spanning Tree Algorithm - 5.1.7

STP is based on an algorithm invented by Radia Perlman while working for Digital Equipment Corporation, and published in the 1985 paper "An Algorithm for Distributed Computation of a Spanning Tree in an Extended LAN." Her spanning tree algorithm (STA) creates a loop-free topology by selecting a single root bridge where all other switches determine a single least-cost path.

Without the loop prevention protocol, loops would occur rendering a redundant switch network inoperable.

Click each button for an explanation of how STA creates a loop-free topology.

STA Scenario Topology

This STA scenario uses an Ethernet LAN with redundant connections between multiple switches.

Select the Root Bridge

The spanning tree algorithm begins by selecting a single root bridge. The figure shows that switch S1 has been selected as the root bridge. In this topology, all links are equal cost (same bandwidth). Each switch will determine a single, least cost path from itself to the root bridge.

Note: The STA and STP refers to switches as bridges. This is because in the early days of Ethernet, switches were referred to as bridges.

Block Redundant Paths

STP ensures that there is only one logical path between all destinations on the network by intentionally blocking redundant paths that could cause a loop, as shown in the figure. When a port is blocked, user data is prevented from entering or leaving that port. Blocking the redundant paths is critical to preventing loops on the network.

Loop-Free Topology

A blocked port has the effect of making that link a non-forwarding link between the two switches, as shown in the figure. Notice that this creates a topology where each switch has only a single path to the root bridge, similar to branches on a tree that connect to the root of the tree.

Link Failure Causes Recalculation

The physical paths still exist to provide redundancy, but these paths are disabled to prevent the loops from occurring. If the path is ever needed to compensate for a network cable or switch failure, STP recalculates the paths and unblocks the necessary ports to allow the redundant path to become active. STP recalculations can also occur any time a new switch or new inter-switch link is added to the network.

The figure shows a link failure between switches S2 and S4 causing STP to recalculate. Notice that the previously redundant link between S4 and S5 is now forwarding to compensate for this failure. There is still only one path between every switch and the root bridge.

STP prevents loops from occurring by configuring a loop-free path through the network using strategically placed "blocking-state" ports. The switches running STP are able to compensate for failures by dynamically unblocking the previously blocked ports and permitting traffic to traverse the alternate paths.

Refer to **Video** in online course

Video - Observe STP Operation - 5.1.8

Click Play for a demonstration of Spanning Tree Protocol.

Refer to **Packet Tracer Activity** for this chapter

Packet Tracer - Investigate STP Loop Prevention - 5.1.9

In this Packet Tracer activity, you will complete the following objectives:

- Create and configure a simple three switch network with STP.
- View STP operation
- Disable STP and view operation again.

Go to the online course to take the quiz and exam.

Check Your Understanding - Purpose of STP - 5.1.10

STP Operations - 5.2

Refer to **Online Course** for Illustration

Steps to a Loop-Free Topology - 5.2.1

Now you know how loops are created and the basics of using spanning tree protocol to prevent them. This topic will take you, step by step, through the operation of STP. Using the STA, STP builds a loop-free topology in a four-step process:

1. Elect the root bridge.
2. Elect the root ports.
3. Elect designated ports.
4. Elect alternate (blocked) ports.

During STA and STP functions, switches use Bridge Protocol Data Units (BPDUs) to share information about themselves and their connections. BPDUs are used to elect the root bridge, root ports, designated ports, and alternate ports. Each BPDU contains a bridge ID (BID) that identifies which switch sent the BPDU. The BID is involved in making many of the STA decisions including root bridge and port roles. As shown in the figure, the BID contains a priority value, the MAC address of the switch, and an extended system ID. The lowest BID value is determined by the combination of these three fields.

Bridge Priority

The default priority value for all Cisco switches is- the decimal value 32768. The range is 0 to 61440 in increments of 4096. A lower bridge priority is preferable. A bridge priority of 0 takes precedence over all other bridge priorities.

Extended System ID

The extended system ID value is a decimal value added to the bridge priority value in the BID to identify the VLAN for this BPDU.

Early implementations of IEEE 802.1D were designed for networks that did not use VLANs. There was a single common spanning tree across all switches. For this reason, in older switches, the extended system ID was not included in the BPDUs. As VLANs became common for network infrastructure segmentation, 802.1D was enhanced to include support for VLANs, which required that the 12-bit VLAN ID be included in the BPDU frame. VLAN information is included in the BPDU frame through the use of the extended system ID.

The extended system ID allows later implementations of STP, such as Rapid STP (RSTP) to have different root bridges for different sets of VLANs. This can allow for redundant, non-forwarding links in a STP topology for one set of VLANs to be used by a different set of VLANs using a different root bridge.

MAC address

When two switches are configured with the same priority and have the same extended system ID, the switch having the MAC address with the lowest value, expressed in hexadecimal, will have the lower BID.

Refer to
Online Course
for Illustration

1. Elect the Root Bridge - 5.2.2

The STA designates a single switch as the root bridge and uses it as the reference point for all path calculations. Switches exchange BPDUs to build the loop-free topology beginning with selecting the root bridge.

An election process determines which switch becomes the root bridge. All switches in the broadcast domain participate in the election process. After a switch boots, it begins to send out BPDU frames every two seconds. These BPDU frames contain the BID of the sending switch and the BID of the root bridge, known as the Root ID.

The switch with the lowest BID will become the root bridge. At first, all switches declare themselves as the root bridge with their own BID set as the Root ID. Eventually, the switches learn through the exchange of BPDUs which switch has the lowest BID and will agree on one root bridge.

In the figure, S1 is elected the root bridge because it has the lowest BID.

Refer to
Online Course
for Illustration

Impact of Default BIDs - 5.2.3

Because the default BID is 32768, it is possible for two or more switches to have the same priority. In this scenario, where the priorities are the same, the switch with the lowest MAC address will become the root bridge. To ensure that the root bridge decision best meets network requirements, it is recommended that the administrator configure the desired root bridge switch with a lower priority.

In the figure, all switches are configured with the same priority of 32769. Here the MAC address becomes the deciding factor as to which switch becomes the root bridge. The switch with the lowest hexadecimal MAC address value is the preferred root bridge. In this example, S2 has the lowest value for its MAC address and is elected as the root bridge for that spanning tree instance.

Note: In the example, the priority of all the switches is 32769. The value is based on the 32768 default bridge priority and the extended system ID (VLAN 1 assignment) associated with each switch (32768+1).

Determine the Root Path Cost - 5.2.4

When the root bridge has been elected for a given spanning tree instance, the STA starts the process of determining the best paths to the root bridge from all destinations in the broadcast domain. The path information, known as the internal root path cost, is determined by the sum of all the individual port costs along the path from the switch to the root bridge.

Note: The BPDU includes the root path cost. This is the cost of the path from the sending switch to the root bridge.

When a switch receives the BPDU, it adds the ingress port cost of the segment to determine its internal root path cost.

The default port costs are defined by the speed at which the port operates. The table shows the default port costs suggested by IEEE. Cisco switches by default use the values as defined by the IEEE 802.1D standard, also known as the short path cost, for both STP and RSTP. However, the IEEE standard suggests using the values defined in the IEEE-802.1w, also known as long path cost, when using 10 Gbps links and faster.

Note: RSTP is discussed in more detail later in this module.

Link Speed	STP Cost: IEEE 802.1D-1998	RSTP Cost: IEEE 802.1w-2004
10 Gbps	2	2,000
1 Gbps	4	20,000
100 Mbps	19	200,000
10 Mbps	100	2,000,000

Although switch ports have a default port cost associated with them, the port cost is configurable. The ability to configure individual port costs gives the administrator the flexibility to manually control the spanning tree paths to the root bridge.

Refer to
Online Course
for Illustration

2. Elect the Root Ports - 5.2.5

After the root bridge has been determined, the STA algorithm is used to select the root port. Every non-root switch will select one root port. The root port is the port closest to the root bridge in terms of overall cost (best path) to the root bridge. This overall cost is known as the internal root path cost.

The internal root path cost is equal to the sum of all the port costs along the path to the root bridge, as shown in the figure. Paths with the lowest cost become preferred, and all other redundant paths are blocked. In the example, the internal root path cost from S2 to the root bridge S1 over path 1 is 19 (based on the IEEE-specified individual port cost) while the internal root path cost over path 2 is 38. Because path 1 has a lower overall path cost to the root bridge, it is the preferred path and F0/1 becomes the root port on S2.

Refer to
Interactive Graphic
in online course

Refer to
Online Course
for Illustration

3. Elect Designated Ports - 5.2.6

The loop prevention part of spanning tree becomes evident during these next two steps. After each switch selects a root port, the switches will then select designated ports.

Every segment between two switches will have one designated port. The designated port is a port on the segment (with two switches) that has the internal root path cost to the root bridge. In other words, the designated port has the best path to receive traffic leading to the root bridge.

What is not a root port or a designated port becomes an alternate or blocked port. The end result is a single path from every switch to the root bridge.

Click each button for an explanation of how STA elects the designated ports.

Designated Ports on Root Bridge

All ports on the root bridge are designated ports, as shown in the figure. This is because the root bridge has the lowest cost to itself.

Designated Port When There is a Root Port

If one end of a segment is a root port, then the other end is a designated port. To demonstrate this, the figure shows that switch S4 is connected to S3. The Fa0/1 interface on S4 is its root port because it has the best and only path to the root bridge. The Fa0/3 interface on S3 at the other end of the segment would therefore, be the designated port.

Note: All switch ports with end devices (hosts) attached are designated ports.

Designated Port When There is No Root Port

This leaves only segments between two switches where neither of the switches is the root bridge. In this case, the port on the switch with the least-cost path to the root bridge is the designated port for the segment. For example, in the figure, the last segment is the one between S2 and S3. Both S2 and S3 have the same path cost to the root bridge. The spanning tree algorithm will use the bridge ID as a tie breaker. Although not shown in the figure, S2 has a lower BID. Therefore, the F0/2 port of S2 will be chosen as the designated port. Designated ports are in forwarding state.

Refer to
Online Course
for Illustration

4. Elect Alternate (Blocked) Ports - 5.2.7

If a port is not a root port or a designated port, then it becomes an alternate (or backup) port. Alternate ports and backup ports are in discarding or blocking state to prevent loops. In the figure, the STA has configured port F0/2 on S3 in the alternate role. Port F0/2 on S3 is in the blocking state and will not forward Ethernet frames. All other inter-switch ports are in forwarding state. This is the loop-prevention part of STP.

Refer to
Interactive Graphic
in online course

Refer to
Online Course
for Illustration

Elect a Root Port from Multiple Equal-Cost Paths - 5.2.8

Root port and designated ports are based on the lowest path cost to the root bridge. But what happens if the switch has multiple equal-cost paths to the root bridge? How does a switch designate a root port?

When a switch has multiple equal-cost paths to the root bridge, the switch will determine a port using the following criteria:

1. Lowest sender BID

2. Lowest sender port priority

3. Lowest sender port ID

Click each criteria for an example and explanation.

1. Lowest Sender BID

The figure shows a topology with four switches, including switch S1 as the root bridge. Examining the port roles, port F0/1 on switch S3 and port F0/3 on switch S4 have been selected as root ports because they have the lowest cost path (root path cost) to the root bridge for their respective switches. S2 has two ports, F0/1 and F0/2 with equal cost paths to the root bridge. In this case the bridge IDs of the neighboring switches, S3 and S4, will be used to break the tie. This is known as the sender's BID. S3 has a BID of 32769.5555.5555.5555 and S4 has a BID of 32769.1111.1111.1111. Because S4 has a lower BID, the F0/1 port of S2, which is the port connected to S4, will be the root port.

2. Lowest Sender Port Priority

To demonstrate these next two criteria, the topology is changed to one where two switches are connected with two equal-cost paths between them. S1 is the root bridge, so both of its ports are designated ports.

S4 has two ports with equal-cost paths to the root bridge. Because both ports are connected to the same switch, the sender's BID (S1) is equal. So the first step is a tie.

Next on the list is the sender's (S1) port priority. The default port priority is 128, so both ports on S1 have the same port priority. This is also a tie. However, if either port on S1 was configured with a lower port priority, S4 would put its adjacent port in forwarding state. The other port on S4 would be a blocking state.

3. Lowest Sender Port ID

The last tie-breaker is the lowest sender's port ID. Switch S4 has received BPDUs from port F0/1 and port F0/2 on S1. Remember the decision is based on the sender's port ID, not the receiver's port ID. Because the port ID of F0/1 on S1 is lower than port F0/2, the port F0/6 on switch S4 will be the root port. This is the port on S4 that is connected to the F0/1 port on S1.

Port F0/5 on S4 will become an alternate port and placed in the blocking state, which is the loop-prevention part of STP.

Refer to
Online Course
for Illustration

STP Timers and Port States - 5.2.9

STP convergence requires three timers, as follows:

- **Hello Timer** - The hello time is the interval between BPDUs. The default is 2 seconds but can be modified to between 1 and 10 seconds.

- **Forward Delay Timer** - The forward delay is the time that is spent in the listening and learning state. The default is 15 seconds but can be modified to between 4 and 30 seconds.

■ **Max Age Timer** - The max age is the maximum length of time that a switch waits before attempting to change the STP topology. The default is 20 seconds but be modified to between 6 and 40 seconds.

Note: The default times can be changed on the root bridge, which dictates the value of these timers for the STP domain.

STP facilitates the logical loop-free path throughout the broadcast domain. The spanning tree is determined through the information learned by the exchange of the BPDU frames between the interconnected switches. If a switch port transitions directly from the blocking state to the forwarding state without information about the full topology during the transition, the port can temporarily create a data loop. For this reason, STP has five ports states, four of which are operational port states as shown in the figure. The disabled state is considered non-operational.

The details of each port state are shown in the table.

Port State	Description
Blocking	The port is an alternate port and does not participate in frame forwarding. The port receives BPDU frames to determine the location and root ID of the root bridge. BPDU frames also determine which port roles each switch port should assume in the final active STP topology. With a Max Age timer of 20 seconds, a switch port that has not received an expected BPDU from a neighbor switch will go into the blocking state.
Listening	After the blocking state, a port will move to the listening state. The port receives BPDUs to determine the path to the root. The switch port also transmits its own BPDU frames and informs adjacent switches that the switch port is preparing to participate in the active topology.
Learning	A switch port transitions to the learning state after the listening state. During the learning state, the switch port receives and processes BPDUs and prepares to participate in frame forwarding. It also begins to populate the MAC address table. However, in the learning state, user frames are not forwarded to the destination.
Forwarding	In the forwarding state, a switch port is considered part of the active topology. The switch port forwards user traffic and sends and receives BPDU frames.
Disabled	A switch port in the disabled state does not participate in spanning tree and does not forward frames. The disabled state is set when the switch port is administratively disabled.

Operational Details of Each Port State - 5.2.10

The table summarizes the operational details of each port state.

Port State	BPDU	MAC Address Table	Forwarding Data Frames
Blocking	Receive only	No update	No
Listening	Receive and send	No update	No
Learning	Receive and send	Updating table	No
Forwarding	Receive and send	Updating table	Yes
Disabled	None sent or received	No update	No

Per-VLAN Spanning Tree - 5.2.11

Up until now, we have discussed STP in an environment where there is only one VLAN. However, STP can be configured to operate in an environment with multiple VLANs.

In Per-VLAN Spanning Tree (PVST) versions of STP, there is a root bridge elected for each spanning tree instance. This makes it possible to have different root bridges for different sets of VLANs. STP operates a separate instance of STP for each individual VLAN. If all ports on all switches are members of VLAN 1, then there is only one spanning tree instance.

Check Your Understanding - STP Operations - 5.2.12

Go to the online course to take the quiz and exam.

Evolution of STP - 5.3

Different Versions of STP - 5.3.1

This topic details the many different versions of STP and other options for preventing loops in your network.

Up to now, we have used the term Spanning Tree Protocol and the acronym STP, which can be misleading. Many professionals generically use these to refer to the various implementations of spanning tree, such as Rapid Spanning Tree Protocol (RSTP) and Multiple Spanning Tree Protocol (MSTP). In order to communicate spanning tree concepts correctly, it is important to refer to the implementation or standard of spanning tree in context.

The latest standard for spanning tree is contained in IEEE-802-1D-2004, the IEEE standard for Local and metropolitan area networks: Media Access Control (MAC) Bridges. This version of the standard states that switches and bridges that comply with the standard will use Rapid Spanning Tree Protocol (RSTP) instead of the older STP protocol specified in the original 802.1d standard. In this curriculum, when the original Spanning Tree Protocol is the context of a discussion, the phrase "original 802.1D spanning tree" is used to avoid confusion. Because the two protocols share much of the same terminology and methods for the loop-free path, the primary focus will be on the current standard and the Cisco proprietary implementations of STP and RSTP.

Several varieties of spanning tree protocols have emerged since the original IEEE 802.1D specification, as shown in the table.

STP Variety	Description
STP	This is the original IEEE 802.1D version (802.1D-1998 and earlier) that provides a loop-free topology in a network with redundant links. Also called Common Spanning Tree (CST), it assumes one spanning tree instance for the entire bridged network, regardless of the number of VLANs.
PVST+	Per-VLAN Spanning Tree (PVST+) is a Cisco enhancement of STP that provides a separate 802.1D spanning tree instance for each VLAN configured in the network. PVST+ supports PortFast, UplinkFast, BackboneFast, BPDU guard, BPDU filter, root guard, and loop guard.
802.1D-2004	This is an updated version of the STP standard, incorporating IEEE 802.1w.

STP Variety	Description
RSTP	Rapid Spanning Tree Protocol (RSTP) or IEEE 802.1w is an evolution of STP that provides faster convergence than STP.
Rapid PVST+	This is a Cisco enhancement of RSTP that uses PVST+ and provides a separate instance of 802.1w per VLAN. Each separate instance supports PortFast, BPDU guard, BPDU filter, root guard, and loop guard.
MSTP	Multiple Spanning Tree Protocol (MSTP) is an IEEE standard inspired by the earlier Cisco proprietary Multiple Instance STP (MISTP) implementation. MSTP maps multiple VLANs into the same spanning tree instance.
MST	Multiple Spanning Tree (MST) is the Cisco implementation of MSTP, which provides up to 16 instances of RSTP and combines many VLANs with the same physical and logical topology into a common RSTP instance. Each instance supports PortFast, BPDU guard, BPDU filter, root guard, and loop guard.

A network professional, whose duties include switch administration, may be required to decide which type of spanning tree protocol to implement.

Cisco switches running IOS 15.0 or later, run PVST+ by default. This version incorporates many of the specifications of IEEE 802.1D-2004, such as alternate ports in place of the former non-designated ports. Switches must be explicitly configured for rapid spanning tree mode in order to run the rapid spanning tree protocol.

RSTP Concepts - 5.3.2

RSTP (IEEE 802.1w) supersedes the original 802.1D while retaining backward compatibility. The 802.1w STP terminology remains primarily the same as the original IEEE 802.1D STP terminology. Most parameters have been left unchanged. Users that are familiar with the original STP standard can easily configure RSTP. The same spanning tree algorithm is used for both STP and RSTP to determine port roles and topology.

RSTP increases the speed of the recalculation of the spanning tree when the Layer 2 network topology changes. RSTP can achieve much faster convergence in a properly configured network, sometimes in as little as a few hundred milliseconds. If a port is configured to be an alternate port it can immediately change to a forwarding state without waiting for the network to converge.

Note: Rapid PVST+ is the Cisco implementation of RSTP on a per-VLAN basis. With Rapid PVST+ an independent instance of RSTP runs for each VLAN.

Refer to
Interactive Graphic
in online course

Refer to
Online Course
for Illustration

RSTP Port States and Port Roles - 5.3.3

The port states and port roles between STP and RSTP are similar.

Click each button for a comparison between STP and RSTP port states and port roles.

STP and RSTP Port States

As shown in the figure, there are only three port states in RSTP that correspond to the three possible operational states in STP. The 802.1D disabled, blocking, and listening states are merged into a unique 802.1w discarding state.

STP and RSTP Port Roles

As shown in the figure, root ports and designated ports are the same for both STP and RSTP. However, there are two RSTP port roles that correspond to the blocking state of STP. In STP, a blocked port is defined as not being the designated or root port. RSTP has two port roles for this purpose.

RSTP Alternate and Backup Ports

As shown in the figure, the alternate port has an alternate path to the root bridge. The backup port is a backup to a shared medium, such as a hub. A backup port is less common because hubs are now considered legacy devices.

Refer to
Online Course
for Illustration

PortFast and BPDU Guard - 5.3.4

When a device is connected to a switch port or when a switch powers up, the switch port goes through both the listening and learning states, each time waiting for the Forward Delay timer to expire. This delay is 15 seconds for each state, listening and learning, for a total of 30 seconds. This delay can present a problem for DHCP clients trying to discover a DHCP server. DHCP messages from the connected host will not be forwarded for the 30 seconds of Forward Delay timers and the DHCP process may timeout. The result is that an IPv4 client will not receive a valid IPv4 address.

Note: Although this may occur with clients sending ICMPv6 Router Solicitation messages, the router will continue to send ICMPv6 Router Advertisement messages so the device will know how to obtain its address information.

When a switch port is configured with PortFast, that port transitions from blocking to forwarding state immediately, bypassing the usual 802.1D STP transition states (the listening and learning states) and avoiding a 30 second delay. You can use PortFast on access ports to allow devices connected to these ports, such as DHCP clients, to access the network immediately, rather than waiting for IEEE 802.1D STP to converge on each VLAN. Because the purpose of PortFast is to minimize the time that access ports must wait for spanning tree to converge, it should only be used on access ports. If you enable PortFast on a port connecting to another switch, you risk creating a spanning tree loop. PortFast is only for use on switch ports that connect to end devices.

In a valid PortFast configuration, BPDUs should never be received on PortFast-enabled switch ports because that would indicate that another bridge or switch is connected to the port. This potentially causes a spanning tree loop. To prevent this type of scenario from occurring, Cisco switches support a feature called BPDU guard. When enabled, BPDU guard immediately puts the switch port in an errdisabled (error-disabled) state on receipt of any BPDU. This protects against potential loops by effectively shutting down the port. The BPDU guard feature provides a secure response to invalid configurations because an administrator must manually put the interface back into service.

Refer to
Online Course
for Illustration

Alternatives to STP - 5.3.5

STP was and still is an Ethernet loop-prevention protocol. Over the years, organizations required greater resiliency and availability in the LAN. Ethernet LANs went from a few interconnected switches connected to a single router, to a sophisticated hierarchical network design including access, distribution and core layer switches, as shown in the figure.

Depending on the implementation, Layer 2 may include not only the access layer, but also the distribution or even the core layers. These designs may include hundreds of switches, with hundreds or even thousands of VLANs. STP has adapted to the added redundancy and complexity with enhancements, as part of RSTP and MSTP.

An important aspect to network design is fast and predictable convergence when there is a failure or change in the topology. Spanning tree does not offer the same efficiencies and predictabilities provided by routing protocols at Layer 3. The figure shows a traditional hierarchical network design with the distribution and core multilayer switches performing routing.

Layer 3 routing allows for redundant paths and loops in the topology, without blocking ports. For this reason, some environments are transitioning to Layer 3 everywhere except where devices connect to the access layer switch. In other words, the connections between access layer switches and distribution switches would be Layer 3 instead of Layer 2, as shown in the next figure.

Although STP will most likely continue to be used as a loop prevention mechanism in the enterprise, on access layer switches, other technologies are also being used, including the following:

- Multi System Link Aggregation (MLAG)
- Shortest Path Bridging (SPB)
- Transparent Interconnect of Lots of Links (TRILL)

Note: These technologies are beyond the scope of this course.

Go to the online course to take the quiz and exam.

Check Your Understanding - Evolution of STP - 5.3.6

Module Practice and Quiz - 5.4

What did I learn in this module? - 5.4.1

Purpose of STP

Redundant paths in a switched Ethernet network may cause both physical and logical Layer 2 loops. A Layer 2 loop can result in MAC address table instability, link saturation, and high CPU utilization on switches and end-devices. This results in the network becoming unusable. Unlike the Layer 3 protocols, IPv4 and IPv6, Layer 2 Ethernet does not include a mechanism to recognize and eliminate endlessly looping frames. Ethernet LANs require a loop-free topology with a single path between any two devices. STP is a loop-prevention network protocol that allows for redundancy while creating a loop-free Layer 2 topology. Without STP, Layer 2 loops can form, causing broadcast, multicast and unknown unicast frames to loop endlessly, bringing down a network. A broadcast storm is an abnormally high number of broadcasts overwhelming the network during a specific amount of time. Broadcast storms can disable a network within seconds by overwhelming switches and end devices. STP is based on an algorithm invented by Radia Perlman. Her spanning tree algorithm (STA) creates a loop-free topology by selecting a single root bridge where all other switches determine a single least-cost path.

STP Operations

Using the STA, STP builds a loop-free topology in a four-step process: elect the root bridge, elect the root ports, elect designated ports, and elect alternate (blocked) ports. During STA and STP functions, switches use BPDUs to share information about themselves and their connections. BPDUs are used to elect the root bridge, root ports, designated ports, and alternate ports. Each BPDU contains a BID that identifies the switch that sent the BPDU. The BID is involved in making many of the STA decisions including root bridge and port roles. The BID contains a priority value, the MAC address of the switch, and an extended system ID. The lowest BID value is determined by the combination of these three fields. The switch with the lowest BID will become the root bridge. Because the default BID is 32,768 it is possible for two or more switches to have the same priority. In this scenario, where the priorities are the same, the switch with the lowest MAC address will become the root bridge. When the root bridge has been elected for a given spanning tree instance, the STA determines the best paths to the root bridge from all destinations in the broadcast domain. The path information, known as the internal root path cost, is determined by the sum of all the individual port costs along the path from the switch to the root bridge. After the root bridge has been determined the STA algorithm selects the root port. The root port is the port closest to the root bridge in terms of overall cost, which is called the internal root path cost. After each switch selects a root port, switches will select designated ports. The designated port is a port on the segment (with two switches) that has the internal root path cost to the root bridge. If a port is not a root port or a designated port, then it becomes an alternate (or backup) port. Alternate ports and backup ports are in discarding or blocking state to prevent loops. When a switch has multiple equal-cost paths to the root bridge, the switch will determine a port using the following criteria: lowest sender BID, then the lowest sender port priority, and finally the lowest sender port ID. STP convergence requires three timers: the hello timer, the forward delay timer, and the max age timer. Port states are blocking, listening, learning, forwarding, and disabled. In PVST versions of STP, there is a root bridge elected for each spanning tree instance. This makes it possible to have different root bridges for different sets of VLANs.

Evolution of STP.

The term Spanning Tree Protocol and the acronym STP can be misleading. STP is often used to refer to the various implementations of spanning tree, such as RSTP and MSTP. RSTP is an evolution of STP that provides faster convergence than STP. RSTP port states are learning, forwarding and discarding. PVST+ is a Cisco enhancement of STP that provides a separate spanning tree instance for each VLAN configured in the network. PVST+ supports PortFast, UplinkFast, BackboneFast, BPDU guard, BPDU filter, root guard, and loop guard. Cisco switches running IOS 15.0 or later, run PVST+ by default. Rapid PVST+ is a Cisco enhancement of RSTP that uses PVST+ and provides a separate instance of 802.1w per VLAN. When a switch port is configured with PortFast, that port transitions from blocking to forwarding state immediately, bypassing the STP listening and learning states and avoiding a 30 second delay. Use PortFast on access ports to allow devices connected to these ports, such as DHCP clients, to access the network immediately, rather than waiting for STP to converge on each VLAN. Cisco switches support a feature called BPDU guard which immediately puts the switch port in an error-disabled state upon receipt of any BPDU to protect against potential loops. Over the years, Ethernet LANs went from a few interconnected switches that were connected to a single router, to a sophisticated hierarchical network design. Depending on the implementation, Layer 2 may include not only the access layer, but also the distribution or even the core layers. These designs may include hundreds of switches, with hundreds or even thousands of VLANs. STP has adapted to the added redundancy and complexity with enhancements as part of RSTP and MSTP. Layer 3 routing allows for redundant paths and loops in the topology, without blocking ports. For this reason, some environments are transitioning to Layer 3 everywhere except where devices connect to the access layer switch.

Go to the online course to take the quiz and exam.

Chapter Quiz - STP Concepts

Your Chapter Notes

CHAPTER 6

EtherChannel

Introduction - 6.0

Why should I take this module? - 6.0.1

Welcome to EtherChannel!

Your network design includes redundant switches and links. You have some version of STP configured to prevent Layer 2 loops. But now, like most network administrators, you realize that you could use more bandwidth and redundancy in your network. Not to worry, Ether-Channel is here to help! EtherChannel aggregates links between devices into bundles. These bundles include redundant links. STP may block one of those links, but it will not block all of them. With EtherChannel your network can have redundancy, loop prevention, and increased bandwidth!

There are two protocols, PAgP and LACP. This module explains them both and also shows you how to configure, verify and troubleshoot them! A Syntax Checker and two Packet Tracer activities help you to better understand these protocols. What are you waiting for?

What will I learn to do in this module? - 6.0.2

Module Title: EtherChannel

Module Objective: Troubleshoot EtherChannel on switched links.

Topic Title	Topic Objective
EtherChannel Operation	Describe EtherChannel technology.
Configure EtherChannel	Configure EtherChannel.
Verify and Troubleshoot EtherChannel	Troubleshoot EtherChannel.

EtherChannel Operation - 6.1

Link Aggregation - 6.1.1

Refer to
Online Course
for Illustration

There are scenarios in which more bandwidth or redundancy between devices is needed than what can be provided by a single link. Multiple links could be connected between devices to increase bandwidth. However, Spanning Tree Protocol (STP), which is enabled on Layer 2 devices like Cisco switches by default, will block redundant links to prevent switching loops, as shown in the figure.

A link aggregation technology is needed that allows redundant links between devices that will not be blocked by STP. That technology is known as EtherChannel.

EtherChannel is a link aggregation technology that groups multiple physical Ethernet links together into one single logical link. It is used to provide fault-tolerance, load sharing, increased bandwidth, and redundancy between switches, routers, and servers.

EtherChannel technology makes it possible to combine the number of physical links between the switches to increase the overall speed of switch-to-switch communication.

Refer to
Online Course
for Illustration

EtherChannel - 6.1.2

EtherChannel technology was originally developed by Cisco as a LAN switch-to-switch technique of grouping several Fast Ethernet or Gigabit Ethernet ports into one logical channel. When an EtherChannel is configured, the resulting virtual interface is called a port channel. The physical interfaces are bundled together into a port channel interface, as shown in the figure.

Advantages of EtherChannel - 6.1.3

EtherChannel technology has many advantages, including the following:

- Most configuration tasks can be done on the EtherChannel interface instead of on each individual port, ensuring configuration consistency throughout the links.

- EtherChannel relies on existing switch ports. There is no need to upgrade the link to a faster and more expensive connection to have more bandwidth.

- Load balancing takes place between links that are part of the same EtherChannel. Depending on the hardware platform, one or more load-balancing methods can be implemented. These methods include source MAC to destination MAC load balancing, or source IP to destination IP load balancing, across the physical links.

- EtherChannel creates an aggregation that is seen as one logical link. When several EtherChannel bundles exist between two switches, STP may block one of the bundles to prevent switching loops. When STP blocks one of the redundant links, it blocks the entire EtherChannel. This blocks all the ports belonging to that EtherChannel link. Where there is only one EtherChannel link, all physical links in the EtherChannel are active because STP sees only one (logical) link.

- EtherChannel provides redundancy because the overall link is seen as one logical connection. Additionally, the loss of one physical link within the channel does not create a change in the topology. Therefore, a spanning tree recalculation is not required. Assuming at least one physical link is present; the EtherChannel remains functional, even if its overall throughput decreases because of a lost link within the EtherChannel.

Refer to
Online Course
for Illustration

Implementation Restrictions - 6.1.4

EtherChannel has certain implementation restrictions, including the following:

- Interface types cannot be mixed. For example, Fast Ethernet and Gigabit Ethernet cannot be mixed within a single EtherChannel.

- Currently each EtherChannel can consist of up to eight compatibly-configured Ethernet ports. EtherChannel provides full-duplex bandwidth up to 800 Mbps (Fast EtherChannel) or 8 Gbps (Gigabit EtherChannel) between one switch and another switch or host.

- The Cisco Catalyst 2960 Layer 2 switch currently supports up to six EtherChannels. However, as new IOSs are developed and platforms change, some cards and platforms may support increased numbers of ports within an EtherChannel link, as well as support an increased number of Gigabit EtherChannels.

- The individual EtherChannel group member port configuration must be consistent on both devices. If the physical ports of one side are configured as trunks, the physical ports of the other side must also be configured as trunks within the same native VLAN. Additionally, all ports in each EtherChannel link must be configured as Layer 2 ports.

- Each EtherChannel has a logical port channel interface, as shown in the figure. A configuration applied to the port channel interface affects all physical interfaces that are assigned to that interface.

AutoNegotiation Protocols - 6.1.5

EtherChannels can be formed through negotiation using one of two protocols, Port Aggregation Protocol (PAgP) or Link Aggregation Control Protocol (LACP). These protocols allow ports with similar characteristics to form a channel through dynamic negotiation with adjoining switches.

Note: It is also possible to configure a static or unconditional EtherChannel without PAgP or LACP.

PAgP Operation - 6.1.6

PAgP (pronounced "Pag - P") is a Cisco-proprietary protocol that aids in the automatic creation of EtherChannel links. When an EtherChannel link is configured using PAgP, PAgP packets are sent between EtherChannel-capable ports to negotiate the forming of a channel. When PAgP identifies matched Ethernet links, it groups the links into an EtherChannel. The EtherChannel is then added to the spanning tree as a single port.

When enabled, PAgP also manages the EtherChannel. PAgP packets are sent every 30 seconds. PAgP checks for configuration consistency and manages link additions and failures between two switches. It ensures that when an EtherChannel is created, all ports have the same type of configuration.

Note: In EtherChannel, it is mandatory that all ports have the same speed, duplex setting, and VLAN information. Any port modification after the creation of the channel also changes all other channel ports.

PAgP helps create the EtherChannel link by detecting the configuration of each side and ensuring that links are compatible so that the EtherChannel link can be enabled when needed. The modes for PAgP as follows:

- **On** - This mode forces the interface to channel without PAgP. Interfaces configured in the on mode do not exchange PAgP packets.

- **PAgP desirable** - This PAgP mode places an interface in an active negotiating state in which the interface initiates negotiations with other interfaces by sending PAgP packets.

- **PAgP auto** - This PAgP mode places an interface in a passive negotiating state in which the interface responds to the PAgP packets that it receives but does not initiate PAgP negotiation.

The modes must be compatible on each side. If one side is configured to be in auto mode, it is placed in a passive state, waiting for the other side to initiate the EtherChannel negotiation. If the other side is also set to auto, the negotiation never starts and the EtherChannel does not form. If all modes are disabled by using the **no** command, or if no mode is configured, then the EtherChannel is disabled.

The on mode manually places the interface in an EtherChannel, without any negotiation. It works only if the other side is also set to on. If the other side is set to negotiate parameters through PAgP, no EtherChannel forms, because the side that is set to on mode does not negotiate.

No negotiation between the two switches means there is no checking to make sure that all the links in the EtherChannel are terminating on the other side, or that there is PAgP compatibility on the other switch.

Refer to **Online Course** for Illustration

PAgP Mode Settings Example - 6.1.7

Consider the two switches in the figure. Whether S1 and S2 establish an EtherChannel using PAgP depends on the mode settings on each side of the channel.

The table shows the various combination of PAgP modes on S1 and S2 and the resulting channel establishment outcome.

PAgP Modes

S1	S2	Channel Establishment
On	On	Yes
On	Desirable/Auto	No
Desirable	Desirable	Yes
Desirable	Auto	Yes
Auto	Desirable	Yes
Auto	Auto	No

LACP Operation - 6.1.8

LACP is part of an IEEE specification (802.3ad) that allows several physical ports to be bundled to form a single logical channel. LACP allows a switch to negotiate an automatic bundle by sending LACP packets to the other switch. It performs a function similar to

PAgP with Cisco EtherChannel. Because LACP is an IEEE standard, it can be used to facilitate EtherChannels in multivendor environments. On Cisco devices, both protocols are supported.

Note: LACP was originally defined as IEEE 802.3ad. However, LACP is now defined in the newer IEEE 802.1AX standard for local and metropolitan area networks.

LACP provides the same negotiation benefits as PAgP. LACP helps create the Ether-Channel link by detecting the configuration of each side and making sure that they are compatible so that the EtherChannel link can be enabled when needed. The modes for LACP are as follows:

- **On** - This mode forces the interface to channel without LACP. Interfaces configured in the on mode do not exchange LACP packets.

- **LACP active** - This LACP mode places a port in an active negotiating state. In this state, the port initiates negotiations with other ports by sending LACP packets.

- **LACP passive** - This LACP mode places a port in a passive negotiating state. In this state, the port responds to the LACP packets that it receives but does not initiate LACP packet negotiation.

Just as with PAgP, modes must be compatible on both sides for the EtherChannel link to form. The on mode is repeated, because it creates the EtherChannel configuration unconditionally, without PAgP or LACP dynamic negotiation.

LACP allows for eight active links, and also eight standby links. A standby link will become active should one of the current active links fail.

Refer to
Online Course
for Illustration

LACP Mode Settings Example - 6.1.9

Consider the two switches in the figure. Whether S1 and S2 establish an EtherChannel using LACP depends on the mode settings on each side of the channel.

The table shows the various combination of LACP modes on S1 and S2 and the resulting channel establishment outcome.

LACP Modes

S1	S2	Channel Establishment
On	On	Yes
On	Active/Passive	No
Active	Active	Yes
Active	Passive	Yes
Passive	Active	Yes
Passive	Passive	No

Go to the online course to take the quiz and exam.

Check Your Understanding - EtherChannel Operation

Configure EtherChannel - 6.2

Refer to **Online Course** for Illustration

Configuration Guidelines - 6.2.1

Now that you know what EtherChannel is, this topic explains how to configure it. The following guidelines and restrictions are useful for configuring EtherChannel:

- **EtherChannel support** - All Ethernet interfaces must support EtherChannel with no requirement that interfaces be physically contiguous.

- **Speed and duplex** - Configure all interfaces in an EtherChannel to operate at the same speed and in the same duplex mode.

- **VLAN match** - All interfaces in the EtherChannel bundle must be assigned to the same VLAN or be configured as a trunk (shown in the figure).

- **Range of VLANs** - An EtherChannel supports the same allowed range of VLANs on all the interfaces in a trunking EtherChannel. If the allowed range of VLANs is not the same, the interfaces do not form an EtherChannel, even when they are set to **auto** or **desirable** mode.

The figure shows a configuration that would allow an EtherChannel to form between S1 and S2.

In the next figure, S1 ports are configured as half duplex. Therefore, an EtherChannel will not form between S1 and S2.

If these settings must be changed, configure them in port channel interface configuration mode. Any configuration that is applied to the port channel interface also affects individual interfaces. However, configurations that are applied to the individual interfaces do not affect the port channel interface. Therefore, making configuration changes to an interface that is part of an EtherChannel link may cause interface compatibility issues.

The port channel can be configured in access mode, trunk mode (most common), or on a routed port.

Refer to **Online Course** for Illustration

LACP Configuration Example - 6.2.2

EtherChannel is disabled by default and must be configured. The topology in the figure will be used to demonstrate an EtherChannel configuration example using LACP.

Configuring EtherChannel with LACP requires the following three steps:

Step 1. Specify the interfaces that compose the EtherChannel group using the **interface range** *interface* global configuration mode command. The **range** keyword allows you to select several interfaces and configure them all together.

Step 2. Create the port channel interface with the **channel-group** *identifier* **mode active** command in interface range configuration mode. The identifier specifies a channel group number. The **mode active** keywords identify this as an LACP EtherChannel configuration.

Step 3.   To change Layer 2 settings on the port channel interface, enter port channel interface configuration mode using the **interface port-channel** command, followed by the interface identifier. In the example, S1 is configured with an LACP EtherChannel. The port channel is configured as a trunk interface with the allowed VLANs specified.

```
S1(config)# interface range FastEthernet 0/1 - 2

S1(config-if-range)# channel-group 1 mode active

Creating a port-channel interface Port-channel 1

S1(config-if-range)# exit

S1(config-if)# interface port-channel 1

S1(config-if)# switchport mode trunk

S1(config-if)# switchport trunk allowed vlan 1,2,20
```

Refer to **Interactive Graphic** in online course

Syntax Checker - Configure EtherChannel - 6.2.3

Configure the EtherChannel for S2 based on the specified requirements

Refer to **Packet Tracer Activity** for this chapter

Packet Tracer - Configure EtherChannel

Three switches have just been installed. There are redundant uplinks between the switches. As configured, only one of these links can be used; otherwise, a bridging loop might occur. However, using only one link utilizes only half of the available bandwidth. EtherChannel allows up to eight redundant links to be bundled together into one logical link. In this lab, you will configure Port Aggregation Protocol (PAgP), a Cisco EtherChannel protocol, and Link Aggregation Control Protocol (LACP), an IEEE 802.3ad open standard version of EtherChannel.

Verify and Troubleshoot EtherChannel - 6.3

Refer to **Online Course** for Illustration

Verify EtherChannel - 6.3.1

As always, when you configure devices in your network, you must verify your configuration. If there are problems, you will also need to be able to troubleshoot and fix them. This topic gives you the commands to verify, as well as some common EtherChannel network problems and their solutions.

Refer to **Interactive Graphic** in online course

The verification command examples will use the topology shown in the figure.

There are a number of commands to verify an EtherChannel configuration. Click each button to for an explanation and command output.

show interfaces port-channel

The **show interfaces port-channel** command displays the general status of the port channel interface. In the figure, the Port Channel 1 interface is up.

```
S1# show interfaces port-channel 1

Port-channel1 is up, line protocol is up (connected)
```

```
    Hardware is EtherChannel, address is c07b.bcc4.a981 (bia c07b.bcc4.a981)
    MTU 1500 bytes, BW 200000 Kbit/sec, DLY 100 usec,
        reliability 255/255, txload 1/255, rxload 1/255
(output omitted)
```

show etherchannel summary

When several port channel interfaces are configured on the same device, use the **show etherchannel summary** command to display one line of information per port channel. In the output, the switch has one EtherChannel configured; group 1 uses LACP.

The interface bundle consists of the FastEthernet0/1 and FastEthernet0/2 interfaces. The group is a Layer 2 EtherChannel and it is in use, as indicated by the letters SU next to the port channel number.

```
S1# show etherchannel summary
Flags:  D - down        P - bundled in port-channel
        I - stand-alone s - suspended
        H - Hot-standby (LACP only)
        R - Layer3       S - Layer2
        U - in use       N - not in use, no aggregation
        f - failed to allocate aggregator
        M - not in use, minimum links not met
        m - not in use, port not aggregated due to minimum links not met
        u - unsuitable for bundling
        w - waiting to be aggregated
        d - default port
        A - formed by Auto LAG
Number of channel-groups in use: 1
Number of aggregators:           1
Group  Port-channel  Protocol    Ports
------+-------------+-----------+-------------------------------------------
1      Po1(SU)       LACP        Fa0/1(P)    Fa0/2(P)
```

show etherchannel port-channel

Use the **show etherchannel port-channel** command to display information about a specific port channel interface, as shown in the output. In the example, the Port Channel 1 interface consists of two physical interfaces, FastEthernet0/1 and FastEthernet0/2. It uses LACP in active mode. It is properly connected to another switch with a compatible configuration, which is why the port channel is said to be in use.

```
S1# show etherchannel port-channel
                  Channel-group listing:

                  ----------------------

Group: 1

----------

                  Port-channels in the group:

                  --------------------------

Port-channel: Po1     (Primary Aggregator)

------------

Age of the Port-channel    = 0d:01h:02m:10s

Logical slot/port    = 2/1            Number of ports = 2

HotStandBy port = null

Port state          = Port-channel Ag-Inuse

Protocol            =   LACP

Port security       = Disabled

Load share deferral = Disabled

Ports in the Port-channel:

Index    Load    Port    EC state          No of bits

------+------+------+------------------+-----------

  0      00    Fa0/1    Active              0

  0      00    Fa0/2    Active              0

Time since last port bundled:    0d:00h:09m:30s    Fa0/2
```

show interfaces etherchannel

On any physical interface member of an EtherChannel bundle, the **show interfaces etherchannel** command can provide information about the role of the interface in the EtherChannel, as shown in the output. The interface FastEthernet0/1 is part of the EtherChannel bundle 1. The protocol for this EtherChannel is LACP.

```
S1# show interfaces f0/1 etherchannel

Port state      = Up Mstr Assoc In-Bndl

Channel group = 1              Mode = Active          Gcchange = -

Port-channel  = Po1           GC   =   -             Pseudo port-channel
= Po1

Port index    = 0             Load = 0x00            Protocol =   LACP

Flags:  S - Device is sending Slow LACPDUs    F - Device is sending fast
LACPDUs.

        A - Device is in active mode.       P - Device is in passive
mode.
```

```
Local information:

                                   LACP port      Admin    Oper     Port
Port      Flags    State    Priority          Key      Number   State

Fa0/1     SA       bndl     32768             0x1      0x1      0x102
0x3D

Partner's information:
                   LACP port                            Admin    Oper     Port
Port

Port      Flags    Priority   Dev ID           Age     key      Key      Number
State

Fa0/1     SA       32768      c025.5cd7.ef00   12s     0x0      0x1      0x102
0x3Dof the port in the current state: 0d:00h:11m:51sllowed vlan 1,2,20
```

Common Issues with EtherChannel Configurations - 6.3.2

All interfaces within an EtherChannel must have the same configuration of speed and duplex mode, native and allowed VLANs on trunks, and access VLAN on access ports. Ensuring these configurations will significantly reduce network problems related to Ether-Channel. Common EtherChannel issues include the following:

- Assigned ports in the EtherChannel are not part of the same VLAN, or not configured as trunks. Ports with different native VLANs cannot form an EtherChannel.

- Trunking was configured on some of the ports that make up the EtherChannel, but not all of them. It is not recommended that you configure trunking mode on individual ports that make up the EtherChannel. When configuring a trunk on an EtherChannel, verify the trunking mode on the EtherChannel.

- If the allowed range of VLANs is not the same, the ports do not form an EtherChannel even when PAgP is set to the **auto** or **desirable** mode.

- The dynamic negotiation options for PAgP and LACP are not compatibly configured on both ends of the EtherChannel.

Note: It is easy to confuse PAgP or LACP with DTP, because they are all protocols used to automate behavior on trunk links. PAgP and LACP are used for link aggregation (EtherChannel). DTP is used for automating the creation of trunk links. When an Ether-Channel trunk is configured, typically EtherChannel (PAgP or LACP) is configured first and then DTP.

Refer to
Online Course
for Illustration

Refer to
Interactive Graphic
in online course

Troubleshoot EtherChannel Example - 6.3.3

In the figure, interfaces F0/1 and F0/2 on switches S1 and S2 are connected with an Ether-Channel. However, the EtherChannel is not operational.

Click each button for the steps to troubleshoot the EtherChannel.

Step 1. View the EtherChannel Summary Information

The output of the **show etherchannel summary** command indicates that the EtherChannel is down.

```
S1# show etherchannel summary
Flags:    D - down         P - bundled in port-channel
          I - stand-alone  s - suspended
          H - Hot-standby (LACP only)
          R - Layer3       S - Layer2
          U - in use       N - not in use, no aggregation
          f - failed to allocate aggregator
          M - not in use, minimum links not met
          m - not in use, port not aggregated due to minimum links not
met
          u - unsuitable for bundling
          w - waiting to be aggregated
          d - default port
          A - formed by Auto LAG
Number of channel-groups in use: 1
Number of aggregators:           1
Group  Port-channel  Protocol     Ports
------+-------------+-----------+-------------------------------
1      Po1(SD)          -          Fa0/1(D)    Fa0/2(D)
```

Step 2. View Port Channel Configuration

In the **show run | begin interface port-channel** output, more detailed output indicates that there are incompatible PAgP modes configured on S1 and S2.

```
S1# show run | begin interface port-channel
interface Port-channel1
 switchport trunk allowed vlan 1,2,20
 switchport mode trunk
!
interface FastEthernet0/1
 switchport trunk allowed vlan 1,2,20
 switchport mode trunk
 channel-group 1 mode on
!
```

```
interface FastEthernet0/2

 switchport trunk allowed vlan 1,2,20

 switchport mode trunk

 channel-group 1 mode on

!======================================
```

S2# **show run | begin interface port-channel**

```
interface Port-channel1

 switchport trunk allowed vlan 1,2,20

 switchport mode trunk

!

interface FastEthernet0/1

 switchport trunk allowed vlan 1,2,20

 switchport mode trunk

 channel-group 1 mode desirable

!

interface FastEthernet0/2

 switchport trunk allowed vlan 1,2,20

 switchport mode trunk

 channel-group 1 mode desirable
```

Step 3. Correct the Misconfiguration

To correct the issue, the PAgP mode on the EtherChannel is changed to desirable.

Note: EtherChannel and STP must interoperate. For this reason, the order in which EtherChannel-related commands are entered is important, which is why you see interface Port-Channel 1 removed and then re-added with the **channel-group** command, as opposed to directly changed. If one tries to change the configuration directly, STP errors cause the associated ports to go into blocking or errdisabled state.

S1(config)# **no interface port-channel 1**

S1(config)# **interface range fa0/1 - 2**

S1(config-if-range)# **channel-group 1 mode desirable**

Creating a port-channel interface Port-channel 1

S1(config-if-range)# **no shutdown**

S1(config-if-range)# **exit**

S1(config)# **interface range fa0/1 - 2**

S1(config-if-range)# **channel-group 1 mode desirable**

S1(config-if-range)# **no shutdown**

```
S1(config-if-range)# interface port-channel 1
S1(config-if)# switchport mode trunk
S1(config-if)# end
S1#
```

Step 4. Verify EtherChannel is Operational

The EtherChannel is now active as verified by the output of the **show etherchannel summary** command.

```
S1# show etherchannel summary
Flags:    D - down         P - bundled in port-channel
          I - stand-alone  s - suspended
          H - Hot-standby (LACP only)
          R - Layer3       S - Layer2
          U - in use       N - not in use, no aggregation
          f - failed to allocate aggregator
          M - not in use, minimum links not met
          m - not in use, port not aggregated due to minimum links not
met
          u - unsuitable for bundling
          w - waiting to be aggregated
          d - default port
          A - formed by Auto LAG
Number of channel-groups in use: 1
Number of aggregators:           1
Group  Port-channel  Protocol    Ports
------+-------------+-----------+-------------------------------
1      Po1(SU)       PAgP        Fa0/1(P)    Fa0/2(P)
```

Refer to **Packet Tracer Activity** for this chapter

Packet Tracer - Troubleshoot EtherChannel - 6.3.4

Four switches were recently configured by a junior technician. Users are complaining that the network is running slowly and would like you to investigate.

Module Practice and Quiz - 6.4

Refer to **Packet Tracer Activity** for this chapter

Packet Tracer - Implement EtherChannel - 6.4.1

You have been tasked with designing an EtherChannel implementation for a company that wants to improve the performance of the switch trunk links. You will try several different ways of implementing the EtherChannel links in order to evaluate which is the best for the company. You will build the topology, configure trunk ports and implement LACP and PAgP EtherChannels.

Refer to
Lab Activity
for this chapter

Lab - Implement EtherChannel - 6.4.2

In this lab, you will complete the following objectives:

- Part 1: Build the Network and Configure Basic Device Settings
- Part 2: Create VLANs and Assign Switch Ports
- Part 3: Configure 802.1Q Trunks between the Switches
- Part 4: Implement and Verify an EtherChannel between the switches

What did I learn in this module? - 6.4.3

EtherChannel Operation

To increase bandwidth or redundancy, multiple links could be connected between devices. However, STP will block redundant links to prevent switching loops. EtherChannel is a link aggregation technology that allows redundant links between devices that will not be blocked by STP. EtherChannel groups multiple physical Ethernet links together into one single logical link. It provides fault-tolerance, load sharing, increased bandwidth, and redundancy between switches, routers, and servers. When an EtherChannel is configured, the resulting virtual interface is called a port channel. EtherChannel has several advantages, as well as some restrictions to implementation. EtherChannels can be formed through negotiation using one of two protocols, PAgP or LACP. These protocols allow ports with similar characteristics to form a channel through dynamic negotiation with adjoining switches. When an EtherChannel link is configured using Cisco-proprietary PAgP, PAgP packets are sent between EtherChannel-capable ports to negotiate the forming of a channel. Modes for PAgP are On, PAgP desirable, and PAgP auto. LACP performs a function similar to PAgP with Cisco EtherChannel. Because LACP is an IEEE standard, it can be used to facilitate EtherChannels in multivendor environments. Modes for LACP are On, LACP active, and LACP passive.

Configure EtherChannel

The following guidelines and restrictions are useful for configuring EtherChannel:

- **EtherChannel support** - All Ethernet interfaces on all modules must support EtherChannel with no requirement that interfaces be physically contiguous, or on the same module.
- **Speed and duplex** - Configure all interfaces in an EtherChannel to operate at the same speed and in the same duplex mode.
- **VLAN match** - All interfaces in the EtherChannel bundle must be assigned to the same VLAN or be configured as a trunk.
- **Range of VLANs** - An EtherChannel supports the same allowed range of VLANs on all the interfaces in a trunking EtherChannel.

Configuring EtherChannel with LACP requires three steps:

Step 1.   Specify the interfaces that compose the EtherChannel group using the interface range interface global configuration mode command.

Step 2.   Create the port channel interface with the channel-group identifier mode active command in interface range configuration mode.

Step 3.   To change Layer 2 settings on the port channel interface, enter port channel interface configuration mode using the interface port-channel command, followed by the interface identifier.

Verify and Troubleshoot EtherChannel.

There are a number of commands to verify an EtherChannel configuration including **show interfaces port-channel**, **show etherchannel summary**, **show etherchannel port-channel**, and **show interfaces etherchannel**. Common EtherChannel issues include the following:

■ Assigned ports in the EtherChannel are not part of the same VLAN, or not configured as trunks. Ports with different native VLANs cannot form an EtherChannel.

■ Trunking was configured on some of the ports that make up the EtherChannel, but not all of them.

■ If the allowed range of VLANs is not the same, the ports do not form an EtherChannel even when PAgP is set to the auto or desirable mode.

■ The dynamic negotiation options for PAgP and LACP are not compatibly configured on both ends of the EtherChannel.

Go to the online course to take the quiz and exam.

Chapter Quiz - EtherChannel

Your Chapter Notes

Introduction - 7.0

Why should I take this module? - 7.0.1

Welcome to DHCPv4!

The Dynamic Host Configuration Protocol (DHCP) dynamically assigns IP addresses to devices. DHCPv4 is for an IPv4 network. (Don't worry, you'll learn about DHCPv6 in another module.) This means that you, the network administrator, do not have to spend your day configuring IP addresses for every device on your network. In a small home or office, that would not be very difficult, but any large network might have hundreds, or even thousands of devices.

In this module, you will learn how to configure a Cisco IOS router to be a DHCPv4 server. Then you will learn how to configure a Cisco IOS router as a client. This module includes a few Syntax Checkers and a Packet Tracer activity to help you try out your new knowledge. DHCPv4 configuration skills will significantly reduce your workload, and who doesn't want that?

What will I learn to do in this module? - 7.0.2

Module Title: DHCPv4

Module Objective: Implement DHCPv4 to operate across multiple LANs.

Topic Title	Topic Objective
DHCPv4 Concepts	Explain how DHCPv4 operates in a small- to medium-sized business network.
Configure a Cisco IOS DHCPv4 Server	Configure a router as a DHCPv4 server.
Configure a DHCPv4 Client	Configure a router as a DHCPv4 client.

DHCPv4 Concepts - 7.1

DHCPv4 Server and Client - 7.1.1

Refer to
Online Course
for Illustration

Dynamic Host Configuration Protocol v4 (DHCPv4) assigns IPv4 addresses and other network configuration information dynamically. Because desktop clients typically make up the bulk of network nodes, DHCPv4 is an extremely useful and timesaving tool for network administrators.

A dedicated DHCPv4 server is scalable and relatively easy to manage. However, in a small branch or SOHO location, a Cisco router can be configured to provide DHCPv4 services without the need for a dedicated server. Cisco IOS software supports an optional, full-featured DHCPv4 server.

The DHCPv4 server dynamically assigns, or leases, an IPv4 address from a pool of addresses for a limited period of time chosen by the server, or until the client no longer needs the address.

Clients lease the information from the server for an administratively defined period. Administrators configure DHCPv4 servers to set the leases to time out at different intervals. The lease is typically anywhere from 24 hours to a week or more. When the lease expires, the client must ask for another address, although the client is typically reassigned the same address.

DHCPv4 Operation - 7.1.2

DHCPv4 works in a client/server mode. When a client communicates with a DHCPv4 server, the server assigns or leases an IPv4 address to that client. The client connects to the network with that leased IPv4 address until the lease expires. The client must contact the DHCP server periodically to extend the lease. This lease mechanism ensures that clients that move or power off do not keep addresses that they no longer need. When a lease expires, the DHCP server returns the address to the pool where it can be reallocated as necessary.

Refer to **Interactive Graphic** in online course

Steps to Obtain a Lease - 7.1.3

When the client boots (or otherwise wants to join a network), it begins a four-step process to obtain a lease:

Refer to **Online Course** for Illustration

1. DHCP Discover (DHCPDISCOVER)

2. DHCP Offer (DHCPOFFER)

3. DHCP Request (DHCPREQUEST)

4. DHCP Acknowledgment (DHCPACK)

Click each button to learn the four-step process to obtain a DHCP lease.

Step 1. DHCP Discover

Step 1. DHCP Discover (DHCPDISCOVER)

The client starts the process using a broadcast DHCPDISCOVER message with its own MAC address to discover available DHCPv4 servers. Because the client has no valid IPv4 information at bootup, it uses Layer 2 and Layer 3 broadcast addresses to communicate with the server. The purpose of the DHCPDISCOVER message is to find DHCPv4 servers on the network.

Step 2. DHCP Offer

Step 2. DHCP Offer (DHCPOFFER)

When the DHCPv4 server receives a DHCPDISCOVER message, it reserves an available IPv4 address to lease to the client. The server also creates an ARP entry consisting of the MAC address of the requesting client and the leased IPv4 address of the client. The DHCPv4 server sends the binding DHCPOFFER message to the requesting client.

Step 3. DHCP Request

Step 3. DHCP Request (DHCPREQUEST)

When the client receives the DHCPOFFER from the server, it sends back a DHCPRE-QUEST message. This message is used for both lease origination and lease renewal. When used for lease origination, the DHCPREQUEST serves as a binding acceptance notice to the selected server for the parameters it has offered and an implicit decline to any other servers that may have provided the client a binding offer.

Many enterprise networks use multiple DHCPv4 servers. The DHCPREQUEST message is sent in the form of a broadcast to inform this DHCPv4 server and any other DHCPv4 servers about the accepted offer.

Step 4. DHCP Acknowledgment

Step 4. DHCP Acknowledgment (DHCPACK)

On receiving the DHCPREQUEST message, the server may verify the lease information with an ICMP ping to that address to ensure it is not being used already, it will create a new ARP entry for the client lease, and reply with a DHCPACK message. The DHCPACK message is a duplicate of the DHCPOFFER, except for a change in the message type field. When the client receives the DHCPACK message, it logs the configuration information and may perform an ARP lookup for the assigned address. If there is no reply to the ARP, the client knows that the IPv4 address is valid and starts using it as its own.

Refer to
Online Course
for Illustration

Steps to Renew a Lease - 7.1.4

Prior to lease expiration, the client begins a two-step process to renew the lease with the DHCPv4 server, as shown in the figure:

1. DHCP Request (DHCPREQUEST)

Before the lease expires, the client sends a DHCPREQUEST message directly to the DHCPv4 server that originally offered the IPv4 address. If a DHCPACK is not received within a specified amount of time, the client broadcasts another DHCPREQUEST so that one of the other DHCPv4 servers can extend the lease.

2. DHCP Acknowledgment (DHCPACK)

On receiving the DHCPREQUEST message, the server verifies the lease information by returning a DHCPACK.

Note: These messages (primarily the DHCPOFFER and DHCPACK) can be sent as unicast or broadcast according to IETF RFC 2131.

Go to the online course to take the quiz and exam.

Check Your Understanding - DHCPv4 Concepts - 7.1.5

Configure a Cisco IOS DHCPv4 Server - 7.2

Refer to **Online Course** for Illustration

Cisco IOS DHCPv4 Server - 7.2.1

Now you have a basic understanding of how DHCPv4 works and how it can make your job a bit easier. If you do not have a separate DHCPv4 server, this topic will show you how to configure a Cisco IOS router to act as one. A Cisco router running Cisco IOS software can be configured to act as a DHCPv4 server. The Cisco IOS DHCPv4 server assigns and manages IPv4 addresses from specified address pools within the router to DHCPv4 clients.

Steps to Configure a Cisco IOS DHCPv4 Server - 7.2.2

Use the following steps to configure a Cisco IOS DHCPv4 server:

Step 1.   Exclude IPv4 addresses.

Step 2.   Define a DHCPv4 pool name.

Step 3.   Configure the DHCPv4 pool.

Step 1. Exclude IPv4 Addresses

The router functioning as the DHCPv4 server assigns all IPv4 addresses in a DHCPv4 address pool unless it is configured to exclude specific addresses. Typically, some IPv4 addresses in a pool are assigned to network devices that require static address assignments. Therefore, these IPv4 addresses should not be assigned to other devices. The command syntax to exclude IPv4 addresses is the following:

```
Router(config)# ip dhcp excluded-address low-address [high-address]
```

A single address or a range of addresses can be excluded by specifying the *low-address* and *high-address* of the range. Excluded addresses should be those addresses that are assigned to routers, servers, printers, and other devices that have been, or will be, manually configured. You can also enter the command multiple times.

Step 2. Define a DHCPv4 Pool Name

Configuring a DHCPv4 server involves defining a pool of addresses to assign.

As shown in the example, the **ip dhcp pool** *pool-name* command creates a pool with the specified name and puts the router in DHCPv4 configuration mode, which is identified by the prompt Router(dhcp-config)#.

The command syntax to define the pool is the following:

```
Router(config)# ip dhcp pool pool-name
Router(dhcp-config)#
```

Step 3. Configure the DHCPv4 Pool

The table lists the tasks to complete the DHCPv4 pool configuration.

The address pool and default gateway router must be configured. Use the **network** statement to define the range of available addresses. Use the **default-router** command to define the default gateway router. Typically, the gateway is the LAN interface of the router closest to the client devices. One gateway is required, but you can list up to eight addresses if there are multiple gateways.

Other DHCPv4 pool commands are optional. For example, the IPv4 address of the DNS server that is available to a DHCPv4 client is configured using the **dns-server** command. The **domain-name** command is used to define the domain name. The duration of the DHCPv4 lease can be changed using the **lease** command. The default lease value is one day. The **netbios-name-server** command is used to define the NetBIOS WINS server.

Task	IOS Command
Define the address pool.	**network** *network-number* [*mask* | / *prefix-length*]
Define the default router or gateway.	**default-router** *address* [*address2....address8*]
Define a DNS server.	**dns-server** *address* [*address2...address8*]
Define the domain name.	**domain-name** *domain*
Define the duration of the DHCP lease.	**lease** {*days* [*hours* [*minutes*]] | **infinite**}
Define the NetBIOS WINS server.	**netbios-name-server** *address* [*address2...address8*]

Note: Microsoft recommends not deploying WINS, instead configure DNS for Windows name resolution and decommission WINS.

Refer to
Online Course
for Illustration

Configuration Example - 7.2.3

The topology for the example configuration is shown in the figure.

The example shows the configuration to make R1 a DHCPv4 server for the 192.168.10.0/24 LAN.

```
R1(config)# ip dhcp excluded-address 192.168.10.1 192.168.10.9
R1(config)# ip dhcp excluded-address 192.168.10.254
R1(config)# ip dhcp pool LAN-POOL-1
```

```
R1(dhcp-config)# network 192.168.10.0 255.255.255.0

R1(dhcp-config)# default-router 192.168.10.1

R1(dhcp-config)# dns-server 192.168.11.5

R1(dhcp-config)# domain-name example.com

R1(dhcp-config)# end

R1#
```

DHCPv4 Verification Commands - 7.2.4

Use the commands in the table to verify that the Cisco IOS DHCPv4 server is operational.

Command	Description
`show running-config	section dhcp`	Displays the DHCPv4 commands configured on the router.
`show ip dhcp binding`	Displays a list of all IPv4 address to MAC address bindings provided by the DHCPv4 service.
`show ip dhcp server statistics`	Displays count information regarding the number of DHCPv4 messages that have been sent and received.

Refer to
Online Course
for Illustration

Refer to
Interactive Graphic
in online course

Verify DHCPv4 is Operational - 7.2.5

The topology shown in the figure is used in the example output. In this example, R1 has been configured to provide DHCPv4 services. PC1 has not been powered up and, therefore, does not have an IP address.

The output for the following commands assumes PC1 has received its IPv4 addressing information from the DHCPv4 server. You may need to enter ipconfig /renew on a Windows PC to force it to send out a DHCPDISCOVER message. Click each button to see the command output verifying that DHCPv4 is operational.

Verify the DHCPv4 Configuration

As shown in the example, the **show running-config | section dhcp** command output displays the DHCPv4 commands configured on R1. The **| section** parameter displays only the commands associated with DHCPv4 configuration.

```
R1# show running-config | section dhcp

ip dhcp excluded-address 192.168.10.1 192.168.10.9

ip dhcp excluded-address 192.168.10.254

ip dhcp pool LAN-POOL-1

 network 192.168.10.0 255.255.255.0

 default-router 192.168.10.1

 dns-server 192.168.11.5

 domain-name example.com
```

Verify DHCPv4 Bindings

As shown in the example, the operation of DHCPv4 can be verified using the **show ip dhcp binding** command. This command displays a list of all IPv4 address to MAC address bindings that have been provided by the DHCPv4 service.

```
R1# show ip dhcp binding

Bindings from all pools not associated with VRF:

IP address      Client-ID/         Lease expiration    Type      State
Interface

                Hardware address/

                User name

192.168.10.10 0100.5056.b3ed.d8 Sep 15 2019 8:42 AM   Automatic  Active
GigabitEthernet0/0/0
```

Verify DHCPv4 Statistics

The output of the **show ip dhcp server statistics** is used to verify that messages are being received or sent by the router. This command displays count information regarding the number of DHCPv4 messages that have been sent and received.

```
R1# show ip dhcp server statistics

Memory usage            19465

Address pools           1

Database agents         0

Automatic bindings      2

Manual bindings         0

Expired bindings        0

Malformed messages      0

Secure arp entries      0

Renew messages          0

Workspace timeouts      0

Static routes           0

Relay bindings          0

Relay bindings active           0

Relay bindings terminated       0

Relay bindings selecting        0

Message                 Received

BOOTREQUEST             0

DHCPDISCOVER            4

DHCPREQUEST             2

DHCPDECLINE             0

DHCPRELEASE             0

DHCPINFORM              0
```

Verify DHCPv4 Client Received IPv4 Addressing

The **ipconfig /all** command, when issued on PC1, displays the TCP/IP parameters, as shown in the example. Because PC1 was connected to the network segment 192.168.10.0/24, it automatically received a DNS suffix, IPv4 address, subnet mask, default gateway, and DNS server address from that pool. No DHCP-specific router interface configuration is required. If a PC is connected to a network segment that has a DHCPv4 pool available, the PC can obtain an IPv4 address from the appropriate pool automatically.

```
C:\Users\Student> ipconfig /all

Windows IP Configuration

    Host Name . . . . . . . . . . . . : ciscolab

    Primary Dns Suffix  . . . . . . . :

    Node Type . . . . . . . . . . . . : Hybrid

    IP Routing Enabled. . . . . . . . : No

    WINS Proxy Enabled. . . . . . . . : No

Ethernet adapter Ethernet0:

    Connection-specific DNS Suffix  . : example.com

    Description . . . . . . . . . . . : Realtek PCIe GBE Family
                                        Controller

    Physical Address. . . . . . . . . : 00-05-9A-3C-7A-00

    DHCP Enabled. . . . . . . . . . . : Yes

    Autoconfiguration Enabled . . . . : Yes

    IPv4 Address. . . . . . . . . . . : 192.168.10.10

    Subnet Mask . . . . . . . . . . . : 255.255.255.0

    Lease Obtained  . . . . . . . . . : Saturday, September 14, 2019
                                        8:42:22AM

    Lease Expires   . . . . . . . . . : Sunday, September 15, 2019
                                        8:42:22AM

    Default Gateway . . . . . . . . . : 192.168.10.1

    DHCP Server . . . . . . . . . . . : 192.168.10.1

    DNS Servers . . . . . . . . . . . : 192.168.11.5
```

Refer to
Online Course
for Illustration

Refer to
Interactive Graphic
in online course

Syntax Checker - Configure DHCPv4 - 7.2.6

In this Syntax Checker activity, you will configure R1 to be the DHCPv4 server for the 192.168.11.0/24 network.

Disable the Cisco IOS DHCPv4 Server - 7.2.7

The DHCPv4 service is enabled by default. To disable the service, use the **no service dhcp** global configuration mode command. Use the **service dhcp** global configuration mode command to re-enable the DHCPv4 server process, as shown in the example. Enabling the service has no effect if the parameters are not configured.

Note: Clearing the DHCP bindings or stopping and restarting the DHCP service may result in duplicate IP addresses being temporarily assigned on the network.

```
R1(config)# no service dhcp
R1(config)# service dhcp
R1(config)#
```

Refer to
Online Course
for Illustration

Refer to
Interactive Graphic
in online course

DHCPv4 Relay - 7.2.8

In a complex hierarchical network, enterprise servers are usually located centrally. These servers may provide DHCP, DNS, TFTP, and FTP services for the network. Network clients are not typically on the same subnet as those servers. In order to locate the servers and receive services, clients often use broadcast messages.

In the figure, PC1 is attempting to acquire an IPv4 address from a DHCPv4 server using a broadcast message. In this scenario, R1 is not configured as a DHCPv4 server and does not forward the broadcast. Because the DHCPv4 server is located on a different network, PC1 cannot receive an IP address using DHCP. R1 must be configured to relay DHCPv4 messages to the DHCPv4 server.

In this scenario, a network administrator is attempting to renew IPv4 addressing information for PC1. Click each button to see the command output as the network administrator resolves this issue.

ipconfig /release

PC1 is a Windows computer. The network administrator releases all current IPv4 addressing information using the **ipconfig /release** command. Notice that the IPv4 address is released and no address is shown.

```
C:\Users\Student> ipconfig /release

Windows IP Configuration

Ethernet adapter Ethernet0:

   Connection-specific DNS Suffix   . :
   Default Gateway . . . . . . . . . :
```

ipconfig /renew

Next, the network administrator attempts to renew the IPv4 addressing information with the **ipconfig /renew** command. This command causes PC1 to broadcast a DHCPDISCOVER message. The output shows that PC1 is unable to locate the DHCPv4 server. Because routers do not forward broadcasts, the request is not successful.

The network administrator could add DHCPv4 servers on R1 for all subnets. However, this would create additional cost and administrative overhead.

```
C:\Users\Student> ipconfig /renew

Windows IP Configuration

An error occurred while renewing interface Ethernet0 : unable to connect
to your DHCP server. Request has timed out.
```

ip helper-address

A better solution is to configure R1 with the **ip helper-address** *address* interface configuration command. This will cause R1 to relay DHCPv4 broadcasts to the DHCPv4 server. As shown in the example, the interface on R1 receiving the broadcast from PC1 is configured to relay DHCPv4 address to the DHCPv4 server at 192.168.11.6.

```
R1(config)# interface g0/0/0

R1(config-if)# ip helper-address 192.168.11.6

R1(config-if)# end

R1#
```

show ip interface

When R1 has been configured as a DHCPv4 relay agent, it accepts broadcast requests for the DHCPv4 service and then forwards those requests as a unicast to the IPv4 address 192.168.11.6. The network administrator can use the **show ip interface** command to verify the configuration.

```
R1# show ip interface g0/0/0

GigabitEthernet0/0/0 is up, line protocol is up

   Internet address is 192.168.10.1/24

   Broadcast address is 255.255.255.255

   Address determined by setup command

   MTU is 1500 bytes

   Helper address is 192.168.11.6

(output omitted)
```

ipconfig /all

As shown in the output, PC1 is now able to acquire an IPv4 address from the DHCPv4 server as verified with the **ipconfig /all** command.

```
C:\Users\Student> ipconfig /all

Windows IP Configuration


Ethernet adapter Ethernet0:

     Connection-specific DNS Suffix   . : example.com

     IPv4 Address. . . . . . . . . . . : 192.168.10.10

     Subnet Mask . . . . . . . . . . . : 255.255.255.0

     Default Gateway . . . . . . . . . : 192.168.10.1
```

Other Service Broadcasts Relayed - 7.2.9

DHCPv4 is not the only service that the router can be configured to relay. By default, the **ip helper-address** command forwards the following eight UDP services:

- Port 37: Time
- Port 49: TACACS
- Port 53: DNS
- Port 67: DHCP/BOOTP server
- Port 68: DHCP/BOOTP client
- Port 69: TFTP
- Port 137: NetBIOS name service
- Port 138: NetBIOS datagram service

Refer to **Packet Tracer Activity** for this chapter

Packet Tracer - Configure DHCPv4 - 7.2.10

In this Packet Tracer Activity, you will complete the following objectives:

- Part 1: Configure a Router as a DHCP Server
- Part 2: Configure DHCP Relay
- Part 3: Configure a Router as a DHCP Client
- Part 4: Verify DHCP and Connectivity

Configure a DHCPv4 Client - 7.3

Refer to **Online Course** for Illustration

Cisco Router as a DHCPv4 Client - 7.3.1

There are scenarios where you might have access to a DHCP server through your ISP. In these instances, you can configure a Cisco IOS router as a DHCPv4 client. This topic walks you through that process.

Sometimes, Cisco routers in a small office or home office (SOHO) and branch sites have to be configured as DHCPv4 clients in a similar manner to client computers. The method used depends on the ISP. However, in its simplest configuration, the Ethernet interface is used to connect to a cable or DSL modem.

To configure an Ethernet interface as a DHCP client, use the **ip address dhcp** interface configuration mode command.

In the figure, assume that an ISP has been configured to provide select customers with IP addresses from the 209.165.201.0/27 network range after the G0/0/1 interface is configured with the **ip address dhcp** command.

Configuration Example - 7.3.2

To configure an Ethernet interface as a DHCP client, use the **ip address dhcp** interface configuration mode command, as shown in the example. This configuration assumes that the ISP has been configured to provide select customers with IPv4 addressing information.

```
SOHO(config)# interface G0/0/1

SOHO(config-if)# ip address dhcp

SOHO(config-if)# no shutdown

Sep 12 10:01:25.773: %DHCP-6-ADDRESS_ASSIGN: Interface
GigabitEthernet0/0/1 assigned DHCP address 209.165.201.12, mask
255.255.255.224, hostname SOHO
```

The **show ip interface g0/1** command confirms that the interface is up and that the address was allocated by a DHCPv4 server.

```
SOHO# show ip interface g0/0/1

GigabitEthernet0/0/1 is up, line protocol is up

    Internet address is 209.165.201.12/27

    Broadcast address is 255.255.255.255

    Address determined by DHCP

(output omitted)
```

Refer to
Online Course
for Illustration

Home Router as a DHCPv4 Client - 7.3.3

Home routers are typically already set to receive IPv4 addressing information automatically from the ISP. This is so that customers can easily set up the router and connect to the internet.

For example, the figure shows the default WAN setup page for a Packet Tracer wireless router. Notice that the internet connection type is set to **Automatic Configuration - DHCP**. This selection is used when the router is connected to a DSL or cable modem and acts as a DHCPv4 client, requesting an IPv4 address from the ISP.

Various manufacturers of home routers will have a similar setup.

Refer to
Online Course
for Illustration

Syntax Checker - Configure a Cisco Router as DHCP Client - 7.3.4

Refer to
Interactive Graphic
in online course

In this Syntax Checker activity, you will configure a Cisco router as DHCP client.

Module Practice and Quiz - 7.4

Refer to **Packet
Tracer Activity**
for this chapter

Packet Tracer - Implement DHCPv4 - 7.4.1

As the network technician for your company, you are tasked with configuring a Cisco router as a DHCP server to provide dynamic allocation of addresses to clients on the network. You are also required to configure the edge router as a DHCP client so that it receives an IP address from the ISP network. Because the server is centralized, you will need to configure the two LAN routers to relay DHCP traffic between the LANs and the router that is serving as the DHCP server.

Refer to
Lab Activity
for this chapter

Lab - Implement DHCPv4 - 7.4.2

In this lab, you will complete the following objectives:

■ Part 1: Build the Network and Configure Basic Device Settings

■ Part 2: Configure and Verify Two DHCPv4 Servers on R1

■ Part 3: Configure and Verify a DHCP Relay on R2

What did I learn in this module? - 7.4.3

DHCPv4 Concepts

The DHCPv4 server dynamically assigns, or leases, an IPv4 address to a client from a pool of addresses for a limited period of time chosen by the server, or until the client no longer needs the address. The DHCPv4 lease process begins with the client sending message requesting the services of a DHCP server. If there is a DHCPv4 server that receives the message it will respond with an IPv4 address and possible other network configuration information. The client must contact the DHCP server periodically to extend the lease. This lease mechanism ensures that clients that move or power off do not keep addresses that they no longer need. When the client boots (or otherwise wants to join a network), it begins a four-step process to obtain a lease: DHCPDISCOVER, then DHCPOFFER, then DHCPREQUEST, and finally DHCPACK. Prior to lease expiration, the client begins a two-step process to renew the lease with the DHCPv4 server: DHCPREQUEST then DHCPACK.

Configure a Cisco IOS DHCPv4 Server

A Cisco router running Cisco IOS software can be configured to act as a DHCPv4 server. Use the following steps to configure a Cisco IOS DHCPv4 server: exclude IPv4 addresses, define a DHCPv4 pool name, and configure the DHCPv4 pool. Verify your configuration using the **show running-config | section dhcp**, **show ip dhcp binding**, and **show ip dhcp server statistics** commands. The DHCPv4 service is enabled, by default. To disable the service, use the **no service dhcp** global configuration mode command. In a complex hierarchical network, enterprise servers are usually located centrally. These servers may provide DHCP, DNS, TFTP, and FTP services for the network. Network clients are not typically on the same subnet as those servers. In order to locate the servers and receive services, clients often use broadcast messages. A PC is attempting to acquire an IPv4 address from a DHCPv4 server using a broadcast message. If the router is not configured as a DHCPv4 server, it will not forward the broadcast. If the DHCPv4 server is located on a different network, the PC cannot receive an IP address using DHCP. The router must be configured to relay DHCPv4 messages to the DHCPv4 server. The network administrator releases all current IPv4 addressing information using the **ipconfig /release** command. Next, the network administrator attempts to renew the IPv4 addressing information with the **ipconfig /renew** command. A better solution is to configure R1 with the **ip helper-address**

address interface configuration command. The network administrator can use the **show ip interface** command to verify the configuration. The PC is now able to acquire an IPv4 address from the DHCPv4 server as verified with the **ipconfig /all** command. By default, the **ip helper-address** command forwards the following eight UDP services:

- Port 37: Time

- Port 49: TACACS

- Port 53: DNS

- Port 67: DHCP/BOOTP server

- Port 68: DHCP/BOOTP client

- Port 69: TFTP

- Port 137: NetBIOS name service

- Port 138: NetBIOS datagram service

Configure a DHCPv4 Client

The Ethernet interface is used to connect to a cable or DSL modem. To configure an Ethernet interface as a DHCP client, use the **ip address dhcp interface** configuration mode command. Home routers are typically already set to receive IPv4 addressing information automatically from the ISP. The internet connection type is set to Automatic Configuration - DHCP. This selection is used when the router is connected to a DSL or cable modem and acts as a DHCPv4 client, requesting an IPv4 address from the ISP.

Go to the online
course to take the
quiz and exam.

Chapter Quiz - DHCPv4

Your Chapter Notes

CHAPTER 8

SLAAC and DHCPv6

Introduction - 8.0

Welcome - 8.0.1

Welcome to SLAAC and DHCPv6!

SLAAC and DHCPv6 are dynamic addressing protocols for an IPv6 network. So, a little bit of configuring will make your day as a network administrator lot easier. In this module, you will learn how to use SLAAC to allow hosts to create their own IPv6 global unicast address, as well as configure a Cisco IOS router to be a DHCPv6 server, a DHCPv6 client, or a DHCPv6 relay agent. This module includes a lab where you will configure DHCPv6 on real equipment!

What will I learn to do in this module? - 8.0.2

Module Title: SLAAC and DHCPv6

Module Objective: Configure dynamic address allocation in IPv6 networks.

Topic Title	Topic Objective
IPv6 Global Unicast Address Assignment	Explain how an IPv6 host can acquire its IPv6 configuration.
SLAAC	Explain the operation of SLAAC.
DHCPv6	Explain the operation of DHCPv6.
Configure DHCPv6 Server	Configure a stateful and stateless DHCPv6 server.

IPv6 GUA Assignment - 8.1

IPv6 Host Configuration - 8.1.1

Refer to
Online Course
for Illustration

First things first. To use either stateless address autoconfiguration (SLAAC) or DHCPv6, you should review global unicast addresses (GUAs) and link-local addresses (LLAs). This topic covers both.

On a router, an IPv6 global unicast address (GUA) is manually configured using the **ipv6 address** *ipv6-address/prefix-length* interface configuration command.

A Windows host can also be manually configured with an IPv6 GUA address configuration, as shown in the figure.

Manually entering an IPv6 GUA can be time consuming and somewhat error prone. Therefore, most Windows host are enabled to dynamically acquire an IPv6 GUA configuration, as shown in the figure.

IPv6 Host Link-Local Address - 8.1.2

When automatic IPv6 addressing is selected, the host will attempt to automatically obtain and configure IPv6 address information on the interface. The host will use one of three methods defined by the Internet Control Message Protocol version 6 (ICMPv6) Router Advertisement (RA) message received on the interface. An IPv6 router that is on the same link as the host sends out RA messages that suggest to the hosts how to obtain their IPv6 addressing information. The IPv6 link-local address is automatically created by the host when it boots and the Ethernet interface is active. The example **ipconfig** output shows an automatically generated link-local address (LLA) on an interface.

In the figure, notice that the interface did not create an IPv6 GUA. The reason is because, in this example, the network segment does not have a router to provide network configuration instructions for the host.

Note: Host operating systems will at times show a link-local address appended with a "%" and a number. This is known as a Zone ID or Scope ID. It is used by the OS to associate the LLA with a specific interface.

Note: DHCPv6 is defined in RFC 3315.

```
C:\PC1> ipconfig
Windows IP Configuration
Ethernet adapter Ethernet0:
    Connection-specific DNS Suffix  .  :
    IPv6 Address. . . . . . . . . . . :
    Link-local IPv6 Address . . . . . : fe80::fb:1d54:839f:f595%21
    IPv4 Address. . . . . . . . . . . : 169.254.202.140
    Subnet Mask . . . . . . . . . . . : 255.255.0.0
    Default Gateway . . . . . . . . . :
C:\PC1>
```

Refer to
Online Course
for Illustration

IPv6 GUA Assignment - 8.1.3

IPv6 was designed to simplify how a host can acquire its IPv6 configuration. By default, an IPv6-enabled router advertises its IPv6 information. This allows a host to dynamically create or acquire its IPv6 configuration.

The IPv6 GUA can be assigned dynamically using stateless and stateful services, as shown in the figure.

All stateless and stateful methods in this module use ICMPv6 RA messages to suggest to the host how to create or acquire its IPv6 configuration. Although host operating systems follow the suggestion of the RA, the actual decision is ultimately up to the host.

Refer to
Online Course
for Illustration

Three RA Message Flags - 8.1.4

The decision of how a client will obtain an IPv6 GUA depends on the settings within the RA message.

An ICMPv6 RA message includes three flags to identify the dynamic options available to a host, as follows:

- **A flag** - This is the Address Autoconfiguration flag. Use Stateless Address Autoconfiguration (SLAAC) to create an IPv6 GUA.

- **O flag** - This is the Other Configuration flag. Other information is available from a stateless DHCPv6 server.

- **M flag** - This is the Managed Address Configuration flag. Use a stateful DHCPv6 server to obtain an IPv6 GUA.

Using different combinations of the A, O and M flags, RA messages inform the host about the dynamic options available.

The figure illustrates these three methods.

Go to the online
course to take the
quiz and exam.

Check Your Understanding - IPv6 GUA Assignment - 8.1.5

SLAAC - 8.2

SLAAC Overview - 8.2.1

Not every network has access to a DHCPv6 server. But every device in an IPv6 network needs a GUA. The SLAAC method enables hosts to create their own unique IPv6 global unicast address without the services of a DHCPv6 server.

SLAAC is a stateless service. This means there is no server that maintains network address information to know which IPv6 addresses are being used and which ones are available.

SLAAC uses ICMPv6 RA messages to provide addressing and other configuration information that would normally be provided by a DHCP server. A host configures its IPv6 address based on the information that is sent in the RA. RA messages are sent by an IPv6 router every 200 seconds.

A host can also send a Router Solicitation (RS) message requesting that an IPv6-enabled router send the host an RA.

SLAAC can be deployed as SLAAC only, or SLAAC with DHCPv6.

Refer to
Online Course
for Illustration

Refer to
Interactive Graphic
in online course

Enabling SLAAC - 8.2.2

Refer to the following topology to see how SLAAC is enabled to provide stateless dynamic GUA allocation.

Assume R1 GigabitEthernet 0/0/1 has been configured with the indicated IPv6 GUA and link-local addresses. Click each button for an explanation of how R1 is enabled for SLAAC.

Verify IPv6 Addresses

The output of the **show ipv6 interface** command displays the current settings on the G0/0/1 interface.

As highlighted, R1 has been assigned the following IPv6 addresses:

- **Link-local IPv6 address** - fe80::1

- **GUA and subnet** - 2001:db8:acad:1::1 and 2001:db8:acad:1::/64

- **IPv6 all-nodes group** - ff02::1

```
R1# show ipv6 interface G0/0/1
GigabitEthernet0/0/1 is up, line protocol is up
  IPv6 is enabled, link-local address is FE80::1
  No Virtual link-local address(es):
  Description: Link to LAN
  Global unicast address(es):
    2001:DB8:ACAD:1::1, subnet is 2001:DB8:ACAD:1::/64
  Joined group address(es):
    FF02::1
    FF02::1:FF00:1
(output omitted)
R1#
```

Enable IPv6 Routing

Although the router interface has an IPv6 configuration, it is still not yet enabled to send RAs containing address configuration information to hosts using SLAAC.

To enable the sending of RA messages, a router must join the IPv6 all-routers group using the **ipv6 unicast-routing** global config command, as show in the output.

```
R1(config)# ipv6 unicast-routing
R1(config)# exit
R1#
```

Verify SLAAC is Enabled

The IPv6 all-routers group responds to the IPv6 multicast address ff02::2. You can use the **show ipv6 interface** command to verify if a router is enabled as shown, in the output.

An IPv6-enabled Cisco router sends RA messages to the IPv6 all-nodes multicast address
ff02::1 every 200 seconds.

```
R1# show ipv6 interface G0/0/1 | section Joined
  Joined group address(es):
    FF02::1
    FF02::2
    FF02::1:FF00:1
R1#
```

SLAAC Only Method - 8.2.3

Refer to
Online Course
for Illustration

The SLAAC only method is enabled by default when the **ipv6 unicast-routing** command is
configured. All enabled Ethernet interfaces with an IPv6 GUA configured will start sending
RA messages with the A flag set to 1, and the O and M flags set to 0, as shown in the figure.

The **A = 1** flag suggests to the client that it create its own IPv6 GUA using the prefix
advertised in the RA. The client can create its own Interface ID using either Extended
Unique Identifier method (EUI-64) or have it randomly generated.

The **O =0** and **M=0** flags instruct the client to use the information in the RA message
exclusively. The RA includes the prefix, prefix-length, DNS server, MTU, and default gateway information. There is no further information available from a DHCPv6 server.

In the example, PC1 is enabled to obtain its IPv6 addressing information automatically.
Because of the settings of the A, O and M flags, PC1 performs SLAAC only, using the
information contained in the RA message sent by R1.

The default gateway address is the source IPv6 address of the RA message, which is the
LLA for R1. The default gateway can only be obtained automatically from the RA message. A DHCPv6 server does not provide this information.

```
C:\PC1> ipconfig

Windows IP Configuration

Ethernet adapter Ethernet0:

   Connection-specific DNS Suffix  . :
   IPv6 Address. . . . . . . . . . . : 2001:db8:acad:1:1de9:c69:73ee:ca8c
   Link-local IPv6 Address . . . . . : fe80::fb:1d54:839f:f595%21
   IPv4 Address. . . . . . . . . . . : 169.254.202.140
   Subnet Mask . . . . . . . . . . . : 255.255.0.0
   Default Gateway . . . . . . . . . : fe80::1%6

C:\PC1>
```

ICMPv6 RS Messages - 8.2.4

Refer to
Online Course
for Illustration

A router sends RA messages every 200 seconds. However, it will also send an RA message
if it receives an RS message from a host.

When a client is configured to obtain its addressing information automatically, it sends an RS message to the IPv6 all-routers multicast address of ff02::2.

The figure illustrates how a host initiates the SLAAC method.

Host Process to Generate Interface ID - 8.2.5

Using SLAAC, a host typically acquires its 64-bit IPv6 subnet information from the router RA. However, it must generate the remainder 64-bit interface identifier (ID) using one of two methods:

- **Randomly generated** - The 64-bit interface ID is randomly generated by the client operating system. This is the method now used by Windows 10 hosts.

- **EUI-64** - The host creates an interface ID using its 48-bit MAC address and inserts the hex value of fffe in the middle of the address. Some operating systems default to the randomly generated interface ID instead of the EUI-64 method, due to privacy concerns. This is because the Ethernet MAC address of the host is used by EUI-64 to create the interface ID.

Note: Windows, Linux, and Mac OS allow for the user to modify the generation of the interface ID to be either randomly generated or to use EUI-64.

For instance, in the following **ipconfig** output, the Windows 10 PC1 host used the IPv6 subnet information contained in the R1 RA and randomly generated a 64-bit interface ID as highlighted in the output.

```
C:\PC1> ipconfig

Windows IP Configuration

Ethernet adapter Ethernet0:

    Connection-specific DNS Suffix  . :

    IPv6 Address. . . . . . . . . . . : 2001:db8:acad:1:1de9:c69:73ee:ca8c

    Link-local IPv6 Address . . . . . : fe80::fb:1d54:839f:f595%21

    IPv4 Address. . . . . . . . . . . : 169.254.202.140

    Subnet Mask . . . . . . . . . . . : 255.255.0.0

    Default Gateway . . . . . . . . . : fe80::1%6

C:\PC1>
```

Duplicate Address Detection - 8.2.6

The process enables the host to create an IPv6 address. However, there is no guarantee that the address is unique on the network.

SLAAC is a stateless process; therefore, a host has the option to verify that a newly created IPv6 address is unique before it can be used. The Duplicate Address Detection (DAD) process is used by a host to ensure that the IPv6 GUA is unique.

DAD is implemented using ICMPv6. To perform DAD, the host sends an ICMPv6 Neighbor Solicitation (NS) message with a specially constructed multicast address, called a solicited-node multicast address. This address duplicates the last 24 bits of IPv6 address of the host.

If no other devices respond with a NA message, then the address is virtually guaranteed to be unique and can be used by the host. If an NA is received by the host, then the address is not unique, and the operating system has to determine a new interface ID to use.

The Internet Engineering Task Force (IETF) recommends that DAD is used on all IPv6 unicast addresses regardless of whether it is created using SLAAC only, obtained using stateful DHCPv6, or manually configured. DAD is not mandatory because a 64-bit interface ID provides 18 quintillion possibilities and the chance that there is a duplication is remote. However, most operating systems perform DAD on all IPv6 unicast addresses, regardless of how the address is configured.

Go to the online course to take the quiz and exam.

Check Your Understanding - SLAAC - 8.2.7

DHCPv6 - 8.3

DHCPv6 Operation Steps - 8.3.1

This topic explains stateless and stateful DHCPv6. Stateless DHCPv6 uses parts of SLAAC to ensure that all the necessary information is supplied to the host. Stateful DHCPv6 does not require SLAAC.

Although DHCPv6 is similar to DHCPv4 in what it provides, the two protocols are independent of each other.

The host begins the DHCPv6 client/server communications after stateless DHCPv6 or stateful DHCPv6 is indicated in the RA.

Server to client DHCPv6 messages use UDP destination port 546 while client to server DHCPv6 messages use UDP destination port 547.

The steps for DHCPv6 operations are as follows:

1. The host sends an RS message.

2. The router responds with an RA message.

3. The host sends a DHCPv6 SOLICIT message.

4. The DHCPv6 server responds with an ADVERTISE message.

5. The host responds to the DHCPv6 server.

6. The DHCPv6 server sends a REPLY message.

Refer to **Interactive Graphic** in online course

Click each button for an explanation and illustration of these DHCPv6 operation steps.

Refer to **Online Course** for Illustration

Step 1

Step 1. Host sends an RS message.

PC1 sends an RS message to all IPv6-enabled routers.

Step 2

Step 2. Router responds with an RA message.

R1 receives the RS and responds with an RA indicating that the client is to initiate communication with a DHCPv6 server.

Step 3

Step 3. Host sends a DHCPv6 SOLICIT message.

The client, now a DHCPv6 client, needs to locate a DHCPv6 server and sends a DHCPv6 SOLICIT message to the reserved IPv6 multicast all-DHCPv6-servers address of ff02::1:2. This multicast address has link-local scope, which means routers do not forward the messages to other networks.

Step 4

Step 4. DHCPv6 server responds with an ADVERTISE message.

One or more DHCPv6 servers respond with a DHCPv6 ADVERTISE unicast message. The ADVERTISE message informs the DHCPv6 client that the server is available for DHCPv6 service.

Step 5

Step 5. Host responds to DHCPv6 server.

The PC1 response depends on whether it is using stateful or stateless DHCPv6:

- **Stateless DHCPv6 client** - The client creates an IPv6 address using the prefix in the RA message and a self-generated Interface ID. The client then sends a DHCPv6 INFORMATION-REQUEST message to the DHCPv6 server requesting additional configuration parameters (e.g., DNS server address).

- **Stateful DHCPv6 client** - The client sends a DHCPv6 REQUEST message to the DHCPv6 server to obtain all necessary IPv6 configuration parameters.

Step 6

Step 6. DHCPv6 sends a REPLY message.

The server sends a DHCPv6 REPLY unicast message to the client. The content of the message varies depending on if it is replying to a REQUEST or INFORMATION-REQUEST message.

Note: The client will use the source IPv6 Link-local address of the RA as its default gateway address. A DHCPv6 server does not provide this information.

Refer to
Online Course
for Illustration

Stateless DHCPv6 Operation - 8.3.2

The stateless DHCPv6 option tells the client to use the information in the RA message for addressing, but additional configuration parameters are available from a DHCPv6 server.

This process is known as stateless DHCPv6 because the server is not maintaining any client state information (i.e., a list of available and allocated IPv6 addresses). The stateless DHCPv6 server is only providing configuration parameters for clients, not IPv6 addresses.

The figure illustrates stateless DHCPv6 operation.

Enable Stateless DHCPv6 on an Interface - 8.3.3

Stateless DHCPv6 is enabled on a router interface using the **ipv6 nd other-config-flag** interface configuration command. This sets the O flag to 1.

The highlighted output confirms the RA will tell receiving hosts to use stateless autoconfigure (A flag = 1) and contact a DHCPv6 server to obtain another configuration information (O flag = 1).

Note: You can use the **no ipv6 nd other-config-flag** to reset the interface to the default SLAAC only option (O flag = 0).

```
R1(config-if)# ipv6 nd other-config-flag

R1(config-if)# end

R1#

R1# show ipv6 interface g0/0/1 | begin ND

  ND DAD is enabled, number of DAD attempts: 1

  ND reachable time is 30000 milliseconds (using 30000)

  ND advertised reachable time is 0 (unspecified)

  ND advertised retransmit interval is 0 (unspecified)

  ND router advertisements are sent every 200 seconds

  ND router advertisements live for 1800 seconds

  ND advertised default router preference is Medium

  Hosts use stateless autoconfig for addresses.

  Hosts use DHCP to obtain other configuration.

R1#
```

Refer to
Online Course
for Illustration

Stateful DHCPv6 Operation - 8.3.4

This option is most similar to DHCPv4. In this case, the RA message tells the client to obtain all addressing information from a stateful DHCPv6 server, except the default gateway address which is the source IPv6 link-local address of the RA.

This is known as stateful DHCPv6 because the DHCPv6 server maintains IPv6 state information. This is similar to a DHCPv4 server allocating addresses for IPv4.

The figure illustrates stateful DHCPv6 operation.

Note: If A=1 and M=1, some operating systems such as Windows will create an IPv6 address using SLAAC and obtain a different address from the stateful DHCPv6 server. In most cases it is recommended to manually set the A flag to 0.

Enable Stateful DHCPv6 on an Interface - 8.3.5

Stateful DHCPv6 is enabled on a router interface using the **ipv6 nd managed-config-flag** interface configuration command. This sets the M flag to 1.

The highlighted output in the example confirms that the RA will tell the host to obtain all IPv6 configuration information from a DHCPv6 server (M flag = 1).

```
R1(config)# int g0/0/1

R1(config-if)# ipv6 nd managed-config-flag

R1(config-if)# end

R1#

R1# show ipv6 interface g0/0/1 | begin ND

  ND DAD is enabled, number of DAD attempts: 1

  ND reachable time is 30000 milliseconds (using 30000)

  ND advertised reachable time is 0 (unspecified)

  ND advertised retransmit interval is 0 (unspecified)

  ND router advertisements are sent every 200 seconds

  ND router advertisements live for 1800 seconds

  ND advertised default router preference is Medium

  Hosts use DHCP to obtain routable addresses.

R1#
```

Go to the online course to take the quiz and exam.

Check Your Understanding - DHCPv6 - 8.3.6

Configure DHCPv6 Server - 8.4

DHCPv6 Router Roles - 8.4.1

Cisco IOS routers are powerful devices. In smaller networks, you do not have to have separate devices to have a DHCPv6 server, client, or relay agent. A Cisco IOS router can be configured to provide DHCPv6 server services.

Specifically, it can be configured to be one of the following:

■ **DHCPv6 Server** - Router provides stateless or stateful DHCPv6 services.

■ **DHCPv6 Client** - Router interface acquires an IPv6 IP configuration from a DHCPv6 server.

■ **DHCPv6 Relay Agent** - Router provides DHCPv6 forwarding services when the client and the server are located on different networks.

Refer to
Online Course
for Illustration

Refer to
Interactive Graphic
in online course

Configure a Stateless DHCPv6 Server - 8.4.2

The stateless DHCPv6 server option requires that the router advertise the IPv6 network addressing information in RA messages. However, the client must contact a DHCPv6 server for more information.

Refer to the sample topology to learn how to configure the stateless DHCPv6 server method.

In this example, R1 will provide SLAAC services for the host IPv6 configuration and DHCPv6 services.

There are five steps to configure and verify a router as a stateless DHCPv6 server:

Step 1.   Enable IPv6 routing.

Step 2.   Define a DHCPv6 pool name.

Step 3.   Configure the DHCPv6 pool.

Step 4.   Bind the DHCPv6 pool to an interface.

Step 5.   Verify that the hosts have received IPv6 addressing information.

Click each button for an example of these steps.

Step 1

Step 1. Enable IPv6 routing.

The **ipv6 unicast-routing** command is required to enable IPv6 routing. Although it is not necessary for the router to be a stateless DHCPv6 server, it is required for the router to source ICMPv6 RA messages.

```
R1(config)# ipv6 unicast-routing

R1(config)#
```

Step 2

Step 2. Define a DHCPv6 pool name.

Create the DHCPv6 pool using the **ipv6 dhcp pool** *POOL-NAME* global config command. This enters DHCPv6 pool sub-configuration mode as identified by the **Router(config-dhcpv6)#** prompt.

Note: The pool name does not have to be uppercase. However, using an uppercase name makes it easier to see in a configuration.

```
R1(config)# ipv6 dhcp pool IPV6-STATELESS

R1(config-dhcpv6)#
```

Step 3

Step 3. Configure the DHCPv6 pool.

R1 will be configured to provide additional DHCP information including DNS server address and domain name, as shown in the command output.

```
R1(config-dhcpv6)# dns-server 2001:db8:acad:1::254

R1(config-dhcpv6)# domain-name example.com

R1(config-dhcpv6)# exit

R1(config)#
```

Step 4

Step 4. Bind the DHCPv6 pool to an interface.

The DHCPv6 pool has to be bound to the interface using the **ipv6 dhcp server** *POOL-NAME* interface config command as shown in the output.

The router responds to stateless DHCPv6 requests on this interface with the information contained in the pool. The O flag needs to be manually changed from 0 to 1 using the interface command **ipv6 nd other-config-flag**. RA messages sent on this interface indicate that additional information is available from a stateless DHCPv6 server. The A flag is 1 by default, telling clients to use SLAAC to create their own GUA.

```
R1(config)# interface GigabitEthernet0/0/1

R1(config-if)# description Link to LAN

R1(config-if)# ipv6 address fe80::1 link-local

R1(config-if)# ipv6 address 2001:db8:acad:1::1/64

R1(config-if)# ipv6 nd other-config-flag

R1(config-if)# ipv6 dhcp server IPV6-STATELESS

R1(config-if)# no shut

R1(config-if)# end

R1#
```

Step 5

Step 5. Verify hosts received IPv6 addressing information.

To verify stateless DHCP on a Windows host, use the **ipconfig /all** command. The example output displays the settings on PC1.

Notice in the output that PC1 created its IPv6 GUA using the 2001:db8:acad:1::/64 prefix. Also notice that the default gateway is the IPv6 link-local address of R1. This confirms that PC1 derived its IPv6 configuration from the RA of R1.

The highlighted output confirms that PC1 has learned the domain name and DNS server address information from the stateless DHCPv6 server.

```
C:\PC1> ipconfig /all

Windows IP Configuration

Ethernet adapter Ethernet0:
```

```
Connection-specific DNS Suffix  . : example.com

Description . . . . . . . . . . .: Intel(R) 82574L Gigabit
                                   Network Connection

Physical Address. . . . . . . . .: 00-05-9A-3C-7A-00

DHCP Enabled. . . . . . . . . . .: Yes

Autoconfiguration Enabled . . . .: Yes

IPv6 Address. . . . . . . . . . .: 2001:db8:acad:1:1dd:a2ea:
                                   66e7 Preferred)

Link-local IPv6 Address . . . . .: fe80::fb:1d54:839f:
                                   f595%21 (Preferred)

IPv4 Address. . . . . . . . . . .: 169.254.102.23
                                   (Preferred)

Subnet Mask . . . . . . . . . . .: 255.255.0.0

Default Gateway . . . . . . . . .: fe80::1%6

DHCPv6 IAID . . . . . . . . . . .: 318768538

DHCPv6 Client DUID. . . . . . . .: 00-01-00-01-21-F3-76-75-
                                   54-E1-AD-DE-DA-9A

DNS Servers . . . . . . . . . . .: 2001:db8:acad:1::1

NetBIOS over Tcpip. . . . . . . .: Enabled

C:\PC1>
```

Refer to **Online Course** for Illustration

Refer to **Interactive Graphic** in online course

Configure a Stateless DHCPv6 Client - 8.4.3

A router can also be a DHCPv6 client and get an IPv6 configuration from a DHCPv6 server, such as a router functioning as a DHCPv6 server. In the figure, R1 is a stateless DHCPv6 server.

There are five steps to configure and verify a router as a stateless DHCPv6 server.

Step 1.   Enable IPv6 routing.

Step 2.   Configure the client router to create an LLA.

Step 3.   Configure the client router to use SLAAC.

Step 4.   Verify that the client router is assigned a GUA.

Step 5.   Verify that the client router received other necessary DHCPv6 information.

Click each button for an example of these steps.

Step 1

Step 1. Enable IPv6 routing.

The DHCPv6 client router needs to have **ipv6 unicast-routing** enabled.

```
R3(config)# ipv6 unicast-routing

R3(config)#
```

Step 2

Step 2. Configure client router to create an LLA.

The client router needs to have a link-local address. An IPv6 link-local address is created on a router interface when a global unicast address is configured. It can also be created without a GUA using the **ipv6 enable** interface configuration command. Cisco IOS uses EUI-64 to create a randomized Interface ID.

In the output, the **ipv6 enable** command is configured on the Gigabit Ethernet 0/0/1 interface of the R3 client router.

```
R3(config)# interface g0/0/1
R3(config-if)# ipv6 enable
R3(config-if)#
```

Step 3

Step 3. Configure client router to use SLAAC.

The client router needs to be configured to use SLAAC to create an IPv6 configuration. The **ipv6 address autoconfig** command enables the automatic configuration of IPv6 addressing using SLAAC.

```
R3(config-if)# ipv6 address autoconfig
R3(config-if)# end
R3#
```

Step 4

Step 4. Verify client router is assigned a GUA.

Use the **show ipv6 interface brief** command to verify the host configuration as shown. The output confirms that the G0/0/1 interface on R3 was assigned a valid GUA.

Note: it may take the interface a few seconds to complete the process.

```
R3# show ipv6 interface brief
GigabitEthernet0/0/0    [up/up]
    unassigned
GigabitEthernet0/0/1    [up/up]
    FE80::2FC:BAFF:FE94:29B1
    2001:DB8:ACAD:1:2FC:BAFF:FE94:29B1
Serial0/1/0             [up/up]
    unassigned
Serial0/1/1             [up/up]
    unassigned
R3#
```

Step 5

Step 5. Verify client router received other DHCPv6 information.

The **show ipv6 dhcp interface g0/0/1** command confirms that the DNS and domain names were also learned by R3.

```
R3# show ipv6 dhcp interface g0/0/1
GigabitEthernet0/0/1 is in client mode
  Prefix State is IDLE (0)
  Information refresh timer expires in 23:56:06
  Address State is IDLE
  List of known servers:
    Reachable via address: FE80::1
    DUID: 000300017079B3923640
    Preference: 0
    Configuration parameters:
      DNS server: 2001:DB8:ACAD:1::254
      Domain name: example.com
      Information refresh time: 0
  Prefix Rapid-Commit: disabled
  Address Rapid-Commit: disabled
R3#
```

Refer to
Online Course
for Illustration

Refer to
Interactive Graphic
in online course

Configure a Stateful DHCPv6 Server - 8.4.4

The stateful DHCP server option requires that the IPv6 enabled router tells the host to contact a DHCPv6 server to obtain all necessary IPv6 network addressing information.

In the figure, R1 will provide stateful DHCPv6 services to all hosts on the local network. Configuring a stateful DHCPv6 server is similar to configuring a stateless server. The most significant difference is that a stateful DHCPv6 server also includes IPv6 addressing information similar to a DHCPv4 server.

There are five steps to configure and verify a router as a stateless DHCPv6 server:

Step 1.   Enable IPv6 routing.

Step 2.   Define a DHCPv6 pool name.

Step 3.   Configure the DHCPv6 pool.

Step 4.   Bind the DHCPv6 pool to an interface.

Step 5.   Verify that the hosts have received IPv6 addressing information.

Click each button for an example of these steps.

Step 1

Step 1. Enable IPv6 routing.

The **ipv6 unicast-routing** command is required to enable IPv6 routing.

```
R1(config)# ipv6 unicast-routing
R1(config)#
```

Step 2

Step 2. Define a DHCPv6 pool name.

Create the DHCPv6 pool using the **ipv6 dhcp pool** *POOL-NAME* global config command.

```
R1(config)# ipv6 dhcp pool IPV6-STATEFUL
R1(config-dhcpv6)#
```

Step 3

Step 3. Configure the DHCPv6 pool.

R1 will be configured to provide IPv6 addressing, DNS server address, and domain name, as shown in the command output. With stateful DHCPv6, all addressing and other configuration parameters must be assigned by the DHCPv6 server. The **address prefix** command is used to indicate the pool of addresses to be allocated by the server. Other information provided by the stateful DHCPv6 server typically includes DNS server address and the domain name, as shown in the output.

Note: This example is setting the DNS server to Google's public DNS server.

```
R1(config-dhcpv6)# address prefix 2001:db8:acad:1::/64
R1(config-dhcpv6)# dns-server 2001:4860:4860::8888
R1(config-dhcpv6)# domain-name example.com
R1(config-dhcpv6)#
```

Step 4

Step 4. Bind the DHCPv6 pool to an interface.

The example shows the full configuration of the GigabitEthernet 0/0/1 interface on R1.

The DHCPv6 pool has to be bound to the interface using the **ipv6 dhcp server** *POOL-NAME* interface config command.

- The M flag is manually changed from 0 to 1 using the interface command **ipv6 nd managed-config-flag**.

- The A flag is manually changed from 1 to 0 using the interface command **ipv6 nd prefix default no-autoconfig**. The A flag can be left at 1, but some client operating systems such as Windows will create a GUA using SLAAC and get a GUA from the stateful DHCPv6 server. Setting the A flag to 0 tells the client not to use SLAAC to create a GUA.

- The **ipv6 dhcp server** command binds the DHCPv6 pool to the interface. R1 will now respond with the information contained in the pool when it receives stateful DHCPv6 requests on this interface.

Note: You can use the **no ipv6 nd managed-config-flag** to set the M flag back to its default of 0. The **no ipv6 nd prefix default no-autoconfig** command sets the A flag back its default of 1.

```
R1(config)# interface GigabitEthernet0/0/1

R1(config-if)# description Link to LAN

R1(config-if)# ipv6 address fe80::1 link-local

R1(config-if)# ipv6 address 2001:db8:acad:1::1/64

R1(config-if)# ipv6 nd managed-config-flag

R1(config-if)# ipv6 nd prefix default no-autoconfig

R1(config-if)# ipv6 dhcp server IPV6-STATEFUL

R1(config-if)# no shut

R1(config-if)# end

R1#
```

Step 5

Step 5. Verify hosts received IPv6 addressing information.

To verify on a Windows host, use the **ipconfig /all** command to verify the stateless DHCP configuration method. The output displays the settings on PC1. The highlighted output shows that PC1 has received its IPv6 GUA from a stateful DHCPv6 server.

```
C:\PC1> ipconfig /all

Windows IP Configuration

Ethernet adapter Ethernet0:

    Connection-specific DNS Suffix  . : example.com

    Description . . . . . . . . . . . : IntelI 82574L Gigabit
                                        Network Connection

    Physical Address. . . . . . . . . : 00-05-9A-3C-7A-00

    DHCP Enabled. . . . . . . . . . . : Yes

    Autoconfiguration Enabled . . . . : Yes

    IPv6 Address. . . . . . . . . . . : 2001:db8:acad:1a43c:fd28:
                                        9d79:9e42 (Preferred)

    Lease Obtained. . . . . . . . . . : Saturday, September 27,
                                        2019, 10:45:30 AM

    Lease Expires . . . . . . . . . . : Monday, September 29,
                                        2019 10:05:04 AM

    Link-local IPv6 Address . . . . . : fe80::192f:6fbc:9db:
                                        b749%6(Preferred)
```

```
         Autoconfiguration IPv4 Address. .  : 169.254.102.73
                                                (Preferred)

         Subnet Mask . . . . . . . . . . .  : 255.255.0.0

         Default Gateway . . . . . . . . .  : fe80::1%6

         DHCPv6 IAID . . . . . . . . . . .  : 318768538

         DHCPv6 Client DUID. . . . . . . .  : 00-01-00-01-21-F3-76-
                                                75-54-E1-AD-DE-DA-9A

         DNS Servers . . . . . . . . . . .  : 2001:4860:4860::8888

         NetBIOS over Tcpip. . . . . . . .  : Enabled

C:\PC1>
```

Configure a Stateful DHCPv6 Client - 8.4.5

A router can also be a DHCPv6 client. The client router needs to have **ipv6 unicast-routing** enabled and an IPv6 link-local address to send and receive IPv6 messages.

Refer to the sample topology to learn how to configure the stateful DHCPv6 client.

There are five steps to configure and verify a router as a stateless DHCPv6 server.

Step 1.   Enable IPv6 routing.

Step 2.   Configure the client router to create an LLA.

Step 3.   Configure the client router to use DHCPv6.

Step 4.   Verify that the client router is assigned a GUA.

Step 5.   Verify that the client router received other necessary DHCPv6 information.

Click each button for an example of these steps.

Step 1

Step 1. Enable IPv6 routing.

The DHCPv6 client router needs to have **ipv6 unicast-routing** enabled.

```
R3(config)# ipv6 unicast-routing
R3(config)#
```

Step 2

Step 2. Configure client router to create an LLA.

In the output, the **ipv6 enable** command is configured on the R3 Gigabit Ethernet 0/0/1 interface. This enables the router to create an IPv6 LLA without needing a GUA.

```
R3(config)# interface g0/0/1
R3(config-if)# ipv6 enable
R3(config-if)#
```

Step 3

Step 3. Configure client router to use DHCPv6.

The **ipv6 address dhcp** command configures R3 to solicit its IPv6 addressing information from a DHCPv6 server.

```
R3(config-if)# ipv6 address dhcp
R3(config-if)# end
R3#
```

Step 4

Step 4. Verify client router is assigned a GUA.

Use the **show ipv6 interface brief** command to verify the host configuration as shown.

```
R3# show ipv6 interface brief
GigabitEthernet0/0/0    [up/up]
    unassigned
GigabitEthernet0/0/1    [up/up]
    FE80::2FC:BAFF:FE94:29B1
    2001:DB8:ACAD:1:B4CB:25FA:3C9:747C
Serial0/1/0             [up/up]
    unassigned
Serial0/1/1             [up/up]
    unassigned
R3#
```

Step 5

Step 5. Verify client router received other DHCPv6 information.

The **show ipv6 dhcp interface g0/0/1** command confirms that the DNS and domain names were learned by R3.

```
R3# show
ipv6 dhcp interface g0/0/1
GigabitEthernet0/0/1 is in client mode
  Prefix State is IDLE
  Address State is OPEN
  Renew for address will be sent in 11:56:33
  List of known servers:
    Reachable via address: FE80::1
    DUID: 000300017079B3923640
    Preference: 0
    Configuration parameters:
```

```
        IA NA: IA ID 0x00060001, T1 43200, T2 69120
          Address: 2001:DB8:ACAD:1:B4CB:25FA:3C9:747C/128
                    preferred lifetime 86400, valid lifetime 172800
                    expires at Sep 29 2019 11:52 AM (172593 seconds)
        DNS server: 2001:4860:4860::8888
        Domain name: example.com
        Information refresh time: 0
    Prefix Rapid-Commit: disabled
    Address Rapid-Commit: disabled
R3#
```

Refer to
Interactive Graphic
in online course

DHCPv6 Server Verification Commands - 8.4.6

Use the **show ipv6 dhcp pool** and **show ipv6 dhcp binding** commands to verify DHCPv6 operation on a router.

Click each button for example output.

show ipv6 dhcp pool

The **show ipv6 dhcp pool** command verifies the name of the DHCPv6 pool and its parameters. The command also identifies the number of active clients. In this example, the IPV6-STATEFUL pool currently has 2 clients, which reflects PC1 and R3 receiving their IPv6 global unicast address from this server.

When a router is providing stateful DHCPv6 services, it also maintains a database of assigned IPv6 addresses.

```
R1# show ipv6 dhcp pool
DHCPv6 pool: IPV6-STATEFUL
   Address allocation prefix: 2001:DB8:ACAD:1::/64 valid 172800 preferred
   86400 (2 in use,  0 conflicts)
   DNS server: 2001:4860:4860::8888
   Domain name: example.com
   Active clients: 2
R1#
```

show ipv6 dhcp binding

Use the **show ipv6 dhcp binding** command output to display the IPv6 link-local address of the client and the global unicast address assigned by the server.

The output displays the current stateful binding on R1. The first client in the output is PC1 and the second client is R3.

This information is maintained by a stateful DHCPv6 server. A stateless DHCPv6 server would not maintain this information.

```
R1# show ipv6 dhcp binding
Client: FE80::192F:6FBC:9DB:B749
  DUID: 0001000125148183005056B327D6
  Username : unassigned
  VRF : default
  IA NA: IA ID 0x03000C29, T1 43200, T2 69120
    Address: 2001:DB8:ACAD:1:A43C:FD28:9D79:9E42
            preferred lifetime 86400, valid lifetime 172800
            expires at Sep 27 2019 09:10 AM (171192 seconds)
Client: FE80::2FC:BAFF:FE94:29B1
  DUID: 0003000100FCBA9429B0
  Username : unassigned
  VRF : default
  IA NA: IA ID 0x00060001, T1 43200, T2 69120
    Address: 2001:DB8:ACAD:1:B4CB:25FA:3C9:747C
            preferred lifetime 86400, valid lifetime 172800
            expires at Sep 27 2019 09:29 AM (172339 seconds)
R1#
```

Configure a DHCPv6 Relay Agent - 8.4.7

Refer to
Online Course
for Illustration

If the DHCPv6 server is located on a different network than the client, then the IPv6 router can be configured as a DHCPv6 relay agent. The configuration of a DHCPv6 relay agent is similar to the configuration of an IPv4 router as a DHCPv4 relay.

In the figure, R3 is configured as a stateful DHCPv6 server. PC1 is on the 2001:db8:acad:2::/64 network and requires the services of a stateful DHCPv6 server to acquire its IPv6 configuration. R1 needs to be configured as the DHCPv6 Relay Agent.

The command syntax to configure a router as a DHCPv6 relay agent is as follows:

```
Router(config-if)# ipv6 dhcp relay destination ipv6-address
[interface-type interface-number]
```

This command is configured on the interface facing the DHCPv6 clients and specifies the DHCPv6 server address and egress interface to reach the server, as shown in the output. The egress interface is only required when the next-hop address is an LLA.

```
R1(config)# interface gigabitethernet 0/0/1
R1(config-if)# ipv6 dhcp relay destination 2001:db8:acad:1::2 G0/0/0
R1(config-if)# exit
R1(config)#
```

Refer to
Interactive Graphic
in online course

Verify the DHCPv6 Relay Agent - 8.4.8

Verify that the DHCPv6 relay agent is operational with the **show ipv6 dhcp interface** and **show ipv6 dhcp binding** commands. Verify Windows hosts received IPv6 addressing information with the **ipconfig /all** command.

Click each button for example output.

show ipv6 dhcp interface

The DHCPv6 relay agent can be verified using the **show ipv6 dhcp interface** command. This will verify that the G0/0/1 interface is in relay mode.

```
R1# show ipv6 dhcp interface
GigabitEthernet0/0/1 is in relay mode
  Relay destinations:
    2001:DB8:ACAD:1::2
    2001:DB8:ACAD:1::2 via GigabitEthernet0/0/0
R1#
```

show ipv6 dhcp binding

On R3, use the **show ipv6 dhcp binding command** to verify if any hosts have been assigned an IPv6 configuration.

Notice that a client link-local address has been assigned an IPv6 GUA. We can assume that this is PC1.

```
R3# show ipv6 dhcp binding
Client: FE80::5C43:EE7C:2959:DA68
  DUID: 0001000124F5CEA2005056B3636D
  Username : unassigned
  VRF : default
  IA NA: IA ID 0x03000C29, T1 43200, T2 69120
    Address: 2001:DB8:ACAD:2:9C3C:64DE:AADA:7857
            preferred lifetime 86400, valid lifetime 172800
            expires at Sep 29 2019 08:26 PM (172710 seconds)
R3#
```

ipconfig /all

Finally, use **ipconfig /all** on PC1 to confirm that it has been assigned an IPv6 configuration. As you can see, PC1 has indeed received its IPv6 configuration from the DHCPv6 server.

```
C:\PC1> ipconfig /all
Windows IP Configuration
```

```
Ethernet adapter Ethernet0:

    Connection-specific DNS Suffix   . : example.com

    Description . . . . . . . . . . : Intel(R) 82574L Gigabit Network
                                       Connection

    Physical Address. . . . . . . . : 00-05-9A-3C-7A-00

    DHCP Enabled. . . . . . . . . . : Yes

    Autoconfiguration Enabled . . . . : Yes

    IPv6 Address. . . . . . . . . . : 2001:db8:acad:2:9c3c:64de:
                                       aada:7857 (Preferred)

    Link-local IPv6 Address . . . . . : fe80::5c43:ee7c:2959:da68%6
                                       (Preferred)

    Lease Obtained  . . . . . . . . . : Saturday, September 27, 2019,
                                       11:45:30 AM

    Lease Expires . . . . . . . . . : Monday, September 29, 2019
                                       11:05:04 AM

    IPv4 Address. . . . . . . . . . : 169.254.102.73 (Preferred)

    Subnet Mask . . . . . . . . . . : 255.255.0.0

    Default Gateway . . . . . . . . : fe80::1%6

    DHCPv6 IAID . . . . . . . . . . : 318768538

    DHCPv6 Client DUID. . . . . . . : 00-01-00-01-21-F3-76-75-54-E1-
                                       AD-DE-DA-9A

    DNS Servers . . . . . . . . . . : 2001:4860:4860::8888

    NetBIOS over Tcpip. . . . . . . : Enabled

C:\PC1>
```

Go to the online course to take the quiz and exam.

Check Your Understanding - Configure DHCPv6 Server - 8.4.9

Module Practice and Quiz - 8.5

Refer to **Lab Activity** for this chapter

Lab - Configure DHCPv6 - 8.5.1

In this lab, you will complete the following objectives:

- Part 1: Build the Network and Configure Basic Device Settings
- Part 2: Verify SLAAC address assignment from R1
- Part 3: Configure and verify a Stateless DHCPv6 Server on R1
- Part 4: Configure and verify a Stateful DHCPv6 Server on R1
- Part 5: Configure and verify a DHCPv6 Relay on R2

What did I learn in this module? - 8.5.2

IPv6 GUA Assignment

On a router, an IPv6 global unicast addresses (GUA) is manually configured using the **ipv6 address** *ipv6-address/prefix-length* interface configuration command. When automatic IPv6 addressing is selected, the host will attempt to automatically obtain and configure IPv6 address information on the interface. The IPv6 link-local address is automatically created by the host when it boots and the Ethernet interface is active. By default, an IPv6-enabled router advertises its IPv6 information enabling a host to dynamically create or acquire its IPv6 configuration. The IPv6 GUA can be assigned dynamically using stateless and stateful services. The decision of how a client will obtain an IPv6 GUA depends on the settings within the RA message. An ICMPv6 RA message includes three flags to identify the dynamic options available to a host:

- **A flag** - This is the Address Autoconfiguration flag. Use SLAAC to create an IPv6 GUA.

- **O flag** - This is the Other Configuration flag. Get Other information from a stateless DHCPv6 server.

- **M flag** - This is the Managed Address Configuration flag. Use a stateful DHCPv6 server to obtain an IPv6 GUA.

SLAAC

The SLAAC method enables hosts to create their own unique IPv6 global unicast address without the services of a DHCPv6 server. SLAAC, which is stateless, uses ICMPv6 RA messages to provide addressing and other configuration information that would normally be provided by a DHCP server. SLAAC can be deployed as SLAAC only, or SLAAC with DHCPv6. To enable the sending of RA messages, a router must join the IPv6 all-routers group using the **ipv6 unicast-routing** global config command. Use the **show ipv6 interface** command to verify if a router is enabled. The SLAAC only method is enabled by default when the ipv6 unicast-routing command is configured. All enabled Ethernet interfaces with an IPv6 GUA configured will start sending RA messages with the A flag set to 1, and the O and M flags set to 0. The A = 1 flag suggests to the client to create its own IPv6 GUA using the prefix advertised in the RA. The O =0 and M=0 flags instructs the client to use the information in the RA message exclusively. A router sends RA messages every 200 seconds. However, it will also send an RA message if it receives an RS message from a host. Using SLAAC, a host typically acquires its 64-bit IPv6 subnet information from the router RA. However, it must generate the remainder 64-bit interface identifier (ID) using one of two methods: randomly generated, or EUI-64. The DAD process is used by a host to ensure that the IPv6 GUA is unique. DAD is implemented using ICMPv6. To perform DAD, the host sends an ICMPv6 NS message with a specially constructed multicast address, called a solicited-node multicast address. This address duplicates the last 24 bits of IPv6 address of the host.

DHCPv6

The host begins the DHCPv6 client/server communications after stateless DHCPv6 or stateful DHCPv6 is indicated in the RA. Server to client DHCPv6 messages use UDP destination port 546, while client to server DHCPv6 messages use UDP destination port 547. The stateless DHCPv6 option informs the client to use the information in the RA message for addressing, but additional configuration parameters are available from a DHCPv6 server. This is called stateless DHCPv6 because the server is not maintaining any client state information. Stateless DHCPv6 is enabled on a router interface using the **ipv6 nd other-config-flag** interface configuration command. This sets the O flag to 1. In stateful DHCPv6, the RA message tells the client to obtain all addressing information from a stateful DHCPv6 server, except the default gateway address which is the source IPv6 link-local address of the RA. It is called stateful because the DHCPv6 server maintains IPv6 state information. Stateful DHCPv6 is enabled on a router interface using the **ipv6 nd managed-config-flag** interface configuration command. This sets the M flag to 1.

Configure DHCPv6 Server

A Cisco IOS router can be configured to provide DHCPv6 server services as one of the following three types: DHCPv6 server, DHCPv6 client, or DHCPv6 relay agent. The stateless DHCPv6 server option requires that the router advertise the IPv6 network addressing information in RA messages. A router can also be a DHCPv6 client and get an IPv6 configuration from a DHCPv6 server. The stateful DHCP server option requires that the IPv6-enabled router tells the host to contact a DHCPv6 server to acquire all required IPv6 network addressing information. For a client router to be a DHCPv6 router, it needs to **have ipv6 unicast-routing** enabled and an IPv6 link-local address to send and receive IPv6 messages. Use the **show ipv6 dhcp pool** and **show ipv6 dhcp binding** commands to verify DHCPv6 operation on a router. If the DHCPv6 server is located on a different network than the client, then the IPv6 router can be configured as a DHCPv6 relay agent using the **ipv6 dhcp relay destination** *ipv6-address [interface-type interface-number]* command. This command is configured on the interface facing the DHCPv6 clients and specifies the DHCPv6 server address and egress interface to reach the server. The egress interface is only required when the next-hop address is an LLA. Verify the DHCPv6 relay agent is operational with the **show ipv6 dhcp interface** and **show ipv6 dhcp binding** commands.

Go to the online course to take the quiz and exam.

Chapter Quiz - SLAAC and DHCPv6

Your Chapter Notes

CHAPTER 9

FHRP Concepts

Introduction - 9.0

Why should I take this module? - 9.0.1

Welcome to FHRP Concepts!

Your network is up and running. You've conquered Layer 2 redundancy without any Layer 2 loops. All your devices get their addresses dynamically. You are *good* at network administration! But, wait. One of your routers, the default gateway router in fact, has gone down. None of your hosts can send any messages outside of the immediate network. It's going to take a while to get this default gateway router operating again. You've got a lot of angry people asking you how soon the network will be 'back up.'

You can avoid this problem easily. First Hop Redundancy Protocols (FHRPs) are the solution you need. This module discusses what FHRP does, and all of the types of FHRPs that are available to you. One of these types is a Cisco-proprietary FHRP called Hot Standby Router Protocol (HSRP). You will learn how HSRP works and then complete a Packet Tracer activity where you will configure and verify HSRP. Don't wait, get started!

What will I learn to do in this module? - 9.0.2

Module Title: FHRP Concepts

Module Objective: Explain how FHRPs provide default gateway services in a redundant network.

Topic Title	Topic Objective
First Hop Redundancy Protocols	Explain the purpose and operation of first hop redundancy protocols.
HSRP	Explain how HSRP operates.

First Hop Redundancy Protocols - 9.1

Default Gateway Limitations - 9.1.1

Refer to
Online Course
for Illustration

If a router or router interface (that serves as a default gateway) fails, the hosts configured with that default gateway are isolated from outside networks. A mechanism is needed to provide alternate default gateways in switched networks where two or more routers are connected to the same VLANs. That mechanism is provided by first hop redundancy protocols (FHRPs).

In a switched network, each client receives only one default gateway. There is no way to use a secondary gateway, even if a second path exists to carry packets off the local segment.

In the figure, R1 is responsible for routing packets from PC1. If R1 becomes unavailable, the routing protocols can dynamically converge. R2 now routes packets from outside networks that would have gone through R1. However, traffic from the inside network associated with R1, including traffic from workstations, servers, and printers configured with R1 as their default gateway, are still sent to R1 and dropped.

Note: For the purposes of the discussion on router redundancy, there is no functional difference between a Layer 3 switch and a router at the distribution layer. In practice, it is common for a Layer 3 switch to act as the default gateway for each VLAN in a switched network. This discussion focuses on the functionality of routing, regardless of the physical device used.

End devices are typically configured with a single IPv4 address for a default gateway. This address does not change when the network topology changes. If that default gateway IPv4 address cannot be reached, the local device is unable to send packets off the local network segment, effectively disconnecting it from other networks. Even if a redundant router exists that could serve as a default gateway for that segment, there is no dynamic method by which these devices can determine the address of a new default gateway.

Note: IPv6 devices receive their default gateway address dynamically from the ICMPv6 Router Advertisement. However, IPv6 devices benefit with a faster failover to the new default gateway when using FHRP.

Router Redundancy - 9.1.2

Refer to **Online Course** for Illustration

One way to prevent a single point of failure at the default gateway is to implement a virtual router. To implement this type of router redundancy, multiple routers are configured to work together to present the illusion of a single router to the hosts on the LAN, as shown in the figure. By sharing an IP address and a MAC address, two or more routers can act as a single virtual router.

The IPv4 address of the virtual router is configured as the default gateway for the workstations on a specific IPv4 segment. When frames are sent from host devices to the default gateway, the hosts use ARP to resolve the MAC address that is associated with the IPv4 address of the default gateway. The ARP resolution returns the MAC address of the virtual router. Frames that are sent to the MAC address of the virtual router can then be physically processed by the currently active router within the virtual router group. A protocol is used to identify two or more routers as the devices that are responsible for processing frames that are sent to the MAC or IP address of a single virtual router. Host devices send traffic to the address of the virtual router. The physical router that forwards this traffic is transparent to the host devices.

A redundancy protocol provides the mechanism for determining which router should take the active role in forwarding traffic. It also determines when the forwarding role must be taken over by a standby router. The transition from one forwarding router to another is transparent to the end devices.

The ability of a network to dynamically recover from the failure of a device acting as a default gateway is known as first-hop redundancy.

Steps for Router Failover - 9.1.3

Refer to
Online Course
for Illustration

When the active router fails, the redundancy protocol transitions the standby router to the new active router role, as shown in the figure. These are the steps that take place when the active router fails:

1. The standby router stops seeing Hello messages from the forwarding router.

2. The standby router assumes the role of the forwarding router.

3. Because the new forwarding router assumes both the IPv4 and MAC addresses of the virtual router, the host devices see no disruption in service.

FHRP Options - 9.1.4

The FHRP used in a production environment largely depends on the equipment and needs of the network. The table lists all the options available for FHRPs.

FHRP Options	Description
Hot Standby Router Protocol (HSRP)	HRSP is a Cisco-proprietary FHRP that is designed to allow for transparent failover of a first-hop IPv4 device. HSRP provides high network availability by providing first-hop routing redundancy for IPv4 hosts on networks configured with an IPv4 default gateway address. HSRP is used in a group of routers for selecting an active device and a standby device. In a group of device interfaces, the active device is the device that is used for routing packets; the standby device is the device that takes over when the active device fails, or when pre-set conditions are met. The function of the HSRP standby router is to monitor the operational status of the HSRP group and to quickly assume packet-forwarding responsibility if the active router fails.
HSRP for IPv6	This is a Cisco-proprietary FHRP that provides the same functionality of HSRP, but in an IPv6 environment. An HSRP IPv6 group has a virtual MAC address derived from the HSRP group number and a virtual IPv6 link-local address derived from the HSRP virtual MAC address. Periodic router advertisements (RAs) are sent for the HSRP virtual IPv6 link-local address when the HSRP group is active. When the group becomes inactive, these RAs stop after a final RA is sent.
Virtual Router Redundancy Protocol version 2 (VRRPv2)	This is a non-proprietary election protocol that dynamically assigns responsibility for one or more virtual routers to the VRRP routers on an IPv4 LAN. This allows several routers on a multiaccess link to use the same virtual IPv4 address. A VRRP router is configured to run the VRRP protocol in conjunction with one or more other routers attached to a LAN. In a VRRP configuration, one router is elected as the virtual router master, with the other routers acting as backups, in case the virtual router master fails.
VRRPv3	This provides the capability to support IPv4 and IPv6 addresses. VRRPv3 works in multi-vendor environments and is more scalable than VRRPv2.

FHRP Options	Description
Gateway Load Balancing Protocol (GLBP)	This is a Cisco-proprietary FHRP that protects data traffic from a failed router or circuit, like HSRP and VRRP, while also allowing load balancing (also called load sharing) between a group of redundant routers.
GLBP for IPv6	This is a Cisco-proprietary FHRP that provides the same functionality of GLBP, but in an IPv6 environment. GLBP for IPv6 provides automatic router backup for IPv6 hosts configured with a single default gateway on a LAN. Multiple first-hop routers on the LAN combine to offer a single virtual first-hop IPv6 router while sharing the IPv6 packet forwarding load.
ICMP Router Discovery Protocol (IRDP)	Specified in RFC 1256, IRDP is a legacy FHRP solution. IRDP allows IPv4 hosts to locate routers that provide IPv4 connectivity to other (nonlocal) IP networks.

Go to the online course to take the quiz and exam.

Check Your Understanding - First Hop Redundancy Protocols - 9.1.5

HSRP - 9.2

HSRP Overview - 9.2.1

Cisco provides HSRP and HSRP for IPv6 as a way to avoid losing outside network access if your default router fails.

HSRP is a Cisco-proprietary FHRP that is designed to allow for transparent failover of a first-hop IP device.

HSRP ensures high network availability by providing first-hop routing redundancy for IP hosts on networks configured with an IP default gateway address. HSRP is used in a group of routers for selecting an active device and a standby device. In a group of device interfaces, the active device is the device that is used for routing packets; the standby device is the device that takes over when the active device fails, or when pre-set conditions are met. The function of the HSRP standby router is to monitor the operational status of the HSRP group and to quickly assume packet-forwarding responsibility if the active router fails.

Refer to **Online Course** for Illustration

HSRP Priority and Preemption - 9.2.2

The role of the active and standby routers is determined during the HSRP election process. By default, the router with the numerically highest IPv4 address is elected as the active router. However, it is always better to control how your network will operate under normal conditions rather than leaving it to chance.

HSRP Priority

HSRP priority can be used to determine the active router. The router with the highest HSRP priority will become the active router. By default, the HSRP priority is 100. If the priorities are equal, the router with the numerically highest IPv4 address is elected as the active router.

To configure a router to be the active router, use the **standby priority** interface command. The range of the HSRP priority is 0 to 255.

HSRP Preemption

By default, after a router becomes the active router, it will remain the active router even if another router comes online with a higher HSRP priority.

To force a new HSRP election process to take place when a higher priority router comes online, preemption must be enabled using the **standby preempt** interface command. Preemption is the ability of an HSRP router to trigger the re-election process. With preemption enabled, a router that comes online with a higher HSRP priority will assume the role of the active router.

Preemption only allows a router to become the active router if it has a higher priority. A router enabled for preemption, with equal priority but a higher IPv4 address will not preempt an active router. Refer to the topology in the figure.

R1 has been configured with the HSRP priority of 150 while R2 has the default HSRP priority of 100. Preemption has been enabled on R1. With a higher priority, R1 is the active router and R2 is the standby router. Due to a power failure affecting only R1, the active router is no longer available and the standby router, R2, assumes the role of the active router. After power is restored, R1 comes back online. Because R1 has a higher priority and preemption is enabled, it will force a new election process. R1 will re-assume the role of the active router and R2 will fall back to the role of the standby router.

Note: With preemption disabled, the router that boots up first will become the active router if there are no other routers online during the election process.

HSRP States and Timers - 9.2.3

A router can either be the active HSRP router responsible for forwarding traffic for the segment, or it can be a passive HSRP router on standby, ready to assume the active role if the active router fails. When an interface is configured with HSRP or is first activated with an existing HSRP configuration, the router sends and receives HSRP hello packets to begin the process of determining which state it will assume in the HSRP group.

The table summarizes the HSRP states.

HSRP State	Description
Initial	This state is entered through a configuration change or when an interface first becomes available.
Learn	The router has not determined the virtual IP address and has not yet seen a hello message from the active router. In this state, the router waits to hear from the active router.
Listen	The router knows the virtual IP address, but the router is neither the active router nor the standby router. It listens for hello messages from those routers.
Speak	The router sends periodic hello messages and actively participates in the election of the active and/or standby router.
Standby	The router is a candidate to become the next active router and sends periodic hello messages.

The active and standby HSRP routers send hello packets to the HSRP group multicast address every 3 seconds by default. The standby router will become active if it does not receive a hello message from the active router after 10 seconds. You can lower these timer settings to speed up the failover or preemption. However, to avoid increased CPU usage and unnecessary standby state changes, do not set the hello timer below 1 second or the hold timer below 4 seconds.

Go to the online course to take the quiz and exam.

Check Your Understanding - 9.2.4

Module Practice and Quiz - 9.3

What did I learn in this module? - 9.3.1

First Hop Redundancy Protocols

If a router or router interface that serves as a default gateway fails, the hosts configured with that default gateway are isolated from outside networks. FHRP provides alternate default gateways in switched networks where two or more routers are connected to the same VLANs. One way to prevent a single point of failure at the default gateway, is to implement a virtual router. With a virtual router, multiple routers are configured to work together to present the illusion of a single router to the hosts on the LAN. When the active router fails, the redundancy protocol transitions the standby router to the new active router role. These are the steps that take place when the active router fails:

1. The standby router stops seeing Hello messages from the forwarding router.

2. The standby router assumes the role of the forwarding router.

3. Because the new forwarding router assumes both the IPv4 and MAC addresses of the virtual router, the host devices see no disruption in service.

The FHRP used in a production environment largely depends on the equipment and needs of the network. These are the options available for FHRPs:

■ HSRP and HSRP for IPv6

■ VRRPv2 and VRRPv3

■ GLBP and GLBP for IPv6

■ IRDP

HSRP

HSRP is a Cisco-proprietary FHRP designed to allow for transparent failover of a first-hop IP device. HSRP is used in a group of routers for selecting an active device and a standby device. In a group of device interfaces, the active device is the device that is used for routing packets; the standby device is the device that takes over when the active device fails, or when pre-set conditions are met. The function of the HSRP standby router is to monitor the operational status of the HSRP group and to quickly assume packet-forwarding responsibility if the active router fails. The router with the highest HSRP priority will become the active router. Preemption is the ability of an HSRP router to trigger the re-election process. With preemption enabled, a router that comes online with a higher HSRP priority will assume the role of the active router. HSRP states include initial, learn, listen, speak, and standby.

Go to the online course to take the quiz and exam.

Chapter Quiz - FHRP Concepts

Refer to **Packet Tracer Activity** for this chapter

Packet Tracer - HSRP Configuration Guide

Note: HSRP configuration is not a required skill for this module, course, or for the CCNA certification. However, we thought you might enjoy implementing HSRP in Packet Tracer. Completing this activity will help you better understand how FHRPs, and specifically HSRP, operates.

In this Packet Tracer activity, you will learn how to configure Hot Standby Router Protocol (HSRP) to provide redundant default gateway devices to hosts on LANs. After configuring HSRP, you will test the configuration to verify that hosts are able to use the redundant default gateway if the current gateway device becomes unavailable.

- Configure an HSRP active router.
- Configure an HSRP standby router.
- Verify HSRP operation.

Your Chapter Notes

CHAPTER 10

LAN Security Concepts

Introduction - 10.0

Why should I take this module? - 10.0.1

Welcome to LAN Security Concepts!

If your career path is in IT, you won't just be building or maintaining networks. You will be responsible for the security of your network. For today's network architects and administrators, security is not an afterthought. It is a top priority for them! In fact, many people in IT now work exclusively in the area of network security.

Do you understand what makes a LAN secure? Do you know what threat actors can do to break network security? Do you know what you can do to stop them? This module is your introduction to the world of network security, so don't wait, click Next!

What will I learn in this module? - 10.0.2

Module Title: LAN Security Concepts

Module Objective: Explain how vulnerabilities compromise LAN security.

Topic Title	Topic Objective
Endpoint Security	Explain how to use endpoint security to mitigate attacks.
Access Control	Explain how AAA and 802.1X are used to authenticate LAN endpoints and devices.
Layer 2 Security Threats	Identify Layer 2 vulnerabilities.
MAC Address Table Attack	Explain how a MAC address table attack compromises LAN security.
LAN Attacks	Explain how LAN attacks compromise LAN security.

Endpoint Security - 10.1

Refer to
Online Course
for Illustration

Network Attacks Today - 10.1.1

The news media commonly covers attacks on enterprise networks. Simply search the internet for "latest network attacks" to find up-to-date information on current attacks. Most likely, these attacks will involve one or more of the following:

- **Distributed Denial of Service (DDoS)** - This is a coordinated attack from many devices, called zombies, with the intention of degrading or halting public access to an organization's website and resources.

- **Data Breach** - This is an attack in which an organization's data servers or hosts are compromised to steal confidential information.

- **Malware** - This is an attack in which an organization's hosts are infected with malicious software that cause a variety of problems. For example, ransomware such as WannaCry, shown in the figure, encrypts the data on a host and locks access to it until a ransom is paid.

Refer to
Interactive Graphic
in online course

Refer to
Online Course
for Illustration

Network Security Devices - 10.1.2

Various network security devices are required to protect the network perimeter from outside access. These devices could include a virtual private network (VPN) enabled router, a next-generation firewall (NGFW), and a network access control (NAC) device.

Click each network security device for more information.

VPN-Enabled Router

A VPN-enabled router provides a secure connection to remote users across a public network and into the enterprise network. VPN services can be integrated into the firewall.

NGFW

An NGFW provides stateful packet inspection, application visibility and control, a next-generation intrusion prevention system (NGIPS), advanced malware protection (AMP), and URL filtering.

NAC

A NAC device includes authentication, authorization, and accounting (AAA) services. In larger enterprises, these services might be incorporated into an appliance that can manage access policies across a wide variety of users and device types. The Cisco Identity Services Engine (ISE) is an example of a NAC device.

Refer to
Online Course
for Illustration

Endpoint Protection - 10.1.3

LAN devices such as switches, wireless LAN controllers (WLCs), and other access point (AP) devices interconnect endpoints. Most of these devices are susceptible to the LAN-related attacks that are covered in this module.

But many attacks can also originate from inside the network. If an internal host is infiltrated, it can become a starting point for a threat actor to gain access to critical system devices, such as servers and sensitive data.

Endpoints are hosts which commonly consist of laptops, desktops, servers, and IP phones, as well as employee-owned devices that are typically referred to as bring your own devices (BYODs). Endpoints are particularly susceptible to malware-related attacks that originate through email or web browsing. These endpoints have typically used traditional host-based security features, such as antivirus/antimalware, host-based firewalls, and host-based intrusion prevention systems (HIPSs). However, today endpoints are best protected by a combination of NAC, host-based AMP software, an email security appliance (ESA), and a web security appliance (WSA). Advanced Malware Protection (AMP) products include endpoint solutions such as Cisco AMP for Endpoints.

The figure is a simple topology representing all the network security devices and endpoint solutions discussed in this module.

Refer to
Online Course
for Illustration

Cisco Email Security Appliance - 10.1.4

Content security appliances include fine-grained control over email and web browsing for an organization's users.

According to the Cisco's Talos Intelligence Group, in June 2019, 85% of all email sent was spam. Phishing attacks are a particularly virulent form of spam. Recall that a phishing attack entices the user to click a link or open an attachment. Spear phishing targets high-profile employees or executives that may have elevated login credentials. This is particularly crucial in today's environment where, according to the SANS Institute, 95% of all attacks on enterprise networks are the result of a successful spear phishing attack.

The Cisco ESA is a device that is designed to monitor Simple Mail Transfer Protocol (SMTP). The Cisco ESA is constantly updated by real-time feeds from the Cisco Talos, which detects and correlates threats and solutions by using a worldwide database monitoring system. This threat intelligence data is pulled by the Cisco ESA every three to five minutes. These are some of the functions of the Cisco ESA:

- Block known threats.
- Remediate against stealth malware that evaded initial detection.
- Discard emails with bad links (as shown in the figure).
- Block access to newly infected sites.
- Encrypt content in outgoing email to prevent data loss.

In the figure, the Cisco ESA discards the email with bad links.

Refer to
Online Course
for Illustration

Cisco Web Security Appliance - 10.1.5

The Cisco Web Security Appliance (WSA) is a mitigation technology for web-based threats. It helps organizations address the challenges of securing and controlling web traffic. The Cisco WSA combines advanced malware protection, application visibility and control, acceptable use policy controls, and reporting.

Cisco WSA provides complete control over how users access the internet. Certain features and applications, such as chat, messaging, video and audio, can be allowed, restricted with time and bandwidth limits, or blocked, according to the organization's requirements. The WSA can perform blacklisting of URLs, URL-filtering, malware scanning, URL categorization, Web application filtering, and encryption and decryption of web traffic.

In the figure, an internal corporate employee uses a smartphone to attempt to connect to a known blacklisted site.

Go to the online
course to take the
quiz and exam.

Check Your Understanding - Endpoint Security

Access Control - 10.2

Authentication with a Local Password - 10.2.1

In the previous topic, you learned that a NAC device provides AAA services. In this topic, you will learn more about AAA and the ways to control access.

Many types of authentication can be performed on networking devices, and each method offers varying levels of security. The simplest method of remote access authentication is to configure a login and password combination on console, vty lines, and aux ports, as shown in the vty lines in the following example. This method is the easiest to implement, but it is also the weakest and least secure. This method provides no accountability and the password is sent in plaintext. Anyone with the password can gain entry to the device.

```
R1(config)# line vty 0 4
R1(config-line)# password ci5c0
R1(config-line)# login
```

SSH is a more secure form of remote access:

- It requires a username and a password, both of which are encrypted during transmission.

- The username and password can be authenticated by the local database method.

- It provides more accountability because the username is recorded when a user logs in.

The following example illustrates SSH and local database methods of remote access.

```
R1(config)# ip domain-name example.com
R1(config)# crypto key generate rsa general-keys modulus 2048
R1(config)# username Admin secret Str0ng3rPa55w0rd
R1(config)# ssh version 2
R1(config)# line vty 0 4
R1(config-line)# transport input ssh
R1(config-line)# login local
```

The local database method has some limitations:

- User accounts must be configured locally on each device. In a large enterprise environment with multiple routers and switches to manage, it can take time to implement and change local databases on each device.

- The local database configuration provides no fallback authentication method. For example, what if the administrator forgets the username and password for that device? With no backup method available for authentication, password recovery becomes the only option.

A better solution is to have all devices refer to the same database of usernames and passwords from a central server.

Refer to
Online Course
for Illustration

AAA Components - 10.2.2

AAA stands for Authentication, Authorization, and Accounting. The AAA concept is similar to using a credit card, as shown in the figure. The credit card identifies who can use it, how much that user can spend, and keeps an account of what items or services the user purchased.

AAA provides the primary framework to set up access control on a network device. AAA is a way to control who is permitted to access a network (authenticate), what they can do while they are there (authorize), and to audit what actions they performed while accessing the network (accounting).

Refer to
Online Course
for Illustration

Authentication - 10.2.3

Local and server-based are two common methods of implementing AAA authentication.

Local AAA Authentication

Local AAA stores usernames and passwords locally in a network device such as the Cisco router. Users authenticate against the local database, as shown in figure. Local AAA is ideal for small networks.

Server-Based AAA Authentication

With the server-based method, the router accesses a central AAA server, as shown in figure. The AAA server contains the usernames and password for all users. The router uses either the Remote Authentication Dial-In User Service (RADIUS) or Terminal Access Controller Access Control System (TACACS+) protocols to communicate with the AAA server. When there are multiple routers and switches, server-based AAA is more appropriate.

Refer to
Online Course
for Illustration

Authorization - 10.2.4

AAA authorization is automatic and does not require users to perform additional steps after authentication. Authorization governs what users can and cannot do on the network after they are authenticated.

Authorization uses a set of attributes that describes the user's access to the network. These attributes are used by the AAA server to determine privileges and restrictions for that user, as shown in the figure.

Refer to
Online Course
for Illustration

Accounting - 10.2.5

AAA accounting collects and reports usage data. This data can be used for such purposes as auditing or billing. The collected data might include the start and stop connection times, executed commands, number of packets, and number of bytes.

A primary use of accounting is to combine it with AAA authentication. The AAA server keeps a detailed log of exactly what the authenticated user does on the device, as shown in the figure. This includes all EXEC and configuration commands issued by the user. The log contains numerous data fields, including the username, the date and time, and the actual command that was entered by the user. This information is useful when troubleshooting devices. It also provides evidence for when individuals perform malicious acts.

Refer to
Online Course
for Illustration

802.1X - 10.2.6

The IEEE 802.1X standard is a port-based access control and authentication protocol. This protocol restricts unauthorized workstations from connecting to a LAN through publicly accessible switch ports. The authentication server authenticates each workstation that is connected to a switch port before making available any services offered by the switch or the LAN.

With 802.1X port-based authentication, the devices in the network have specific roles, as shown in the figure.

- **Client (Supplicant)** - This is a device running 802.1X-compliant client software, which is available for wired or wireless devices.

- **Switch (Authenticator)** - The switch acts as an intermediary between the client and the authentication server. It requests identifying information from the client, verifies that information with the authentication server, and relays a response to the client. Another device that could act as authenticator is a wireless access point.

- **Authentication server** - The server validates the identity of the client and notifies the switch or wireless access point that the client is or is not authorized to access the LAN and switch services.

Go to the online
course to take the
quiz and exam.

Check Your Understanding - Access Control - 10.2.7

Layer 2 Security Threats

Refer to
Online Course
for Illustration

Layer 2 Vulnerabilities - 10.3.1

The previous two topics discussed securing endpoints. In this topic, you will continue to learn about ways to secure the LAN by focusing on the frames found in the data link layer (Layer 2) and the switch.

Recall that the OSI reference model is divided into seven layers which work independently of each other. The figure shows the function of each layer and the core elements that can be exploited.

Network administrators routinely implement security solutions to protect the elements in Layer 3 up through Layer 7. They use VPNs, firewalls, and IPS devices to protect these elements. However, if Layer 2 is compromised, then all the layers above it are also affected. For example, if a threat actor with access to the internal network captured Layer 2 frames, then all the security implemented on the layers above would be useless. The threat actor could cause a lot of damage on the Layer 2 LAN networking infrastructure.

Switch Attack Categories - 10.3.2

Security is only as strong as the weakest link in the system, and Layer 2 is considered to be that weak link. This is because LANs were traditionally under the administrative control of a single organization. We inherently trusted all persons and devices connected to our LAN. Today, with BYOD and more sophisticated attacks, our LANs have become more vulnerable to penetration. Therefore, in addition to protecting Layer 3 to Layer 7, network security professionals must also mitigate attacks to the Layer 2 LAN infrastructure.

The first step in mitigating attacks on the Layer 2 infrastructure is to understand the underlying operation of Layer 2 and the threats posed by the Layer 2 infrastructure.

Attacks against the Layer 2 LAN infrastructure are described in the table and are discussed in more detail later in this module.

Layer 2 Attacks

Category	Examples
MAC Table Attacks	Includes MAC address flooding attacks.
VLAN Attacks	Includes VLAN hopping and VLAN double-tagging attacks. It also includes attacks between devices on a common VLAN.
DHCP Attacks	Includes DHCP starvation and DHCP spoofing attacks.
ARP Attacks	Includes ARP spoofing and ARP poisoning attacks.
Address Spoofing Attacks	Includes MAC address and IP address spoofing attacks.
STP Attacks	Includes Spanning Tree Protocol manipulation attacks.

Switch Attack Mitigation Techniques - 10.3.3

The table provides an overview of Cisco solutions to help mitigate Layer 2 attacks.

Layer 2 Attack Mitigation

Solution	Description
Port Security	Prevents many types of attacks including MAC address flooding attacks and DHCP starvation attacks.
DHCP Snooping	Prevents DHCP starvation and DHCP spoofing attacks.
Dynamic ARP Inspection (DAI)	Prevents ARP spoofing and ARP poisoning attacks.
IP Source Guard (IPSG)	Prevents MAC and IP address spoofing attacks.

These Layer 2 solutions will not be effective if the management protocols are not secured. For example, the management protocols Syslog, Simple Network Management Protocol (SNMP), Trivial File Transfer Protocol (TFTP), telnet, File Transfer Protocol (FTP) and most other common protocols are insecure; therefore, the following strategies are recommended:

- Always use secure variants of these protocols such as SSH, Secure Copy Protocol (SCP), Secure FTP (SFTP), and Secure Socket Layer/Transport Layer Security (SSL/TLS).

- Consider using out-of-band management network to manage devices.

- Use a dedicated management VLAN where nothing but management traffic resides.

- Use ACLs to filter unwanted access.

Go to the online course to take the quiz and exam.

Check Your Understanding - Layer 2 Security Threats - 10.3.4

MAC Address Table Attack - 10.4

Switch Operation Review - 10.4.1

In this topic, the focus is still on switches, specifically their MAC address tables and how these tables are vulnerable to attacks.

Recall that to make forwarding decisions, a Layer 2 LAN switch builds a table based on the source MAC addresses in received frames. Shown in the figure, this is called a MAC address table. MAC address tables are stored in memory and are used to more efficiently forward frames.

```
S1# show mac address-table dynamic

         Mac Address Table
-------------------------------------------

Vlan    Mac Address       Type       Ports
----    -----------       --------   -----

   1    0001.9717.22e0    DYNAMIC    Fa0/4

   1    000a.f38e.74b3    DYNAMIC    Fa0/1

   1    0090.0c23.ceca    DYNAMIC    Fa0/3

   1    00d0.ba07.8499    DYNAMIC    Fa0/2

S1#
```

Refer to
Online Course
for Illustration

MAC Address Table Flooding - 10.4.2

All MAC tables have a fixed size and consequently, a switch can run out of resources in which to store MAC addresses. MAC address flooding attacks take advantage of this limitation by bombarding the switch with fake source MAC addresses until the switch MAC address table is full.

When this occurs, the switch treats the frame as an unknown unicast and begins to flood all incoming traffic out all ports on the same VLAN without referencing the MAC table. This condition now allows a threat actor to capture all of the frames sent from one host to another on the local LAN or local VLAN.

Note: Traffic is flooded only within the local LAN or VLAN. The threat actor can only capture traffic within the local LAN or VLAN to which the threat actor is connected.

The figure shows how a threat actor can easily use the network attack tool **macof** to overflow a MAC address table.

If the threat actor stops **macof** from running or is discovered and stopped, the switch eventually ages out the older MAC address entries from the table and begins to act like a switch again.

MAC Address Table Attack Mitigation - 10.4.3

What makes tools such as **macof** so dangerous is that an attacker can create a MAC table overflow attack very quickly. For instance, a Catalyst 6500 switch can store 132,000 MAC addresses in its MAC address table. A tool such as **macof** can flood a switch with up to 8,000 bogus frames per second; creating a MAC address table overflow attack in a matter of a few seconds. The example shows a sample output of the **macof** command on a Linux host.

```
# macof -i eth1

36:a1:48:63:81:70 15:26:8d:4d:28:f8 0.0.0.0.26413 > 0.0.0.0.49492: S
1094191437:1094191437(0) win 512

16:e8:8:0:4d:9c da:4d:bc:7c:ef:be 0.0.0.0.61376 > 0.0.0.0.47523: S
446486755:446486755(0) win 512

18:2a:de:56:38:71 33:af:9b:5:a6:97 0.0.0.0.20086 > 0.0.0.0.6728: S
105051945:105051945(0) win 512

e7:5c:97:42:ec:1 83:73:1a:32:20:93 0.0.0.0.45282 > 0.0.0.0.24898: S
1838062028:1838062028(0) win 512

62:69:d3:1c:79:ef 80:13:35:4:cb:d0 0.0.0.0.11587 > 0.0.0.0.7723: S
1792413296:1792413296(0) win 512

c5:a:b7:3e:3c:7a 3a:ee:c0:23:4a:fe 0.0.0.0.19784 > 0.0.0.0.57433: S
1018924173:1018924173(0) win 512

88:43:ee:51:c7:68 b4:8d:ec:3e:14:bb 0.0.0.0.283 > 0.0.0.0.11466: S
727776406:727776406(0) win 512

b8:7a:7a:2d:2c:ae c2:fa:2d:7d:e7:bf 0.0.0.0.32650 > 0.0.0.0.11324: S
605528173:605528173(0) win 512

e0:d8:1e:74:1:e 57:98:b6:5a:fa:de 0.0.0.0.36346 > 0.0.0.0.55700: S
2128143986:2128143986(0) win 512
```

Another reason why these attack tools are dangerous is because they not only affect the local switch, they can also affect other connected Layer 2 switches. When the MAC address table of a switch is full, it starts flooding out all ports including those connected to other Layer 2 switches.

To mitigate MAC address table overflow attacks, network administrators must implement port security. Port security will only allow a specified number of source MAC addresses to be learned on the port. Port security is further discussed in another module.

Go to the online course to take the quiz and exam.

Check Your Understanding - MAC Address Table Attacks - 10.4.4

LAN Attacks - 10.5

Refer to **Video** in online course

Video - VLAN and DHCP Attacks - 10.5.1

This topic investigates the many different types of LAN attacks and their mitigation techniques. Like the previous topics, these attacks tend to be specific to switches and Layer 2.

Click Play in the figure to view a video about VLAN and DHCP attacks.

Refer to **Online Course** for Illustration

VLAN Hopping Attacks - 10.5.2

A VLAN hopping attack enables traffic from one VLAN to be seen by another VLAN without the aid of a router. In a basic VLAN hopping attack, the threat actor configures a host to act like a switch to take advantage of the automatic trunking port feature enabled by default on most switch ports.

The threat actor configures the host to spoof 802.1Q signaling and Cisco-proprietary Dynamic Trunking Protocol (DTP) signaling to trunk with the connecting switch. If successful, the switch establishes a trunk link with the host, as shown in the figure. Now the threat actor can access all the VLANs on the switch. The threat actor can send and receive traffic on any VLAN, effectively hopping between VLANs.

Refer to **Interactive Graphic** in online course

Refer to **Online Course** for Illustration

VLAN Double-Tagging Attack - 10.5.3

A threat actor in specific situations could embed a hidden 802.1Q tag inside the frame that already has an 802.1Q tag. This tag allows the frame to go to a VLAN that the original 802.1Q tag did not specify.

Click each step for an example and explanation of a double-tagging attack.

Step 1

The threat actor sends a double-tagged 802.1Q frame to the switch. The outer header has the VLAN tag of the threat actor, which is the same as the native VLAN of the trunk port. For the purposes of this example, assume that this is VLAN 10. The inner tag is the victim VLAN, in this example, VLAN 20.

Step 2

The frame arrives on the first switch, which looks at the first 4-byte 802.1Q tag. The switch sees that the frame is destined for VLAN 10, which is the native VLAN. The switch forwards the packet out all VLAN 10 ports after stripping the VLAN 10 tag. The frame is not retagged because it is part of the native VLAN. At this point, the VLAN 20 tag is still intact and has not been inspected by the first switch.

Step 3

The frame arrives at the second switch which has no knowledge that it was supposed to be for VLAN 10. Native VLAN traffic is not tagged by the sending switch as specified in the

802.1Q specification. The second switch looks only at the inner 802.1Q tag that the threat actor inserted and sees that the frame is destined for VLAN 20, the target VLAN. The second switch sends the frame on to the target or floods it, depending on whether there is an existing MAC address table entry for the target.

A VLAN double-tagging attack is unidirectional and works only when the attacker is connected to a port residing in the same VLAN as the native VLAN of the trunk port. The idea is that double tagging allows the attacker to send data to hosts or servers on a VLAN that otherwise would be blocked by some type of access control configuration. Presumably the return traffic will also be permitted, thus giving the attacker the ability to communicate with devices on the normally blocked VLAN.

VLAN Attack Mitigation

VLAN hopping and VLAN double-tagging attacks can be prevented by implementing the following trunk security guidelines, as discussed in a previous module:

- Disable trunking on all access ports.

- Disable auto trunking on trunk links so that trunks must be manually enabled.

- Be sure that the native VLAN is only used for trunk links.

Refer to
Online Course
for Illustration

DHCP Messages - 10.5.4

DHCP servers dynamically provide IP configuration information including IP address, subnet mask, default gateway, DNS servers, and more to clients. A review of the sequence of the DHCP message exchange between client and server is shown in the figure.

Refer to
Interactive Graphic
in online course

DHCP Attacks - 10.5.5

Refer to
Online Course
for Illustration

Two types of DHCP attacks are DHCP starvation and DHCP spoofing. Both attacks are mitigated by implementing DHCP snooping.

DHCP Starvation Attack

The goal of the DHCP Starvation attack is to create a DoS for connecting clients. DHCP starvation attacks require an attack tool such as Gobbler.

Gobbler has the ability to look at the entire scope of leasable IP addresses and tries to lease them all. Specifically, it creates DHCP discovery messages with bogus MAC addresses.

DHCP Spoofing Attack

A DHCP spoofing attack occurs when a rogue DHCP server is connected to the network and provides false IP configuration parameters to legitimate clients. A rogue server can provide a variety of misleading information:

- **Wrong default gateway** - The rogue server provides an invalid gateway or the IP address of its host to create a man-in-the-middle attack. This may go entirely undetected as the intruder intercepts the data flow through the network.

- **Wrong DNS server** - The rogue server provides an incorrect DNS server address pointing the user to a nefarious website.

■ **Wrong IP address** - The rogue server provides an invalid IP address effectively creating a DoS attack on the DHCP client.

Click each step for an example and explanation of a DHCP spoofing attack.

Step 1

Threat Actor Connects Rogue DHCP Server

A threat actor successfully connects a rogue DHCP server to a switch port on the same subnet and VLANs as the target clients. The goal of the rogue server is to provide clients with false IP configuration information.

Step 2

Client Broadcasts DHCP Discovery Messages

A legitimate client connects to the network and requires IP configuration parameters. Therefore, the client broadcasts a DHCP Discovery request looking for a response from a DHCP server. Both servers will receive the message and respond.

Step 3

Legitimate and Rogue DHCP Reply

The legitimate DHCP server responds with valid IP configuration parameters. However, the rogue server also responds with a DHCP offer containing IP configuration parameters defined by the threat actor. The client will reply to the first offer received.

Step 4

Client Accepts Rogue DHCP Offer

The rogue offer was received first, and therefore, the client broadcasts a DHCP request accepting the IP parameters defined by the threat actor. The legitimate and rogue server will receive the request.

Step 5

Rogue Server Acknowledges

The rogue server unicasts a reply to the client to acknowledge its request. The legitimate server will cease communicating with the client.

Video - ARP Attacks, STP Attacks, and CDP Reconnaissance - 10.5.6

Click Play in the figure to view a video about VLAN and DHCP attacks.

ARP Attacks - 10.5.7

Recall that hosts broadcast ARP Requests to determine the MAC address of a host with a particular IP address. This is typically done to discover the MAC address of the default gateway. All hosts on the subnet receive and process the ARP Request. The host with the matching IP address in the ARP Request sends an ARP Reply.

According to the ARP RFC, a client is allowed to send an unsolicited ARP Reply called a "gratuitous ARP." When a host sends a gratuitous ARP, other hosts on the subnet store the MAC address and IP address contained in the gratuitous ARP in their ARP tables.

The problem is that an attacker can send a gratuitous ARP message containing a spoofed MAC address to a switch, and the switch would update its MAC table accordingly. Therefore, any host can claim to be the owner of any IP and MAC address combination they choose. In a typical attack, a threat actor can send unsolicited ARP Replies to other hosts on the subnet with the MAC Address of the threat actor and the IP address of the default gateway.

There are many tools available on the internet to create ARP man-in-the-middle attacks including dsniff, Cain & Abel, ettercap, Yersinia, and others. IPv6 uses ICMPv6 Neighbor Discovery Protocol for Layer 2 address resolution. IPv6 includes strategies to mitigate Neighbor Advertisement spoofing, similar to the way IPv6 prevents a spoofed ARP Reply.

ARP spoofing and ARP poisoning are mitigated by implementing DAI.

Click each step for an example and explanation of ARP spoofing and ARP poisoning.

Step 1

Normal State with Converged MAC Tables

Each device has an accurate MAC table with the correct IP and MAC addresses for the other devices on the LAN.

Step 2

ARP Spoofing Attack

The threat actor sends two spoofed gratuitous ARP Replies in an attempt to replace R1 as the default gateway:

1. The first one informs all devices on the LAN that the threat actor's MAC address (CC:CC:CC) maps to R1's IP address, 10.0.0.1.

2. The second one informs all devices on the LAN that the threat actor's MAC address (CC:CC:CC) maps to PC1's IP address, 10.0.0.11.

Step 3

ARP Poisoning Attack with Man-in-the-Middle Attack

R1 and PC1 remove the correct entry for each other's MAC address and replace it with PC2's MAC address. The threat actor has now poisoned the ARP caches of all devices on the subnet. ARP poisoning leads to various man-in-the-middle attacks, posing a serious security threat to the network.

Address Spoofing Attack - 10.5.8

Refer to
Online Course
for Illustration

IP addresses and MAC addresses can be spoofed for a variety of reasons. IP address spoofing is when a threat actor hijacks a valid IP address of another device on the subnet, or uses a random IP address. IP address spoofing is difficult to mitigate, especially when it is used inside a subnet in which the IP belongs.

MAC address spoofing attacks occur when the threat actors alter the MAC address of their host to match another known MAC address of a target host. The attacking host then sends a frame throughout the network with the newly-configured MAC address. When the switch receives the frame, it examines the source MAC address. The switch overwrites the current MAC table entry and assigns the MAC address to the new port, as shown in the figure. It then inadvertently forwards frames destined for the target host to the attacking host.

When the target host sends traffic, the switch will correct the error, realigning the MAC address to the original port. To stop the switch from returning the port assignment to its correct state, the threat actor can create a program or script that will constantly send frames to the switch so that the switch maintains the incorrect or spoofed information. There is no security mechanism at Layer 2 that allows a switch to verify the source of MAC addresses, which is what makes it so vulnerable to spoofing.

IP and MAC address spoofing can be mitigated by implementing IPSG.

Refer to
Online Course
for Illustration

STP Attack - 10.5.9

Network attackers can manipulate the Spanning Tree Protocol (STP) to conduct an attack by spoofing the root bridge and changing the topology of a network. Attackers can make their hosts appear as root bridges; and therefore, capture all traffic for the immediate switched domain.

To conduct an STP manipulation attack, the attacking host broadcasts STP bridge protocol data units (BPDUs) containing configuration and topology changes that will force spanning-tree recalculations, as shown in the figure. The BPDUs sent by the attacking host announce a lower bridge priority in an attempt to be elected as the root bridge.

If successful, the attacking host becomes the root bridge, as shown in the figure, and can now capture a variety of frames that would otherwise not be accessible.

This STP attack is mitigated by implementing BPDU Guard on all access ports. BPDU Guard is discussed in more detail later in the course.

Refer to
Online Course
for Illustration

CDP Reconnaissance - 10.5.10

The Cisco Discovery Protocol (CDP) is a proprietary Layer 2 link discovery protocol. It is enabled on all Cisco devices by default. CDP can automatically discover other CDP-enabled devices and help auto-configure their connection. Network administrators also use CDP to help configure and troubleshoot network devices.

CDP information is sent out CDP-enabled ports in periodic, unencrypted broadcasts. CDP information includes the IP address of the device, IOS software version, platform, capabilities, and the native VLAN. The device receiving the CDP message updates its CDP database.

CDP information is extremely useful in network troubleshooting. For example, CDP can be used to verify Layer 1 and 2 connectivity. If an administrator cannot ping a directly connected interface, but still receives CDP information, then the problem is most likely related to the Layer 3 configuration.

However, the information provided by CDP can also be used by a threat actor to discover network infrastructure vulnerabilities.

In the figure, a sample Wireshark capture displays the contents of a CDP packet. The attacker is able to identify the Cisco IOS software version used by the device. This allows the attacker to determine whether there were any security vulnerabilities specific to that particular version of IOS.

CDP broadcasts are sent unencrypted and unauthenticated. Therefore, an attacker could interfere with the network infrastructure by sending crafted CDP frames containing bogus device information to directly-connected Cisco devices.

To mitigate the exploitation of CDP, limit the use of CDP on devices or ports. For example, disable CDP on edge ports that connect to untrusted devices.

To disable CDP globally on a device, use the **no cdp run** global configuration mode command. To enable CDP globally, use the **cdp run** global configuration command.

To disable CDP on a port, use the **no cdp enable** interface configuration command. To enable CDP on a port, use the **cdp enable** interface configuration command.

Note: Link Layer Discovery Protocol (LLDP) is also vulnerable to reconnaissance attacks. Configure **no lldp run** to disable LLDP globally. To disable LLDP on the interface, configure **no lldp transmit** and **no lldp receive**.

> Go to the online course to take the quiz and exam.

Check Your Understanding - LAN Attacks - 10.5.11

Module Practice and Quiz - 10.6

What did I learn in this module? - 10.6.1

Endpoints are particularly susceptible to malware-related attacks that originate through email or web browsing, such as DDOS, date breaches, and malware. These endpoints have typically used traditional host-based security features, such as antivirus/antimalware, host-based firewalls, and host-based intrusion prevention systems (HIPSs). Endpoints are best protected by a combination of NAC, host-based AMP software, an email security appliance (ESA), and a web security appliance (WSA). Cisco WSA can perform blacklisting of URLs, URL-filtering, malware scanning, URL categorization, Web application filtering, and encryption and decryption of web traffic.

AAA controls who is permitted to access a network (authenticate), what they can do while they are there (authorize), and to audit what actions they performed while accessing the network (accounting). Authorization uses a set of attributes that describes the user's access to the network. Accounting is combined with AAA authentication. The AAA server keeps a detailed log of exactly what the authenticated user does on the device. The IEEE 802.1X standard is a port-based access control and authentication protocol that restricts unauthorized workstations from connecting to a LAN through publicly accessible switch ports.

If Layer 2 is compromised, then all layers above it are also affected. The first step in mitigating attacks on the Layer 2 infrastructure is to understand the underlying operation of Layer 2 and the Layer 2 solutions: Port Security, DHCP Snooping, DAI, and IPSG. These won't work unless management protocols are secured.

MAC address flooding attacks bombard the switch with fake source MAC addresses until the switch MAC address table is full. At this point, the switch treats the frame as an unknown unicast and begins to flood all incoming traffic out all ports on the same VLAN without referencing the MAC table. The threat actor can now capture all of the frames sent from one host to another on the local LAN or local VLAN. The threat actor uses **macof** to rapidly generate many random source and destination MAC and IP. To mitigate MAC table overflow attacks, network administrators must implement port security.

A VLAN hopping attack enables traffic from one VLAN to be seen by another VLAN without the aid of a router. The threat actor configures a host to act like a switch to take advantage of the automatic trunking port feature enabled by default on most switch ports.

A VLAN double-tagging attack is unidirectional and works only when the threat actor is connected to a port residing in the same VLAN as the native VLAN of the trunk port. Double tagging allows the threat actor to send data to hosts or servers on a VLAN that otherwise would be blocked by some type of access control configuration. Return traffic will also be permitted, letting the threat actor communicate with devices on the normally blocked VLAN.

VLAN hopping and VLAN double-tagging attacks can be prevented by implementing the following trunk security guidelines:

- Disable trunking on all access ports.

- Disable auto trunking on trunk links so that trunks must be manually enabled.

- Be sure that the native VLAN is only used for trunk links.

DHCP Attack: DHCP servers dynamically provide IP configuration information including IP address, subnet mask, default gateway, DNS servers, and more to clients. Two types of DHCP attacks are DHCP starvation and DHCP spoofing. Both attacks are mitigated by implementing DHCP snooping.

ARP Attack: A threat actor sends a gratuitous ARP message containing a spoofed MAC address to a switch, and the switch updates its MAC table accordingly. Now the threat actor sends unsolicited ARP Replies to other hosts on the subnet with the MAC Address of the threat actor and the IP address of the default gateway. ARP spoofing and ARP poisoning are mitigated by implementing DAI.

Address Spoofing Attack: IP address spoofing is when a threat actor hijacks a valid IP address of another device on the subnet or uses a random IP address. MAC address spoofing attacks occur when the threat actors alter the MAC address of their host to match another known MAC address of a target host. IP and MAC address spoofing can be mitigated by implementing IPSG.

STP Attack: Threat actors manipulate STP to conduct an attack by spoofing the root bridge and changing the topology of a network. Threat actors make their hosts appear as root bridges; therefore, capturing all traffic for the immediate switched domain. This STP attack is mitigated by implementing BPDU Guard on all access ports

CDP Reconnaissance: CDP information is sent out CDP-enabled ports in periodic, unencrypted broadcasts. CDP information includes the IP address of the device, IOS software version, platform, capabilities, and the native VLAN. The device receiving the CDP message updates its CDP database. the information provided by CDP can also be used by a threat actor to discover network infrastructure vulnerabilities. To mitigate the exploitation of CDP, limit the use of CDP on devices or ports.

Go to the online course to take the quiz and exam.

Chapter Quiz - LAN Security Concepts

Your Chapter Notes

CHAPTER 11

Switch Security Configuration

Introduction - 11.0

Why should I take this module? - 11.0.1

Welcome to Switch Security Configuration!

An important part of your responsibility as a network professional is to keep the network secure. Most of the time we only think about security attacks coming from outside the network, but threats can come from within the network as well. These threats can range any-where from an employee innocently adding an Ethernet switch to the corporate network so they can have more ports, to malicious attacks caused by a disgruntled employee. It is your job to keep the network safe and ensuring that business operations continue uncompromised.

How do we keep the network safe and stable? How do we protect it from malicious attacks from within the network? How do we make sure employees are not adding switches, servers and other devices to the network that might compromise network operations?

This module is your introduction to keeping your network secure from within!

What will I learn in this module? - 11.0.2

Module Title: Switch Security Configuration

Module Objective: Configure switch security to mitigate LAN attacks.

Topic Title	Topic Objective
Implement Port Security	Implement port security to mitigate MAC address table attacks.
Mitigate VLAN Attacks	Explain how to configure DTP and native VLAN to mitigate VLAN attacks.
Mitigate DHCP Attacks	Explain how to configure DHCP snooping to mitigate DHCP attacks.
Mitigate ARP Attacks	Explain how to configure ARP inspection to mitigate ARP attacks.
Mitigate STP Attacks	Explain how to configure PortFast and BPDU Guard to mitigate STP attacks.

Implement Port Security - 11.1

Secure Unused Ports - 11.1.1

Layer 2 devices are considered to be the weakest link in a company's security infrastructure. Layer 2 attacks are some of the easiest for hackers to deploy but these threats can also be mitigated with some common Layer 2 solutions.

All switch ports (interfaces) should be secured before the switch is deployed for production use. How a port is secured depends on its function.

A simple method that many administrators use to help secure the network from unauthorized access is to disable all unused ports on a switch. For example, if a Catalyst 2960 switch has 24 ports and there are three Fast Ethernet connections in use, it is good practice to disable the 21 unused ports. Navigate to each unused port and issue the Cisco IOS **shutdown** command. If a port must be reactivated at a later time, it can be enabled with the **no shutdown** command.

To configure a range of ports, use the **interface range** command.

```
Switch(config)# interface range type module/first-number - last-number
```

For example, to shutdown ports for Fa0/8 through Fa0/24 on S1, you would enter the following command.

```
S1(config)# interface range fa0/8 - 24

S1(config-if-range)# shutdown

%LINK-5-CHANGED: Interface FastEthernet0/8, changed state to
administratively down

(output omitted)

%LINK-5-CHANGED: Interface FastEthernet0/24, changed state to
administratively down

S1(config-if-range)#
```

Refer to
Online Course
for Illustration

Mitigate MAC Address Table Attacks - 11.1.2

The simplest and most effective method to prevent MAC address table overflow attacks is to enable port security.

Port security limits the number of valid MAC addresses allowed on a port. It allows an administrator to manually configure MAC addresses for a port or to permit the switch to dynamically learn a limited number of MAC addresses. When a port configured with port security receives a frame, the source MAC address of the frame is compared to the list of secure source MAC addresses that were manually configured or dynamically learned on the port.

By limiting the number of permitted MAC addresses on a port to one, port security can be used to control unauthorized access to the network, as shown in the figure.

Enable Port Security - 11.1.3

Notice in the example, the **switchport port-security** command was rejected. This is because port security can only be configured on manually configured access ports or manually configured trunk ports. By default, Layer 2 switch ports are set to dynamic auto (trunking on). Therefore, in the example, the port is configured with the **switchport mode access** interface configuration command.

Note: Trunk port security is beyond the scope of this course.

```
S1(config)# interface f0/1

S1(config-if)# switchport port-security

Command rejected: FastEthernet0/1 is a dynamic port.

S1(config-if)# switchport mode access

S1(config-if)# switchport port-security

S1(config-if)# end

S1#
```

Use the **show port-security interface** command to display the current port security settings for FastEthernet 0/1, as shown in the example. Notice how port security is enabled, the violation mode is shutdown, and how the maximum number of MAC addresses is 1. If a device is connected to the port, the switch will automatically add the device's MAC address as a secure MAC. In this example, no device is connected to the port.

```
S1# show port-security interface f0/1

Port Security                 : Enabled

Port Status                   : Secure-shutdown

Violation Mode                : Shutdown

Aging Time                    : 0 mins

Aging Type                    : Absolute

SecureStatic Address Aging    : Disabled

Maximum MAC Addresses         : 1

Total MAC Addresses           : 0

Configured MAC Addresses      : 0

Sticky MAC Addresses          : 0

Last Source Address:Vlan      : 0000.0000.0000:0

Security Violation Count      : 0

S1#
```

Note: If an active port is configured with the **switchport port-security** command and more than one device is connected to that port, the port will transition to the error-disabled state. This condition is discussed later in this topic.

After port security is enabled, other port security specifics can be configured, as shown in the example.

```
S1(config-if)# switchport port-security ?

  aging       Port-security aging commands

  mac-address Secure mac address
```

```
    maximum       Max secure addresses

    violation     Security violation mode

    <cr>
S1(config-if)# switchport port-security
```

Limit and Learn MAC Addresses - 11.1.4

To set the maximum number of MAC addresses allowed on a port, use the following command:

```
Switch(config-if)# switchport port-security maximum value
```

The default port security value is 1. The maximum number of secure MAC addresses that can be configured depends the switch and the IOS. In this example, the maximum is 8192.

```
S1(config)# interface f0/1

S1(config-if)# switchport port-security maximum ?

   <1-8192>  Maximum addresses

S1(config-if)# switchport port-security maximum
```

The switch can be configured to learn about MAC addresses on a secure port in one of three ways:

1. Manually Configured

The administrator manually configures a static MAC address(es) by using the following command for each secure MAC address on the port:

```
Switch(config-if)# switchport port-security mac-address mac-address
```

2. Dynamically Learned

When the **switchport port-security** command is entered, the current source MAC for the device connected to the port is automatically secured but is not added to the startup configuration. If the switch is rebooted, the port will have to re-learn the device's MAC address.

3. Dynamically Learned – Sticky

The administrator can enable the switch to dynamically learn the MAC address and "stick" them to the running configuration by using the following command:

```
Switch(config-if)# switchport port-security mac-address sticky
```

Saving the running configuration will commit the dynamically learned MAC address to NVRAM.

The following example demonstrates a complete port security configuration for FastEthernet 0/1. The administrator specifies a maximum of 4 MAC addresses, manually configures one secure MAC address, and then configures the port to dynamically learn additional secure MAC addresses up to the 4 secure MAC address maximum. Use the **show port-security interface** and the **show port-security address** command to verify the configuration.

```
S1(config)# interface fa0/1
S1(config-if)# switchport mode access
S1(config-if)# switchport port-security
S1(config-if)# switchport port-security maximum 4
S1(config-if)# switchport port-security mac-address aaaa.bbbb.1234
S1(config-if)# switchport port-security mac-address sticky
S1(config-if)# end
S1# show port-security interface fa0/1
Port Security               : Enabled
Port Status                 : Secure-up
Violation Mode              : Shutdown
Aging Time                  : 0 mins
Aging Type                  : Absolute
SecureStatic Address Aging  : Disabled
Maximum MAC Addresses       : 4
Total MAC Addresses         : 1
Configured MAC Addresses    : 1
Sticky MAC Addresses        : 0
Last Source Address:Vlan    : 0000.0000.0000:0
Security Violation Count    : 0
S1# show port-security address
              Secure Mac Address Table
-------------------------------------------------------------------------
Vlan    Mac Address      Type              Ports    Remaining Age
                                                     (mins)
----    -----------      ----              -----    --------------
   1    aaaa.bbbb.1234   SecureConfigured  Fa0/1        -
-------------------------------------------------------------------------
Total Addresses in System (excluding one mac per port)    : 0
Max Addresses limit in System (excluding one mac per port) : 8192

S1#
```

Port Security Aging - 11.1.5

Port security aging can be used to set the aging time for static and dynamic secure addresses on a port. Two types of aging are supported per port:

- **Absolute** - The secure addresses on the port are deleted after the specified aging time.

- **Inactivity** - The secure addresses on the port are deleted only if they are inactive for the specified aging time.

Use aging to remove secure MAC addresses on a secure port without manually deleting the existing secure MAC addresses. Aging time limits can also be increased to ensure past secure MAC addresses remain, even while new MAC addresses are added. Aging of statically configured secure addresses can be enabled or disabled on a per-port basis.

Use the **switchport port-security aging** command to enable or disable static aging for the secure port, or to set the aging time or type.

```
Switch(config-if)# switchport port-security aging { static | time time |
type {absolute | inactivity}}
```

The parameters for the command are described in the table.

Parameter	Description
`static`	Enable aging for statically configured secure addresses on this port.
`time` *time*	Specify the aging time for this port. The range is 0 to 1440 minutes. If the time is 0, aging is disabled for this port.
`type` `absolute`	Set the absolute aging time. All the secure addresses on this port age out exactly after the time (in minutes) specified and are removed from the secure address list.
`type` `inactivity`	Set the inactivity aging type. The secure addresses on this port age out only if there is no data traffic from the secure source address for the specified time period.

Note: MAC addresses are shown as 24 bits for simplicity.

The example shows an administrator configuring the aging type to 10 minutes of inactivity and by using the **show port-security interface** command to verify the configuration.

```
S1(config)# interface fa0/1
S1(config-if)# switchport port-security aging time 10
S1(config-if)# switchport port-security aging type inactivity
S1(config-if)# end
S1# show port-security interface fa0/1
Port Security                 : Enabled
Port Status                   : Secure-shutdown
Violation Mode                : Restrict
Aging Time                    : 10 mins
Aging Type                    : Inactivity
```

```
SecureStatic Address Aging   : Disabled

Maximum MAC Addresses        : 4

Total MAC Addresses          : 1

Configured MAC Addresses     : 1

Sticky MAC Addresses         : 0

Last Source Address:Vlan     : 0050.56be.e4dd:1

Security Violation Count     : 1
```

Port Security Violation Modes - 11.1.6

If the MAC address of a device attached to the port differs from the list of secure addresses, then a port violation occurs. By default, the port enters the error-disabled state.

To set the port security violation mode, use the following command:

```
Switch(config-if)# switchport port-security violation { protect |
restrict | shutdown}
```

The following tables show how a switch reacts based on the configured violation mode.

Security Violation Mode Descriptions

Mode	Description
shutdown (default)	The port transitions to the error-disabled state immediately, turns off the port LED, and sends a syslog message. It increments the violation counter. When a secure port is in the error-disabled state, an administrator must re-enable it by entering the **shutdown** and **no shutdown** commands.
restrict	The port drops packets with unknown source addresses until you remove a sufficient number of secure MAC addresses to drop below the maximum value or increase the maximum value. This mode causes the Security Violation counter to increment and generates a syslog message.
protect	This is the least secure of the security violation modes. The port drops packets with unknown MAC source addresses until you remove a sufficient number of secure MAC addresses to drop below the maximum value or increase the maximum value. No syslog message is sent.

Security Violation Mode Comparison

Violation Mode	Discards Offending Traffic	Sends Syslog Message	Increase Violation Counter	Shuts Down Port
Protect	Yes	No	No	No
Restrict	Yes	Yes	Yes	No
Shutdown	Yes	Yes	Yes	Yes

The following example shows an administrator changing the security violation to "restrict". The output of the **show port-security interface** command confirms that the change has been made.

```
S1(config)# interface f0/1
S1(config-if)# switchport port-security violation restrict
S1(config-if)# end
S1#
S1# show port-security interface f0/1
Port Security               : Enabled
Port Status                 : Secure-shutdown
Violation Mode              : Restrict
Aging Time                  : 0 mins
Aging Type                  : Absolute
SecureStatic Address Aging  : Disabled
Maximum MAC Addresses       : 4
Total MAC Addresses         : 1
Configured MAC Addresses    : 1
Sticky MAC Addresses        : 0
Last Source Address:Vlan    : 0050.56be.e4dd:1
Security Violation Count    : 1
S1#
```

Ports in error-disabled State - 11.1.7

When a port is shutdown and placed in the error-disabled state, no traffic is sent or received on that port. A series of port security related messages display on the console, as shown in the following example.

```
*Sep 20 06:44:54.966: %PM-4-ERR_DISABLE: psecure-violation error
detected on Fa0/18, putting Fa0/18 in err-disable state

*Sep 20 06:44:54.966: %PORT_SECURITY-2-PSECURE_VIOLATION: Security
violation occurred, caused by MAC address 000c.292b.4c75 on port
FastEthernet0/18.

*Sep 20 06:44:55.973: %LINEPROTO-5-PPDOWN: Line protocol on Interface
FastEthernet0/18, changed state to down

*Sep 20 06:44:56.971: %LINK-3-UPDOWN: Interface FastEthernet0/18,
changed state to down
```

Note: The port protocol and link status are changed to down and the port LED is turned off.

In the example, the **show interface** command identifies the port status as **err-disabled**. The output of the **show port-security interface** command now shows the port status as **secure-shutdown**. The Security Violation counter increments by 1.

```
S1# show interface fa0/18

FastEthernet0/18 is down, line protocol is down (err-disabled)

(output omitted)

S1# show port-security interface fa0/18

Port Security            : Enabled

Port Status              : Secure-shutdown

Violation Mode           : Shutdown

Aging Time               : 0 mins

Aging Type               : Absolute

SecureStatic Address Aging : Disabled

Maximum MAC Addresses    : 1

Total MAC Addresses      : 1

Configured MAC Addresses : 1

Sticky MAC Addresses     : 0

Last Source Address:Vlan : c025.5cd7.ef01:1

Security Violation Count : 1

S1#
```

The administrator should determine what caused the security violation If an unauthorized device is connected to a secure port, the security threat is eliminated before re-enabling the port.

To re-enable the port, first use the **shutdown** command, then, use the **no shutdown** command to make the port operational, as shown in the example.

```
S1(config)# interface fa0/18

S1(config-if)# shutdown

*Sep 20  07:11:18.845: %LINK-5-CHANGED: Interface FastEthernet0/18,
changed state to administratively down

S1(config-if)# no shutdown

*Sep 20  07:11:32.006: %LINK-3-UPDOWN: Interface FastEthernet0/18,
changed state to up

*Sep 20  07:11:33.013: %LINEPROTO-5-UPDOWN: Line protocol on Interface
FastEthernet0/18, changed state to up

S1(config-if)#
```

Verify Port Security - 11.1.8

After configuring port security on a switch, check each interface to verify that the port security is set correctly, and check to ensure that the static MAC addresses have been configured correctly.

Port Security for All Interfaces

To display port security settings for the switch, use the **show port-security** command. The example indicates that all 24 interfaces are configured with the **switchport port-security** command because the maximum allowed is 1 and the violation mode is shutdown. No devices are connected. Therefore , the CurrentAddr (Count) is 0 for each interface.

```
S1# show port-security

Secure Port MaxSecureAddr CurrentAddr SecurityViolation   Security Action
               (Count)      (Count)      (Count)
-----------------------------------------------------------------------------
      Fa0/1        1            0            0                 Shutdown
      Fa0/2        1            0            0                 Shutdown
      Fa0/3        1            0            0                 Shutdown
(output omitted)
      Fa0/24       1            0            0                 Shutdown
-----------------------------------------------------------------------------

Total Addresses in System (excluding one mac per port)      : 0
Max Addresses limit in System (excluding one mac per port)  : 4096
Switch#
```

Port Security for a Specific Interface

Use the **show port-security interface** command to view details for a specific interface, as shown previously and in this example.

```
S1# show port-security interface fastethernet 0/18
Port Security               : Enabled
Port Status                 : Secure-up
Violation Mode              : Shutdown
Aging Time                  : 0 mins
Aging Type                  : Absolute
SecureStatic Address Aging  : Disabled
Maximum MAC Addresses       : 1
Total MAC Addresses         : 1
Configured MAC Addresses    : 0
Sticky MAC Addresses        : 0
Last Source Address:Vlan    : 0025.83e6.4b01:1
Security Violation Count    : 0
S1#
```

Verify Learned MAC Addresses

To verify that MAC addresses are "sticking" to the configuration, use the **show run** command as shown in the example for FastEthernet 0/19.

```
S1# show run | begin interface FastEthernet0/19

interface FastEthernet0/19

switchport mode access

switchport port-security maximum 10

switchport port-security

switchport port-security mac-address sticky

switchport port-security mac-address sticky 0025.83e6.4b02

(output omitted)

S1#
```

Verify Secure MAC Addresses

To display all secure MAC addresses that are manually configured or dynamically learned on all switch interfaces, use the **show port-security address** command as shown in the example.

```
S1# show port-security address

Secure Mac Address Table

-----------------------------------------------------------------------

Vlan    Mac Address      Type          Ports     Remaining Age
                                                  (mins)

----    -----------      ----          -----     ------------

1       0025.83e6.4b01   SecureDynamic  Fa0/18       -

1       0025.83e6.4b02   SecureSticky   Fa0/19       -

-----------------------------------------------------------------------

Total Addresses in System (excluding one mac per port)      : 0

Max Addresses limit in System (excluding one mac per port) : 8192

S1#
```

Refer to
Interactive Graphic
in online course

Syntax Checker - Implement Port Security - 11.1.9

Implement port security for a switch interface based on the specified requirements

Refer to **Packet Tracer Activity** for this chapter

Packet Tracer - Implement Port Security

In this activity, you will configure and verify port security on a switch. Port security allows you to restrict a port's ingress traffic by limiting the MAC addresses that are allowed to send traffic into the port.

Mitigate VLAN Attacks - 11.2

VLAN Attacks Review - 11.2.1

As a quick review, a VLAN hopping attack can be launched in one of three ways:

- Spoofing DTP messages from the attacking host to cause the switch to enter trunking mode. From here, the attacker can send traffic tagged with the target VLAN, and the switch then delivers the packets to the destination.

- Introducing a rogue switch and enabling trunking. The attacker can then access all the VLANs on the victim switch from the rogue switch.

- Another type of VLAN hopping attack is a double-tagging (or double-encapsulated) attack. This attack takes advantage of the way hardware on most switches operate.

Steps to Mitigate VLAN Hopping Attacks - 11.2.2

Use the following steps to mitigate VLAN hopping attacks:

Step 1.   Disable DTP (auto trunking) negotiations on non-trunking ports by using the **switchport mode access** interface configuration command.

Step 2.   Disable unused ports and put them in an unused VLAN.

Step 3.   Manually enable the trunk link on a trunking port by using the **switchport mode trunk** command.

Step 4.   Disable DTP (auto trunking) negotiations on trunking ports by using the **switchport nonegotiate** command.

Step 5.   Set the native VLAN to a VLAN other than VLAN 1 by using the **switchport trunk native vlan** *vlan_number* command.

For example, assume the following:

- FastEthernet ports 0/1 through fa0/16 are active access ports

- FastEthernet ports 0/17 through 0/24 are not currently in use

- FastEthernet ports 0/21 through 0/24 are trunk ports.

VLAN hopping can be mitigated by implementing the following configuration.

```
S1(config)# interface range fa0/1 - 16

S1(config-if-range)# switchport mode access

S1(config-if-range)# exit

S1(config)#

S1(config)# interface range fa0/17 - 20

S1(config-if-range)# switchport mode access

S1(config-if-range)# switchport access vlan 1000

S1(config-if-range)# exit
```

```
S1(config)#

S1(config)# interface range fa0/21 - 24

S1(config-if-range)# switchport mode trunk

S1(config-if-range)# switchport nonegotiate

S1(config-if-range)# switchport trunk native vlan 999

S1(config-if-range)# end

S1#
```

- FastEthernet ports 0/1 to 0/16 are access ports and therefore trunking is disabled by explicitly making them access ports.

- FastEthernet ports 0/17 to 0/20 are unused ports and are disabled and assigned to an unused VLAN.

- FastEthernet ports 0/21 to 0/24 are trunk links and are manually enabled as trunks with DTP disabled. The native VLAN is also changed from the default VLAN 1 to an unused VLAN 999.

Refer to
Interactive Graphic
in online course

Syntax Checker - Mitigate VLAN Hopping Attacks - 11.2.3

Mitigate VLAN hopping attacks on the switch based on the specified requirements.

Mitigate DHCP Attacks - 11.3

DHCP Attack Review - 11.3.1

The goal of a DHCP starvation attack is to create a Denial of Service (DoS) for connecting clients. DHCP starvation attacks require an attack tool such as Gobbler. Recall that DHCP starvation attacks can be effectively mitigated by using port security because Gobbler uses a unique source MAC address for each DHCP request sent.

However, mitigating DHCP spoofing attacks requires more protection. Gobbler could be configured to use the actual interface MAC address as the source Ethernet address, but specify a different Ethernet address in the DHCP payload. This would render port security ineffective because the source MAC address would be legitimate.

DHCP spoofing attacks can be mitigated by using DHCP snooping on trusted ports.

Refer to
Online Course
for Illustration

DHCP Snooping - 11.3.2

DHCP snooping does not rely on source MAC addresses. Instead, DHCP snooping determines whether DHCP messages are from an administratively configured trusted or untrusted source. It then filters DHCP messages and rate-limits DHCP traffic from untrusted sources.

Devices under your administrative control, such as switches, routers, and servers, are trusted sources. Any device beyond the firewall or outside your network is an untrusted source. In addition, all access ports are generally treated as untrusted sources. The figure shows an example of trusted and untrusted ports.

Notice that the rouge DHCP server would be on an untrusted port after enabling DHCP snooping. All interfaces are treated as untrusted by default. Trusted interfaces are typically trunk links and ports directly connected to a legitimate DHCP server. These interfaces must be explicitly configured as trusted.

A DHCP table is built that includes the source MAC address of a device on an untrusted port and the IP address assigned by the DHCP server to that device. The MAC address and IP address are bound together. Therefore, this table is called the DHCP snooping binding table.

Steps to Implement DHCP Snooping - 11.3.3

Use the following steps to enable DHCP snooping:

Step 1.   Enable DHCP snooping by using the **ip dhcp snooping** global configuration command.

Step 2.   On trusted ports, use the **ip dhcp snooping trust** interface configuration command.

Step 3:   Limit the number of DHCP discovery messages that can be received per second on untrusted ports by using the **ip dhcp snooping limit rate** interface configuration command.

Step 4.   Enable DHCP snooping by VLAN, or by a range of VLANs, by using the **ip dhcp snooping** *vlan* global configuration command.

Refer to
Online Course
for Illustration

DHCP Snooping Configuration Example - 11.3.4

The reference topology for this DHCP snooping example is shown in the figure. Notice that F0/5 is an untrusted port because it connects to a PC. F0/1 is a trusted port because it connects to the DHCP server.

The following is an example of how to configure DHCP snooping on S1. Notice how DHCP snooping is first enabled. Then the upstream interface to the DHCP server is explicitly trusted. Next, the range of FastEthernet ports from F0/5 to F0/24 are untrusted by default, so a rate limit is set to six packets per second. Finally, DHCP snooping is enabled on VLANS 5, 10, 50, 51, and 52.

```
S1(config)# ip dhcp snooping

S1(config)# interface f0/1

S1(config-if)# ip dhcp snooping trust

S1(config-if)# exit

S1(config)# interface range f0/5 - 24

S1(config-if-range)# ip dhcp snooping limit rate 6

S1(config-if)# exit

S1(config)# ip dhcp snooping vlan 5,10,50-52

S1(config)# end

S1#
```

Use the **show ip dhcp snooping** privileged EXEC command to verify DHCP snooping and **show ip dhcp snooping binding** to view the clients that have received DHCP information, as shown in the example.

Note: DHCP snooping is also required by Dynamic ARP Inspection (DAI), which is the next topic

```
S1# show ip dhcp snooping
Switch DHCP snooping is enabled
DHCP snooping is configured on following VLANs:
5,10,50-52
DHCP snooping is operational on following VLANs:
none
DHCP snooping is configured on the following L3 Interfaces:
Insertion of option 82 is enabled
    circuit-id default format: vlan-mod-port
    remote-id: 0cd9.96d2.3f80 (MAC)
Option 82 on untrusted port is not allowed
Verification of hwaddr field is enabled
Verification of giaddr field is enabled
DHCP snooping trust/rate is configured on the following Interfaces:
Interface                 Trusted       Allow option    Rate limit (pps)
----------------------    -------       ------------    ----------------
FastEthernet0/1           yes           yes             unlimited
    Custom circuit-ids:
FastEthernet0/5           no            no              6
    Custom circuit-ids:
FastEthernet0/6           no            no              6
    Custom circuit-ids:
S1# show ip dhcp snooping binding
MacAddress        IpAddress      Lease(sec) Type          VLAN Interface
----------------- -------------- ---------- ------------- ---- --------
00:03:47:B5:9F:AD 192.168.10.10 193185     dhcp-snooping 5
FastEthernet0/5
```

Refer to
Interactive Graphic
in online course

Syntax Checker - Mitigate DHCP Attacks - 11.3.5

Implement DHCP snooping for a switch based on the following topology and specified requirements.

Mitigate ARP Attacks - 11.4

Dynamic ARP Inspection - 11.4.1

In a typical ARP attack, a threat actor can send unsolicited ARP replies to other hosts on the subnet with the MAC Address of the threat actor and the IP address of the default gateway. To prevent ARP spoofing and the resulting ARP poisoning, a switch must ensure that only valid ARP Requests and Replies are relayed.

Dynamic ARP inspection (DAI) requires DHCP snooping and helps prevent ARP attacks by:

- Not relaying invalid or gratuitous ARP Replies out to other ports in the same VLAN.

- Intercepting all ARP Requests and Replies on untrusted ports.

- Verifying each intercepted packet for a valid IP-to-MAC binding.

- Dropping and logging ARP Replies coming from invalid to prevent ARP poisoning.

- Error-disabling the interface if the configured DAI number of ARP packets is exceeded.

DAI Implementation Guidelines - 11.4.2

Refer to
Online Course
for Illustration

To mitigate the chances of ARP spoofing and ARP poisoning, follow these DAI implementation guidelines:

- Enable DHCP snooping globally.

- Enable DHCP snooping on selected VLANs.

- Enable DAI on selected VLANs.

- Configure trusted interfaces for DHCP snooping and ARP inspection.

It is generally advisable to configure all access switch ports as untrusted and to configure all uplink ports that are connected to other switches as trusted.

The sample topology in the figure identifies trusted and untrusted ports.

DAI Configuration Example - 11.4.3

In the previous topology, S1 is connecting two users on VLAN 10. DAI will be configured to mitigate against ARP spoofing and ARP poisoning attacks.

As shown in the example, DHCP snooping is enabled because DAI requires the DHCP snooping binding table to operate. Next, DHCP snooping and ARP inspection are enabled for the PCs on VLAN10. The uplink port to the router is trusted, and therefore, is configured as trusted for DHCP snooping and ARP inspection.

```
S1(config)# ip dhcp snooping

S1(config)# ip dhcp snooping vlan 10

S1(config)# ip arp inspection vlan 10

S1(config)# interface fa0/24

S1(config-if)# ip dhcp snooping trust

S1(config-if)# ip arp inspection trust
```

DAI can also be configured to check for both destination or source MAC and IP addresses:

- **Destination MAC** - Checks the destination MAC address in the Ethernet header against the target MAC address in ARP body.

- **Source MAC** - Checks the source MAC address in the Ethernet header against the sender MAC address in the ARP body.

- **IP address** - Checks the ARP body for invalid and unexpected IP addresses including addresses 0.0.0.0, 255.255.255.255, and all IP multicast addresses.

The **ip arp inspection validate {[src-mac] [dst-mac] [ip]}** global configuration command is used to configure DAI to drop ARP packets when the IP addresses are invalid. It can be used when the MAC addresses in the body of the ARP packets do not match the addresses that are specified in the Ethernet header. Notice in the following example how only one command can be configured. Therefore, entering multiple **ip arp inspection validate** commands overwrites the previous command. To include more than one validation method, enter them on the same command line as shown and verified in the following output.

```
S1(config)# ip arp inspection validate ?
  dst-mac   Validate destination MAC address
  ip        Validate IP addresses
  src-mac   Validate source MAC address
S1(config)# ip arp inspection validate src-mac
S1(config)# ip arp inspection validate dst-mac
S1(config)# ip arp inspection validate ip
S1(config)# do show run | include validate
ip arp inspection validate ip
S1(config)# ip arp inspection validate src-mac dst-mac ip
S1(config)# do show run | include validate
ip arp inspection validate src-mac dst-mac ip
S1(config)#
```

Refer to
Interactive Graphic
in online course

Syntax Checker - Mitigate ARP Attacks - 11.4.4

Implement DAI for a switch based on the following topology and specified requirements.

Mitigate STP Attacks - 11.5

Refer to
Online Course
for Illustration

PortFast and BPDU Guard - 11.5.1

Recall that network attackers can manipulate the Spanning Tree Protocol (STP) to conduct an attack by spoofing the root bridge and changing the topology of a network. To mitigate

Spanning Tree Protocol (STP) manipulation attacks, use PortFast and Bridge Protocol Data Unit (BPDU) Guard:

- **PortFast** - PortFast immediately brings an interface configured as an access or trunk port to the forwarding state from a blocking state, bypassing the listening and learning states. Apply to all end-user ports. PortFast should only be configured on ports attached to end devices.

- **BPDU Guard** - BPDU guard immediately error disables a port that receives a BPDU. Like PortFast, BPDU guard should only be configured on interfaces attached to end devices.

In the figure, the access ports for S1 should be configured with PortFast and BPDU Guard.

Configure PortFast - 11.5.2

PortFast bypasses the STP listening and learning states to minimize the time that access ports must wait for STP to converge. If PortFast is enabled on a port connecting to another switch, there is a risk of creating a spanning-tree loop.

PortFast can be enabled on an interface by using the **spanning-tree portfast** interface configuration command. Alternatively, Portfast can be configured globally on all access ports by using the **spanning-tree portfast default** global configuration command.

To verify whether PortFast is enabled globally you can use either the **show running-config | begin span** command or the **show spanning-tree summary** command. To verify if PortFast is enabled an interface, use the **show running-config interface** *type/number* command, as shown in the following example. The **show spanning-tree interface** *type/number* **detail** command can also be used for verification.

Notice that when PortFast is enabled, warning messages are displayed.

```
S1(config)# interface fa0/1

S1(config-if)# switchport mode access

S1(config-if)# spanning-tree portfast

%Warning: portfast should only be enabled on ports connected to a single

 host. Connecting hubs, concentrators, switches, bridges, etc... to this

 interface when portfast is enabled, can cause temporary bridging loops.

 Use with CAUTION

%Portfast has been configured on FastEthernet0/1 but will only

 have effect when the interface is in a non-trunking mode.

S1(config-if)# exit

S1(config)# spanning-tree portfast default

%Warning: this command enables portfast by default on all interfaces.
You should now disable portfast explicitly on switched ports leading to
hubs, switches and bridges as they may create temporary bridging loops.
```

```
S1(config)# exit

S1# show running-config | begin span

spanning-tree mode pvst

spanning-tree portfast default

spanning-tree extend system-id

!

interface FastEthernet0/1

 switchport mode access

 spanning-tree portfast

!

interface FastEthernet0/2

!

interface FastEthernet0/3

!

interface FastEthernet0/4

!

interface FastEthernet0/5

!

(output omitted)

S1#
```

Configure BPDU Guard - 11.5.3

Even though PortFast is enabled, the interface will still listen for BPDUs. Unexpected BPDUs might be accidental, or part of an unauthorized attempt to add a switch to the network.

If any BPDUs are received on a BPDU Guard enabled port, that port is put into error-disabled state. This means the port is shut down and must be manually re-enabled or automatically recovered through the **errdisable recovery cause psecure_violation** global command.

BPDU Guard can be enabled on a port by using the **spanning-tree bpduguard enable** interface configuration command. Alternatively, Use the **spanning-tree portfast bpduguard default** global configuration command to globally enable BPDU guard on all PortFast-enabled ports.

To display information about the state of spanning tree, use the **show spanning-tree summary** command. In the example, PortFast default and BPDU Guard are both enabled as the default state for ports configured as access mode.

Note: Always enable BPDU Guard on all PortFast-enabled ports.

```
S1(config)# interface fa0/1
S1(config-if)# spanning-tree bpduguard enable
S1(config-if)# exit
S1(config)# spanning-tree portfast bpduguard default
S1(config)# end
S1# show spanning-tree summary
Switch is in pvst mode
Root bridge for: none
Extended system ID              is enabled
Portfast Default                is enabled
PortFast BPDU Guard Default     is enabled
Portfast BPDU Filter Default    is disabled
Loopguard Default               is disabled
EtherChannel misconfig guard    is enabled
UplinkFast                      is disabled
BackboneFast                    is disabled
Configured Pathcost method used is short
(output omitted)
S1#
```

Refer to
Interactive Graphic
in online course

Syntax Checker - Mitigate STP Attacks - 11.5.4

Implement PortFast and BPDU Guard for a switch based on the following topology and specified requirements

Module Practice and Quiz - 11.6

Refer to **Packet Tracer Activity** for this chapter

Packet Tracer - Switch Security Configuration - 11.6.1

In this Packet Tracer activity, you will:

- Secure unused ports
- Implement port security
- Mitigate VLAN hopping attacks
- Mitigate DHCP attacks
- Mitigate ARP attacks
- Mitigate STP attacks
- Verify the switch security configuration

Refer to
Lab Activity
for this chapter

Lab - Switch Security Configuration - 11.6.2

In this lab, you will:

- Secure unused ports
- Implement port security
- Mitigate VLAN hopping attacks
- Mitigate DHCP attacks
- Mitigate ARP attacks
- Mitigate STP attacks
- Verify the switch security configuration

What did I learn in this module? - 11.6.3

All switch ports (interfaces) should be secured before the switch is deployed for production use. The simplest and most effective method to prevent MAC address table overflow attacks is to enable port security. By default, Layer 2 switch ports are set to dynamic auto (trunking on). The switch can be configured to learn about MAC addresses on a secure port in one of three ways: manually configured, dynamically learned, and dynamically learned – sticky. Port security aging can be used to set the aging time for static and dynamic secure addresses on a port. Two types of aging are supported per port: absolute and inactivity. If the MAC address of a device attached to the port differs from the list of secure addresses, then a port violation occurs. By default, the port enters the error-disabled state. When a port is shutdown and placed in the error-disabled state, no traffic is sent or received on that port. To display port security settings for the switch, use the **show port-security** command.

To mitigate VLAN hopping attacks:

Step 1. Disable DTP negotiations on non-trunking ports.

Step 2. Disable unused ports.

Step 3. Manually enable the trunk link on a trunking port.

Step 4. Disable DTP negotiations on trunking ports.

Step 5. Set the native VLAN to a VLAN other than VLAN 1.

The goal of a DHCP starvation attack is to create a Denial of Service (DoS) for connecting clients. DHCP spoofing attacks can be mitigated by using DHCP snooping on trusted ports. DHCP snooping determines whether DHCP messages are from an administratively-configured trusted or untrusted source. It then filters DHCP messages and rate-limits DHCP traffic from untrusted sources. Use the following steps to enable DHCP snooping:

Step 1. Enable DHCP snooping.

Step 2. On trusted ports, use the **ip dhcp snooping trust** interface configuration command.

Step 3. Limit the number of DHCP discovery messages that can be received per second on untrusted ports.

Step 4.   Enable DHCP snooping by VLAN, or by a range of VLANs.

Dynamic ARP inspection (DAI) requires DHCP snooping and helps prevent ARP attacks by:

- Not relaying invalid or gratuitous ARP Replies out to other ports in the same VLAN.
- Intercepting all ARP Requests and Replies on untrusted ports.
- Verifying each intercepted packet for a valid IP-to-MAC binding.
- Dropping and logging ARP Replies coming from invalid to prevent ARP poisoning.
- Error-disabling the interface if the configured DAI number of ARP packets is exceeded.

To mitigate the chances of ARP spoofing and ARP poisoning, follow these DAI implementation guidelines:

- Enable DHCP snooping globally.
- Enable DHCP snooping on selected VLANs.
- Enable DAI on selected VLANs.
- Configure trusted interfaces for DHCP snooping and ARP inspection.

As a general guideline, configure all access switch ports as untrusted and all uplink ports that are connected to other switches as trusted.

DAI can also be configured to check for both destination or source MAC and IP addresses:

- **Destination MAC** - Checks the destination MAC address in the Ethernet header against the target MAC address in ARP body.
- **Source MAC** - Checks the source MAC address in the Ethernet header against the sender MAC address in the ARP body.
- **IP address** - Checks the ARP body for invalid and unexpected IP addresses including addresses 0.0.0.0, 255.255.255.255, and all IP multicast addresses.

To mitigate Spanning Tree Protocol (STP) manipulation attacks, use PortFast and Bridge Protocol Data Unit (BPDU) Guard:

- **PortFast** - PortFast immediately brings an interface configured as an access or trunk port to the forwarding state from a blocking state, bypassing the listening and learning states. Apply to all end-user ports. PortFast should only be configured on ports attached to end devices. PortFast bypasses the STP listening and learning states to minimize the time that access ports must wait for STP to converge. If PortFast is enabled on a port connecting to another switch, there is a risk of creating a spanning-tree loop.
- **BPDU Guard** - BPDU guard immediately error disables a port that receives a BPDU. Like PortFast, BPDU guard should only be configured on interfaces attached to end devices. BPDU Guard can be enabled on a port by using the **spanning-tree bpduguard enable** interface configuration command. Alternatively, Use the **spanning-tree portfast bpduguard default** global configuration command to globally enable BPDU guard on all PortFast-enabled ports.

Go to the online
course to take the
quiz and exam.

Chapter Quiz - Switch Security Configuration

Your Chapter Notes

CHAPTER 12

WLAN Concepts

Introduction - 12.0

Why should I take this module? - 12.0.1

Welcome to WLAN Concepts!

Do you use a wireless connection at home, work or school? Ever wonder how it works?

There are many ways to connect wirelessly. Like everything else involving networks, these connection types are best used in particular situations. They require specific devices and are also prone to certain types of attacks. And of course, there are solutions to mitigate these attacks. Want to learn more? The WLAN Concepts module gives you the foundational knowledge you need to understand what Wireless LANs are, what they can do, and how to protect them.

If you are curious, don't wait, get started today!

What will I learn in this module? - 12.0.2

Module Title: WLAN Concepts

Module Objective: Explain how WLANs enable network connectivity.

Topic Title	Topic Objective
Introduction to Wireless	Describe WLAN technology and standards.
Components of WLANs	Describe the components of a WLAN infrastructure.
WLAN Operation	Explain how wireless technology enables WLAN operation.
CAPWAP Operation	Explain how a WLC uses CAPWAP to manage multiple APs.
Channel Management	Describe channel management in a WLAN.
WLAN Threats	Describe threats to WLANs.
Secure WLANs	Describe WLAN security mechanisms.

Introduction to Wireless - 12.1

Benefits of Wireless - 12.1.1

Refer to
Online Course
for Illustration

A Wireless LAN (WLAN) is a type of wireless network that is commonly used in homes, offices, and campus environments. Networks must support people who are on the move. People connect using computers, laptops, tablets, and smart phones. There are many different network infrastructures that provide network access, such as wired LANs, service provider networks, and cell phone networks. But it's the WLAN that makes mobility possible within the home and business environments.

In businesses with a wireless infrastructure in place, there can be a cost savings any time equipment changes, or when relocating an employee within a building, reorganizing equipment or a lab, or moving to temporary locations or project sites. A wireless infrastructure can adapt to rapidly changing needs and technologies.

Refer to
Interactive Graphic
in online course

Refer to
Online Course
for Illustration

Types of Wireless Networks - 12.1.2

Wireless networks are based on the Institute of Electrical and Electronics Engineers (IEEE) standards and can be classified broadly into four main types: WPAN, WLAN, WMAN, and WWAN.

Click each wireless network type for more information.

WPAN

Wireless Personal-Area Networks (WPAN) - Uses low powered transmitters for a short-range network, usually 20 to 30 ft. (6 to 9 meters). Bluetooth and ZigBee based devices are commonly used in WPANs. WPANs are based on the 802.15 standard and a 2.4-GHz radio frequency.

WLAN

Wireless LANs (WLAN) - Uses transmitters to cover a medium-sized network, usually up to 300 feet. WLANs are suitable for use in a home, office, and even a campus environment. WLANs are based on the 802.11 standard and a 2.4-GHz or 5-GHz radio frequency.

WMAN

Wireless MANs (WMAN) - Uses transmitters to provide wireless service over a larger geographic area. WMANs are suitable for providing wireless access to a metropolitan city or specific district. WMANs use specific licensed frequencies.

WWAN

Wireless Wide-Area Networks (WWANs) - Uses transmitters to provide coverage over an extensive geographic area. WWANs are suitable for national and global communications. WWANs also use specific licensed frequencies.

Refer to
Interactive Graphic
in online course

Refer to
Online Course
for Illustration

Wireless Technologies - 12.1.3

Wireless technology uses the unlicensed radio spectrum to send and receive data. The unlicensed spectrum is accessible to anyone who has a wireless router and wireless technology in the device they are using.

Click each wireless technology for more information.

Bluetooth

Bluetooth - An IEEE 802.15 WPAN standard that uses a device-pairing process to communicate over distances up to 300 ft. (100m). It can be found in smart home devices, audio connections, automobiles, and other devices that require a short distance connection. There are two types of Bluetooth radios:

- **Bluetooth Low Energy (BLE)** - This supports multiple network technologies including mesh topology to large scale network devices.

- **Bluetooth Basic Rate/Enhanced Rate (BR/EDR)** - This supports point to point topologies and is optimized for audio streaming.

WiMAX

WiMAX (Worldwide Interoperability for Microwave Access) - WiMAX is an alternative to broadband wired internet connections, competing with DSL and cable. However, it is typically used in areas that are not yet connected to a DSL or cable provider. It is an IEEE 802.16 WWAN standard that provides high-speed wireless broadband access of up to 30 miles (50 km). WiMAX operates in a similar way to Wi-Fi, but at higher speeds, over greater distances, and for a greater number of users. It uses a network of WiMAX towers that are similar to cell phone towers. WiMAX transmitters and cellular transmitters may share space on the same tower, as shown in the figure.

Cellular Broadband

Cellular Broadband - Cellular 4G/5G are wireless mobile networks primarily used by cellular phones but can be used in automobiles, tablets, and laptops. Cellular networks are multi-access networks carrying both data and voice communications. A cell site is created by a cellular tower transmitting signals in a given area. Interconnecting cell sites form the cellular network. The two types of cellular networks are Global System for Mobile (GSM) and Code Division Multiple Access (CDMA). GSM is internationally recognized, while CDMA is primarily used in the US.

The 4th Generation GSM network (4G) is the current mobile network. 4G delivers speeds that are 10 times the previous 3G networks. The new 5G holds the promise of delivering 100 times faster speeds than 4G and connecting more devices to the network than ever before.

Satellite Broadband

Satellite Broadband - Provides network access to remote sites through the use of a directional satellite dish that is aligned with a specific geostationary Earth orbit satellite. It is usually more expensive and requires a clear line of sight. Typically, it is used by rural homeowners and businesses where cable and DSL are not available.

802.11 Standards - 12.1.4

The world of wireless communications is vast. However, for particular job-related skills, we want to focus on specific aspects of Wi Fi. The best place to start is with the IEEE 802.11 WLAN standards. These standards define how radio frequencies are used for wireless links. Most of the standards specify that wireless devices have one antenna to transmit and receive wireless signals on the specified radio frequency (2.4 GHz or 5 GHz). Some of the newer standards that transmit and receive at higher speeds require access points (APs) and wireless clients to have multiple antennas using the multiple-input and multiple-output (MIMO) technology. MIMO uses multiple antennas as both the transmitter and receiver to improve communication performance. Up to four antennas can be supported.

Various implementations of the IEEE 802.11 standard have been developed over the years. The table highlights these standards.

IEEE WLAN Standard	Radio Frequency	Description
802.11	GHz	• speeds of up to 2 Mbps
802.11a	5 GHz	• speeds of up to 54 Mbps • small coverage area • less effective at penetrating building structures • not interoperable with the 802.11b and 802.11g
802.11b	2.4 GHz	• speeds of up to 11 Mbps • longer range than 802.11a • better able to penetrate building structures
802.11g	2.4 GHz	• speeds of up to 54 Mbps • backward compatible with 802.11b with reduced bandwidth capacity
802.11n	2.4 GHz 5 GHz	• data rates range from 150 Mbps to 600 Mbps with a distance range of up to 70 m (230 feet) • APs and wireless clients require multiple antennas using MIMO technology • backward compatible with 802.11a/b/g devices with limiting data rates
802.11ac	5 GHz	• provides data rates ranging from 450 Mbps to 1.3 Gbps (1300 Mbps) using MIMO technology • Up to eight antennas can be supported • backwards compatible with 802.11a/n devices with limiting data rates
802.11ax	2.4 GHz 5 GHz	• released in 2019 - latest standard • also known as High-Efficiency Wireless (HEW) • higher data rates • increased capacity • handles many connected devices • improved power efficiency • 1 GHz and 7 GHz capable when those frequencies become available • Search the internet for Wi-Fi Generation 6 for more information

Refer to
Online Course
for Illustration

Radio Frequencies - 12.1.5

All wireless devices operate in the radio waves range of the electromagnetic spectrum. WLAN networks operate in the 2.4 GHz frequency band and the 5 GHz band. Wireless LAN devices have transmitters and receivers tuned to specific frequencies of the radio waves range, as shown in the figure. Specifically, the following frequency bands are allocated to 802.11 wireless LANs:

■ 2.4 GHz (UHF) - 802.11b/g/n/ax

■ 5 GHz (SHF) - 802.11a/n/ac/ax

Refer to
Interactive Graphic
in online course

Refer to
Online Course
for Illustration

Wireless Standards Organizations - 12.1.6

Standards ensure interoperability between devices that are made by different manufacturers. Internationally, the three organizations influencing WLAN standards are the ITU-R, the IEEE, and the Wi-Fi Alliance.

Click each button for more information about the standards organization.

ITU

The International Telecommunication Union (ITU) regulates the allocation of the radio frequency spectrum and satellite orbits through the ITU-R. ITU-R stands for the ITU Radiocommunication Sector.

IEEE

The IEEE specifies how a radio frequency is modulated to carry information. It maintains the standards for local and metropolitan area networks (MAN) with the IEEE 802 LAN/MAN family of standards. The dominant standards in the IEEE 802 family are 802.3 Ethernet and 802.11 WLAN.

Wi-Fi Alliance

The Wi-Fi Alliance is a global, non-profit, industry trade association devoted to promoting the growth and acceptance of WLANs. It is an association of vendors whose objective is to improve the interoperability of products that are based on the 802.11 standard by certifying vendors for conformance to industry norms and adherence to standards.

Go to the online
course to take the
quiz and exam.

Check Your Understanding - Introduction to Wireless - 12.1.7

WLAN Components - 12.2

Refer to **Video**
in online course

Video - WLAN Components - 12.2.1

In the previous topic you learned about the benefits of wireless, types of wireless networks, 802.11 standards, and radio frequencies. Here we will learn about WLAN components.

Click Play to view a video about WLAN components.

Refer to
Online Course
for Illustration

Wireless NICs - 12.2.2

Wireless deployments require a minimum of two devices that have a radio transmitter and a radio receiver tuned to the same radio frequencies:

- End devices with wireless NICs
- A network device, such as a wireless router or wireless AP

To communicate wirelessly, laptops, tablets, smart phones, and even the latest automobiles include integrated wireless NICs that incorporate a radio transmitter/receiver. However, if a device does not have an integrated wireless NIC, then a USB wireless adapter can be used, as shown in the figure.

Note: Many wireless devices you are familiar with do not have visible antennas. They are embedded inside smartphones, laptops, and wireless home routers.

Refer to
Online Course
for Illustration

Wireless Home Router - 12.2.3

The type of infrastructure device that an end device associates and authenticates with varies based on the size and requirement of the WLAN.

For example, a home user typically interconnects wireless devices using a small, wireless router, as shown in the figure. The wireless router serves as an:

- **Access point** - This provides 802.11a/b/g/n/ac wireless access.

- **Switch** - This provides a four-port, full-duplex, 10/100/1000 Ethernet switch to interconnect wired devices.

- **Router** - This provides a default gateway for connecting to other network infrastructures, such as the internet.

A wireless router is commonly implemented as a small business or residential wireless access device. The wireless router advertises its wireless services by sending beacons containing its shared service set identifier (SSID). Devices wirelessly discover the SSID and attempt to associate and authenticate with it to access the local network and internet.

Most wireless routers also provide advanced features, such as high-speed access, support for video streaming, IPv6 addressing, quality of service (QoS), configuration utilities, and USB ports to connect printers or portable drives.

Additionally, home users who want to extend their network services can implement Wi-Fi range extenders. A device can connect wirelessly to the extender, which boosts its communications to be repeated to the wireless router.

Refer to
Online Course
for Illustration

Wireless Access Points - 12.2.4

While range extenders are easy to set up and configure, the best solution would be to install another wireless access point to provide dedicated wireless access to the user devices. Wireless clients use their wireless NIC to discover nearby APs advertising their SSID. Clients then attempt to associate and authenticate with an AP. After being authenticated, wireless users have access to network resources. The Cisco Meraki Go APs are shown in the figure.

Refer to
Interactive Graphic
in online course

AP Categories - 12.2.5

APs can be categorized as either autonomous APs or controller-based APs.

Refer to
Online Course
for Illustration

Click each button for a topology and explanation of each type.

Autonomous APs

These are standalone devices configured using a command line interface or a GUI, as shown in the figure. Autonomous APs are useful in situations where only a couple of APs are required in the organization. A home router is an example of an autonomous AP because the entire AP configuration resides on the device. If the wireless demands increase, more APs would be required. Each AP would operate independent of other APs and each AP would require manual configuration and management. This would become overwhelming if many APs were needed.

Controller-based APs

These devices require no initial configuration and are often called lightweight APs (LAPs). LAPs use the Lightweight Access Point Protocol (LWAPP) to communicate with a WLAN controller (WLC), as shown in the next figure. Controller-based APs are useful in situations where many APs are required in the network. As more APs are added, each AP is automatically configured and managed by the WLC.

Notice in the figure that the WLC has four ports connected to the switching infrastructure. These four ports are configured as a link aggregation group (LAG) to bundle them together. Much like how EtherChannel operates, LAG provides redundancy and load-balancing. All the ports on the switch that are connected to the WLC need to be trunking and configured with EtherChannel on. However, LAG does not operate exactly like EtherChannel. The WLC does not support Port Aggregation Protocol (PaGP) or Link Aggregation Control Protocol (LACP).

Refer to
Interactive Graphic
in online course

Wireless Antennas - 12.2.6

Most business class APs require external antennas to make them fully functioning units.

Refer to
Online Course
for Illustration

Click each antenna for more information.

Omnidirectional Antennas

Omnidirectional antennas such as the one shown in the figure provide 360-degree coverage and are ideal in houses, open office areas, conference rooms, and outside areas.

Directional Antennas

Directional antennas focus the radio signal in a given direction. This enhances the signal to and from the AP in the direction the antenna is pointing This provides a stronger signal strength in one direction and reduced signal strength in all other directions. Examples of directional Wi-Fi antennas include Yagi and parabolic dish antennas.

MIMO Antennas

Multiple Input Multiple Output (MIMO) uses multiple antennas to increase available bandwidth for IEEE 802.11n/ac/ax wireless networks. Up to eight transmit and receive antennas can be used to increase throughput.

Go to the online course to take the quiz and exam.

Check Your Understanding - WLAN Components - 12.2.7

WLAN Operation - 12.3

Refer to **Video** in online course

Video - WLAN Operation - 12.3.1

The previous topic covered WLAN components. This topic will cover WLAN operation.

Click Play to view a video about WLAN operation.

Refer to **Interactive Graphic** in online course

Refer to **Online Course** for Illustration

802.11 Wireless Topology Modes - 12.3.2

Wireless LANs can accommodate various network topologies. The 802.11 standard identifies two main wireless topology modes: Ad hoc mode and Infrastructure mode. Tethering is also a mode sometimes used to provide quick wireless access.

Click each wireless topology mode for more information.

Ad hoc mode

Ad hoc mode - This is when two devices connect wirelessly in a peer-to-peer (P2P) manner without using APs or wireless routers. Examples include wireless clients connecting directly to each other using Bluetooth or Wi-Fi Direct. The IEEE 802.11 standard refers to an ad hoc network as an independent basic service set (IBSS).

Infrastructure mode

Infrastructure mode - This is when wireless clients interconnect via a wireless router or AP, such as in WLANs. APs connect to the network infrastructure using the wired distribution system, such as Ethernet.

Tethering

Tethering - A variation of the ad hoc topology is when a smart phone or tablet with cellular data access is enabled to create a personal hotspot. This feature is sometimes referred to as tethering. A hotspot is usually a temporary quick solution that enables a smart phone to provide the wireless services of a Wi-Fi router. Other devices can associate and authenticate with the smart phone to use the internet connection.

Refer to **Interactive Graphic** in online course

Refer to **Online Course** for Illustration

BSS and ESS - 12.3.3

Infrastructure mode defines two topology building blocks: A Basic Service Set (BSS) and an Extended Service Set (ESS).

Click BSS and ESS for more information.

BSS

Basic Service Set

A BSS consists of a single AP interconnecting all associated wireless clients. Two BSSs are shown in the figure. The circles depict the coverage area for the BSS, which is called the

Basic Service Area (BSA). If a wireless client moves out of its BSA, it can no longer directly communicate with other wireless clients within the BSA.

The Layer 2 MAC address of the AP is used to uniquely identify each BSS, which is called the Basic Service Set Identifier (BSSID). Therefore, the BSSID is the formal name of the BSS and is always associated with only one AP.

ESS

Extended Service Set

When a single BSS provides insufficient coverage, two or more BSSs can be joined through a common distribution system (DS) into an ESS. An ESS is the union of two or more BSSs interconnected by a wired DS. Each ESS is identified by a SSID and each BSS is identified by its BSSID.

Wireless clients in one BSA can now communicate with wireless clients in another BSA within the same ESS. Roaming mobile wireless clients may move from one BSA to another (within the same ESS) and seamlessly connect.

The rectangular area in the figure depicts the coverage area within which members of an ESS may communicate. This area is called the Extended Service Area (ESA).

Refer to
Online Course
for Illustration

802.11 Frame Structure - 12.3.4

Recall that all Layer 2 frames consist of a header, payload, and Frame Check Sequence (FCS) section. The 802.11 frame format is similar to the Ethernet frame format, except that it contains more fields, as shown in the figure.

All 802.11 wireless frames contain the following fields:

- **Frame Control** - This identifies the type of wireless frame and contains subfields for protocol version, frame type, address type, power management, and security settings.

- **Duration** - This is typically used to indicate the remaining duration needed to receive the next frame transmission.

- **Address1** - This usually contains the MAC address of the receiving wireless device or AP.

- **Address2** - This usually contains the MAC address of the transmitting wireless device or AP.

- **Address3** - This sometimes contains the MAC address of the destination, such as the router interface (default gateway) to which the AP is attached.

- **Sequence Control** - This contains information to control sequencing and fragmented frames.

- **Address4** - This usually missing because it is used only in ad hoc mode.

- **Payload** - This contains the data for transmission.

- **FCS** - This is used for Layer 2 error control.

CSMA/CA - 12.3.5

WLANs are half-duplex, shared media configurations. Half-duplex means that only one client can transmit or receive at any given moment. Shared media means that wireless clients can all transmit and receive on the same radio channel. This creates a problem because a wireless client cannot hear while it is sending, which makes it impossible to detect a collision.

To resolve this problem, WLANs use carrier sense multiple access with collision avoidance (CSMA/CA) as the method to determine how and when to send data on the network. A wireless client does the following:

1. Listens to the channel to see if it is idle, which means that is senses no other traffic is currently on the channel. The channel is also called the carrier.

2. Sends a ready to send (RTS) message to the AP to request dedicated access to the network.

3. Receives a clear to send (CTS) message from the AP granting access to send.

4. If the wireless client does not receive a CTS message, it waits a random amount of time before restarting the process.

5. After it receives the CTS, it transmits the data.

6. All transmissions are acknowledged. If a wireless client does not receive an acknowledgment, it assumes a collision occurred and restarts the process.

Wireless Client and AP Association - 12.3.6

Refer to
Online Course
for Illustration

For wireless devices to communicate over a network, they must first associate with an AP or wireless router. An important part of the 802.11 process is discovering a WLAN and subsequently connecting to it. Wireless devices complete the following three stage process, as shown in the figure:

- Discover a wireless AP
- Authenticate with AP
- Associate with AP

In order to have a successful association, a wireless client and an AP must agree on specific parameters. Parameters must then be configured on the AP and subsequently on the client to enable the negotiation of a successful association.

- **SSID** - The SSID name appears in the list of available wireless networks on a client. In larger organizations that use multiple VLANs to segment traffic, each SSID is mapped to one VLAN. Depending on the network configuration, several APs on a network can share a common SSID.

- **Password** - This is required from the wireless client to authenticate to the AP.

- **Network mode** - This refers to the 802.11a/b/g/n/ac/ad WLAN standards. APs and wireless routers can operate in a Mixed mode meaning that they can simultaneously support clients connecting via multiple standards.

- **Security mode** - This refers to the security parameter settings, such as WEP, WPA, or WPA2. Always enable the highest security level supported.

- **Channel settings** - This refers to the frequency bands used to transmit wireless data. Wireless routers and APs can scan the radio frequency channels and automatically select an appropriate channel setting. The channel can also be set manually if there is interference with another AP or wireless device.

Refer to
Interactive Graphic
in online course

Refer to
Online Course
for Illustration

Passive and Active Discover Mode - 12.3.7

Wireless devices must discover and connect to an AP or wireless router. Wireless clients connect to the AP using a scanning (probing) process. This process can be passive or active.

Click each mode for more information.

Passive mode

In passive mode, the AP openly advertises its service by periodically sending broadcast beacon frames containing the SSID, supported standards, and security settings. The primary purpose of the beacon is to allow wireless clients to learn which networks and APs are available in a given area. This allows the wireless clients to choose which network and AP to use.

Active mode

In active mode, wireless clients must know the name of the SSID. The wireless client initiates the process by broadcasting a probe request frame on multiple channels. The probe request includes the SSID name and standards supported. APs configured with the SSID will send a probe response that includes the SSID, supported standards, and security settings. Active mode may be required if an AP or wireless router is configured to not broadcast beacon frames.

A wireless client could also send a probe request without a SSID name to discover nearby WLAN networks. APs configured to broadcast beacon frames would respond to the wireless client with a probe response and provide the SSID name. APs with the broadcast SSID feature disabled do not respond.

Go to the online
course to take the
quiz and exam.

Check Your Understanding - WLAN Operation - 12.3.8

CAPWAP Operation - 12.4

Refer to **Video**
in online course

Video - CAPWAP - 12.4.1

In the previous topic you learned about WLAN operation. Now you will learn about Control and Provisioning of Wireless Access Points (CAPWAP).

Click Play to view a video about Control and Provisioning of Wireless Access Points (CAPWAP) protocol.

Refer to
Online Course
for Illustration

Introduction to CAPWAP - 12.4.2

CAPWAP is an IEEE standard protocol that enables a WLC to manage multiple APs and WLANs. CAPWAP is also responsible for the encapsulation and forwarding of WLAN client traffic between an AP and a WLC.

CAPWAP is based on LWAPP but adds additional security with Datagram Transport Layer Security (DTLS). CAPWAP establishes tunnels on User Datagram Protocol (UDP) ports. CAPWAP can operate either over IPv4 or IPv6, as shown in the figure, but uses IPv4 by default.

IPv4 and IPv6 can use UDP ports 5246 and 5247. However, CAPWAP tunnels use different IP protocols in the frame header. IPv4 uses IP protocol 17 and IPv6 uses IP protocol 136.

Split MAC Architecture - 12.4.3

A key component of CAPWAP is the concept of a split media access control (MAC). The CAPWAP split MAC concept does all of the functions normally performed by individual APs and distributes them between two functional components:

- AP MAC Functions
- WLC MAC Functions

The table shows some of the MAC functions performed by each.

AP MAC Functions	WLC MAC Functions
Beacons and probe responses	Authentication
Packet acknowledgements and retransmissions	Association and re-association of roaming clients
Frame queueing and packet prioritization	Frame translation to other protocols
MAC layer data encryption and decryption	Termination of 802.11 traffic on a wired interface

Refer to
Online Course
for Illustration

DTLS Encryption - 12.4.4

DTLS is a protocol which provides security between the AP and the WLC. It allows them to communicate using encryption and prevents eavesdropping or tampering.

DTLS is enabled by default to secure the CAPWAP control channel but is disabled by default for the data channel, as shown in the figure. All CAPWAP management and control traffic exchanged between an AP and WLC is encrypted and secured by default to provide control plane privacy and prevent Man-In-the-Middle (MITM) attacks.

CAPWAP data encryption is optional and is enabled per AP. Data encryption requires a DTLS license to be installed on the WLC prior to being enabled on an AP. When enabled, all WLAN client traffic is encrypted at the AP before being forwarded to the WLC and vice versa.

Refer to
Online Course
for Illustration

FlexConnect APs - 12.4.5

FlexConnect is a wireless solution for branch office and remote office deployments. It lets you configure and control access points in a branch office from the corporate office through a WAN link, without deploying a controller in each office.

There are two modes of operation for the FlexConnect AP.

- **Connected mode** - The WLC is reachable. In this mode the FlexConnect AP has CAPWAP connectivity with its WLC and can send traffic through the CAPWAP tunnel, as shown in the figure. The WLC performs all its CAPWAP functions.
- **Standalone mode** - The WLC is unreachable. The FlexConnect has lost or failed to establish CAPWAP connectivity with its WLC. In this mode, a FlexConnect AP can assume some of the WLC functions such as switching client data traffic locally and performing client authentication locally.

Go to the online course to take the quiz and exam.

Check Your Understanding - CAPWAP Operation - 12.4.6

Channel Management - 12.5

Refer to **Interactive Graphic** in online course

Frequency Channel Saturation - 12.5.1

Refer to **Online Course** for Illustration

Wireless LAN devices have transmitters and receivers tuned to specific frequencies of radio waves to communicate. A common practice is for frequencies to be allocated as ranges. Such ranges are then split into smaller ranges called channels.

If the demand for a specific channel is too high, that channel is likely to become oversaturated. The saturation of the wireless medium degrades the quality of the communication. Over the years, a number of techniques have been created to improve wireless communication and alleviate saturation. These techniques mitigate channel saturation by using the channels in a more efficient way.

Click each frequency channel saturation technique for more information.

DSSS

Direct-Sequence Spread Spectrum (DSSS) - This is a modulation technique designed to spread a signal over a larger frequency band. Spread spectrum techniques were developed during war time to make it more difficult for enemies to intercept or jam a communication signal. It does this by spreading the signal over a wider frequency which effectively hides the discernable peak of the signal, as shown in the figure. A properly configured receiver can reverse the DSSS modulation and re-construct the original signal. DSSS is used by 802.11b devices to avoid interference from other devices using the same 2.4 GHz frequency.

FHSS

Frequency-Hopping Spread Spectrum (FHSS) - This relies on spread spectrum methods to communicate. It transmits radio signals by rapidly switching a carrier signal among many frequency channels. With the FHSS, the sender and receiver must be synchronized to "know" which channel to jump to. This channel hopping process allows for a more efficient usage of the channels, decreasing channel congestion. FHSS was used by the original 802.11 standard. Walkie-talkies and 900 MHz cordless phones also use FHSS, and Bluetooth uses a variation of FHSS.

OFDM

Orthogonal Frequency-Division Multiplexing (OFDM) - This is a subset of frequency division multiplexing in which a single channel uses multiple sub-channels on adjacent frequencies. Sub-channels in an OFDM system are precisely orthogonal to one another which allow the sub-channels to overlap without interfering. OFDM is used by a number of communication systems including 802.11a/g/n/ac. The new 802.11ax uses a variation of OFDM called Orthogonal frequency-division multiaccess (OFDMA).

Refer to **Online Course** for Illustration

Channel Selection - 12.5.2

A best practice for WLANs requiring multiple APs is to use non-overlapping channels. For example, the 802.11b/g/n standards operate in the 2.4 GHz to 2.5GHz spectrum. The

2.4 GHz band is subdivided into multiple channels. Each channel is allotted 22 MHz bandwidth and is separated from the next channel by 5 MHz. The 802.11b standard identifies 11 channels for North America, as shown in the figure (13 in Europe and 14 in Japan).

Note: Search the internet for 2.4 GHz channels to learn more about the variations for different countries.

Interference occurs when one signal overlaps a channel reserved for another signal, causing possible distortion. The best practice for 2.4GHz WLANs that require multiple APs is to use non-overlapping channels, although most modern APs will do this automatically. If there are three adjacent APs, use channels 1, 6, and 11, as shown in the figure.

For the 5GHz standards 802.11a/n/ac, there are 24 channels. The 5GHz band is divided into three sections. Each channel is separated from the next channel by 20 MHz. The figure shows the first section of eight channels for the 5GHz band. Although there is a slight overlap, the channels do not interfere with one another. 5GHz wireless can provide faster data transmission for wireless clients in heavily populated wireless networks because of the large amount of non-overlapping wireless channels.

Note: Search the internet for 5GHz channels to learn more about the other 16 channels available and to learn more about the variations for different countries.

As with 2.4GHz WLANs, choose non-interfering channels when configuring multiple 5GHz APs that are adjacent to each other, as shown in the figure.

Refer to
Online Course
for Illustration

Plan a WLAN Deployment - 12.5.3

The number of users supported by a WLAN depends on the geographical layout of the facility, including the number of bodies and devices that can fit in a space, the data rates users expect, the use of non-overlapping channels by multiple APs in an ESS, and transmit power settings.

When planning the location of APs, the approximate circular coverage area is important (as shown in the figure), but there are some additional recommendations:

- If APs are to use existing wiring or if there are locations where APs cannot be placed, note these locations on the map.

- Note all potential sources of interference which can include microwave ovens, wireless video cameras, fluorescent lights, motion detectors, or any other device that uses the 2.4 GHz range.

- Position APs above obstructions.

- Position APs vertically near the ceiling in the center of each coverage area, if possible.

- Position APs in locations where users are expected to be. For example, conference rooms are typically a better location for APs than a hallway.

- If an IEEE 802.11 network has been configured for mixed mode, the wireless clients may experience slower than normal speeds in order to support the older wireless standards.

When estimating the expected coverage area of an AP, realize that this value varies depending on the WLAN standard or mix of standards that are deployed, the nature of the facility, and the transmit power that the AP is configured for. Always consult the specifications for the AP when planning for coverage areas.

Go to the online course to take the quiz and exam.

Check Your Understanding - Channel Management - 12.5.4

WLAN Threats - 12.6

Refer to **Video** in online course

Video - WLAN Threats - 12.6.1

The previous topics covered the WLAN components and configuration. Here you will learn about WLAN threats.

Click Play to view a video about threats to WLANs.

Wireless Security Overview - 12.6.2

A WLAN is open to anyone within range of an AP and the appropriate credentials to associate to it. With a wireless NIC and knowledge of cracking techniques, an attacker may not have to physically enter the workplace to gain access to a WLAN.

Attacks can be generated by outsiders, disgruntled employees, and even unintentionally by employees. Wireless networks are specifically susceptible to several threats, including:

- **Interception of data** - Wireless data should be encrypted to prevent it from being read by eavesdroppers.

- **Wireless intruders** - Unauthorized users attempting to access network resources can be deterred through effective authentication techniques.

- **Denial of Service (DoS) Attacks** - Access to WLAN services can be compromised either accidentally or maliciously. Various solutions exist depending on the source of the DoS attack.

- **Rogue APs** - Unauthorized APs installed by a well-intentioned user or for malicious purposes can be detected using management software.

Refer to **Online Course** for Illustration

DoS Attacks - 12.6.3

Wireless DoS attacks can be the result of:

- **Improperly configured devices** - Configuration errors can disable the WLAN. For instance, an administrator could accidently alter a configuration and disable the network, or an intruder with administrator privileges could intentionally disable a WLAN.

- **A malicious user intentionally interfering with the wireless communication** - Their goal is to disable the wireless network completely or to the point where no legitimate device can access the medium.

- **Accidental interference** - WLANs are prone to interference from other wireless devices including microwave ovens, cordless phones, baby monitors, and more, as shown in the figure. The 2.4 GHz band is more prone to interference than the 5 GHz band.

Rogue Access Points - 12.6.4

Refer to **Online Course** for Illustration

A rogue AP is an AP or wireless router that has been connected to a corporate network without explicit authorization and against corporate policy. Anyone with access to the premises can install (maliciously or non-maliciously) an inexpensive wireless router that can potentially allow access to a secure network resource.

Once connected, the rogue AP can be used by an attacker to capture MAC addresses, capture data packets, gain access to network resources, or launch a man-in-the-middle attack.

A personal network hotspot could also be used as a rogue AP. For example, a user with secure network access enables their authorized Windows host to become a Wi-Fi AP. Doing so circumvents the security measures and other unauthorized devices can now access network resources as a shared device.

To prevent the installation of rogue APs, organizations must configure WLCs with rogue AP policies, as shown in the figure, and use monitoring software to actively monitor the radio spectrum for unauthorized APs.

Man-in-the-Middle Attack - 12.6.5

Refer to **Online Course** for Illustration

In a man-in-the-middle (MITM) attack, the hacker is positioned in between two legitimate entities in order to read or modify the data that passes between the two parties. There are many ways in which to create a MITM attack.

A popular wireless MITM attack is called the "evil twin AP" attack, where an attacker introduces a rogue AP and configures it with the same SSID as a legitimate AP, as shown in the figure. Locations offering free Wi-Fi, such as airports, cafes, and restaurants, are particularly popular spots for this type of attack due to the open authentication.

Wireless clients attempting to connect to a WLAN would see two APs with the same SSID offering wireless access. Those near the rogue AP find the stronger signal and most likely associate with it. User traffic is now sent to the rogue AP, which in turn captures the data and forwards it to the legitimate AP, as shown in the figure. Return traffic from the legitimate AP is sent to the rogue AP, captured, and then forwarded to the unsuspecting user. The attacker can steal the user's passwords, personal information, gain access to their device, and compromise the system.

Defeating an attack like an MITM attack depends on the sophistication of the WLAN infrastructure and the vigilance in monitoring activity on the network. The process begins with identifying legitimate devices on the WLAN. To do this, users must be authenticated. After all of the legitimate devices are known, the network can be monitored for abnormal devices or traffic.

Check Your Understanding - WLAN Threats - 12.6.6

Go to the online course to take the quiz and exam.

Secure WLANs - 12.7

Video - Secure WLANs - 12.7.1

Refer to **Video** in online course

The previous topic explained the WLAN threats. What can you do to secure the WLAN?

Click Play to view a video about techniques for securing WLANs.

Refer to
Online Course
for Illustration

SSID Cloaking and MAC Address Filtering - 12.7.2

Wireless signals can travel through solid matter, such as ceilings, floors, walls, outside of the home, or office space. Without stringent security measures in place, installing a WLAN can be the equivalent of putting Ethernet ports everywhere, even outside.

To address the threats of keeping wireless intruders out and protecting data, two early security features were used and are still available on most routers and APs: SSID cloaking and MAC address filtering.

SSID Cloaking

APs and some wireless routers allow the SSID beacon frame to be disabled, as shown in the figure. Wireless clients must manually configure the SSID to connect to the network.

MAC Addresses Filtering

An administrator can manually permit or deny clients wireless access based on their physical MAC hardware address. In the figure, the router is configured to permit two MAC addresses. Devices with different MAC addresses will not be able to join the 2.4GHz WLAN.

Refer to
Online Course
for Illustration

802.11 Original Authentication Methods - 12.7.3

Although these two features would deter most users, the reality is that neither SSID cloaking nor MAC address filtering would deter a crafty intruder. SSIDs are easily discovered even if APs do not broadcast them and MAC addresses can be spoofed. The best way to secure a wireless network is to use authentication and encryption systems.

Two types of authentication were introduced with the original 802.11 standard:

- **Open system authentication** - Any wireless client should easily be able to connect and should only be used in situations where security is of no concern, such as those providing free internet access like cafes, hotels, and in remote areas. The wireless client is responsible for providing security such as using a virtual private network (VPN) to connect securely. VPNs provide authentication and encryption services. VPNs are beyond the scope of this topic.

- **Shared key authentication** - Provides mechanisms, such as WEP, WPA, WPA2, and WPA3 to authenticate and encrypt data between a wireless client and AP. However, the password must be pre-shared between both parties to connect.

The following chart summarizes these authentication methods.

Shared Key Authentication Methods - 12.7.4

There are four shared key authentication techniques available, as described in the table. Until the availability of WPA3 devices becomes ubiquitous, wireless networks should use the WPA2 standard.

Authentication Method	Description
Wired Equivalent Privacy (WEP)	The original 802.11 specification designed to secure the data using the Rivest Cipher 4 (RC4) encryption method with a static key. However, the key never changes when exchanging packets. This makes it easy to hack. WEP is no longer recommended and should never be used.
Wi-Fi Protected Access (WPA)	A Wi-Fi Alliance standard that uses WEP, but secures the data with the much stronger Temporal Key Integrity Protocol (TKIP) encryption algorithm. TKIP changes the key for each packet, making it much more difficult to hack.
WPA2	WPA2 is the current industry standard for securing wireless networks. It uses the Advanced Encryption Standard (AES) for encryption. AES is currently considered the strongest encryption protocol.
WPA3	The next generation of Wi-Fi security. All WPA3-enabled devices use the latest security methods, disallow outdated legacy protocols, and require the use of Protected Management Frames (PMF). However, devices with WPA3 are not yet readily available.

Authenticating a Home User - 12.7.5

Refer to
Online Course
for Illustration

Home routers typically have two choices for authentication: WPA and WPA2. WPA2 is the stronger of the two. The figure shows the option to select one of two WPA2 authentication methods:

- **Personal** - Intended for home or small office networks, users authenticate using a pre-shared key (PSK). Wireless clients authenticate with the wireless router using a pre-shared password. No special authentication server is required.

- **Enterprise** - Intended for enterprise networks but requires a Remote Authentication Dial-In User Service (RADIUS) authentication server. Although more complicated to set up, it provides additional security. The device must be authenticated by the RADIUS server and then users must authenticate using 802.1X standard, which uses the Extensible Authentication Protocol (EAP) for authentication.

In the figure, the administrator is configuring the wireless router with WPA2 Personal authentication on the 2.4 GHz band.

Encryption Methods - 12.7.6

Refer to
Online Course
for Illustration

Encryption is used to protect data. If an intruder has captured encrypted data, they would not be able to decipher it in any reasonable amount of time.

The WPA and WPA2 standards use the following encryption protocols:

- **Temporal Key Integrity Protocol (TKIP)** - TKIP is the encryption method used by WPA. It provides support for legacy WLAN equipment by addressing the original flaws associated with the 802.11 WEP encryption method. It makes use of WEP, but encrypts the Layer 2 payload using TKIP, and carries out a Message Integrity Check (MIC) in the encrypted packet to ensure the message has not been altered.

- **Advanced Encryption Standard (AES)** - AES is the encryption method used by WPA2. It is the preferred method because it is a far stronger method of encryption. It uses the Counter Cipher Mode with Block Chaining Message Authentication Code Protocol (CCMP) that allows destination hosts to recognize if the encrypted and non-encrypted bits have been altered.

In the figure, the administrator is configuring the wireless router to use WPA2 with AES encryption on the 2.4 GHz band.

Refer to
Online Course
for Illustration

Authentication in the Enterprise - 12.7.7

In networks that have stricter security requirements, an additional authentication or login is required to grant wireless clients such access. The Enterprise security mode choice requires an Authentication, Authorization, and Accounting (AAA) RADIUS server.

- **RADIUS Server IP address** - This is the reachable address of the RADIUS server.

- **UDP port numbers** - Officially assigned UDP ports 1812 for RADIUS Authentication, and 1813 for RADIUS Accounting, but can also operate using UDP ports 1645 and 1646, as shown in the figure.

- **Shared key** - Used to authenticate the AP with the RADIUS server.

In the figure, the administrator is configuring the wireless router with WPA2 Enterprise authentication using AES encryption. The RADIUS server IPv4 address is configured as well with a strong password to be used between the wireless router and the RADIUS server.

The shared key is not a parameter that must be configured on a wireless client. It is only required on the AP to authenticate with the RADIUS server. User authentication and authorization is handled by the 802.1X standard, which provides a centralized, server-based authentication of end users.

The 802.1X login process uses EAP to communicate with the AP and RADIUS server. EAP is a framework for authenticating network access. It can provide a secure authentication mechanism and negotiate a secure private key which can then be used for a wireless encryption session using TKIP or AES encryption.

WPA3 - 12.7.8

At the time of this writing, devices that support WPA3 authentication were not readily available. However, WPA2 is no longer considered secure. WPA3, if available, is the recommended 802.11 authentication method. WPA3 includes four features:

- WPA3-Personal
- WPA3-Enterprise
- Open Networks
- Internet of Things (IoT) Onboarding

WPA3-Personal

In WPA2-Personal, threat actors can listen in on the "handshake" between a wireless client and the AP and use a brute force attack to try and guess the PSK. WPA3-Personal thwarts this attack by using Simultaneous Authentication of Equals (SAE), a feature specified in the IEEE 802.11-2016. The PSK is never exposed, making it impossible for the threat actor to guess.

WPA3-Enterprise

WPA3-Enterprise still uses 802.1X/EAP authentication. However, it requires the use of a 192-bit cryptographic suite and eliminates the mixing of security protocols for previous 802.11 standards. WPA3-Enterprise adheres to the Commercial National Security Algorithm (CNSA) Suite which is commonly used in high security Wi-Fi networks.

Open Networks

Open networks in WPA2 send user traffic in unauthenticated, clear text. In WPA3, open or public Wi-Fi networks still do not use any authentication. However, they do use Opportunistic Wireless Encryption (OWE) to encrypt all wireless traffic.

IoT Onboarding

Although WPA2 included Wi-Fi Protected Setup (WPS) to quickly onboard devices without configuring them first, WPS is vulnerable to a variety of attacks and is not recommended. Furthermore, IoT devices are typically headless, meaning they have no built-in GUI for configuration, and needed any easy way to get connected to the wireless network. The Device Provisioning Protocol (DPP) was designed to address this need. Each headless device has a hardcoded public key. The key is typically stamped on the outside of the device or its packaging as a Quick Response (QR) code. The network administrator can scan the QR code and quickly onboard the device. Although not strictly part of the WPA3 standard, DPP will replace WPS over time.

Go to the online course to take the quiz and exam.

Check Your Understanding - Secure WLANs - 12.7.9

Module Practice and Quiz - 12.8

What did I learn in this module? - 12.8.1

A Wireless LAN (WLAN) is a type of wireless network that is commonly used in homes, offices, and campus environments. Wireless networks are based on IEEE standards and can be classified into four main types: WPAN, WLAN, WMAN, and WWAN. Wireless LAN technologies uses the unlicensed radio spectrum to send and receive data. Examples of this technology are Bluetooth, WiMAX, Cellular Broadband, and Satellite Broadband. The IEEE 802.11 WLAN standards define how radio frequencies are used for wireless links. WLAN networks operate in the 2.4 GHz frequency band and the 5 GHz band. Standards ensure interoperability between devices that are made by different manufacturers. Internationally, the three organizations influencing WLAN standards are the ITU-R, the IEEE, and the Wi-Fi Alliance.

To communicate wirelessly, most devices include integrated wireless NICs that incorporate a radio transmitter/receiver. The wireless router serves as an access point, a switch, and a router. Wireless clients use their wireless NIC to discover nearby APs advertising their SSID. Clients then attempt to associate and authenticate with an AP. After being authenticated, wireless users have access to network resources. APs can be categorized as either autonomous APs or controller-based APs. There are three types of antennas for business class APs: omnidirectional, directional, and MIMO.

The 802.11 standard identifies two main wireless topology modes: Ad hoc mode and Infrastructure mode. Tethering is used to provide quick wireless access. Infrastructure mode defines two topology building blocks: A Basic Service Set (BSS) and an Extended Service Set (ESS). All 802.11 wireless frames contain the following fields: frame control, duration, address 1, address 2, address 3, sequence control, address 4, payload, and FCS. WLANs use CSMA/CA as the method to determine how and when to send data on the network. Part of the 802.11 process is discovering a WLAN and subsequently connecting to it. Wireless devices discover a wireless AP, authenticate with it, and then associate with it. Wireless clients connect to the AP using a scanning process which may be passive or active.

CAPWAP is an IEEE standard protocol that enables a WLC to manage multiple APs and WLANs. The CAPWAP split MAC concept does all of the functions normally performed by individual APs and distributes them between two functional components: AP MAC functions and WLC MAC functions. DTLS is a protocol which provides security between the AP and the WLC. FlexConnect is a wireless solution for branch office and remote office deployments. You configure and control access points in a branch office from the corporate office through a WAN link, without deploying a controller in each office. There are two modes of operation for the FlexConnect AP: connected and standalone.

Wireless LAN devices have transmitters and receivers tuned to specific frequencies of radio waves to communicate. Frequencies are allocated as ranges. Ranges are then split into smaller ranges called channels: DSSS, FHSS, and OFDM. The 802.11b/g/n standards operate in the 2.4 GHz to 2.5GHz spectrum. The 2.4 GHz band is subdivided into multiple channels. Each channel is allotted 22 MHz bandwidth and is separated from the next channel by 5 MHz. When planning the location of APs, the approximate circular coverage area is important.

Wireless networks are susceptible to threats, including: data interception, wireless intruders, DoS attacks, and rogue APs. Wireless DoS attacks can be the result of: improperly configured devices, a malicious user intentionally interfering with the wireless communication, and accidental interference. A rogue AP is an AP or wireless router that has been connected to a corporate network without explicit authorization. When connected, a threat actor can use the rogue AP to capture MAC addresses, capture data packets, gain access to network resources, or launch a MITM attack. In a MITM attack, the threat actor is positioned in between two legitimate entities to read or modify the data that passes between the two parties. A popular wireless MITM attack is called the "evil twin AP" attack, where a threat actor introduces a rogue AP and configures it with the same SSID as a legitimate AP. To prevent the installation of rogue APs, organizations must configure WLCs with rogue AP policies.

To keep wireless intruders out and protect data, two early security features are still available on most routers and APs: SSID cloaking and MAC address filtering. There are four shared key authentication techniques available: WEP, WPA, WPA2, and WPA3 (Devices with WPA3 are not yet readily available). Home routers typically have two choices for authentication: WPA and WPA2. WPA2 is the stronger of the two. Encryption is used to protect data. The WPA and WPA2 standards use the following encryption protocols: TKIP and AES. In networks that have stricter security requirements, an additional authentication or login is required to grant wireless clients access. The Enterprise security mode choice requires an Authentication, Authorization, and Accounting (AAA) RADIUS server.

Go to the online course to take the quiz and exam.

Chapter Quiz - WLAN Concepts

Your Chapter Notes

CHAPTER 13

WLAN Configuration

Introduction - 13.0

Why should I take this module? - 13.0.1

Welcome to WLAN Configuration!

Some of us remember getting on the internet using dial up. Dial up involved using your landline phone. Your landline phone was unavailable to make or receive calls while you were on the internet. Your dial up connection to the internet was very slow. It basically meant that, for most people, your computer was always in one place in your home or school.

Then we were able to connect to the internet without using our landlines. But our computers were still hardwired to the devices that connected them to the internet. Today we can connect to the internet using wireless devices that lets us take our phones, laptops, and tablets almost anywhere. It's nice to have this freedom of movement, but it requires special end and intermediary devices and a good understanding of wireless protocols. Want to know more? Then this is the module for you!

What will I learn to do in this module? - 13.0.2

Module Title: WLAN Configuration

Module Objective: Implement a WLAN using a wireless router and WLC.

Topic Title	Topic Objective
Remote Site WLAN Configuration	Configure a WLAN to support a remote site.
Configure a Basic WLAN on the WLC	Configure a WLC WLAN to use the management interface and WPA2 PSK authentication.
Configure a WPA2 Enterprise WLAN on the WLC	Configure a WLC WLAN to use a VLAN interface, a DHCP server, and WPA2 Enterprise authentication.
Troubleshoot WLAN Issues	Troubleshoot common wireless configuration issues.

Remote Site WLAN Configuration - 13.1

Video - Configure a Wireless Network - 13.1.1

Refer to **Video**
in online course

Click Play in the figure to view a demonstration of how to configure a wireless network.

Refer to
Online Course
for Illustration

The Wireless Router - 13.1.2

Remote workers, small branch offices, and home networks often use a small office and home router. These routers are sometimes called an integrated router because they typically include a switch for wired clients, a port for an internet connection (sometimes labeled "WAN"), and wireless components for wireless client access, as shown for the Cisco Meraki MX64W in the figure. For the rest of this module, small office and home routers are referred to as wireless routers.

The next figure shows a topology depicting the physical connection of a wired laptop to the wireless router, which is then connected to a cable or DSL modem for internet connectivity.

These wireless routers typically provide WLAN security, DHCP services, integrated Name Address Translation (NAT), quality of service (QoS), as well as a variety of other features. The feature set will vary based on the router model.

Note: Cable or DSL modem configuration is usually done by the service provider's representative either on-site or remotely through a walkthrough with you on the phone. If you buy the modem, it will come with documentation for how to connect it to your service provider which will most likely include contacting your service provider for more information.

Refer to
Online Course
for Illustration

Log in to the Wireless Router - 13.1.3

Most wireless routers are ready for service out of the box. They are preconfigured to be connected to the network and provide services. For example, the wireless router uses DHCP to automatically provide addressing information to connected devices. However, wireless router default IP addresses, usernames, and passwords can easily be found on the internet. Just enter the search phrase "default wireless router IP address" or "default wireless router passwords" to see a listing of many websites that provide this information. For example, username and password for the wireless router in the figure is "admin". Therefore, your first priority should be to change these defaults for security reasons.

To gain access to the wireless router's configuration GUI, open a web browser. In the address field, enter the default IP address for your wireless router. The default IP address can be found in the documentation that came with the wireless router or you can search the internet. The figure shows the IPv4 address 192.168.0.1, which is a common default for many manufacturers. A security window prompts for authorization to access the router GUI. The word admin is commonly used as the default username and password. Again, check your wireless router's documentation or search the internet.

Refer to
Interactive Graphic
in online course

Basic Network Setup - 13.1.4

Basic network setup includes the following steps:

Refer to
Online Course
for Illustration

1. Log in to the router from a web browser.

2. Change the default administrative password.

3. Log in with the new administrative password.

4. Change the default DHCP IPv4 addresses.

5. Renew the IP address.

6. Log in to the router with the new IP address.

Click each step for more information and an example GUI.

1. Log in to the router from a web browser.

After logging in, a GUI opens. The GUI will have tabs or menus to help you navigate to various router configuration tasks. It is often necessary to save the settings changed in one window before proceeding to another window. At this point, it is a best practice to make changes to the default settings.

Click the next step.

2. Change the default administrative password.

To change the default login password, find the administration portion of the router's GUI. In this example, the Administration tab was selected. This is where the router password can be changed. On some devices, such as the one in the example, you can only change the password. The username remains admin or whatever the default username is for the router you are configuring.

Click the next step.

3. Log in with the new administrative password.

After you save the new password, the wireless router will request authorization again. Enter the username and new password, as shown in the example.

Click the next step.

4. Change the default DHCP IPv4 addresses.

Change the default router IPv4 address. It is a best practice to use private IPv4 addressing inside your network. The IPv4 address 10.10.10.1 is used in the example but it could be any private IPv4 address you choose.

Click the next step.

5. Renew the IP address.

When you click save, you will temporarily lose access to the wireless router. Open a command window and renew your IP address with the ipconfig /renew command, as shown in the example.

Click the next step.

6. Log in to the router with the new IP address.

Enter the router's new IP address to regain access to the router configuration GUI, as shown in the example. You are now ready to continue configuring the router for wireless access.

Refer to
Interactive Graphic
in online course

Refer to
Online Course
for Illustration

Basic Wireless Setup - 13.1.5

Basic wireless setup includes the following steps:

1. View the WLAN defaults.

2. Change the network mode.

3. Configure the SSID.

4. Configure the channel.

5. Configure the security mode.

6. Configure the passphrase.

Click each step for more information and an example GUI.

1. View the WLAN defaults.

Out of the box, a wireless router provides wireless access to devices using a default wireless network name and password. The network name is called the Service Set Identified (SSID). Locate the basic wireless settings for your router to change these defaults, as shown in the example.

Click the next step.

2. Change the network mode.

Some wireless routers allow you to select which 802.11 standard to implement. The example shows that "Legacy" has been selected. This means wireless devices connecting to the wireless router can have a variety of wireless NICs installed. Today's wireless routers configured for legacy or mixed mode most likely support 802.11a, 802.11n, and 802.11ac NICs.

Click the next step.

3. Configure the SSID.

Assign an SSID to the WLANs. OfficeNet is used in the example for all three WLANs (the third WLAN is not shown). The wireless router announces its presence by sending broadcasts advertising its SSID. This allows wireless hosts to automatically discover the name of the wireless network. If the SSID broadcast is disabled, you must manually enter the SSID on each wireless device that connects to the WLAN.

Click the next step.

4. Configure the channel.

Devices configured with the same channel within the 2.4GHz band may overlap and cause distortion, slowing down the wireless performance and potentially break network connections. The solution to avoid interference is to configure non-overlapping channels on the wireless routers and access points that are near to each other. Specifically, channels 1, 6, and 11 are non-overlapping. In the example, the wireless router is configured to use channel 6.

Click the next step.

5. Configure the security mode.

Out of the box, a wireless router may have no WLAN security configured. In the example, the personal version of Wi-Fi Protected Access version 2 (WPA2 Personal) is selected for all three WLANs. WPA2 with Advanced Encryption Standard (AES) encryption is currently the strongest security mode.

Click the next step.

6. Configure the passphrase.

WPA2 personal uses a passphrase to authenticate wireless clients. WPA2 personal is easier to use in a small office or home environment because it does not require an authentication server. Larger organizations implement WPA2 enterprise and require wireless clients to authenticate with a username and password.

Refer to Online Course for Illustration

Configure a Wireless Mesh Network - 13.1.6

In a small office or home network, one wireless router may suffice to provide wireless access to all the clients. However, if you want to extend the range beyond approximately 45 meters indoors and 90 meters outdoors, you can add wireless access points. As shown in the wireless mesh network in the figure, two access points are configured with the same WLAN settings from our previous example. Notice that the channels selected are 1 and 11 so that the access points do not interfere with channel 6 configured previously on the wireless router.

Extending a WLAN in a small office or home has become increasingly easier. Manufacturers have made creating a wireless mesh network (WMN) simple through smartphone apps. You buy the system, disperse the access points, plug them in, download the app, and configure your WMN in a few steps. Search the internet for "best wi-fi mesh network system" to find reviews of current offerings.

Refer to Online Course for Illustration

NAT for IPv4 - 13.1.7

On a wireless router, if you look for a page like the Status page shown in the figure, you will find the IPv4 addressing information that the router uses to send data to the internet. Notice that the IPv4 address is 209.165.201.11 is a different network than the 10.10.10.1 address assigned to the router's LAN interface. All the devices on the router's LAN will get assigned addresses with the 10.10.10 prefix.

The 209.165.201.11 IPv4 address is publicly routable on the internet. Any address with the 10 in the first octet is a private IPv4 address and cannot be routed on the internet. Therefore, the router will use a process called Network Address Translation (NAT) to convert private IPv4 addresses to internet-routable IPv4 addresses. With NAT, a private (local) source IPv4 address is translated to a public (global) address. The process is reversed for incoming packets. The router is able to translate many internal IPv4 addresses into public addresses, by using NAT.

Some ISPs use private addressing to connect to customer devices. However, eventually, your traffic will leave the provider's network and be routed on the internet. To see the IP addresses for your devices, search the internet for "what is my IP address." Do this for other devices on the same network and you will see that they all share the same public IPv4 address. NAT makes this possible by tracking the source port numbers for every session established by a device. If your ISP has IPv6 enabled, you will see a unique IPv6 address for each device.

Refer to Online Course for Illustration

Quality of Service - 13.1.8

Many wireless routers have an option for configuring Quality of Service (QoS). By configuring QoS, you can guarantee that certain traffic types, such as voice and video, are prioritized over traffic that is not as time-sensitive, such as email and web browsing. On some wireless routers, traffic can also be prioritized on specific ports.

The figure is a simplified mockup of a QoS interface based on a Netgear GUI. You will usually find the QoS settings in the advanced menus. If you have a wireless router available, investigate the QoS settings. Sometimes, these might be listed under "bandwidth control" or something similar. Consult the wireless router's documentation or search the internet for "qos settings" for your router's make and model.

Refer to
Online Course
for Illustration

Port Forwarding - 13.1.9

Wireless routers typically block TCP and UDP ports to prevent unauthorized access in and out of a LAN. However, there are situations when specific ports must be opened so that certain programs and applications can communicate with devices on different networks. Port forwarding is a rule-based method of directing traffic between devices on separate networks.

When traffic reaches the router, the router determines if the traffic should be forwarded to a certain device based on the port number found with the traffic. For example, a router might be configured to forward port 80, which is associated with HTTP. When the router receives a packet with the destination port of 80, the router forwards the traffic to the server inside the network that serves web pages. In the figure, port forwarding is enabled for port 80 and is associated with the web server at IPv4 address 10.10.10.50.

Port triggering allows the router to temporarily forward data through inbound ports to a specific device. You can use port triggering to forward data to a computer only when a designated port range is used to make an outbound request. For example, a video game might use ports 27000 to 27100 for connecting with other players. These are the trigger ports. A chat client might use port 56 for connecting the same players so that they can interact with each other. In this instance, if there is gaming traffic on an outbound port within the triggered port range, inbound chat traffic on port 56 is forwarded to the computer that is being used to play the video game and chat with friends. When the game is over and the triggered ports are no longer in use, port 56 is no longer allowed to send traffic of any type to this computer.

Refer to **Packet Tracer Activity** for this chapter

Packet Tracer - Configure a Wireless Network - 13.1.10

In this activity, you will configure a wireless router and an access point to accept wireless clients and route IP packets.

Refer to **Lab Activity** for this chapter

Lab - Configure a Wireless Network - 13.1.11

In this lab, you will configure basic settings on a wireless router and connect a PC to router wirelessly.

Configure a Basic WLAN on the WLC - 13.2

Refer to **Video** in online course

Video - Configure a Basic WLAN on the WLC - 13.2.1

In the previous topic you learned about remote site WLAN configuration. This topic is about configuring a basic WLAN on the WLC.

Click Play in the figure to view a demonstration of configuring a Cisco 3504 WLC with basic WLAN connectivity.

Refer to
Online Course
for Illustration

WLC Topology - 13.2.2

The topology and addressing scheme used for the videos and this topic are shown in the figure and the table. The access point (AP) is a controller-based AP as opposed to an autonomous AP. Recall that controller-based APs require no initial configuration and are often called lightweight APs (LAPs). LAPs use the Lightweight Access Point Protocol (LWAPP) to communicate with a WLAN controller (WLC). Controller-based APs are useful in situations where many APs are required in the network. As more APs are added, each AP is automatically configured and managed by the WLC.

Addressing Table

Device	Interface	IP Address	Subnet Mask
R1	F0/0	172.16.1.1	255.255.255.0
R1	F0/1.1	192.168.200.1	255.255.255.0
S1	VLAN 1	DHCP	
WLC	Management	192.168.200.254	255.255.255.0
AP1	Wired 0	192.168.200.3	255.255.255.0
PC-A	NIC	172.16.1.254	255.255.255.0
PC-B	NIC	DHCP	
Wireless Laptop	NIC	DHCP	

Refer to
Online Course
for Illustration

Log in to the WLC - 13.2.3

Configuring a wireless LAN controller (WLC) is not that much different from configuring a wireless router. The big difference is that a WLC controls APs and provides more services and management capabilities, many of which are beyond the scope of this module.

Note: The figures in this topic that show the graphical user interface (GUI) and menus are from a Cisco 3504 Wireless Controller. However, other WLC models will have similar menus and features.

The figure shows the user logging into the WLC with credentials that were configured during initial setup.

The **Network Summary** page is a dashboard that provides a quick overview of the number of configured wireless networks, associated access points (APs), and active clients. You can also see the number of rogue access points and clients, as shown in the figure.

Refer to
Online Course
for Illustration

View AP Information - 13.2.4

Click **Access Points** from the left menu to view an overall picture of the AP's system information and performance, as shown in the next figure. The AP is using IP address

192.168.200.3. Because Cisco Discovery Protocol (CDP) is active on this network, the WLC knows that the AP is connected to the FastEthernet 0/1 port on the switch.

This AP in the topology is a Cisco Aironet 1815i which means you can use the command-line and a limited set of familiar IOS commands. In the example, the network administrator pinged the default gateway, pinged the WLC, and verified the wired interface.

```
AP1# ping 192.168.200.1

Sending 5, 100-byte ICMP Echos to 192.168.200.1, timeout is 2 seconds

!!!!!

Success rate is 100 percent (5/5), round-trip min/avg/max = 1069812.242/
1071814.785/1073817.215 ms

AP1# ping 192.168.200.254

Sending 5, 100-byte ICMP Echos to 192.168.200.254, timeout is 2 seconds

!!!!!

Success rate is 100 percent (5/5), round-trip min/avg/max = 1055820.953/
1057820.738/1059819.928 ms

AP1# show interface wired 0

wired0     Link encap:Ethernet   HWaddr 2C:4F:52:60:37:E8

           inet addr:192.168.200.3   Bcast:192.168.200.255   Mask:
           255.255.255.255

           UP BROADCAST RUNNING PROMISC MULTICAST   MTU:1500   Metric:1

           RX packets:2478 errors:0 dropped:3 overruns:0 frame:0

           TX packets:1494 errors:0 dropped:0 overruns:0 carrier:0

           collisions:0 txqueuelen:80

           RX bytes:207632 (202.7 KiB)   TX bytes:300872 (293.8 KiB)

AP1#
```

Refer to **Online Course** for Illustration

Advanced Settings - 13.2.5

Most WLC will come with some basic settings and menus that users can quickly access to implement a variety of common configurations. However, as a network administrator, you will typically access the advanced settings. For the Cisco 3504 Wireless Controller, click **Advanced** in the upper right-hand corner to access the advanced **Summary** page, as shown in the figure. From here, you can access all the features of the WLC.

Refer to **Online Course** for Illustration

Refer to **Interactive Graphic** in online course

Configure a WLAN - 13.2.6

Wireless LAN Controllers have ports and interfaces. Ports are the sockets for the physical connections to the wired network. They resemble switch ports. Interfaces are virtual. They are created in software and are very similar to VLAN interfaces. In fact, each interface that will carry traffic from a WLAN is configured on the WLC as a different VLAN. The Cisco 3504 WLC can support 150 access points and 4096 VLANs, however it only has five physical ports, as shown in the figure. This means that each physical port can support many APs and WLANs. The ports on the WLC are essentially trunk ports that can carry traffic from multiple VLANs to a switch for distribution to multiple APs. Each AP can support multiple WLANs.

Basic WLAN configuration on the WLC includes the following steps:

1. Create the WLAN

2. Apply and Enable the WLAN

3. Select the Interface

4. Secure the WLAN

5. Verify the WLAN is Operational

6. Monitor the WLAN

7. View Wireless Client Information

Click each step for more information and an example GUI.

1. Create the WLAN

In the figure, the administrator is creating a new WLAN that will use **Wireless_LAN** as the name and service set identifier (SSID). The ID is an arbitrary value that is used to identify the WLAN in display output on the WLC.

2. Apply and Enable the WLAN

After clicking **Apply**, the network administrator must enable the WLAN before it can be accessed by users, as shown in the figure. The Enable checkbox allows the network administrator to configure a variety of features for the WLAN, as well as additional WLANs, before enabling them for wireless client access. From here, the network administrator can configure a variety of settings for the WLAN including security, QoS, policies, and other advanced settings.

3. Select the Interface

When you create a WLAN, you must select the interface that will carry the WLAN traffic. The next figure shows the selection of an interface that has already been created on the WLC. We will learn how to create interfaces later in this module.

4. Secure the WLAN

Click the Security tab to access all the available options for securing the LAN. The network administrator wants to secure Layer 2 with WPA2-PSK. WPA2 and 802.1X are set by default. In the Layer 2 Security drop down box, verify that **WPA+WPA2** is selected (not shown). Click PSK and enter the pre-shared key, as shown in the figure. Then click **Apply**. This will enable the WLAN with WPA2-PSK authentication. Wireless clients that know the pre-shared key can now associate and authenticate with the AP.

5. Verify the WLAN is Operational

Click **WLANs** in the menu on the left to view the newly configured WLAN. In the figure, you can verify that WLAN ID 1 is configured with **Wireless_LAN** as the name and SSID, it is enabled, and is using WPA2 PSK security.

6. Monitor the WLAN

Click the **Monitor** tab at the top to access the advanced **Summary** page again. Here you can see that the **Wireless_LAN** now has one client using its services, as shown in the figure.

7. View Wireless Client Details

Click **Clients** in the left menu to view more information about the clients connected to the WLAN, as shown in the figure. One client is attached to **Wireless_LAN** through AP1 and was given the IP address 192.168.5.2. DHCP services in this topology are provided by the router.

Refer to **Packet Tracer Activity** for this chapter

Packet Tracer - Configure a Basic WLAN on the WLC - 13.2.7

In this lab, you will explore some of the features of a wireless LAN controller. You will create a new WLAN on the controller and implement security on that LAN. Then you will configure a wireless host to connect to the new WLAN through an AP that is under the control of the WLC. Finally, you will verify connectivity.

Configure a WPA2 Enterprise WLAN on the WLC - 13.3

Refer to **Video** in online course

Video - Define an SNMP and RADIUS Server on the WLC - 13.3.1

The previous topic covered configuring a basic WLAN on the WLC. Now you will learn about configuring a WPA2 Enterprise WLAN.

Click Play in the figure to view a demonstration of configuring SNMP and RADIUS services on the WLC.

Refer to **Online Course** for Illustration

SNMP and RADIUS - 13.3.2

In the figure, PC-A is running Simple Network Management Protocol (SNMP) and Remote Authentication Dial-In User Service (RADIUS) server software. SNMP is used to monitor the network. The network administrator wants the WLC to forward all SNMP log messages, called traps, to the SNMP server.

In addition, for WLAN user authentication, the network administrator wants to use a RADIUS server for authentication, authorization, and accounting (AAA) services. Instead of entering a publicly known pre-shared key to authenticate, as they do with WPA2-PSK, users will enter their own username and password credentials. The credentials will be verified by the RADIUS server. This way, individual user access can be tracked and audited if necessary and user accounts can be added or modified from a central location. The RADIUS server is required for WLANs that are using WPA2 Enterprise authentication.

Note: SNMP server and RADIUS server configuration is beyond the scope of this module.

Refer to
Online Course
for Illustration

Configure SNMP Server Information - 13.3.3

Click the **MANAGEMENT** tab to access a variety of management features. SNMP is listed at the top of the menu on the left. Click **SNMP** to expand the sub-menus, and then click **Trap Receivers**. Click **New...** to configure a new SNMP trap receiver, as shown in the figure.

Enter the SNMP Community name and the IP address (IPv4 or IPv6) for the SNMP server. Click **Apply**. The WLC will now forward SNMP log messages to the SNMP server.

Refer to
Online Course
for Illustration

Configure RADIUS Server Information - 13.3.4

In our example configuration, the network administrator wants to configure a WLAN using WPA2 Enterprise, as opposed to WPA2 Personal or WPA2 PSK. Authentication will be handled by the RADIUS server running on PC-A.

To configure the WLC with the RADIUS server information, click the **SECURITY** tab > **RADIUS** > **Authentication**. No RADIUS servers are currently configured. Click **New...** to add PC-A as the RADIUS server.

Enter the IPv4 address for PC-A and the shared secret. This is the password used between the WLC and the RADIUS server. It is not for users. Click **Apply**, as shown in the figure.

After clicking **Apply**, the list of configured **RADIUS Authentication Servers** refreshes with the new server listed, as shown in the figure.

Refer to **Video**
in online course

Video - Configure a VLAN for a New WLAN - 13.3.5

Click Play in the figure to view a demonstration of configuring a VLAN on the WLC.

Refer to
Online Course
for Illustration

Topology with VLAN 5 Addressing - 13.3.6

Each WLAN configured on the WLC needs its own virtual interface. The WLC has five physical ports for data traffic. Each physical port can be configured to support multiple WLANs, each on its own virtual interface. Physical ports can also be aggregated to create high-bandwidth links.

The network administrator has decided that the new WLAN will use interface VLAN 5 and network 192.168.5.0/24. R1 already has a subinterface configured and active for VLAN 5, as shown in the topology and **show ip interface brief** output.

```
R1# show ip interface brief

Interface           IP-Address      OK? Method Status        Protocol

FastEthernet0/0     172.16.1.1      YES manual up            up

FastEthernet0/1     unassigned      YES unset  up            up

FastEthernet0/1.1   192.168.200.1   YES manual up            up

FastEthernet0/1.5   192.168.5.254   YES manual up            up

(output omitted)

R1#
```

Refer to
Interactive Graphic
in online course

Refer to
Online Course
for Illustration

Configure a New Interface - 13.3.7

VLAN interface configuration on the WLC includes the following steps:

1. Create a new interface.

2. Configure the VLAN name and ID.

3. Configure the port and interface address.

4. Configure the DHCP server address.

5. Apply and Confirm.

6. Verify Interfaces.

Click each step for more information and an example GUI.

1. Create a new interface.

To add a new interface, click **CONTROLLER > Interfaces > New...**, as shown in the figure.

2. Configure the VLAN name and ID.

In the figure, the network administrator configures the interface name as **vlan5** and the VLAN ID as **5**. Clicking **Apply** will create the new interface.

3. Configure the port and interface address.

On the **Edit** page for the interface, configure the physical port number. G1 in the topology is Port Number 1 on the WLC. Then configure the VLAN 5 interface addressing. In the figure, VLAN 5 is assigned IPv4 address 192.168.5.254/24. R1 is the default gateway at IPv4 address 192.168.5.1.

4. Configure the DHCP server address.

In larger enterprises, WLCs will be configured to forward DHCP messages to a dedicated DHCP server. Scroll down the page to configure the primary DHCP server as IPv4 address 192.168.5.1, as shown in the figure. This is the default gateway router address. The router is configured with a DHCP pool for the WLAN network. As hosts join the WLAN that is associated with the VLAN 5 interface, they will receive addressing information from this pool.

5. Apply and Confirm.

Scroll to the top and click **Apply**, as shown in the figure. Click **OK** for the warning message.

6. Verify Interfaces.

Click **Interfaces**. The new **vlan5** interface is now shown in the list of interfaces with its IPv4 address, as shown in the figure.

Refer to **Video**
in online course

Refer to
Interactive Graphic
in online course

Refer to
Online Course
for Illustration

Video - Configure a DHCP Scope - 13.3.8

Click Play in the figure to view a demonstration of configuring DHCP services.

Configure a DHCP Scope - 13.3.9

DHCP scope configuration includes the following steps:

1. Create a new DHCP scope.
2. Name the DHCP scope.
3. Verify the new DHCP scope.
4. Configure and enable the new DHCP scope.
5. Verify the enable DHCP scope

Click each step for more information and an example GUI.

1. Create a new DHCP scope.

A DHCP scope is very similar to a DHCP pool on a router. It can include a variety of information including a pool of addresses to assign to DHCP clients, DNS server information, lease times, and more. To configure a new DHCP scope, click **Internal DHCP Server > DHCP Scope > New...**, as shown in the figure.

2. Name the DHCP scope.

On the next screen, name the scope. Because this scope will apply to the wireless management network, the network administrator uses **Wireless_Management** as the Scope Name and clicks **Apply**.

3. Verify the new DHCP scope.

You are returned to the **DHCP Scopes** page and can verify the scope is ready to be configured. Click the new Scope Name to configure the DHCP scope.

4. Configure and enable the new DHCP scope.

On the Edit screen for the **Wireless_Management** scope, configure a pool of addresses for the 192.168.200.0/24 network starting at .240 and ending at .249. The network address and subnet mask are configured. The default router IPv4 address is configured, which is the subinterface for R1 at 192.168.200.1. For this example, the rest of the scope is left unchanged. The network administrator selects **Enabled** from the Status drop down and clicks **Apply**.

5. Verify the enable DHCP scope

The network administrator is returned to the **DHCP Scopes** page and can verify the scope is ready to be allocated to a new WLAN.

Refer to **Video**
in online course

Video - Configure a WPA2 Enterprise WLAN - 13.3.10

Click Play in the figure to view a demonstration of configuring a new WLAN with WPA2 Enterprise on the WLC.

Refer to
Interactive Graphic
in online course

Configure a WPA2 Enterprise WLAN - 13.3.11

Refer to
Online Course
for Illustration

By default, all newly created WLANs on the WLC will use WPA2 with Advanced Encryption System (AES). 802.1X is the default key management protocol used to communicate with the RADIUS server. Because the network administrator already configured the WLC with the IPv4 address of the RADIUS server running on PC-A, the only configuration left to do is to create a new WLAN to use interface **vlan5**.

Configuring a new WLAN on the WLC includes the following steps:

1. Create a new WLAN.

2. Configure the WLAN name and SSID.

3. Enable the WLAN for VLAN 5.

4. Verify AES and 802.1X defaults.

5. Configure WLAN security to use the RADIUS server.

6. Verify the new WLAN is available.

Click each step for more information and an example GUI.

1. Create a new WLAN.

Click the **WLANs** tab and then **Go** to create a new WLAN, as shown in the figure.

2. Configure the WLAN name and SSID.

Fill in the profile name and SSID. In order to be consistent with the VLAN that was previously configured, choose an ID of **5**. However, any available value can be used. Click **Apply** to create the new WLAN, as shown in the figure.

3. Enable the WLAN for VLAN 5.

The WLAN is created but it still needs to be enabled and associated with the correct VLAN interface. Change the status to **Enabled** and choose **vlan5** from the Interface/Interface Group(G) dropdown list. Click **Apply** and click **OK** to accept the popup message, as shown in the figure.

4. Verify AES and 802.1X defaults.

Click the **Security** tab to view the default security configuration for the new WLAN. The WLAN will use WPA2 security with AES encryption. Authentication traffic is handled by 802.1X between the WLC and the RADIUS server.

5. Configure the RADIUS server.

We now need to select the RADIUS server that will be used to authenticate users for this WLAN. Click the **AAA Servers** tab. In the dropdown box select the RADIUS server that was configured on the WLC previously. Apply your changes.

6. Verify that the new WLAN is available.

To verify the new WLAN is listed and enabled, click **Back** or the **WLANs** submenu on the left. Both the **Wireless_LAN** WLAN and the **CompanyName** WLAN are listed. In the figure, notice that both are enabled. **Wireless_LAN** is using WPA2 with PSK authentication. **CompanyNam**e is using WPA2 security with 802.1X authentication.

Refer to **Packet Tracer Activity** for this chapter

Packet Tracer - Configure a WPA2 Enterprise WLAN on the WLC - 13.3.12

In this activity, you will configure a new WLAN on a wireless LAN controller (WLC), including the VLAN interface that it will use. You will configure the WLAN to use a RADIUS server and WPA2-Enterprise to authenticate users. You will also configure the WLC to use an SNMP server.

Troubleshoot WLAN Issues - 13.4

Troubleshooting Approaches - 13.4.1

In the previous topics, you learned about WLAN configuration. Here we will discuss troubleshooting WLAN issues.

Network problems can be simple or complex, and can result from a combination of hardware, software, and connectivity issues. Technicians must be able to analyze the problem and determine the cause of the error before they can resolve the network issue. This process is called troubleshooting.

Troubleshooting any sort of network problem should follow a systematic approach. A common and efficient troubleshooting methodology is based on the scientific method and can be broken into the six main steps shown in the table.

Step	Title	Description
1	Identify the Problem	The first step in the troubleshooting process is to identify the problem. While tools can be used in this step, a conversation with the user is often very helpful.
2	Establish a Theory of Probable Causes	After you have talked to the user and identified the problem, you can try and establish a theory of probable causes. This step often yields more than a few probable causes to the problem.
3	Test the Theory to Determine Cause	Based on the probable causes, test your theories to determine which one is the cause of the problem. A technician will often apply a quick procedure to test and see if it solves the problem. If a quick procedure does not correct the problem, you might need to research the problem further to establish the exact cause.
4	Establish a Plan of Action to Resolve the Problem and Implement the Solution	After you have determined the exact cause of the problem, establish a plan of action to resolve the problem and implement the solution.

Step	Title	Description
5	Verify Full System Functionality and Implement Preventive Measures	After you have corrected the problem, verify full functionality and, if applicable, implement preventive measures.
6	Document Findings, Actions, and Outcomes	In the final step of the troubleshooting process, document your findings, actions, and outcomes. This is very important for future reference.

To assess the problem, determine how many devices on the network are experiencing the problem. If there is a problem with one device on the network, start the troubleshooting process at that device. If there is a problem with all devices on the network, start the troubleshooting process at the device where all other devices are connected. You should develop a logical and consistent method for diagnosing network problems by eliminating one problem at a time.

Refer to
Online Course
for Illustration

Wireless Client Not Connecting - 13.4.2

When troubleshooting a WLAN, a process of elimination is recommended.

In the figure, a wireless client is not connecting to the WLAN.

If there is no connectivity, check the following:

- Confirm the network configuration on the PC using the **ipconfig** command. Verify that the PC has received an IP address via DHCP or is configured with a static IP address.

- Confirm that the device can connect to the wired network. Connect the device to the wired LAN and ping a known IP address.

- If necessary, reload drivers as appropriate for the client. It may be necessary to try a different wireless NIC.

- If the wireless NIC of the client is working, check the security mode and encryption settings on the client. If the security settings do not match, the client cannot gain access to the WLAN.

If the PC is operational but the wireless connection is performing poorly, check the following:

- How far is the PC from an AP? Is the PC out of the planned coverage area (BSA)?

- Check the channel settings on the wireless client. The client software should detect the appropriate channel as long as the SSID is correct.

- Check for the presence of other devices in the area that may be interfering with the 2.4 GHz band. Examples of other devices are cordless phones, baby monitors, microwave ovens, wireless security systems, and potentially rogue APs. Data from these devices can cause interference in the WLAN and intermittent connection problems between a wireless client and AP.

Next, ensure that all the devices are actually in place. Consider a possible physical security issue. Is there power to all devices and are they powered on?

Finally, inspect links between cabled devices looking for bad connectors or damaged or missing cables. If the physical plant is in place, verify the wired LAN by pinging devices, including the AP. If connectivity still fails at this point, perhaps something is wrong with the AP or its configuration.

When the user PC is eliminated as the source of the problem, and the physical status of devices is confirmed, begin investigating the performance of the AP. Check the power status of the AP.

Refer to
Online Course
for Illustration

Troubleshooting When the Network Is Slow - 13.4.3

To optimize and increase the bandwidth of 802.11 dual-band routers and APs, either:

- **Upgrade your wireless clients** - Older 802.11b, 802.11g, and even 802.11n devices can slow the entire WLAN. For the best performance, all wireless devices should support the same highest acceptable standard. Although 802.11ax was released in 2019, 802.11ac is most likely that highest standard that enterprises can currently enforce.

- **Split the traffic** - The easiest way to improve wireless performance is to split the wireless traffic between the 802.11n 2.4 GHz band and the 5 GHz band. Therefore, 802.11n (or better) can use the two bands as two separate wireless networks to help manage the traffic. For example, use the 2.4 GHz network for basic internet tasks, such as web browsing, email, and downloads, and use the 5 GHz band for streaming multimedia, as shown in the figure.

There are several reasons for using a split-the-traffic approach:

- The 2.4 GHz band may be suitable for basic Internet traffic that is not time-sensitive.

- The bandwidth may still be shared with other nearby WLANs.

- The 5 GHz band is much less crowded than the 2.4 GHz band; ideal for streaming multimedia.

- The 5 GHz band has more channels; therefore, the channel chosen is likely interference-free.

By default, dual-band routers and APs use the same network name on both the 2.4 GHz band and the 5 GHz band. The simplest way to segment traffic is to rename one of the wireless networks. With a separate, descriptive name, it is easier to connect to the right network.

To improve the range of a wireless network, ensure the wireless router or AP location is free of obstructions, such as furniture, fixtures, and tall appliances. These block the signal, which shortens the range of the WLAN. If this still does not solve the problem, then a Wi-Fi Range Extender or deploying the Powerline wireless technology may be used.

Refer to
Online Course
for Illustration

Updating Firmware - 13.4.4

Most wireless routers and APs offer upgradable firmware. Firmware releases may contain fixes for common problems reported by customers as well as security vulnerabilities.

You should periodically check the router or AP for updated firmware. In the figure, the network administrator is verifying that the firmware is up to date on a Cisco Meraki AP.

On a WLC, there will most likely be the ability to upgrade the firmware on all APs that the WLC controls. In the next figure, the network administrator is downloading the firmware image that will be used to upgrade all the APs.

Users will be disconnected from the WLAN and the internet until the upgrade finishes. The wireless router may need to reboot several times before normal network operations are restored.

Refer to Packet Tracer Activity for this chapter

Packet Tracer - Troubleshoot WLAN Issues - 13.4.5

Now that you have learned how to configure wireless in home and enterprise networks, you need to learn how to troubleshoot in both wireless environments. Your goal is to enable connectivity between hosts on the networks to the Web Server by both IP address and URL. Connectivity between the home and enterprise networks is not required.

Module Practice and Summary - 13.5

Refer to Packet Tracer Activity for this chapter

Packet Tracer - WLAN Configuration - 13.5.1

In this activity, you will configure both a wireless home router and a WLC-based network. You will implement both WPA2-PSK and WPA2-Enterprise security.

What did I learn in this module? - 13.5.2

Remote workers, small branch offices, and home networks often use a wireless router, which typically include a switch for wired clients, a port for an internet connection (sometimes labeled "WAN"), and wireless components for wireless client access. Most wireless routers are preconfigured to be connected to the network and provide services. The wireless router uses DHCP to automatically provide addressing information to connected devices. Your first priority should be to change the username and password of your wireless router. Use your router's interface to complete basic network and wireless setup. If you want to extend the range beyond approximately 45 meters indoors and 90 meters outdoors, you can add wireless access points. The router will use a process called Network Address Translation (NAT) to convert private IPv4 addresses to Internet-routable IPv4 addresses. By configuring QoS, you can guarantee that certain traffic types, such as voice and video, are prioritized over traffic that is not as time-sensitive, such as email and web browsing.

Lightweight APs (LAPs) use the Lightweight Access Point Protocol (LWAPP) to communicate with a WLAN controller (WLC). Configuring a wireless LAN controller (WLC) is similar to configuring a wireless router except that a WLC controls APs and provides more services and management capabilities. Use the WLC interface to view an overall picture of the AP's system information and performance, to access advanced settings and to configure a WLAN.

SNMP is used monitor the network. The WLC is set to forward all SNMP log messages, called traps, to the SNMP server. For WLAN user authentication, a RADIUS server is used for authentication, accounting, and auditing (AAA) services. Individual user access can be tracked and audited. Use the WLC interface to configure SNMP server and RADIUS server information, VLAN interfaces, DHCP scope, and a WPA2 Enterprise WLAN.

There are six steps to the troubleshooting process. When troubleshooting a WLAN, a process of elimination is recommended. Common problems are: no connectivity and poorly performing wireless connection when the PC is operational. To optimize and increase the bandwidth of 802.11 dual-band routers and APs, either: upgrade your wireless clients or split the traffic. Most wireless routers and APs offer upgradable firmware. Firmware releases may contain fixes for common problems reported by customers as well as security vulnerabilities. You should periodically check the router or AP for updated firmware.

Go to the online course to take the quiz and exam.

Chapter Quiz - WLAN Configuration

Your Chapter Notes

CHAPTER 14

Routing Concepts

Introduction - 14.0

Why should I take this module? - 14.0.1

Welcome to Routing Concepts!

No matter how effectively you set up your network, something will always stop working correctly, or even stop working completely. This is a simple truth about networking. So, even though you already know quite a bit about routing, you still need to know *how* your routers actually work. This knowledge is critical if you want to be able to troubleshoot your network. This module goes into detail about the workings of a router. Jump in!

What will I learn to do in this module? - 14.0.2

Module Title: Routing Concepts

Module Objective: Explain how routers use information in packets to make forwarding decisions.

Topic Title	Topic Objective
Path Determination	Explain how routers determine the best path.
Packet Forwarding	Explain how routers forward packets to the destination.
Basic Router Configuration Review	Configure basic settings on a router.
IP Routing Table	Describe the structure of a routing table.
Static and Dynamic Routing	Compare static and dynamic routing concepts.

Path Determination - 14.1

Two Functions of Router - 14.1.1

Before a router forwards a packet anywhere, it has to determine the best path for the packet to take. This topic explains how routers make this determination.

Ethernet switches are used to connect end devices and other intermediary devices, such as other Ethernet switches, to the same network. A router connects multiple networks, which means that it has multiple interfaces that each belong to a different IP network.

When a router receives an IP packet on one interface, it determines which interface to use to forward the packet to the destination. This is known as routing. The interface that the router uses to forward the packet may be the final destination, or it may be a network connected to another router that is used to reach the destination network. Each network that a router connects to typically requires a separate interface, but this may not always be the case.

The primary functions of a router are to determine the best path to forward packets based on the information in its routing table, and to forward packets toward their destination.

Refer to
Interactive Graphic
in online course

Router Functions Example - 14.1.2

The router uses its IP routing table to determine which path (route) to use to forward a packet. Click Play in the figure to follow a packet from the source PC to the destination PC. Watch how both R1 and R2 use their respective IP routing tables to first determine the best path, and then forward the packet.

Best Path Equals Longest Match - 14.1.3

What is meant by the router must determine the best path in the routing table? The best path in the routing table is also known as the longest match. The longest match is a process the router uses to find a match between the destination IP address of the packet and a routing entry in the routing table.

The routing table contains route entries consisting of a prefix (network address) and prefix length. For there to be a match between the destination IP address of a packet and a route in the routing table, a minimum number of far-left bits must match between the IP address of the packet and the route in the routing table. The prefix length of the route in the routing table is used to determine the minimum number of far-left bits that must match. Remember that an IP packet only contains the destination IP address and not the prefix length.

The longest match is the route in the routing table that has the greatest number of far-left matching bits with the destination IP address of the packet. The route with the greatest number of equivalent far-left bits, or the longest match, is always the preferred route.

Note: The term prefix length will be used to refer to the network portion of both IPv4 and IPv6 addresses.

IPv4 Address Longest Match Example - 14.1.4

In the table, an IPv4 packet has the destination IPv4 address 172.16.0.10. The router has three route entries in its IPv4 routing table that match this packet: 172.16.0.0/12, 172.16.0.0/18, and 172.16.0.0/26. Of the three routes, 172.16.0.0/26 has the longest match and would be chosen to forward the packet. Remember, for any of these routes to be considered a match there must be at least the number of matching bits indicated by the subnet mask of the route.

Destination IPv4 Address		Address in Binary
172.16.0.10		10101100.00010000.00000000.00001010
Route Entry	Prefix/Prefix Length	Address in Binary
1	172.16.0.0/12	10101100.00010000.00000000.00001010
2	172.16.0.0/18	10101100.00010000.00000000.00001010
3	172.16.0.0/26	10101100.00010000.00000000.00001010

IPv6 Address Longest Match Example - 14.1.5

In the table, an IPv6 packet has the destination IPv6 address 2001:db8:c000::99. This example shows three route entries, but only two of them are a valid match, with one of those being the longest match. The first two route entries have prefix lengths that have the required number of matching bits as indicated by the prefix length. The first route entry with a prefix length of /40 matches the 40 far-left bits in the IPv6 address. The second route entry has a prefix length of /48 and with all 48 bits matching the destination IPv6 address, and is the longest match. The third route entry is not a match because its /64 prefix requires 64 matching bits. For the prefix 2001:db8:c000:5555::/64 to be a match, the first 64 bits must the destination IPv6 address of the packet. Only the first 48 bits match, so this route entry is not considered a match.

For the destination IPv6 packet with the address **2001:db8:c000::**99, consider the following three route entries:

Route Entry	Prefix/Prefix Length	Does it match?
1	**2001:db8:c000::/40**	Match of 40 bits
2	**2001:db8:c000::/48**	Match of 48 bits (longest match)
3	**2001:db8:c000:5555::/64**	Does not match 64 bits

Refer to **Online Course** for Illustration

Refer to **Interactive Graphic** in online course

Build the Routing Table - 14.1.6

A routing table consists of prefixes and their prefix lengths. But how does the router learn about these networks? How does R1 in the figure populate its routing table?

Click each button for more information about the different ways a router learns routes.

Directly Connected Networks

Directly connected networks are networks that are configured on the active interfaces of a router. A directly connected network is added to the routing table when an interface is configured with an IP address and subnet mask (prefix length) and is active (up and up).

Remote Networks

Remote networks are networks that are not directly connected to the router. Routers learn about remote networks in two ways:

- **Static routes** - Added to the routing table when a route is manually configured.

- **Dynamic routing protocols** - Added to the routing table when routing protocols dynamically learn about the remote network. Dynamic routing protocols include Enhanced Interior Gateway Routing Protocol (EIGRP), Open Shortest Path First (OSPF), as well as several others.

Default Route

A default route specifies a next-hop router to use when the routing table does not contain a specific route that matches the destination IP address. The default route can be entered manually as a static route or learned automatically from a dynamic routing protocol.

A default route over IPv4 has a route entry of 0.0.0.0/0 and a default route over IPv6 has a route entry of ::/0. The /0 prefix length indicates that zero bits or no bits need to match the destination IP address for this route entry to be used. If there are no routes with a longer match, more than 0 bits, then the default route is used to forward the packet. The default route is sometimes referred to as a gateway of last resort.

Go to the online course to take the quiz and exam.

Check Your Understanding - Path Determination - 14.1.7

Packet Forwarding - 14.2

Refer to **Online Course** for Illustration

Refer to **Interactive Graphic** in online course

Packet Forwarding Decision Process - 14.2.1

Now that the router has determined the best path for a packet based on the longest match, it must determine how to encapsulate the packet and forward it out the correct egress interface.

The figure demonstrates how a router first determines the best path, and then forwards the packet.

Click each button for a description of the three things a router can do with a packet after it has determined the best path.

Forwards the Packet to a Device on a Directly Connected Network

If the route entry indicates that the egress interface is a directly connected network, this means that the destination IP address of the packet belongs to a device on the directly connected network. Therefore, the packet can be forwarded directly to the destination device. The destination device is typically an end device on an Ethernet LAN, which means the packet must be encapsulated in an Ethernet frame.

To encapsulate the packet in the Ethernet frame, the router needs to determine the destination MAC address associated with the destination IP address of the packet. The process varies based on whether the packet is an IPv4 or IPv6 packet:

- **IPv4 packet** - The router checks its ARP table for the destination IPv4 address and an associated Ethernet MAC address. If there is no match, the router sends an ARP Request. The destination device will return an ARP Reply with its MAC address. The router can now forward the IPv4 packet in an Ethernet frame with the proper destination MAC address.

- **IPv6 packet** - The router checks its neighbor cache for the destination IPv6 address and an associated Ethernet MAC address. If there is no match, the router sends an ICMPv6 Neighbor Solicitation (NS) message. The destination device will return an ICMPv6 Neighbor Advertisement (NA) message with its MAC address. The router can now forward the IPv6 packet in an Ethernet frame with the proper destination MAC address.

Forwards the Packet to a Next-Hop Router

If the route entry indicates that the destination IP address is on a remote network, this means the destination IP address of the packet belongs to a device on network that is not directly connected. Therefore, the packet must be forwarded to another router, specifically a next-hop router. The next-hop address is indicated in the route entry.

If the forwarding router and the next-hop router are on an Ethernet network, a similar process (ARP and ICMPv6 Neighbor Discovery) will occur for determining the destination MAC address of the packet as described previously. The difference is that the router will search for the IP address of the next-hop router in its ARP table or neighbor cache, instead of the destination IP address of the packet.

Note: This process will vary for other types of Layer 2 networks.

Drops the Packet - No Match in Routing Table

If there is no match between the destination IP address and a prefix in the routing table, and if there is no default route, the packet will be dropped.

Refer to **Interactive Graphic** in online course

End-to-End Packet Forwarding - 14.2.2

The primary responsibility of the packet forwarding function is to encapsulate packets in the appropriate data link frame type for the outgoing interface. For example, the data link frame format for a serial link could be Point-to-Point (PPP) protocol, High-Level Data Link Control (HDLC) protocol, or some other Layer 2 protocol.

Click each button and play the animations of PC1 sending a packet to PC2. Notice how the contents and format of the data link frame change at each hop.

PC1 Sends Packet to PC2

In the first animation, PC1 sends a packet to PC2. Note that if an ARP entry does not exist in the ARP table for the default gateway of 192.168.1.1, PC1 sends an ARP request. Router R1 would then return an ARP reply.

R1 Forwards the Packet to PC2

R1 now forwards the packet to PC2. Because the exit interface is on an Ethernet network, R1 must resolve the next-hop IPv4 address with a destination MAC address using its ARP table. If an ARP entry does not exist in the ARP table for the next-hop interface of 192.168.2.2, R1 sends an ARP request. R2 would then return an ARP Reply.

R2 Forwards the Packet to R3

R2 now forwards the packet to R3. Because the exit interface is not an Ethernet network, R2 does not have to resolve the next-hop IPv4 address with a destination MAC address. When the interface is a point-to-point (P2P) serial connection, the router encapsulates the IPv4 packet into the proper data link frame format used by the exit interface (HDLC, PPP, etc.). Because there are no MAC addresses on serial interfaces, R2 sets the data link destination address to an equivalent of a broadcast.

R3 Forwards the Packet to PC2

R3 now forwards the packet to PC2. Because the destination IPv4 address is on a directly connected Ethernet network, R3 must resolve the destination IPv4 address of the packet with its associated MAC address. If the entry is not in the ARP table, R3 sends an ARP request out of its FastEthernet 0/0 interface. PC2 would then return an ARP reply with its MAC address.

Refer to
Interactive Graphic
in online course

Refer to
Online Course
for Illustration

Packet Forwarding Mechanisms - 14.2.3

As mentioned previously, the primary responsibility of the packet forwarding function is to encapsulate packets in the appropriate data link frame type for the outgoing interface. The more efficiently a router can perform this task, the faster packets can be forwarded by the router. Routers support the following three packet forwarding mechanisms:

- Process switching
- Fast switching
- Cisco Express Forwarding (CEF)

Assume that there is a traffic flow which consists of five packets. They are all going to the same destination. Click each button for more information about the packet forwarding mechanisms.

Process Switching

An older packet forwarding mechanism still available for Cisco routers. When a packet arrives on an interface, it is forwarded to the control plane where the CPU matches the destination address with an entry in its routing table, and then determines the exit interface and forwards the packet. It is important to understand that the router does this for every packet, even if the destination is the same for a stream of packets. This process-switching mechanism is very slow and is rarely implemented in modern networks. Contrast this with fast switching.

Fast Switching

Fast switching is another, older packet forwarding mechanism which was the successor to process switching. Fast switching uses a fast-switching cache to store next-hop information. When a packet arrives on an interface, it is forwarded to the control plane where the CPU searches for a match in the fast-switching cache. If it is not there, it is process-switched and forwarded to the exit interface. The flow information for the packet is also stored in the fast-switching cache. If another packet going to the same destination arrives on an interface, the next-hop information in the cache is re-used without CPU intervention.

With fast switching, notice how only the first packet of a flow is process-switched and added to the fast-switching cache. The next four packets are quickly processed based on the information in the fast-switching cache.

CEF

Cisco Express Forwarding (CEF)

CEF is the most recent and default Cisco IOS packet-forwarding mechanism. Like fast switching, CEF builds a Forwarding Information Base (FIB), and an adjacency table. However, the table entries are not packet-triggered like fast switching but change-triggered, such as when something changes in the network topology. Therefore, when a network has converged, the FIB and adjacency tables contain all the information that a router would have to consider when forwarding a packet. Cisco Express Forwarding is the fastest forwarding mechanism and the default on Cisco routers and multilayer switches.

CEF builds the FIB and adjacency tables after the network has converged. All five packets are quickly processed in the data plane.

A common analogy used to describe these three different packet-forwarding mechanisms is as follows:

- Process switching solves a problem by doing math long hand, even if it is the identical problem that was just solved.

- Fast switching solves a problem by doing math long hand one time and remembering the answer for subsequent identical problems.

- CEF solves every possible problem ahead of time in a spreadsheet.

Go to the online course to take the quiz and exam.

Check Your Understanding - Packet Forwarding - 14.2.4

Basic Router Configuration Review - 14.3

Refer to
Online Course
for Illustration

Topology - 14.3.1

A router creates a routing table to help it determine where to forward packets. But before diving into the details of the IP routing table, this topic reviews basic router configuration and verification tasks. You will also complete a Packet Tracer activity to refresh your skills.

The topology in the figure will be used for configuration and verification examples. It will also be used in the next topic to discuss the IP routing table.

Configuration Commands - 14.3.2

The following examples show the full configuration for R1.

```
Router> enable
Router# configure terminal
Enter configuration commands, one per line. End with CNTL/Z.
Router(config)# hostname R1
R1(config)# enable secret class
R1(config)# line console 0
R1(config-line)# logging synchronous
R1(config-line)# password cisco
R1(config-line)# login
R1(config-line)# exit
R1(config)# line vty 0 4
R1(config-line)# password cisco
```

```
R1(config-line)# login

R1(config-line)# transport input ssh telnet

R1(config-line)# exit

R1(config)# service password-encryption

R1(config)# banner motd #

Enter TEXT message. End with a new line and the #

**************************************************

WARNING: Unauthorized access is prohibited!

**************************************************

#

R1(config)# ipv6 unicast-routing

R1(config)# interface gigabitethernet 0/0/0

R1(config-if)# description Link to LAN 1

R1(config-if)# ip address 10.0.1.1 255.255.255.0

R1(config-if)# ipv6 address 2001:db8:acad:1::1/64

R1(config-if)# ipv6 address fe80::1:a link-local

R1(config-if)# no shutdown

R1(config-if)# exit

R1(config)# interface gigabitethernet 0/0/1

R1(config-if)# description Link to LAN 2

R1(config-if)# ip address 10.0.2.1 255.255.255.0

R1(config-if)# ipv6 address 2001:db8:acad:2::1/64

R1(config-if)# ipv6 address fe80::1:b link-local

R1(config-if)# no shutdown

R1(config-if)# exit

R1(config)# interface serial 0/1/1

R1(config-if)# description Link to R2

R1(config-if)# ip address 10.0.3.1 255.255.255.0

R1(config-if)# ipv6 address 2001:db8:acad:3::1/64

R1(config-if)# ipv6 address fe80::1:c link-local

R1(config-if)# no shutdown

R1(config-if)# exit

R1# copy running-config startup-config

Destination filename [startup-config]?

Building configuration...

[OK]

R1#
```

Refer to
Online Course
for Illustration

Refer to
Interactive Graphic
in online course

Verification Commands - 14.3.3

Common verification commands include the following:

- show ip interface brief
- show running-config interface *interface-type number*
- show interfaces
- show ip interface
- show ip route
- ping

In each case, replace **ip** with **ipv6** for the IPv6 version of the command. The figure shows the topology again for easy reference.

Click each button for the command output for R1.

show ip interface brief

```
R1# show ip interface brief

Interface            IP-Address    OK? Method Status                Protocol
GigabitEthernet0/0/0 10.0.1.1      YES manual up                          up
GigabitEthernet0/0/1 10.0.2.1      YES manual up                          up
Serial0/1/0          unassigned    YES unset  administratively down down
Serial0/1/1          10.0.3.1      YES manual up                          up
GigabitEthernet0     unassigned    YES unset  down                      down
R1#
```

show ipv6 interface brief

```
R1# show ipv6 interface brief
GigabitEthernet0/0/0     [up/up]
    FE80::1:A
    2001:DB8:ACAD:1::1
GigabitEthernet0/0/1     [up/up]
    FE80::1:B
    2001:DB8:ACAD:2::1
Serial0/1/0              [administratively down/down]
    unassigned
Serial0/1/1              [up/up]
    FE80::1:C
    2001:DB8:ACAD:3::1
```

```
GigabitEthernet0          [down/down]
    unassigned
R1#
```

show running-config interface

```
R1# show running-config interface gigabitethernet 0/0/0
Building configuration...
Current configuration : 189 bytes
!
interface GigabitEthernet0/0/0
 description Link to LAN 1
 ip address 10.0.1.1 255.255.255.0
 negotiation auto
 ipv6 address FE80::1:A link-local
 ipv6 address 2001:DB8:ACAD:1::1/64
end
R1#
```

show interfaces

```
R1# show interfaces gigabitEthernet 0/0/0
GigabitEthernet0/0/0 is up, line protocol is up
  Hardware is ISR4321-2x1GE, address is a0e0.af0d.e140 (bia a0e0.af0d.
  e140)
  Internet address is 10.0.1.1/24
  MTU 1500 bytes, BW 100000 Kbit/sec, DLY 100 usec,
     reliability 255/255, txload 1/255, rxload 1/255
  Encapsulation ARPA, loopback not set
  Keepalive not supported
  Full Duplex, 100Mbps, link type is auto, media type is RJ45
  output flow-control is off, input flow-control is off
  ARP type: ARPA, ARP Timeout 04:00:00
  Last input 00:00:00, output 00:00:06, output hang never
  Last clearing of "show interface" counters never
  Input queue: 0/375/0/0 (size/max/drops/flushes); Total output drops: 0
  Queueing strategy: fifo
  Output queue: 0/40 (size/max)
```

```
    5 minute input rate 2000 bits/sec, 1 packets/sec
    5 minute output rate 0 bits/sec, 0 packets/sec
        57793 packets input, 10528767 bytes, 0 no buffer
        Received 19711 broadcasts (0 IP multicasts)
        0 runts, 0 giants, 0 throttles
        0 input errors, 0 CRC, 0 frame, 0 overrun, 0 ignored
        0 watchdog, 36766 multicast, 0 pause input
        10350 packets output, 1280030 bytes, 0 underruns
        0 output errors, 0 collisions, 1 interface resets
        0 unknown protocol drops
        0 babbles, 0 late collision, 0 deferred
        0 lost carrier, 0 no carrier, 0 pause output
        0 output buffer failures, 0 output buffers swapped out
R1#
```

show ip interface

```
R1# show ip interface gigabitethernet 0/0/0
GigabitEthernet0/0/0 is up, line protocol is up
    Internet address is 10.0.1.1/24
    Broadcast address is 255.255.255.255
    Address determined by setup command
    MTU is 1500 bytes
    Helper address is not set
    Directed broadcast forwarding is disabled
    Multicast reserved groups joined: 224.0.0.5 224.0.0.6
    Outgoing Common access list is not set
    Outgoing access list is not set
    Inbound Common access list is not set
    Inbound  access list is not set
    Proxy ARP is enabled
    Local Proxy ARP is disabled
    Security level is default
    Split horizon is enabled
    ICMP redirects are always sent
    ICMP unreachables are always sent
    ICMP mask replies are never sent
```

```
IP fast switching is enabled

IP Flow switching is disabled

IP CEF switching is enabled

IP CEF switching turbo vector

IP Null turbo vector

Associated unicast routing topologies:

        Topology "base", operation state is UP

IP multicast fast switching is enabled

IP multicast distributed fast switching is disabled

IP route-cache flags are Fast, CEF

Router Discovery is disabled

IP output packet accounting is disabled

IP access violation accounting is disabled

TCP/IP header compression is disabled

RTP/IP header compression is disabled

Probe proxy name replies are disabled

Policy routing is disabled

Network address translation is disabled

BGP Policy Mapping is disabled

Input features: MCI Check

IPv4 WCCP Redirect outbound is disabled

IPv4 WCCP Redirect inbound is disabled

IPv4 WCCP Redirect exclude is disabled
R1#
```

show ipv6 interface

```
R1# show ipv6 interface gigabitethernet 0/0/0
GigabitEthernet0/0/0 is up, line protocol is up
  IPv6 is enabled, link-local address is FE80::1:A
  No Virtual link-local address(es):
  Global unicast address(es):
    2001:DB8:ACAD:1::1, subnet is 2001:DB8:ACAD:1::/64
  Joined group address(es):
    FF02::1
    FF02::2
    FF02::5
    FF02::6
```

```
       FF02::1:FF00:1

       FF02::1:FF01:A

    MTU is 1500 bytes

    ICMP error messages limited to one every 100 milliseconds

    ICMP redirects are enabled

    ICMP unreachables are sent

    ND DAD is enabled, number of DAD attempts: 1

    ND reachable time is 30000 milliseconds (using 30000)

    ND advertised reachable time is 0 (unspecified)

    ND advertised retransmit interval is 0 (unspecified)

    ND router advertisements are sent every 200 seconds

    ND router advertisements live for 1800 seconds

    ND advertised default router preference is Medium

    Hosts use stateless autoconfig for addresses.

R1#
```

show ip route

```
R1# show ip route

Codes: L - local, C - connected, S - static, R - RIP, M - mobile, B - BGP

(Output omitted)

Gateway of last resort is not set

       10.0.0.0/8 is variably subnetted, 6 subnets, 2 masks

C         10.0.1.0/24 is directly connected, GigabitEthernet0/0/0

L         10.0.1.1/32 is directly connected, GigabitEthernet0/0/0

C         10.0.2.0/24 is directly connected, GigabitEthernet0/0/1

L         10.0.2.1/32 is directly connected, GigabitEthernet0/0/1

C         10.0.3.0/24 is directly connected, Serial0/1/1

L         10.0.3.1/32 is directly connected, Serial0/1/1

R1#
```

show ipv6 route

```
R1# show ipv6 route

IPv6 Routing Table - default - 5 entries

Codes: C - Connected, L - Local, S - Static, U - Per-user Static route

(Output omitted)
```

```
C    2001:DB8:ACAD:1::/64 [0/0]

       via GigabitEthernet0/0/0, directly connected

L    2001:DB8:ACAD:1::1/128 [0/0]

       via GigabitEthernet0/0/0, receive

C    2001:DB8:ACAD:2::/64 [0/0]

       via GigabitEthernet0/0/1, directly connected

L    2001:DB8:ACAD:2::1/128 [0/0]

       via GigabitEthernet0/0/1, receive

C    2001:DB8:ACAD:3::/64 [0/0]

       via Serial0/1/1, directly connected

L    2001:DB8:ACAD:3::1/128 [0/0]

       via Serial0/1/1, receive

L    FF00::/8 [0/0]

       via Null0, receive

R1#
```

ping

The following **ping** output assumes the S0/1/0 interface on R2 is configured and active.

```
R1# ping 10.0.3.2

Type escape sequence to abort.

Sending 5, 100-byte ICMP Echos to 10.0.3.2, timeout is 2 seconds:

!!!!!

Success rate is 100 percent (5/5), round-trip min/avg/max = 2/2/2 ms

R1# ping 2001:db8:acad:3::2

Type escape sequence to abort.

Sending 5, 100-byte ICMP Echos to 2001:DB8:ACAD:3::2, timeout is 2 seconds:

!!!!!

Success rate is 100 percent (5/5), round-trip min/avg/max = 2/2/2 ms

R1#
```

Refer to
Online Course
for Illustration

Filter Command Output - 14.3.4

Another useful feature that improves user experience in the command-line interface (CLI) is filtering **show** output. Filtering commands can be used to display specific sections of output. To enable the filtering command, enter a pipe (l) character after the **show** command and then enter a filtering parameter and a filtering expression.

The filtering parameters that can be configured after the pipe include:

- **section** - This displays the entire section that starts with the filtering expression.
- **include** - This includes all output lines that match the filtering expression.
- **exclude** - This excludes all output lines that match the filtering expression.
- **begin** - This displays all the output lines from a certain point, starting with the line that matches the filtering expression.

Note: Output filters can be used in combination with any **show** command.

The figure again shows the topology for your convenience

These examples demonstrate some of the more common uses of filtering parameters.

```
R1# show running-config | section line vty
line vty 0 4
 password 7 121A0C0411044C
 login
 transport input telnet ssh
R1#

R1# show ipv6 interface brief | include up
GigabitEthernet0/0/0    [up/up]
GigabitEthernet0/0/1    [up/up]
Serial0/1/1             [up/up]
R1#

R1# show ip interface brief | exclude unassigned
Interface            IP-Address      OK? Method Status        Protocol
GigabitEthernet0/0/0  192.168.10.1    YES manual up            up
GigabitEthernet0/0/1  192.168.11.1    YES manual up            up
Serial0/1/1           209.165.200.225 YES manual up            up
R1#

R1# show ip route | begin Gateway
Gateway of last resort is not set
      192.168.10.0/24 is variably subnetted, 2 subnets, 2 masks
C        192.168.10.0/24 is directly connected, GigabitEthernet0/0/0
L        192.168.10.1/32 is directly connected, GigabitEthernet0/0/0
      192.168.11.0/24 is variably subnetted, 2 subnets, 2 masks
C        192.168.11.0/24 is directly connected, GigabitEthernet0/0/1
L        192.168.11.1/32 is directly connected, GigabitEthernet0/0/1
```

```
              209.165.200.0/24 is variably subnetted, 2 subnets, 2 masks
C        209.165.200.224/30 is directly connected, Serial0/1/1
L        209.165.200.225/32 is directly connected, Serial0/1/1
R1#
```

Refer to **Packet Tracer Activity** for this chapter

Packet Tracer - Basic Router Configuration Review - 14.3.5

Routers R1 and R2 each have two LANs. R1 is already configured. Your task is to configure the appropriate addressing for R2 and verify connectivity between the LANs.

IP Routing Table - 14.4

Refer to **Online Course** for Illustration

Refer to **Interactive Graphic** in online course

Route Sources - 14.4.1

How does a router know where it can send packets? It creates a routing table that is based on the network in which it is located.

A routing table contains a list of routes to known networks (prefixes and prefix lengths). The source of this information is derived from the following:

- Directly connected networks
- Static routes
- Dynamic routing protocols

In the figure, R1 and R2 are using the dynamic routing protocol OSPF to share routing information. In addition, R2 is configured with a default static route to ISP.

Click each button to see the full routing table for each router after directly connected networks, static routing, and dynamic routing is configured. The rest of this topic will demonstrate how these tables are populated.

R1 Routing Table

```
R1# show ip route
Codes: L - local, C - connected, S - static, R - RIP, M - mobile,
B - BGP
        D - EIGRP, EX - EIGRP external, O - OSPF, IA - OSPF inter area
        N1 - OSPF NSSA external type 1, N2 - OSPF NSSA external type 2
        E1 - OSPF external type 1, E2 - OSPF external type 2
        i - IS-IS, su - IS-IS summary, L1 - IS-IS level-1, L2 - IS-IS
            level-2
        ia - IS-IS inter area, * - candidate default, U - per-user
            static route
        o - ODR, P - periodic downloaded static route, H - NHRP,
            l - LISP
```

```
            a - application route

            + - replicated route, % - next hop override, p - overrides
                from PfR

Gateway of last resort is 10.0.3.2 to network 0.0.0.0

O*E2    0.0.0.0/0 [110/1] via 10.0.3.2, 00:51:34, Serial0/1/1

        10.0.0.0/8 is variably subnetted, 8 subnets, 2 masks

C          10.0.1.0/24 is directly connected, GigabitEthernet0/0/0

L          10.0.1.1/32 is directly connected, GigabitEthernet0/0/0

C          10.0.2.0/24 is directly connected, GigabitEthernet0/0/1

L          10.0.2.1/32 is directly connected, GigabitEthernet0/0/1

C          10.0.3.0/24 is directly connected, Serial0/1/1

L          10.0.3.1/32 is directly connected, Serial0/1/1

O          10.0.4.0/24 [110/50] via 10.0.3.2, 00:24:22, Serial0/1/1

O          10.0.5.0/24 [110/50] via 10.0.3.2, 00:24:15, Serial0/1/1

R1#
```

R2 Routing Table

```
R2# show ip route

Codes: L - local, C - connected, S - static, R - RIP, M - mobile,
B - BGP

        D - EIGRP, EX - EIGRP external, O - OSPF, IA - OSPF inter area

        N1 - OSPF NSSA external type 1, N2 - OSPF NSSA external type 2

        E1 - OSPF external type 1, E2 - OSPF external type 2

        i - IS-IS, su - IS-IS summary, L1 - IS-IS level-1, L2 - IS-IS
            level-2

        ia - IS-IS inter area, * - candidate default, U - per-user
             static route

        o - ODR, P - periodic downloaded static route, H - NHRP,
            l - LISP

        a - application route

        + - replicated route, % - next hop override, p - overrides
            from PfR

Gateway of last resort is 209.165.200.226 to network 0.0.0.0

S*    0.0.0.0/0 [1/0] via 209.165.200.226

        10.0.0.0/8 is variably subnetted, 8 subnets, 2 masks

O          10.0.1.0/24 [110/65] via 10.0.3.1, 00:31:38, Serial0/1/0

O          10.0.2.0/24 [110/65] via 10.0.3.1, 00:31:38, Serial0/1/0

C          10.0.3.0/24 is directly connected, Serial0/1/0
```

```
L        10.0.3.2/32 is directly connected, Serial0/1/0

C        10.0.4.0/24 is directly connected, GigabitEthernet0/0/0

L        10.0.4.1/32 is directly connected, GigabitEthernet0/0/0

C        10.0.5.0/24 is directly connected, GigabitEthernet0/0/1

L        10.0.5.1/32 is directly connected, GigabitEthernet0/0/1

      209.165.200.0/24 is variably subnetted, 2 subnets, 2 masks

C        209.165.200.224/30 is directly connected, Serial0/1/1

L        209.165.200.225/32 is directly connected, Serial0/1/1

R2#
```

In the routing tables for R1 and R2, notice that the sources for each route are identified by a code. The code identifies how the route was learned. For instance, common codes include the following:

- **L** - Identifies the address assigned to a router interface. This allows the router to efficiently determine when it receives a packet for the interface instead of being forwarded.

- **C** - Identifies a directly connected network.

- **S** - Identifies a static route created to reach a specific network.

- **O** - Identifies a dynamically learned network from another router using the OSPF routing protocol.

- ***** - This route is a candidate for a default route.

Routing Table Principles - 14.4.2

There are three routing table principles as described in the table. These are issues that are addressed by the proper configuration of dynamic routing protocols or static routes on all the routers between the source and destination devices.

Routing Table Principle	Example
Every router makes its decision alone, based on the information it has in its own routing table.	• R1 can only forward packets using its own routing table. • R1 does not know what routes are in the routing tables of other routers (e.g., R2).
The information in a routing table of one router does not necessarily match the routing table of another router.	Just because R1 has route in its routing table to a network in the internet via R2, that does not mean that R2 knows about that same network.
Routing information about a path does not provide return routing information.	R1 receives a packet with the destination IP address of PC1 and the source IP address of PC3. Just because R1 knows to forward the packet out its G0/0/0 interface, doesn't necessarily mean that it knows how to forward packets originating from PC1 back to the remote network of PC3.

Refer to
Online Course
for Illustration

Routing Table Entries - 14.4.3

As a network administrator, it is imperative to know how to interpret the content of IPv4 and IPv6 routing tables. The figure displays IPv4 and IPv6 routing table entries on R1 for the route to remote network 10.0.4.0/24 and 2001:db8:acad:4::/64. Both these routes were learned dynamically from the OSPF routing protocol.

Directly Connected Networks - 14.4.4

Before a router can learn about any remote networks, it must have at least one active interface configured with an IP address and subnet mask (prefix length). This is known as a directly connected network or a directly connected route. Routers add a directly connected route to its routing table when an interface is configured with an IP address and is activated.

A directly connected network is denoted by a status code of C in the routing table. The route contains a network prefix and prefix length.

The routing table also contains a local route for each of its directly connected networks, indicated by the status code of **L**. This is the IP address that is assigned to the interface on that directly connected network. For IPv4 local routes the prefix length is /32 and for IPv6 local routes the prefix length is /128. This means the destination IP address of the packet must match all the bits in the local route for this route to be a match. The purpose of the local route is to efficiently determine when it receives a packet for the interface instead of a packet that needs to be forwarded.

Directly connected networks and local routes are shown in the following output.

```
R1# show ip route

Codes: L - local, C - connected, S - static, R - RIP, M - mobile,
B - BGP

(Output omitted)

C        10.0.1.0/24 is directly connected, GigabitEthernet0/0/0

L        10.0.1.1/32 is directly connected, GigabitEthernet0/0/0

R1#

R1# show ipv6 route

IPv6 Routing Table - default - 10 entries

Codes: C - Connected, L - Local, S - Static, U - Per-user Static route

(Output omitted)


C    2001:DB8:ACAD:1::/64 [0/0]

     via GigabitEthernet0/0/0, directly connected

L    2001:DB8:ACAD:1::1/128 [0/0]

     via GigabitEthernet0/0/0, receive

R1#
```

Refer to
Online Course
for Illustration

Static Routes - 14.4.5

After directly connected interfaces are configured and added to the routing table, static or dynamic routing can be implemented for accessing remote networks.

Static routes are manually configured. They define an explicit path between two networking devices. Unlike a dynamic routing protocol, static routes are not automatically updated and must be manually reconfigured if the network topology changes. The benefits of using static routes include improved security and resource efficiency. Static routes use less bandwidth than dynamic routing protocols, and no CPU cycles are used to calculate and communicate routes. The main disadvantage to using static routes is the lack of automatic reconfiguration if the network topology changes.

Static routing has three primary uses:

- It provides ease of routing table maintenance in smaller networks that are not expected to grow significantly.

- It uses a single default route to represent a path to any network that does not have a more specific match with another route in the routing table. Default routes are used to send traffic to any destination beyond the next upstream router.

- It routes to and from stub networks. A stub network is a network accessed by a single route, and the router has only one neighbor.

The figure shows an example of stub networks. Notice that any network attached to R1 would only have one way to reach other destinations, whether to networks attached to R2, or to destinations beyond R2. This means that networks 10.0.1.0/24 and 10.0.2.0/24 are stub networks and R1 is a stub router.

In this example, a static route can be configured on R2 to reach the R1 networks. Additionally, because R1 has only one way to send out non-local traffic, a default static route can be configured on R1 to point to R2 as the next hop for all other networks.

Refer to
Online Course
for Illustration

Static Routes in the IP Routing Table - 14.4.6

For demonstrating static routing, the topology in the figure is simplified to show only one LAN attached to each router. The figure shows IPv4 and IPv6 static routes configured on R1 to reach the 10.0.4.0/24 and 2001:db8:acad:4::/64 networks on R2. The configuration commands are for demonstration only and are discussed in another module.

The output shows the IPv4 and IPv6 static routing entries on R1 that can reach the 10.0.4.0/24 and 2001:db8:acad:4::/64 networks on R2. Notice that both routing entries use the status code of **S** indicating that the route was learned by a static route. Both entries also include the IP address of the next hop router, via *ip-address*. The **static** parameter at the end of the command displays only static routes.

```
R1# show ip route static

Codes: L - local, C - connected, S - static, R - RIP, M - mobile,
B - BGP

(output omitted)


        10.0.0.0/8 is variably subnetted, 8 subnets, 2 masks
```

```
S          10.0.4.0/24 [1/0] via 10.0.3.2
R1# show ipv6 route static
IPv6 Routing Table - default - 8 entries
Codes: C - Connected, L - Local, S - Static, U - Per-user Static route
(output omitted)


S    2001:DB8:ACAD:4::/64 [1/0]
        via 2001:DB8:ACAD:3::2
```

Refer to
Online Course
for Illustration

Dynamic Routing Protocols - 14.4.7

Dynamic routing protocols are used by routers to automatically share information about the reachability and status of remote networks. Dynamic routing protocols perform several activities, including network discovery and maintaining routing tables.

Important advantages of dynamic routing protocols are the ability to select a best path, and the ability to automatically discover a new best path when there is a change in the topology.

Network discovery is the ability of a routing protocol to share information about the networks that it knows about with other routers that are also using the same routing protocol. Instead of depending on manually configured static routes to remote networks on every router, a dynamic routing protocol allows the routers to automatically learn about these networks from other routers. These networks, and the best path to each, are added to the routing table of the router, and identified as a network learned by a specific dynamic routing protocol.

The figure shows routers R1 and R2 using a common routing protocol to share network information.

Dynamic Routes in the IP Routing Table - 14.4.8

A previous example used static routes to the 10.0.4.0/24 and 2001:db8:acad:4::/64 networks. These static routes are no longer configured and OSPF is now being used to dynamically learn all the networks connected to R1 and R2. The following examples show the IPv4 and IPv6 OSPF routing entries on R1 that can reach these networks on R2. Notice that both routing entries use the status code of O to indicate the route was learned by the OSPF routing protocol. Both entries also include the IP address of the next-hop router, via *ip-address*.

Note: IPv6 routing protocols use the link-local address of the next-hop router.

Note: OSPF routing configuration for IPv4 and IPv6 is beyond the scope of this course.

```
R1# show ip route
Codes: L - local, C - connected, S - static, R - RIP, M - mobile,
B - BGP

        D - EIGRP, EX - EIGRP external, O - OSPF, IA - OSPF inter area
(output omitted for brevity)
```

```
O          10.0.4.0/24 [110/50] via 10.0.3.2, 00:24:22, Serial0/1/1

O          10.0.5.0/24 [110/50] via 10.0.3.2, 00:24:15, Serial0/1/1

R1# show ipv6 route

IPv6 Routing Table - default - 10 entries

(Output omitted)

          NDr - Redirect, RL - RPL, O - OSPF Intra, OI - OSPF Inter

O    2001:DB8:ACAD:4::/64 [110/50]

     via FE80::2:C, Serial0/1/1

O    2001:DB8:ACAD:5::/64 [110/50]

     via FE80::2:C, Serial0/1/1
```

Refer to **Online Course** for Illustration

Default Route - 14.4.9

A default route is similar to a default gateway on a host. The default route specifies a next-hop router to use when the routing table does not contain a specific route that matches the destination IP address.

A default route can be either a static route or learned automatically from a dynamic routing protocol. A default route has an IPv4 route entry of 0.0.0.0/0 or an IPv6 route entry of ::/0. This means that zero or no bits need to match between the destination IP address and the default route.

Most enterprise routers have a default route in their routing table. This is to reduce the number of routes in a routing table.

A router, such as a home or small office router that only has one LAN, may reach all its remote networks through a default route. This is useful when the router has only directly connected networks and one exit point to a service provider router.

In the figure, routers R1 and R2 are using OSPF to share routing information about their own networks (10.0.x.x/24 and 2001:db8:acad:x::/64 networks). R2 has a static default route to the ISP router. R2 will forward any packets with a destination IP address that does not specifically match one of the networks in its routing table to the ISP router. This would include all packets destined for the internet.

R2 has shared its default route with R1 using OSPF. R1 will now have a default route in its routing table that it learned dynamically from OSPF. R1 will also forward any packets with a destination IP address that does not specifically match one of the networks in its routing table to R2.

The following examples show the IPv4 and IPv6 routing table entries for the static default routes configured on R2.

```
R2# show ip route

(Output omitted)

S*    0.0.0.0/0 [1/0] via 209.165.200.226

R2#

R2# show ipv6 route

(Output omitted)
```

```
S    ::/0 [1/0]
       via 2001:DB8:FEED:224::2
R2#
```

Structure of an IPv4 Routing Table - 14.4.10

IPv4 was standardized in the early 1980s using the now obsolete classful addressing architecture. The IPv4 routing table is organized using this same classful structure. In the **show ip route** output, notice that some route entries are left justified while others are indented. This is based on how the routing process searches the IPv4 routing table for the longest match. This was all because of classful addressing. Although the lookup process no longer uses classes, the structure of the IPv4 routing table still retains in this format.

```
Router# show ip route

(Output omitted)

      192.168.1.0/24 is variably subnetted, 2 subnets, 2 masks
C        192.168.1.0/24 is directly connected, GigabitEthernet0/0
L        192.168.1.1/32 is directly connected, GigabitEthernet0/0
O     192.168.2.0/24 [110/65] via 192.168.12.2, 00:32:33, Serial0/0/0
O     192.168.3.0/24 [110/65] via 192.168.13.2, 00:31:48, Serial0/0/1
      192.168.12.0/24 is variably subnetted, 2 subnets, 2 masks
C        192.168.12.0/30 is directly connected, Serial0/0/0
L        192.168.12.1/32 is directly connected, Serial0/0/0
      192.168.13.0/24 is variably subnetted, 2 subnets, 2 masks
C        192.168.13.0/30 is directly connected, Serial0/0/1
L        192.168.13.1/32 is directly connected, Serial0/0/1
      192.168.23.0/30 is subnetted, 1 subnets
O        192.168.23.0/30 [110/128] via 192.168.12.2, 00:31:38,
Serial0/0/0
Router#
```

Note: The IPv4 routing table in the example is not from any router in the topology used in this module.

Although the details of the structure are beyond the scope of this module, it is helpful to recognize the structure of the table. An indented entry is known as a child route. A route entry is indented if it is the subnet of a classful address (class A, B or C network). Directly connected networks will always be indented (child routes) because the local address of the interface is always entered in the routing table as a /32. The child route will include the route source and all the forwarding information such as the next-hop address. The classful network address of this subnet will be shown above the route entry, less indented, and without a source code. That route is known as a parent route.

Note: This is just a brief introduction to the structure of an IPv4 routing table and does not cover details or specifics of this architecture.

The next example shows the IPv4 routing table of R1 in the topology. Notice that all of the networks in the topology are subnets, which are child routes, of the class A network and parent route10.0.0.0/8.

```
R1# show ip route

(output omitted for brevity)

O*E2  0.0.0.0/0 [110/1] via 10.0.3.2, 00:51:34, Serial0/1/1

         10.0.0.0/8 is variably subnetted, 8 subnets, 2 masks

C        10.0.1.0/24 is directly connected, GigabitEthernet0/0/0

L        10.0.1.1/32 is directly connected, GigabitEthernet0/0/0

C        10.0.2.0/24 is directly connected, GigabitEthernet0/0/1

L        10.0.2.1/32 is directly connected, GigabitEthernet0/0/1

C        10.0.3.0/24 is directly connected, Serial0/1/1

L        10.0.3.1/32 is directly connected, Serial0/1/1

O        10.0.4.0/24 [110/50] via 10.0.3.2, 00:24:22, Serial0/1/1

O        10.0.5.0/24 [110/50] via 10.0.3.2, 00:24:15, Serial0/1/1

R1#
```

Structure of an IPv6 Routing Table - 14.4.11

The concept of classful addressing was never part of IPv6, so the structure of an IPv6 routing table is very straight forward. Every IPv6 route entry is formatted and aligned the same way.

```
R1# show ipv6 route

(output omitted for brevity)

OE2 ::/0 [110/1], tag 2

     via FE80::2:C, Serial0/0/1

C    2001:DB8:ACAD:1::/64 [0/0]

     via GigabitEthernet0/0/0, directly connected

L    2001:DB8:ACAD:1::1/128 [0/0]

     via GigabitEthernet0/0/0, receive

C    2001:DB8:ACAD:2::/64 [0/0]

     via GigabitEthernet0/0/1, directly connected

L    2001:DB8:ACAD:2::1/128 [0/0]

     via GigabitEthernet0/0/1, receive

C    2001:DB8:ACAD:3::/64 [0/0]

     via Serial0/1/1, directly connected
```

```
L    2001:DB8:ACAD:3::1/128 [0/0]

        via Serial0/1/1, receive

O    2001:DB8:ACAD:4::/64 [110/50]

        via FE80::2:C, Serial0/1/1

O    2001:DB8:ACAD:5::/64 [110/50]

        via FE80::2:C, Serial0/1/1

L    FF00::/8 [0/0]

        via Null0, receive

R1#
```

Administrative Distance - 14.4.12

A route entry for a specific network address (prefix and prefix length) can only appear once in the routing table. However, it is possible that the routing table learns about the same network address from more than one routing source.

Except for very specific circumstances, only one dynamic routing protocol should be implemented on a router. However, it is possible to configure both OSPF and EIGRP on a router, and both routing protocols may learn of the same destination network. Each routing protocol may decide on a different path to reach the destination based on the metric of that routing protocol.

This raises a few questions, such as the following:

- How does the router know which source to use?

- Which route should it install in the routing table? The route learned from OSPF, or the route learned from EIGRP?

Cisco IOS uses what is known as the administrative distance (AD) to determine the route to install into the IP routing table. The AD represents the "trustworthiness" of the route. The lower the AD, the more trustworthy the route source. Because EIGRP has an AD of 90 and OSPF has an AD of 110, the EIGRP route entry would be installed in the routing table.

Note: The AD does not necessarily represent which dynamic routing protocol is best.

A more common example is a router learning the same network address from a static route and a dynamic routing protocol, such as OSPF. A static route has an AD of 1, whereas an OSPF-discovered route has an AD of 110. Given two separate route sources to the same destination, the router chooses to install the route with the lowest AD. When a router has the choice of a static route and an OSPF route, the static route takes precedence.

Note: Directly connected networks have the lowest AD of 0. Only a directly connected network can have an AD of 0.

The table lists various routing protocols and their associated ADs.

Route Source	Administrative Distance
Directly connected	0
Static route	1
EIGRP summary route	5
External BGP	20
Internal EIGRP	90
OSPF	110
IS-IS	115
RIP	120
External EIGRP	170
Internal BGP	200

Go to the online course to take the quiz and exam.

Check Your Understanding - IP Routing Table - 14.4.13

Static and Dynamic Routing - 14.5

Static or Dynamic? - 14.5.1

The previous topic discussed the ways that a router creates its routing table. So, you now know that routing, like IP addressing, can be either static or dynamic. Should you use static or dynamic routing? The answer is both! Static and dynamic routing are not mutually exclusive. Rather, most networks use a combination of dynamic routing protocols and static routes.

Static Routes

Static routes are commonly used in the following scenarios:

- As a default route forwarding packets to a service provider
- For routes outside the routing domain and not learned by the dynamic routing protocol
- When the network administrator wants to explicitly define the path for a specific network
- For routing between stub networks

Static routes are useful for smaller networks with only one path to an outside network. They also provide security in a larger network for certain types of traffic, or links to other networks that need more control.

Dynamic Routing Protocols

Dynamic routing protocols help the network administrator manage the time-consuming and exacting process of configuring and maintaining static routes. Dynamic routing protocols are implemented in any type of network consisting of more than just a few routers.

Dynamic routing protocols are scalable and automatically determine better routes if there is a change in the topology.

Dynamic routing protocols are commonly used in the following scenarios:

- In networks consisting of more than just a few routers

- When a change in the network topology requires the network to automatically determine another path

- For scalability. As the network grows, the dynamic routing protocol automatically learns about any new networks.

The table shows a comparison of some the differences between dynamic and static routing.

Feature	Dynamic Routing	Static Routing
Configuration complexity	Independent of network size	Increases with network size
Topology changes	Automatically adapts to topology changes	Administrator intervention required
Scalability	Suitable for simple to complex network topologies	Suitable for simple topologies
Security	Security must be configured	Security is inherent
Resource Usage	Uses CPU, memory, and link bandwidth	No additional resources needed
Path Predictability	Route depends on topology and routing protocol used	Explicitly defined by the administrator

Dynamic Routing Evolution - 14.5.2

Refer to
Online Course
for Illustration

Dynamic routing protocols have been used in networks since the late 1980s. One of the first routing protocols was RIP. RIPv1 was released in 1988, but some of the basic algorithms within the protocol were used on the Advanced Research Projects Agency Network (ARPANET) as early as 1969.

As networks evolved and became more complex, new routing protocols emerged. The RIP protocol was updated to RIPv2 to accommodate growth in the network environment. However, RIPv2 still does not scale to the larger network implementations of today. To address the needs of larger networks, two advanced routing protocols were developed: OSPF and Intermediate System-to-Intermediate System (IS-IS). Cisco developed the Interior Gateway Routing Protocol (IGRP), which was later replaced by Enhanced IGRP (EIGRP), which also scales well in larger network implementations.

Additionally, there was the need to connect the different routing domains of different organizations and provide routing between them. The Border Gateway Protocol (BGP), the successor of Exterior Gateway Protocol (EGP) is used between Internet Service Providers (ISPs). BGP is also used between ISPs and some private organizations to exchange routing information.

The figure displays the timeline of when the various protocols were introduced.

To support IPv6 communication, newer versions of the IP routing protocols have been developed, as shown in the IPv6 row in the table.

The table classifies the current routing protocols. Interior Gateway Protocols (IGPs) are routing protocols used to exchange routing information within a routing domain administered by a single organization. There is only one EGP and it is BGP. BGP is used to exchange routing information between different organizations, known as autonomous systems (AS). BGP is used by ISPs to route packets over the internet. Distance vector, link-state, and path vector routing protocols refer to the type of routing algorithm used to determine best path.

	Interior Gateway Protocols				Exterior Gateway Protocols
	Distance Vector		Link-State		Path Vector
IPv4	RIPv2	EIGRP	OSPFv2	IS-IS	BGP-4
IPv6	RIPng	EIGRP for IPv6	OSPFv3	IS-IS for IPv6	BGP-MP

Refer to Interactive Graphic in online course

Dynamic Routing Protocol Concepts - 14.5.3

A routing protocol is a set of processes, algorithms, and messages that are used to exchange routing information and populate the routing table with the choice of best paths. The purpose of dynamic routing protocols includes the following:

- Discovery of remote networks
- Maintaining up-to-date routing information
- Choosing the best path to destination networks
- Ability to find a new best path if the current path is no longer available

The main components of dynamic routing protocols include the following:

- **Data structures** - Routing protocols typically use tables or databases for their operations. This information is kept in RAM.
- **Routing protocol messages** - Routing protocols use various types of messages to discover neighboring routers, exchange routing information, and other tasks to learn and maintain accurate information about the network.
- **Algorithm** - An algorithm is a finite list of steps used to accomplish a task. Routing protocols use algorithms for facilitating routing information and for the best path determination.

Routing protocols allow routers to dynamically share information about remote networks and automatically offer this information to their own routing tables. Click Play to see an animation of this process.

Routing protocols determine the best path, or route, to each network. That route is then offered to the routing table. The route will be installed in the routing table if there is not another routing source with a lower AD. A primary benefit of dynamic routing protocols is that routers exchange routing information when there is a topology change. This exchange allows routers to automatically learn about new networks and to find alternate paths when there is a link failure to a current network.

Refer to
Interactive Graphic
in online course

Best Path - 14.5.4

Before a path to a remote network is offered to the routing table, the dynamic routing protocol must determine the best path to that network. Determining the best path may involve the evaluation of multiple paths to the same destination network and selecting the optimum or shortest path to reach that network. Whenever multiple paths to the same network exist, each path uses a different exit interface on the router to reach that network.

The best path is selected by a routing protocol based on the value or metric it uses to determine the distance to reach a network. A metric is the quantitative value used to measure the distance to a given network. The best path to a network is the path with the lowest metric.

Dynamic routing protocols typically use their own rules and metrics to build and update routing tables. The routing algorithm generates a value, or a metric, for each path through the network. Metrics can be based on either a single characteristic or several characteristics of a path. Some routing protocols can base route selection on multiple metrics, combining them into a single metric.

The following table lists common dynamic protocols and their metrics.

Routing Protocol	Metric
Routing Information Protocol (RIP)	• The metric is "hop count". • Each router along a path adds a hop to the hop count. • A maximum of 15 hops allowed.
Open Shortest Path First (OSPF)	• The metric is "cost" which is the based on the cumulative bandwidth from source to destination. • Faster links are assigned lower costs compared to slower (higher cost) links.
Enhanced Interior Gateway Routing Protocol (EIGRP)	• It calculates a metric based on the slowest bandwidth and delay values. • It could also include load and reliability into the metric calculation.

The animation in the figure highlights how the path may be different depending on the metric being used. If the best path fails, the dynamic routing protocol will automatically select a new best path if one exists.

Refer to
Interactive Graphic
in online course

Load Balancing - 14.5.5

What happens if a routing table has two or more paths with identical metrics to the same destination network?

When a router has two or more paths to a destination with equal cost metrics, then the router forwards the packets using both paths equally. This is called equal cost load balancing. The routing table contains the single destination network, but has multiple exit interfaces, one for each equal cost path. The router forwards packets using the multiple exit interfaces listed in the routing table.

If configured correctly, load balancing can increase the effectiveness and performance of the network.

Equal cost load balancing is implemented automatically by dynamic routing protocols. It is enabled with static routes when there are multiple static routes to the same destination network using different next-hop routers.

Note: Only EIGRP supports unequal cost load balancing.

The animation in the figure provides an example of equal cost load balancing.

Go to the online course to take the quiz and exam.

Check Your Understanding - Dynamic and Static Routing - 14.5.6

Module Practice and Quiz - 14.6

What did I learn in this module? - 14.6.1

Path Determination

The primary functions of a router are to determine the best path to forward packets based on the information in its routing table, and to forward packets toward their destination. The best path in the routing table is also known as the longest match. The longest match is the route in the routing table that has the greatest number of far-left matching bits with the destination IP address of the packet. Directly connected networks are networks that are configured on the active interfaces of a router. A directly connected network is added to the routing table when an interface is configured with an IP address and subnet mask (prefix length) and is active (up and up). Routers learn about remote networks in two ways: static routes are added to the routing table when a route is manually configured, and with dynamic routing protocols. Using dynamic routing protocols such as EIGRP and OSPF, routes are added to the routing table when routing protocols dynamically learn about the remote network.

Packet Forwarding

After a router determines the correct path, it can forward the packet on a directly connected network, it can forward the packet to a next-hop router, or it can drop the packet. The primary responsibility of the packet forwarding function is to encapsulate packets in the appropriate data link frame type for the outgoing interface. Routers support three packet forwarding mechanisms: process switching, fast switching, and CEF. The following steps describe the packet forwarding process:

1. The data link frame with an encapsulated IP packet arrives on the ingress interface.

2. The router examines the destination IP address in the packet header and consults its IP routing table.

3. The router finds the longest matching prefix in the routing table.

4. The router encapsulates the packet in a data link frame and forwards it out the egress interface. The destination could be a device connected to the network or a next-hop router.

5. However, if there is no matching route entry the packet is dropped.

Basic Router Configuration Review

There are several configuration and verification commands for routers, including **show ip route**, **show ip interface**, **show ip interface brief** and **show running-config**. To reduce the amount of command output, use a filter. Filtering commands can be used to display specific sections of output. To enable the filtering command, enter a pipe (|) character after the **show** command and then enter a filtering parameter and a filtering expression. The filtering parameters that can be configured after the pipe include the following:

- **section** - Shows entire section that starts with the filtering expression

- **include** - Includes all output lines that match the filtering expression

- **exclude** - Excludes all output lines that match the filtering expression

- **begin** - Shows all the output lines from a certain point, starting with the line that matches the filtering expression

IP Routing Table

A routing table contains a list of routes known networks (prefixes and prefix lengths). The source of this information is derived from directly connected networks, static routes, and dynamic routing protocols. Common routing table codes include:

- **L** - Identifies the address assigned to a router interface. This allows the router to efficiently determine when it receives a packet for the interface instead of being forwarded.

- **C** - Identifies a directly connected network.

- **S** - Identifies a static route created to reach a specific network.

- **O** - Identifies a dynamically learned network from another router using the OSPF routing protocol.

- ***** - This route is a candidate for a default route.

Every router makes its decision alone, based on the information it has in its own routing table. The information in a routing table of one router does not necessarily match the routing table of another router. Routing information about a path does not provide return routing information. Routing table entries include the route source, destination network, AD, metric, next-hop, route timestamp, and exit interface. To learn about remote networks, a router must have at least one active interface configured with an IP address and subnet mask (prefix length), called a directly connected network. Static routes are manually configured and define an explicit path between two networking devices. Dynamic routing protocols can discover a network, maintain routing tables, select a best path, and automatically discover a new best path if the topology changes. The default route specifies a next-hop router to use when the routing table does not contain a specific route that matches the destination IP address. A default route can be either a static route or learned automatically from a dynamic routing protocol. A default route has an IPv4 route entry of 0.0.0.0/0 or an IPv6 route entry of ::/0. IPv4 routing tables still have a structure based on classful addressing represented by levels of indentation. IPv6 routing tables do not use the IPv4 routing table structure. Cisco IOS uses what is known as the administrative distance (AD) to determine the route to install into the IP routing table. The AD represents the "trustworthiness" of the route. The lower the AD, the more trustworthy the route source.

Static and Dynamic Routing

Static routes are commonly used:

- As a default route forwarding packets to a service provider.

- For routes outside the routing domain and not learned by the dynamic routing protocol.

- When the network administrator wants to explicitly define the path for a specific network.

- For routing between stub networks.

Dynamic routing protocol are commonly used:

- In networks consisting of more than just a few routers

- When a change in the network topology requires the network to automatically determine another path

- For scalability. As the network grows, the dynamic routing protocol automatically learns about any new networks.

Current routing protocols include IGPs and EGPs. IGPs exchange routing information within a routing domain administered by a single organization. The only EGP is BGP. BGP exchanges routing information between different organizations. BGP is used by ISPs to route packets over the internet. Distance vector, link-state, and path vector routing protocols refer to the type of routing algorithm used to determine best path. The main components of dynamic routing protocols are data structures, routing protocol messages, and algorithms. The best path is selected by a routing protocol based on the value or metric it uses to determine the distance to reach a network. A metric is the quantitative value used to measure the distance to a given network. The best path to a network is the path with the lowest metric. When a router has two or more paths to a destination with equal cost metrics, then the router forwards the packets using both paths equally. This is called equal cost load balancing.

Go to the online course to take the quiz and exam.

Chapter Quiz - Routing Concepts

Your Chapter Notes

CHAPTER 15

IP Static Routing

Introduction - 15.0

Why should I take this module? - 15.0.1

Welcome to IP Static Routing!

There are so many different ways to dynamically route a packet that you might wonder why anybody would take the time to manually configure a static route. It is kind of like handwashing all of your clothes when you have a perfectly good washing machine. But you know that some clothing items cannot go in the washing machine. Some items benefit from being washed by hand. There is a similarity in networking. As it turns out, there are many situations where a manually configured a static route is your best option.

There are different kinds of static routes, and each is perfect for solving (or avoiding) a specific type of network problem. Many networks use both dynamic and static routing, so network administrators need to know how to configure, verify, and troubleshoot static routes. You are taking this course because you want to become a network administrator, or you want to improve your existing network administrator skills. You will be glad you took this module, because you will use these skills frequently! And because this module is about configuring static routes, there are several Syntax Checker activities, followed by a Packet Tracer and a Lab where you can hone your skills!

What will I learn to do in this module? - 15.0.2

Module Title: IP Static Routing

Module Objective: Configure IPv4 and IPv6 static routes.

Topic Title	Topic Objective
Static Routes	Describe the command syntax for static routes.
Configure IP Static Routes	Configure IPv4 and IPv6 static routes.
Configure IP Default Static Routes	Configure IPv4 and IPv6 default static routes.
Configure Floating Static Routes	Configure a floating static route to provide a backup connection.
Configure Static Host Routes	Configure IPv4 and IPv6 static host routes that direct traffic to a specific host.

Static Routes - 15.1

Types of Static Routes - 15.1.1

Static routes are commonly implemented on a network. This is true even when there is a dynamic routing protocol configured. For instance, an organization could configure a default static route to the service provider and advertise this route to other corporate routers using the dynamic routing protocol.

Static routes can be configured for IPv4 and IPv6. Both protocols support the following types of static routes:

- Standard static route
- Default static route
- Floating static route
- Summary static route

Static routes are configured using the **ip route** and **ipv6 route** global configuration commands.

Next-Hop Options - 15.1.2

When configuring a static route, the next hop can be identified by an IP address, exit interface, or both. How the destination is specified creates one of the three following types of static route:

- **Next-hop route** - Only the next-hop IP address is specified
- **Directly connected static route** - Only the router exit interface is specified
- **Fully specified static route** - The next-hop IP address and exit interface are specified

IPv4 Static Route Command - 15.1.3

IPv4 static routes are configured using the following global configuration command:

```
Router(config)# ip route network-address subnet-mask { ip-address |
exit-intf [ip-address]} [distance]
```

Note: Either the *ip-address*, *exit-intf,* or the *ip-address* and *exit-intf* parameters must be configured.

The table describes the **ip route** command parameters.

Parameter	Description
network-address	Identifies the destination IPv4 network address of the remote network to add to the routing table.
subnet-mask	• Identifies the subnet mask of the remote network. • The subnet mask can be modified to summarize a group of networks and create a summary static route.
ip-address	• Identifies the next-hop router IPv4 address. • Typically used with broadcast networks (i.e., Ethernet). • Could create a recursive static route where the router performs an additional lookup to find the exit interface.

Parameter	Description
exit-intf	• Identifies the exit interface to forward packets. • Creates a directly connected static route. • Typically used in a point-to-point configuration.
exit-intf ip-address	Creates a fully specified static route because it specifies the exit interface and next-hop IPv4 address.
distance	• Optional command that can be used to assign an administrative distance value between 1 and 255. • Typically used to configure a floating static route by setting an administrative distance that is higher than a dynamically learned route.

IPv6 Static Route Command - 15.1.4

IPv6 static routes are configured using the following global configuration command:

```
Router(config)# ipv6 route ipv6-prefix/prefix-length {ipv6-address |
exit-intf [ipv6-address]} [distance]
```

Most of parameters are identical to the IPv4 version of the command.

The table shows the various **ipv6 route** command parameters and their descriptions.

Parameter	Description
ipv6-prefix	Identifies the destination IPv6 network address of the remote network to add to the routing table.
/prefix-length	Identifies the prefix length of the remote network.
ipv6-address	• Identifies the next-hop router IPv6 address. • Typically used with broadcast networks (i.e., Ethernet) • Could create a recursive static route where the router performs an additional lookup to find the exit interface.
exit-intf	• Identifies the exit interface to forward packets. • Creates a directly connected static route. • Typically used in a point-to-point configuration.
exit-intf ipv6-address	Creates a fully specified static route because it specifies the exit interface and next-hop IPv6 address.
distance	• Optional command that can be used to assign an administrative distance value between 1 and 255. • Typically used to configure a floating static route by setting an administrative distance that is higher than a dynamically learned route.

Note: The **ipv6 unicast-routing** global configuration command must be configured to enable the router to forward IPv6 packets.

Refer to
Online Course
for Illustration

Dual-Stack Topology - 15.1.5

The figure shows a dual-stack network topology. Currently, no static routes are configured for either IPv4 or IPv6.

Refer to
Interactive Graphic
in online course

IPv4 Starting Routing Tables - 15.1.6

Click each button to see the IPv4 routing table of each router and ping results. Notice that each router has entries only for directly connected networks and associated local addresses.

R1 IPv4 Routing Table

```
R1# show ip route | begin Gateway

Gateway of last resort is not set

      172.16.0.0/16 is variably subnetted, 4 subnets, 2 masks
C        172.16.2.0/24 is directly connected, Serial0/1/0
L        172.16.2.1/32 is directly connected, Serial0/1/0
C        172.16.3.0/24 is directly connected, GigabitEthernet0/0/0
L        172.16.3.1/32 is directly connected, GigabitEthernet0/0/0
R1#
```

R2 IPv4 Routing Table

```
R2# show ip route | begin Gateway

Gateway of last resort is not set

      172.16.0.0/16 is variably subnetted, 4 subnets, 2 masks
C        172.16.1.0/24 is directly connected, GigabitEthernet0/0/0
L        172.16.1.1/32 is directly connected, GigabitEthernet0/0/0
C        172.16.2.0/24 is directly connected, Serial0/1/0
L        172.16.2.2/32 is directly connected, Serial0/1/0
      192.168.1.0/24 is variably subnetted, 2 subnets, 2 masks
C        192.168.1.0/24 is directly connected, Serial0/1/1
L        192.168.1.2/32 is directly connected, Serial0/1/1
R2#
```

R3 IPv4 Routing Table

```
R3# show ip route | begin Gateway

Gateway of last resort is not set

      192.168.1.0/24 is variably subnetted, 2 subnets, 2 masks
C        192.168.1.0/24 is directly connected, Serial0/1/1
```

```
L          192.168.1.1/32 is directly connected, Serial0/1/1
      192.168.2.0/24 is variably subnetted, 2 subnets, 2 masks
C          192.168.2.0/24 is directly connected, GigabitEthernet0/0/0
L          192.168.2.1/32 is directly connected, GigabitEthernet0/0/0
R3#
```

R1 Can Ping R2

None of the routers have knowledge of any networks beyond the directly connected interfaces. This means each router can only reach directly connected networks, as demonstrated in the following ping tests.

A **ping** from R1 to the serial 0/1/0 interface of R2 should be successful because it is a directly-connected network.

```
R1# ping 172.16.2.2
Type escape sequence to abort.
Sending 5, 100-byte ICMP Echos to 172.16.2.2, timeout is 2 seconds:
!!!!!
```

R1 Cannot Ping R3 LAN

However, a **ping** from R1 to the R3 LAN should fail because R1 does not have an entry in its routing table for the R3 LAN network.

```
R1# ping 192.168.2.1
Type escape sequence to abort.
Sending 5, 100-byte ICMP Echos to 192.168.2.1, timeout is 2 seconds:
.....
Success rate is 0 percent (0/5)
```

Refer to
Interactive Graphic
in online course

IPv6 Starting Routing Tables - 15.1.7

Click each button to see the IPv6 routing table of each router and ping results. Notice that each router has entries only for directly connected networks and associated local addresses.

R1 IPv6 Routing Table

```
R1# show ipv6 route | begin C
C    2001:DB8:ACAD:2::/64 [0/0]
        via Serial0/1/0, directly connected
L    2001:DB8:ACAD:2::1/128 [0/0]
        via Serial0/1/0, receive
```

```
C    2001:DB8:ACAD:3::/64 [0/0]

       via GigabitEthernet0/0/0, directly connected

L    2001:DB8:ACAD:3::1/128 [0/0]

       via GigabitEthernet0/0/0, receive

L    FF00::/8 [0/0]

       via Null0, receive

R1#
```

R2 IPv6 Routing Table

```
R2# show ipv6 route | begin C

C    2001:DB8:ACAD:1::/64 [0/0]

       via GigabitEthernet0/0/0, directly connected

L    2001:DB8:ACAD:1::1/128 [0/0]

       via GigabitEthernet0/0/0, receive

C    2001:DB8:ACAD:2::/64 [0/0]

       via Serial0/1/0, directly connected

L    2001:DB8:ACAD:2::2/128 [0/0]

       via Serial0/1/0, receive

C    2001:DB8:CAFE:1::/64 [0/0]

       via Serial0/1/1, directly connected

L    2001:DB8:CAFE:1::2/128 [0/0]

       via Serial0/1/1, receive

L    FF00::/8 [0/0]

       via Null0, receive

R2#
```

R3 IPv6 Routing Table

```
R3# show ipv6 route | begin C

C    2001:DB8:CAFE:1::/64 [0/0]

       via Serial0/1/1, directly connected

L    2001:DB8:CAFE:1::1/128 [0/0]

       via Serial0/1/1, receive

C    2001:DB8:CAFE:2::/64 [0/0]

       via GigabitEthernet0/0/0, directly connected

L    2001:DB8:CAFE:2::1/128 [0/0]

       via GigabitEthernet0/0/0, receive
```

```
L    FF00::/8 [0/0]

     via Null0, receive

R3#
```

R1 Can Ping R2

None of the routers have knowledge of any networks beyond the directly connected interfaces.

A **ping** from R1 to the serial 0/1/0 interface on R2 should be successful.

```
R1# ping 2001:db8:acad:2::2

Type escape sequence to abort.

Sending 5, 100-byte ICMP Echos to 2001:DB8:ACAD:2::2, timeout is 2
seconds:

!!!!!

Success rate is 100 percent (5/5), round-trip min/avg/max = 2/2/3 ms
```

R1 Cannot Ping R3 LAN

However, a **ping** to the R3 LAN is unsuccessful. This is because R1 does not have an entry in its routing table for that network.

```
R1# ping 2001:DB8:cafe:2::1

Type escape sequence to abort.

Sending 5, 100-byte ICMP Echos to 2001:DB8:CAFE:2::1, timeout is
2 seconds:

% No valid route for destination

Success rate is 0 percent (0/1)
```

Check Your Understanding - Static Routes - 15.1.8

Configure IP Static Routes - 15.2

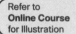

IPv4 Next-Hop Static Route - 15.2.1

The commands to configure standard static routes varies slightly between IPv4 and IPv6. This topic shows you how to configure standard next-hop, directly connected, and full specified static routes for both IPv4 and Ipv6.

In a next-hop static route, only the next-hop IP address is specified. The exit interface is derived from the next hop. For example, three next-hop IPv4 static routes are configured on R1 using the IP address of the next hop, R2.

The commands to configure R1 with the IPv4 static routes to the three remote networks are as follows:

```
R1(config)# ip route 172.16.1.0 255.255.255.0 172.16.2.2
R1(config)# ip route 192.168.1.0 255.255.255.0 172.16.2.2
R1(config)# ip route 192.168.2.0 255.255.255.0 172.16.2.2
```

The routing table for R1 now has routes to the three remote IPv4 networks.

```
R1# show ip route | begin Gateway
Gateway of last resort is not set

      172.16.0.0/16 is variably subnetted, 5 subnets, 2 masks
S        172.16.1.0/24 [1/0] via 172.16.2.2
C        172.16.2.0/24 is directly connected, Serial0/1/0
L        172.16.2.1/32 is directly connected, Serial0/1/0
C        172.16.3.0/24 is directly connected, GigabitEthernet0/0/0
L        172.16.3.1/32 is directly connected, GigabitEthernet0/0/0
S     192.168.1.0/24 [1/0] via 172.16.2.2
S     192.168.2.0/24 [1/0] via 172.16.2.2
R1#
```

IPv6 Next-Hop Static Route - 15.2.2

The commands to configure R1 with the IPv6 static routes to the three remote networks are as follows:

```
R1(config)# ipv6 unicast-routing
R1(config)# ipv6 route 2001:db8:acad:1::/64 2001:db8:acad:2::2
R1(config)# ipv6 route 2001:db8:cafe:1::/64 2001:db8:acad:2::2
R1(config)# ipv6 route 2001:db8:cafe:2::/64 2001:db8:acad:2::2
```

The routing table for R1 now has routes to the three remote IPv6 networks.

```
R1# show ipv6 route
IPv6 Routing Table - default - 8 entries
Codes: C - Connected, L - Local, S - Static, U - Per-user Static route
       B - BGP, R - RIP, H - NHRP, I1 - ISIS L1
       I2 - ISIS L2, IA - ISIS interarea, IS - ISIS summary, D - EIGRP
       EX - EIGRP external, ND - ND Default, NDp - ND Prefix,
          DCE - Destination
       NDr - Redirect, RL - RPL, O - OSPF Intra, OI - OSPF Inter
       OE1 - OSPF ext 1, OE2 - OSPF ext 2, ON1 - OSPF NSSA ext 1
       ON2 - OSPF NSSA ext 2, la - LISP alt, lr - LISP site-registrations
```

```
                   ld - LISP dyn-eid, lA - LISP away, le - LISP extranet-policy
                   a - Application
S     2001:DB8:ACAD:1::/64 [1/0]
        via 2001:DB8:ACAD:2::2
C     2001:DB8:ACAD:2::/64 [0/0]
        via Serial0/1/0, directly connected
L     2001:DB8:ACAD:2::1/128 [0/0]
        via Serial0/1/0, receive
C     2001:DB8:ACAD:3::/64 [0/0]
        via GigabitEthernet0/0/0, directly connected
L     2001:DB8:ACAD:3::1/128 [0/0]
        via GigabitEthernet0/0/0, receive
S     2001:DB8:CAFE:1::/64 [1/0]
        via 2001:DB8:ACAD:2::2
S     2001:DB8:CAFE:2::/64 [1/0]
        via 2001:DB8:ACAD:2::2
L     FF00::/8 [0/0]
        via Null0, receive
```

IPv4 Directly Connected Static Route - 15.2.3

Refer to **Online Course** for Illustration

When configuring a static route, another option is to use the exit interface to specify the next-hop address. The figure shows the topology again.

Three directly connected IPv4 static routes are configured on R1 using the exit interface.

```
R1(config)# ip route 172.16.1.0 255.255.255.0 s0/1/0
R1(config)# ip route 192.168.1.0 255.255.255.0 s0/1/0
R1(config)# ip route 192.168.2.0 255.255.255.0 s0/1/0
```

The IPv4 routing table for R1 shows that when a packet is destined for the 192.168.2.0/24 network, R1 looks for a match in the routing table, and finds that it can forward the packet out of its Serial 0/1/0 interface.

Note: Using a next-hop address is generally recommended. Directly connected static routes should only be used with point-to-point serial interfaces, as in this example.

```
R1# show ip route | begin Gateway
Gateway of last resort is not set
      172.16.0.0/16 is variably subnetted, 5 subnets, 2 masks
S        172.16.1.0/24 is directly connected, Serial0/1/0
```

```
C          172.16.2.0/24 is directly connected, Serial0/1/0
L          172.16.2.1/32 is directly connected, Serial0/1/0
C          172.16.3.0/24 is directly connected, GigabitEthernet0/0/0
L          172.16.3.1/32 is directly connected, GigabitEthernet0/0/0
S       192.168.1.0/24 is directly connected, Serial0/1/0
S       192.168.2.0/24 is directly connected, Serial0/1/0
```

IPv6 Directly Connected Static Route - 15.2.4

In the example, three directly connected IPv6 static routes are configured on R1 using the exit interface.

R1(config)# **ipv6 route 2001:db8:acad:1::/64 s0/1/0**

R1(config)# **ipv6 route 2001:db8:cafe:1::/64 s0/1/0**

R1(config)# **ipv6 route 2001:db8:cafe:2::/64 s0/1/0**

The IPv6 routing table for R1 in the example output shows that when a packet is destined for the 2001:db8:cafe:2::/64 network, R1 looks for a match in the routing table and finds that it can forward the packet out of its Serial 0/1/0 interface.

Note: Using a next-hop address is generally recommended. Directly connected static routes should only be used with point-to-point serial interfaces, as in this example.

```
R1# show ipv6 route
IPv6 Routing Table - default - 8 entries
Codes: C - Connected, L - Local, S - Static, U - Per-user Static route
       B - BGP, R - RIP, H - NHRP, I1 - ISIS L1
       I2 - ISIS L2, IA - ISIS interarea, IS - ISIS summary, D - EIGRP
       EX - EIGRP external, ND - ND Default, NDp - ND Prefix,
          DCE - Destination
       NDr - Redirect, RL - RPL, O - OSPF Intra, OI - OSPF Inter
       OE1 - OSPF ext 1, OE2 - OSPF ext 2, ON1 - OSPF NSSA ext 1
       ON2 - OSPF NSSA ext 2, la - LISP alt, lr - LISP site-registrations
       ld - LISP dyn-eid, lA - LISP away, le - LISP extranet-policy
       a - Application
S    2001:DB8:ACAD:1::/64 [1/0]
     via Serial0/1/0, directly connected
C    2001:DB8:ACAD:2::/64 [0/0]
     via Serial0/1/0, directly connected
L    2001:DB8:ACAD:2::1/128 [0/0]
     via Serial0/1/0, receive
```

```
C    2001:DB8:ACAD:3::/64 [0/0]

        via GigabitEthernet0/0/0, directly connected
L    2001:DB8:ACAD:3::1/128 [0/0]

        via GigabitEthernet0/0/0, receive
S    2001:DB8:CAFE:1::/64 [1/0]

        via Serial0/1/0, directly connected
S    2001:DB8:CAFE:2::/64 [1/0]

        via Serial0/1/0, directly connected
L    FF00::/8 [0/0]

        via Null0, receiveIPv6 Routing Table - default - 8 entries
R1#
```

Refer to Online Course for Illustration

IPv4 Fully Specified Static Route - 15.2.5

In a fully specified static route, both the exit interface and the next-hop IP address are specified. This form of static route is used when the exit interface is a multi-access interface and it is necessary to explicitly identify the next hop. The next hop must be directly connected to the specified exit interface. Using an exit interface is optional, however it is necessary to use a next-hop address.

Suppose that the network link between R1 and R2 is an Ethernet link and that the GigabitEthernet 0/0/1 interface of R1 is connected to that network, as shown in the figure.

The difference between an Ethernet multi-access network and a point-to-point serial network is that a point-to-point serial network has only one other device on that network, the router at the other end of the link. With Ethernet networks, there may be many different devices sharing the same multi-access network, including hosts and even multiple routers.

It is recommended that when the exit interface is an Ethernet network, that the static route includes a next-hop address. You can also use a fully specified static route that includes both the exit interface and the next-hop address.

```
R1(config)# ip route 172.16.1.0 255.255.255.0 GigabitEthernet 0/0/1
172.16.2.2

R1(config)# ip route 192.168.1.0 255.255.255.0 GigabitEthernet 0/0/1
172.16.2.2

R1(config)# ip route 192.168.2.0 255.255.255.0 GigabitEthernet 0/0/1
172.16.2.2
```

When forwarding packets to R2, the exit interface is GigabitEthernet 0/0/1 and the next-hop IPv4 address is 172.16.2.2 as shown in the show ip route output from R1.

```
R1# show ip route | begin Gateway

Gateway of last resort is not set

        172.16.0.0/16 is variably subnetted, 5 subnets, 2 masks

S       172.16.1.0/24 [1/0] via 172.16.2.2, GigabitEthernet0/0/1
```

```
C          172.16.2.0/24 is directly connected, GigabitEthernet0/0/1
L          172.16.2.1/32 is directly connected, GigabitEthernet0/0/1
C          172.16.3.0/24 is directly connected, GigabitEthernet0/0/0
L          172.16.3.1/32 is directly connected, GigabitEthernet0/0/0
S      192.168.1.0/24 [1/0] via 172.16.2.2, GigabitEthernet0/0/1
S      192.168.2.0/24 [1/0] via 172.16.2.2, GigabitEthernet0/0/1
```

Refer to
Online Course
for Illustration

IPv6 Fully Specified Static Route - 15.2.6

In a fully specified IPv6 static route, both the exit interface and the next-hop IPv6 address are specified. There is a situation in IPv6 when a fully specified static route must be used. If the IPv6 static route uses an IPv6 link-local address as the next-hop address, use a fully specified static route. The figure shows an example of a fully specified IPv6 static route using an IPv6 link-local address as the next-hop address.

```
R1(config)# ipv6 route 2001:db8:acad:1::/64 fe80::2

%Interface has to be specified for a link-local nexthop

R1(config)# ipv6 route 2001:db8:acad:1::/64 s0/1/0 fe80::2
```

In the example, a fully specified static route is configured using the link-local address of R2 as the next-hop address. Notice that IOS requires that an exit interface be specified.

The reason a fully specified static route must be used is because IPv6 link-local addresses are not contained in the IPv6 routing table. Link-local addresses are only unique on a given link or network. The next-hop link-local address may be a valid address on multiple networks connected to the router. Therefore, it is necessary that the exit interface be included.

The following example shows the IPv6 routing table entry for this route. Notice that both the next-hop link-local address and the exit interface are included.

```
R1# show ipv6 route static | begin 2001:db8:acad:1::/64

S   2001:DB8:ACAD:1::/64 [1/0]
    via FE80::2, Seria0/1/0
```

Refer to
Online Course
for Illustration

Refer to
Interactive Graphic
in online course

Verify a Static Route - 15.2.7

Along with **show ip route**, **show ipv6 route**, **ping** and **traceroute**, other useful commands to verify static routes include the following:

- **show ip route static**
- **show ip route** *network*
- **show running-config** | section ip route

Replace **ip** with **ipv6** for the IPv6 versions of the command.

Reference the figure when reviewing the command examples.

Click each button for example output for IPv4 and IPv6 static routes.

Display Only IPv4 Static Routes

This output shows only the IPv4 static routes in the routing table. Also note where the filter begins the output, excluding all the codes.

```
R1# show ip route static | begin Gateway
Gateway of last resort is not set
        172.16.0.0/16 is variably subnetted, 5 subnets, 2 masks
S          172.16.1.0/24 [1/0] via 172.16.2.2
S       192.168.1.0/24 [1/0] via 172.16.2.2
S       192.168.2.0/24 [1/0] via 172.16.2.2
R1#
```

Display a Specific IPv4 Network

This command will show output for only the specified network in the routing table.

```
R1# show ip route 192.168.2.1
Routing entry for 192.168.2.0/24
  Known via "static", distance 1, metric 0
  Routing Descriptor Blocks:
  * 172.16.2.2
      Route metric is 0, traffic share count is 1
R1#
```

Display the IPv4 Static Route Configuration

This command filters the running configuration for only IPv4 static routes.

```
R1# show running-config | section ip route
ip route 172.16.1.0 255.255.255.0 172.16.2.2
ip route 192.168.1.0 255.255.255.0 172.16.2.2
ip route 192.168.2.0 255.255.255.0 172.16.2.2
R1#
```

Display Only IPv6 Static Routes

This output shows only the IPv6 static routes in the routing table. Also note where the filter begins the output, excluding all the codes.

```
R1# show ipv6 route static
IPv6 Routing Table - default - 8 entries
Codes: C - Connected, L - Local, S - Static, U - Per-user Static route
       B - BGP, R - RIP, H - NHRP, I1 - ISIS L1
       I2 - ISIS L2, IA - ISIS interarea, IS - ISIS summary, D - EIGRP
```

```
        EX - EIGRP external, ND - ND Default, NDp - ND Prefix,
            DCE - Destination
        NDr - Redirect, RL - RPL, O - OSPF Intra, OI - OSPF Inter
        OE1 - OSPF ext 1, OE2 - OSPF ext 2, ON1 - OSPF NSSA ext 1
        ON2 - OSPF NSSA ext 2, la - LISP alt, lr - LISP site-registrations
        ld - LISP dyn-eid, lA - LISP away, le - LISP extranet-policy
        a - Application
S    2001:DB8:ACAD:1::/64 [1/0]
     via 2001:DB8:ACAD:2::2
S    2001:DB8:CAFE:1::/64 [1/0]
     via 2001:DB8:ACAD:2::2
S    2001:DB8:CAFE:2::/64 [1/0]
     via 2001:DB8:ACAD:2::2
R1#
```

Display a Specific IPv6 Network

This command will show output for only the specified network in the routing table.

```
R1# show ipv6 route 2001:db8:cafe:2::
Routing entry for 2001:DB8:CAFE:2::/64
  Known via "static", distance 1, metric 0
  Route count is 1/1, share count 0
  Routing paths:
    2001:DB8:ACAD:2::2
      Last updated 00:23:55 ago
R1#
```

Display the IPv6 Static Route Configuration

This command filters the running configuration for only IPv6 static routes.

```
R1# show running-config | section ipv6 route
ipv6 route 2001:DB8:ACAD:1::/64 2001:DB8:ACAD:2::2
ipv6 route 2001:DB8:CAFE:1::/64 2001:DB8:ACAD:2::2
ipv6 route 2001:DB8:CAFE:2::/64 2001:DB8:ACAD:2::2
R1#
```

Refer to
Interactive Graphic
in online course

Syntax Checker - Configure Static Routes - 15.2.8

Configure static routes based on the specified requirements.

Configure IP Default Static Routes - 15.3

Refer to
Online Course
for Illustration

Default Static Route - 15.3.1

This topic shows you how to configure a default route for IPv4 and IPv6. It also explains the situations in which a default route is a good choice. A default route is a static route that matches all packets. Instead of routers storing routes for all of the networks in the internet, they can store a single default route to represent any network that is not in the routing table.

Routers commonly use default routes that are either configured locally or learned from another router, using a dynamic routing protocol. A default route does not require any far-left bits to match between the default route and the destination IP address. A default route is used when no other routes in the routing table match the destination IP address of the packet. In other words, if a more specific match does not exist, then the default route is used as the Gateway of Last Resort.

Default static routes are commonly used when connecting an edge router to a service provider network, or a stub router (a router with only one upstream neighbor router).

The figure shows a typical default static route scenario.

IPv4 Default Static Route

The command syntax for an IPv4 default static route is similar to any other IPv4 static route, except that the network address is **0.0.0.0** and the subnet mask is **0.0.0.0**. The 0.0.0.0 0.0.0.0 in the route will match any network address.

Note: An IPv4 default static route is commonly referred to as a quad-zero route.

The basic command syntax for an IPv4 default static route is as follows:

```
Router(config)# ip route 0.0.0.0 0.0.0.0 {ip-address | exit-intf}
```

IPv6 Default Static Route

The command syntax for an IPv6 default static route is similar to any other IPv6 static route, except that the ipv6-prefix/prefix-length is **::/0**, which matches all routes.

The basic command syntax for an IPv6 default static route is as follows:

```
Router(config)# ipv6 route ::/0 {ipv6-address | exit-intf}
```

Refer to
Online Course
for Illustration

Configure a Default Static Route - 15.3.2

In the figure, R1 could be configured with three static routes, one to reach each of the remote networks in the example topology. However, R1 is a stub router because it is only connected to R2. Therefore, it would be more efficient to configure a single default static route.

The example shows an IPv4 default static route configured on R1. With the configuration shown in the example, any packets not matching more specific route entries are forwarded to R2 at 172.16.2.2.

```
R1(config)# ip route 0.0.0.0 0.0.0.0 172.16.2.2
```

An IPv6 default static route is configured in similar fashion. With this configuration any packets not matching more specific IPv6 route entries are forwarded to R2 at 2001:db8:acad:2::2

```
R1(config)# ipv6 route ::/0 2001:db8:acad:2::2
```

Refer to
Online Course
for Illustration

Verify a Default Static Route - 15.3.3

Verify IPv4 Default Static Route

The **show ip route static** command output from R1 displays the contents of the static routes in the routing table. Note the asterisk (*) next to the route with code 'S'. As displayed in the codes table in the **show ip route** output, the asterisk indicates that this static route is a candidate default route, which is why it is selected as the Gateway of Last Resort.

```
R1# show ip route static

Codes: L - local, C - connected, S - static, R - RIP, M - mobile,
B - BGP

D - EIGRP, EX - EIGRP external, O - OSPF, IA - OSPF inter area

N1 - OSPF NSSA external type 1, N2 - OSPF NSSA external type 2

E1 - OSPF external type 1, E2 - OSPF external type 2

i - IS-IS, su - IS-IS summary, L1 - IS-IS level-1, L2 - IS-IS level-2

ia - IS-IS inter area, * - candidate default, U - per-user static route

o - ODR, P - periodic downloaded static route, H - NHRP, l - LISP

+ - replicated route, % - next hop override


Gateway of last resort is 172.16.2.2 to network 0.0.0.0


S* 0.0.0.0/0 [1/0] via 172.16.2.2


R1#
```

Verify IPv6 Default Static Route

This example shows the **show ipv6 route static** command output to display the contents of the routing table.

```
R1# show ipv6 route static

IPv6 Routing Table - default - 8 entries

Codes: C - Connected, L - Local, S - Static, U - Per-user Static route

       B - BGP, R - RIP, H - NHRP, I1 - ISIS L1

       I2 - ISIS L2, IA - ISIS interarea, IS - ISIS summary, D - EIGRP

       EX - EIGRP external, ND - ND Default, NDp - ND Prefix,
          DCE - Destination

       NDr - Redirect, RL - RPL, O - OSPF Intra, OI - OSPF Inter
```

```
                OE1 - OSPF ext 1, OE2 - OSPF ext 2, ON1 - OSPF NSSA ext 1
                ON2 - OSPF NSSA ext 2, la - LISP alt, lr - LISP site-registrations
                ld - LISP dyn-eid, lA - LISP away, le - LISP extranet-policy
                a - Application
S     ::/0 [1/0]
        via 2001:DB8:ACAD:2::2
R1#
```

Notice that the static default route configuration uses the /0 mask for IPv4 default routes and the ::/0 prefix for IPv6 default routes. Remember that the IPv4 subnet mask and IPv6 prefix-length in a routing table determines how many bits must match between the destination IP address of the packet and the route in the routing table. A /0 mask or ::/0 prefix indicates that none of the bits are required to match. As long as a more specific match does not exist, the default static route matches all packets.

Refer to
Interactive Graphic
in online course

Syntax Checker - Configure Default Static Routes - 15.3.4

Configure and verify default static routes based on the specified requirements.

Configure Floating Static Routes - 15.4

Refer to
Online Course
for Illustration

Floating Static Routes - 15.4.1

As with the other topics in this module, you will learn how to configure IPv4 and IPv6 floating static routes and when to use them.

Another type of static route is a floating static route. Floating static routes are static routes that are used to provide a backup path to a primary static or dynamic route, in the event of a link failure. The floating static route is only used when the primary route is not available.

To accomplish this, the floating static route is configured with a higher administrative distance than the primary route. The administrative distance represents the trustworthiness of a route. If multiple paths to the destination exist, the router will choose the path with the lowest administrative distance.

For example, assume that an administrator wants to create a floating static route as a backup to an EIGRP-learned route. The floating static route must be configured with a higher administrative distance than EIGRP. EIGRP has an administrative distance of 90. If the floating static route is configured with an administrative distance of 95, the dynamic route learned through EIGRP is preferred to the floating static route. If the EIGRP-learned route is lost, the floating static route is used in its place.

In the figure, the branch router typically forwards all traffic to the HQ router over the private WAN link. In this example, the routers exchange route information using EIGRP. A floating static route, with an administrative distance of 91 or higher, could be configured to serve as a backup route. If the private WAN link fails and the EIGRP route disappears from the routing table, the router selects the floating static route as the best path to reach the HQ LAN.

By default, static routes have an administrative distance of 1, making them preferable to routes learned from dynamic routing protocols. For example, the administrative distances of some common interior gateway dynamic routing protocols are:

- EIGRP = 90

- OSPF = 110

- IS-IS = 115

The administrative distance of a static route can be increased to make the route less desirable than that of another static route or a route learned through a dynamic routing protocol. In this way, the static route "floats" and is not used when the route with the better administrative distance is active. However, if the preferred route is lost, the floating static route can take over, and traffic can be sent through this alternate route.

Refer to
Online Course
for Illustration

Configure IPv4 and IPv6 Floating Static Routes - 15.4.2

IP floating static routes are configured by using the **distance** argument to specify an administrative distance. If no administrative distance is configured, the default value (1) is used.

Refer to the topology in the figure and the **ip route** and **ipv6 route** commands issued on R1. In this scenario, the preferred default route from R1 is to R2. The connection to R3 should be used for backup only.

```
R1(config)# ip route 0.0.0.0 0.0.0.0 172.16.2.2

R1(config)# ip route 0.0.0.0 0.0.0.0 10.10.10.2 5

R1(config)# ipv6 route ::/0 2001:db8:acad:2::2

R1(config)# ipv6 route ::/0 2001:db8:feed:10::2 5
```

R1 is configured with IPv4 and IPv6 default static routes pointing to R2. Because no administrative distance is configured, the default value (1) is used for these static routes. R1 is also configured with IPv4 and IPv6 floating static default routes pointing to R3 with an administrative distance of 5. This value is greater than the default value of 1 and therefore; this route floats and is not present in the routing table unless the preferred route fails.

The **show ip route** and **show ipv6 route** output verifies that the default routes to R2 are installed in the routing table. Note that the IPv4 floating static route to R3 is not present in the routing table.

```
R1# show ip route static | begin Gateway

Gateway of last resort is 172.16.2.2 to network 0.0.0.0


S*    0.0.0.0/0 [1/0] via 172.16.2.2

R1# show ipv6 route static | begin S :

S    ::/0 [1/0]

     via 2001:DB8:ACAD:2::2

R1#
```

Use the **show run** command to verify that floating static routes are in the configuration. For example, the following command output verifies that both IPv6 static default routes are in the running configuration.

```
R1# show run | include ipv6 route
ipv6 route ::/0 2001:db8:feed:10::2 5
ipv6 route ::/0 2001:db8:acad:2::2
R1#
```

Refer to
Online Course
for Illustration

Test the Floating Static Route - 15.4.3

In the figure, what would happen if R2 failed?

To simulate this failure, both serial interfaces of R2 are shut down, as shown in the configuration.

```
R2(config)# interface s0/1/0
R2(config-if)# shut
*Sep 18 23:36:27.000: %LINK-5-CHANGED: Interface Serial0/1/0, changed
state to administratively down
*Sep 18 23:36:28.000: %LINEPROTO-5-UPDOWN: Line protocol on Interface
Serial0/1/0, changed state to down
R2(config-if)# interface s0/1/1
R2(config-if)# shut
*Sep 18 23:36:41.598: %LINK-5-CHANGED: Interface Serial0/1/1, changed
state to administratively down
*Sep 18 23:36:42.598: %LINEPROTO-5-UPDOWN: Line protocol on Interface
Serial0/1/1, changed state to down
```

Notice that R1 automatically generates messages indicating that the serial interface to R2 is down.

```
R1#
*Sep 18 23:35:48.810: %LINK-3-UPDOWN: Interface Serial0/1/0, changed
state to down
R1#
*Sep 18 23:35:49.811: %LINEPROTO-5-UPDOWN: Line protocol on Interface
Serial0/1/0, changed state to down
R1#
```

A look at the IP routing tables of R1 verifies that the floating static default routes are now installed as the default routes and are pointing to R3 as the next-hop router.

```
R1# show ip route static | begin Gateway
Gateway of last resort is 10.10.10.2 to network 0.0.0.0
S*    0.0.0.0/0 [5/0] via 10.10.10.2
```

```
R1# show ipv6 route static | begin ::
S    ::/0 [5/0]
       via 2001:DB8:FEED:10::2
R1#
```

Refer to
Interactive Graphic
in online course

Syntax Checker - Configure Floating Static Route - 15.4.4

Configure and verify floating static routes based on the specified requirements.

Configure Static Host Routes - 15.5

Host Routes - 15.5.1

This topic shows you how to configure an IPv4 and IPv6 static host route and when to use them.

A host route is an IPv4 address with a 32-bit mask, or an IPv6 address with a 128-bit mask. The following shows the three ways a host route can be added to the routing table:

- Automatically installed when an IP address is configured on the router (as shown in the figures)

- Configured as a static host route

- Host route automatically obtained through other methods (discussed in later courses)

Refer to
Online Course
for Illustration

Automatically Installed Host Routes - 15.5.2

Cisco IOS automatically installs a host route, also known as a local host route, when an interface address is configured on the router. A host route allows for a more efficient process for packets that are directed to the router itself, rather than for packet forwarding. This is in addition to the connected route, designated with a C in the routing table for the network address of the interface.

When an active interface on a router is configured with an IP address, a local host route is automatically added to the routing table. The local routes are marked with L in the output of the routing table.

For example, refer to the topology in the figure.

The IP addresses assigned to the Branch Serial0/1/0 interface are 198.51.100.1/30 and 2001:db8:acad:1::1/64. The local routes for the interface are installed by the IOS in the IPv4 and IPv6 routing tables, as shown in the example.

```
Branch# show ip route | begin Gateway
Gateway of last resort is not set
       198.51.100.0/24 is variably subnetted, 2 subnets, 2 masks
C         198.51.100.0/30 is directly connected, Serial0/1/0
L         198.51.100.1/32 is directly connected, Serial0/1/0
```

```
Branch# show ipv6 route | begin ::
C    2001:DB8:ACAD:1::/64 [0/0]
        via Serial0/1/0, directly connected
L    2001:DB8:ACAD:1::1/128 [0/0]
        via Serial0/1/0, receive
L    FF00::/8 [0/0]
        via Null0, receive
```

Refer to
Online Course
for Illustration

Static Host Routes - 15.5.3

A host route can be a manually configured static route to direct traffic to a specific destination device, such as the server shown in the figure. The static route uses a destination IP address and a 255.255.255.255 (/32) mask for IPv4 host routes, and a /128 prefix length for IPv6 host routes.

Configure Static Host Routes - 15.5.4

The example shows the IPv4 and IPv6 static host route configuration on the Branch router to access the server.

```
Branch(config)# ip route 209.165.200.238 255.255.255.255 198.51.100.2
Branch(config)# ipv6 route 2001:db8:acad:2::238/128 2001:db8:acad:1::2
Branch(config)# exit
Branch#
```

Verify Static Host Routes - 15.5.5

A review of both the IPv4 and IPv6 route tables verifies that the routes are active.

```
Branch# show ip route | begin Gateway
Gateway of last resort is not set
        198.51.100.0/24 is variably subnetted, 2 subnets, 2 masks
C         198.51.100.0/30 is directly connected, Serial0/1/0
L         198.51.100.1/32 is directly connected, Serial0/1/0
        209.165.200.0/32 is subnetted, 1 subnets
S         209.165.200.238 [1/0] via 198.51.100.2
Branch# show ipv6 route
(Output omitted)
C    2001:DB8:ACAD:1::/64 [0/0]
        via Serial0/1/0, directly connected
L    2001:DB8:ACAD:1::1/128 [0/0]
        via Serial0/1/0, receive
```

```
S    2001:DB8:ACAD:2::238/128 [1/0]

       via 2001:DB8:ACAD:1::2

Branch#
```

Configure IPv6 Static Host Route with Link-Local Next-Hop - 15.5.6

For IPv6 static routes, the next-hop address can be the link-local address of the adjacent router. However, you must specify an interface type and an interface number when using a link-local address as the next hop, as shown in the example. First, the original IPv6 static host route is removed, then a fully specified route configured with the IPv6 address of the server and the IPv6 link-local address of the ISP router.

Branch(config)# **no ipv6 route 2001:db8:acad:2::238/128 2001:db8:acad:1::2**

Branch(config)# **ipv6 route 2001:db8:acad:2::238/128 serial 0/1/0 fe80::2**

```
Branch# show ipv6 route | begin ::
C    2001:DB8:ACAD:1::/64 [0/0]

       via Serial0/1/0, directly connected
L    2001:DB8:ACAD:1::1/128 [0/0]

       via Serial0/1/0, receive
S    2001:DB8:ACAD:2::238/128 [1/0]

       via FE80::2, Serial0/1/0

Branch#
```

Refer to
Interactive Graphic
in online course

Syntax Checker - Configure Static Host Routes - 15.5.7

Configure and verify static host routes based on the specified requirements

Module Practice and Quiz - 15.6

Refer to Packet
Tracer Activity
for this chapter

Packet Tracer - Configure IPv4 and IPv6 Static and Default Routes - 15.6.1

In this Packet Tracer summary activity, you will configure static, default, and floating static routes for both the IPv4 and IPv6 protocols.

Refer to
Lab Activity
for this chapter

Lab - Configure IPv4 and IPv6 Static and Default Routes - 15.6.2

In this lab, you will complete the following objectives:

■ Part 1: Build the Network and Configure Basic Device Settings

■ Part 2: Configure and Verify IP and IPv6 Addressing on R1 and R2

- Part 3: Configure and Verify Static and Default Routing for IPv4 on R1 and R2
- Part 4: Configure and Verify Static and Default Routing for IPv6 on R1 and R2

What did I learn in this module? - 15.6.3

Static Routes

Static routes can be configured for IPv4 and IPv6. Both protocols support the following types of static routes: standard static route, default static route, floating static route, and summary static route. Static routes are configured using the ip route and ipv6 route global configuration commands. When configuring a static route, the next hop can be identified by an IP address, exit interface, or both. How the destination is specified creates one of the three following types of static route: next-hop, directly connected, and fully specified. IPv4 static routes are configured using the following global configuration command: **ip route** *network-address subnet-mask* { *ip-address* | *exit-intf* [*ip=address*] } [**distance**]. IPv6 static routes are configured using the following global configuration command: **ipv6 route** *ipv6-prefix/prefix-length* { *ipv6-address* | *exit-intf* [*ipv6-address*]} [**distance**]. The command to start an IPv4 routing table is **show ip route | begin Gateway**. The command to start an IPv6 routing table is **show ipv6 route | begin C**.

Configure IP Static Routes

In a next-hop static route, only the next-hop IP address is specified. The exit interface is derived from the next hop. When configuring a static route, another option is to use the exit interface to specify the next-hop address. Directly connected static routes should only be used with point-to-point serial interfaces. In a fully specified static route, both the exit interface and the next-hop IP address are specified. This form of static route is used when the exit interface is a multi-access interface and it is necessary to explicitly identify the next hop. The next hop must be directly connected to the specified exit interface. In a fully specified IPv6 static route, both the exit interface and the next-hop IPv6 address are specified. Along with **show ip route**, **show ipv6 route**, **ping** and **traceroute**, other useful commands to verify static routes include: **show ip route static**, **show ip route** *network*, and **show running-config | section ip route**. Replace ip with ipv6 for the IPv6 versions of the command.

Configure IP Default Static Routes

A default route is a static route that matches all packets. A default route does not require any far-left bits to match between the default route and the destination IP address. Default static routes are commonly used when connecting an edge router to a service provider network, and a stub router. The command syntax for an IPv4 default static route is similar to any other IPv4 static route, except that the network address is 0.0.0.0 and the subnet mask is 0.0.0.0. The 0.0.0.0 0.0.0.0 in the route will match any network address. The command syntax for an IPv6 default static route is similar to any other IPv6 static route, except that the ipv6-prefix/prefix-length is ::/0, which matches all routes. To verify an IPv4 default static route, use the **show ip route static** command. For IPV6 use the **show ipv6 route static** command.

Configure Floating Static Routes

Floating static routes are static routes that are used to provide a backup path to a primary static or dynamic route in the event of a link failure. The floating static route is configured with a higher administrative distance than the primary route. By default, static routes have an administrative distance of 1, making them preferable to routes learned from dynamic routing protocols. The administrative distances of some common interior gateway dynamic routing protocols are EIGRP = 90, OSPF = 110, and IS-IS = 115. IP floating static routes are configured by using the **distance** argument to specify an administrative distance. If no administrative distance is configured, the default value (1) is used. The **show ip route** and **show ipv6 route** output verifies that the default routes to a router are installed in the routing table.

Configure Static Host Routes

A host route is an IPv4 address with a 32-bit mask or an IPv6 address with a 128-bit mask. There are three ways a host route can be added to the routing table: automatically installed when an IP address is configured on the router, configured as a static host route, or automatically obtained through other methods not covered in this module. Cisco IOS automatically installs a host route, also known as a local host route, when an interface address is configured on the router. A host route can be a manually configured static route to direct traffic to a specific destination device. For IPv6 static routes, the next-hop address can be the link-local address of the adjacent router; however, you must specify an interface type and an interface number when using a link-local address as the next hop. To do this, the original IPv6 static host route is removed, then a fully specified route is configured with the IPv6 address of the server and the IPv6 link-local address of the ISP router.

Go to the online course to take the quiz and exam.

Chapter Quiz - IP Static Routing

Your Chapter Notes

CHAPTER 16

Troubleshoot Static and Default Routes

Introduction - 16.0

Why should I take this module? - 16.0.1

Welcome to Troubleshoot Static and Default Routes!

Well done! You have come to the final module in the Switching, Routing, and Wireless Essentials v7.0 (SRWE) course. This course gave you the in-depth knowledge and skills you need to set up switches and routers (including wireless devices) on your growing network. You really are good at network administration!

But what makes a good network administrator into a great one? The ability to effectively troubleshoot. The best way to gain network troubleshooting skills is simple: always be troubleshooting. In this module, you will troubleshoot both static and default routes. There is a Syntax Checker, a Packet Tracer, and a hands-on Lab where you can hone your troubleshooting skills. Let's get to it!

What will I learn to do in this module? - 16.0.2

Module Title: Troubleshoot Static and Default Routes

Module Objective: Troubleshoot static and default route configurations.

Topic Title	Topic Objective
Packet Processing with Static Routes	Explain how a router processes packets when a static route is configured.
Troubleshoot IPv4 Static and Default Route Configuration	Troubleshoot common static and default route configuration issues.

Packet Processing with Statics Routes - 16.1

Refer to
Interactive Graphic
in online course

Static Routes and Packet Forwarding - 16.1.1

Before diving into the troubleshooting portion of this module, this topic provides a brief review of how packets are forwarded in static routes. In the figure, click Play to see the animation where PC1 is sending a packet to PC3.

The following describes the packet forwarding process with static routes, as demonstrated in the animation:

1. The packet arrives on the GigabitEthernet 0/0/0 interface of R1.

2. R1 does not have a specific route to the destination network, 192.168.2.0/24. Therefore, R1 uses the default static route.

3. R1 encapsulates the packet in a new frame. Because the link to R2 is a point-to-point link, R1 adds an "all 1s" address for the Layer 2 destination address.

4. The frame is forwarded out of the Serial 0/1/0 interface. The packet arrives on the Serial 0/1/0 interface on R2.

5. R2 de-encapsulates the frame and looks for a route to the destination. R2 has a static route to 192.168.2.0/24 out of the Serial 0/1/1 interface.

6. R2 encapsulates the packet in a new frame. Because the link to R3 is a point-to-point link, R2 adds an "all 1s" address for the Layer 2 destination address.

7. The frame is forwarded out of the Serial 0/1/1 interface. The packet arrives on the Serial 0/1/1 interface on R3.

8. R3 de-encapsulates the frame and looks for a route to the destination. R3 has a connected route to 192.168.2.0/24 out of the GigabitEthernet 0/0/0 interface.

9. R3 looks up the ARP table entry for 192.168.2.10 to find the Layer 2 Media Access Control (MAC) address for PC3. If no entry exists, R3 sends an Address Resolution Protocol (ARP) request out of the GigabitEthernet 0/0/0 interface, and PC3 responds with an ARP reply, which includes the PC3 MAC address.

10. R3 encapsulates the packet in a new frame with the MAC address of the GigabitEthernet 0/0/0 interface as the source Layer 2 address, and the MAC address of PC3 as the destination MAC address.

11. The frame is forwarded out of GigabitEthernet 0/0/0 interface. The packet arrives on the network interface card (NIC) interface of PC3.

Refer to
Online Course
for Illustration

Check Your Understanding - Packet Processing with Static Routes - 16.1.2

Go to the online course to take the quiz and exam.

Troubleshoot IPv4 Static and Default Route Configuration - 16.2

Network Changes - 16.2.1

No matter how well you set up your network, you will have to be ready to troubleshoot some problem. Networks are frequently subject to events that can cause their status to change. For example, an interface can fail, or a service provider drops a connection. Links can become oversaturated, or an administrator may enter a wrong configuration.

When there is a change in the network, connectivity may be lost. Network administrators are responsible for pinpointing and solving the problem. To find and solve these issues, a network administrator must be familiar with tools to help isolate routing problems quickly.

Refer to
Online Course
for Illustration

Common Troubleshooting Commands - 16.2.2

Common IOS troubleshooting commands include the following:

Refer to
Interactive Graphic
in online course

■ ping

■ traceroute

- show ip route
- show ip interface brief
- show cdp neighbors detail

The figure shows the topology used to demonstrate these commands.

Click each button for an example and explanation of these common troubleshooting commands.

ping

The example displays the result of an extended ping from the source interface of R1 to the LAN interface of R3. An extended ping is an enhanced version of the ping utility. Extended ping enables you to specify the source IP address for the ping packets.

```
R1# ping 192.168.2.1 source 172.16.3.1

Type escape sequence to abort.

Sending 5, 100-byte ICMP Echos to 192.168.2.1, timeout is 2 seconds:

Packet sent with a source address of 172.16.3.1

!!!!!

Success rate is 100 percent (5/5), round-trip min/avg/max = 3/3/5 ms

R1#
```

traceroute

This example displays the result of a traceroute from R1 to the R3 LAN. Note that each hop route returns an ICMP reply.

```
R1# traceroute 192.168.2.1

Type escape sequence to abort.

Tracing the route to 192.168.2.1

VRF info: (vrf in name/id, vrf out name/id)

  1 172.16.2.2 1 msec 2 msec 1 msec

  2 192.168.1.1 2 msec 3 msec *

R1#
```

show ip route

The **show ip route** command in this example displays the routing table of R1.

```
R1# show ip route | begin Gateway

Gateway of last resort is not set

      172.16.0.0/16 is variably subnetted, 5 subnets, 2 masks

S        172.16.1.0/24 [1/0] via 172.16.2.2

C        172.16.2.0/24 is directly connected, Serial0/1/0

L        172.16.2.1/32 is directly connected, Serial0/1/0
```

```
C          172.16.3.0/24 is directly connected, GigabitEthernet0/0/0

L          172.16.3.1/32 is directly connected, GigabitEthernet0/0/0

S      192.168.1.0/24 [1/0] via 172.16.2.2

S      192.168.2.0/24 [1/0] via 172.16.2.2

R1#
```

show ip interface brief

A quick status of all interfaces on the router is shown using the **show ip interface brief** command in this example.

```
R1# show ip interface brief

Interface              IP-Address      OK? Method Status          Protocol

GigabitEthernet0/0/0   172.16.3.1      YES manual up              up

GigabitEthernet0/0/1   unassigned      YES unset  up              up

Serial0/1/0            172.16.2.1      YES manual up              up

Serial0/1/1            unassigned      YES unset  up              up

R1#
```

show cdp neighbors

The **show cdp neighbors** command provides a list of directly connected Cisco devices. This command validates Layer 2 (and therefore Layer 1) connectivity. For example, if a neighbor device is listed in the command output, but it cannot be pinged, then Layer 3 addressing should be investigated.

```
R1# show cdp neighbors

Capability Codes: R - Router, T - Trans Bridge, B - Source Route Bridge

                  S - Switch, H - Host, I - IGMP, r - Repeater,
                  P - Phone,

                  D - Remote, C - CVTA, M - Two-port Mac Relay

Device ID    Local Intrfce   Holdtme    Capability  Platform   Port ID

Switch       Gig 0/0/1       129             S I    WS-C3560-  Fas 0/5

R2           Ser 0/1/0       156           R S I    ISR4221/K  Ser 0/1/0

R3           Ser 0/1/1       124           R S I    ISR4221/K  Ser 0/1/0

Total cdp entries displayed : 3

R1#
```

Refer to
Online Course
for Illustration

Refer to
Interactive Graphic
in online course

Solve a Connectivity Problem - 16.2.3

Finding a missing (or misconfigured) route is a relatively straightforward process if the right tools are used in a methodical manner.

For instance, the user at PC1 reports that he cannot access resources on the R3 LAN. This can be confirmed by pinging the LAN interface of R3 using the LAN interface of R1 as the source. Again, we will use the topology in the figure to demonstrate how to troubleshoot this connectivity problem.

Click each button to see how troubleshooting commands are used to solve a connectivity problem.

Ping the Remote LAN

The network administrator can test connectivity between the two LANs from R1 instead of PC1. This can be done by sourcing the ping from the G0/0/0 interface on R1 to the G0/0/0 interface on R3, as shown in the example. The ping results show that there is no connectivity between these LANs.

```
R1# ping 192.168.2.1 source g0/0/0
Type escape sequence to abort.
Sending 5, 100-byte ICMP Echos to 192.168.2.1, timeout is 2 seconds:
Packet sent with a source address of 172.16.3.1
.....
Success rate is 0 percent (0/5)
```

Ping the Next-Hop Router

Next, a ping to the S0/1/0 interface on R2 is successful. This ping is sourced from the S0/1/0 interface of R1. Therefore, the issue is not loss of connectivity between R1 and R2.

```
R1# ping 172.16.2.2
Type escape sequence to abort.
Sending 5, 100-byte ICMP Echos to 172.16.2.1, timeout is 2 seconds:
!!!!!
Success rate is 100 percent (5/5), round-trip min/avg/max = 3/3/4 ms
```

Ping R3 LAN from S0/1/0

A ping from R1 to the R3 interface 192.168.2.1 is successful as well. This ping is sourced from the S0/1/0 interface on R1. R3 has a route back to the network between R1 and R2, 172.16.2.0/24. This confirms that R1 can reach the remote LAN on R3. However, packets sourced from the LAN on R1 cannot. This indicates that either R2 or R3 may have an incorrect or missing route to the LAN on R1.

```
R1# ping 192.168.2.1
Type escape sequence to abort.
Sending 5, 100-byte ICMP Echos to 192.168.2.1, timeout is 2 seconds:
!!!!!
Success rate is 100 percent (5/5), round-trip min/avg/max = 3/3/4 ms
```

Verify the R2 Routing Table

The next step is to investigate the routing tables of R2 and R3. The routing table for R2 is shown in the example. Notice that the 172.16.3.0/24 network is configured incorrectly. The static route to the 172.16.3.0/24 network has been configured using the next-hop address 192.168.1.1. Therefore, packets destined for the 172.16.3.0/24 network are sent back to R3 instead of to R1.

```
R2# show ip route | begin Gateway
Gateway of last resort is not set

      172.16.0.0/16 is variably subnetted, 5 subnets, 2 masks
C        172.16.1.0/24 is directly connected, GigabitEthernet0/0/0
L        172.16.1.1/32 is directly connected, GigabitEthernet0/0/0
C        172.16.2.0/24 is directly connected, Serial0/1/0
L        172.16.2.2/32 is directly connected, Serial0/1/0
S        172.16.3.0/24 [1/0] via 192.168.1.1
      192.168.1.0/24 is variably subnetted, 2 subnets, 2 masks
C        192.168.1.0/24 is directly connected, Serial0/1/1
L        192.168.1.2/32 is directly connected, Serial0/1/1
S     192.168.2.0/24 [1/0] via 192.168.1.1
R2#
```

Correct the R2 Static Route Configuration

Next, the running configuration does, in fact, reveal the incorrect **ip route** statement. The incorrect route is removed, and the correct route is then entered.

```
R2# show running-config | include ip route
ip route 172.16.3.0 255.255.255.0 192.168.1.1
ip route 192.168.2.0 255.255.255.0 192.168.1.1
R2#
R2# configure terminal
Enter configuration commands, one per line.  End with CNTL/Z.
R2(config)# no ip route 172.16.3.0 255.255.255.0 192.168.1.1
R2(config)# ip route 172.16.3.0 255.255.255.0 172.16.2.1
R2(config)#
```

Verify New Static Route is Installed

The routing table on R2 is checked once again to confirm the route entry to the LAN on R1, 172.16.3.0, is correct and pointing toward R1.

```
R2(config) # exit
R2#
*Sep 20 02:21:51.812: %SYS-5-CONFIG_I: Configured from console by
console
```

```
R2# show ip route | begin Gateway
Gateway of last resort is not set

      172.16.0.0/16 is variably subnetted, 5 subnets, 2 masks
C        172.16.1.0/24 is directly connected, GigabitEthernet0/0/0
L        172.16.1.1/32 is directly connected, GigabitEthernet0/0/0
C        172.16.2.0/24 is directly connected, Serial0/1/0
L        172.16.2.2/32 is directly connected, Serial0/1/0
S        172.16.3.0/24 [1/0] via 172.16.2.1
      192.168.1.0/24 is variably subnetted, 2 subnets, 2 masks
C        192.168.1.0/24 is directly connected, Serial0/1/1
L        192.168.1.2/32 is directly connected, Serial0/1/1
S     192.168.2.0/24 [1/0] via 192.168.1.1
R2#
```

Ping the Remote LAN Again

Next, a ping from R1 sourced from G0/0/0 is used to verify that R1 can now reach the LAN interface of R3. As a last step in confirmation, the user on PC1 should also test connectivity to the 192.168.2.0/24 LAN.

```
R1# ping 192.168.2.1 source g0/0/0
Type escape sequence to abort.
Sending 5, 100-byte ICMP Echos to 192.168.2.1, timeout is 2 seconds:
Packet sent with a source address of 172.16.3.1
!!!!!
Success rate is 100 percent (5/5), round-trip min/avg/max = 4/4/4 ms
```

<table>
<tr><td>Refer to
Interactive Graphic
in online course</td></tr>
</table>

Syntax Checker - Troubleshoot IPv4 Static and Default Routes - 16.2.4

Troubleshoot IPv4 Static and Default Routes based on the specified requirements

Module Practice and Quiz - 16.3

<table>
<tr><td>Refer to **Packet Tracer Activity** for this chapter</td></tr>
</table>

Packet Tracer - Troubleshoot Static and Default Routes - 16.3.1

In this activity you will troubleshoot and static and default routes and repair any errors that you find.

■ Troubleshoot IPv4 static routes.

■ Troubleshoot IPv6 static routes.

- Configure IPv4 static routes.
- Configure IPv4 default routes.
- Configure IPv6 static routes.

Lab - Troubleshoot Static and Default Routes - 16.3.2

In this lab, you will complete the following objectives:

- Evaluate Network Operation
- Gather information, create an action plan, and implement corrections

What did I learn in this module? - 16.3.3

Packet Processing with Static Routes

1. The packet arrives on the interface of R1.

2. R1 does not have a specific route to the destination network; therefore, R1 uses the default static route.

3. R1 encapsulates the packet in a new frame. Because the link to R2 is a point-to-point link, R1 adds an "all 1s" address for the Layer 2 destination address.

4. The frame is forwarded out of the appropriate interface. The packet arrives on the interface on R2.

5. R2 de-encapsulates the frame and looks for a route to the destination. R2 has a static route to the destination network out of one of its interfaces.

6. R2 encapsulates the packet in a new frame. Because the link to R3 is a point-to-point link, R2 adds an "all 1s" address for the Layer 2 destination address.

7. The frame is forwarded out of the appropriate interface. The packet arrives on the interface on R3.

8. R3 de-encapsulates the frame and looks for a route to the destination. R3 has a connected route to the destination network out of one of its interfaces.

9. R3 looks up the ARP table entry for the destination network to find the Layer 2 MAC address for PC3. If no entry exists, R3 sends an ARP request out of one of its interfaces, and PC3 responds with an ARP reply, which includes the PC3 MAC address.

10. R3 encapsulates the packet in a new frame with the MAC address of the appropriate interface as the source Layer 2 address and the MAC address of PC3 as the destination MAC address.

11. The frame is forwarded out of the appropriate interface. The packet arrives on the network interface card (NIC) interface of PC3.

Troubleshoot IPv4 Static and Default Route Configuration

Networks are frequently subject to events that can cause their status to change. An interface can fail, or a service provider drops a connection. Links can become oversaturated, or an administrator may enter a wrong configuration. Common IOS troubleshooting commands include the following:

- ping
- traceroute
- show ip route
- show ip interface brief
- show cdp neighbors detail

Go to the online course to take the quiz and exam.

Chapter Quiz - Troubleshoot Static and Default Routes

Your Chapter Notes

U

V

W